Cayman's 1794 Wreck of the Ten Sail

Cayman's 1794 Wreck of the Ten Sail

Peace, War, and Peril in the Caribbean

MARGARET E. LESHIKAR-DENTON

THE UNIVERSITY OF ALABAMA PRESS
Tuscaloosa

The University of Alabama Press
Tuscaloosa, Alabama 35487-0380
uapress.ua.edu

Typeface: Caslon

Cover image: A French 12-pounder frigate seen from abeam running before the wind; engraving by Pierre Ozanne (1737–1813), ca. 1780, from the collection of Jean Boudriot and used with permission
Cover design: David Nees

Cataloging-in-Publication data is available from the Library of Congress.
ISBN: 978-0-8173-2045-4 (cloth)
ISBN: 978-0-8173-5965-2 (paper)
E-ISBN: 978-0-8173-9275-8

For all the volunteers
who helped bring the history and archaeology to light

Admiral Sir John Lawford, KCB, by Lea, painted on glass. From *One Hundred Silhouette Portraits from the Collection of Francis Wellesley* (Oxford: Oxford University Press, 1912). Reproduced courtesy of the National Portrait Gallery.

Contents

Illustrations

FIGURES

MAPS

Preface

A cannon shot roared from the darkness. "Breakers ahead! Close to us!" cried a seaman from a topsail yard of His Majesty's ship Convert, *on an eighteenth-century passage to Europe from the Caribbean. Captain John Lawford bounded up on deck as Grand Cayman's jagged eastern reefs appeared in every direction. To his surprise and dismay, the ship firing distress was ahead of its escort, as were several others—not collected, as they should have been, with the Jamaica fleet sailing under* Convert's *protection. Fifty-eight merchant ships were in peril—but not from the French, from whom* Convert, *formerly* L'Inconstante, *was a recent prize. Royal Navy gunners signaled the convoy, laden with West Indian wood, cotton, sugar, and rum, to disperse and save themselves. A merchantman on the opposite tack crashed into* Convert's *bow, foiling her escape. As the crews of the two wooden ships disentangled their rigging,* Convert *struck and bilged. It was three o'clock in the morning, 8 February 1794.*[1]

The story of the most famous shipwreck disaster in the history of the Cayman Islands has been passed through generations for over 225 years. Details vary depending on who is doing the telling, but all refer to this momentous maritime event as the Wreck of the Ten Sail.[2] Surviving archival documents and remains of the ships in the sea confirm that the narrative is more than folklore. It is a legend based on a historical event in which ten British ships, traveling from Jamaica in a convoy of fifty-nine vessels, wrecked on the eastern reefs of Grand Cayman in 1794.

The Wreck of the Ten Sail has historical significance far beyond the boundaries of the Cayman Islands. It is tied to British and French history during the French Revolution, when these and other European nations were competing for military and commercial dominance around the globe. The Wreck of the Ten Sail attests to the worldwide distribution of European war and trade at the close of the eighteenth century (map 1).

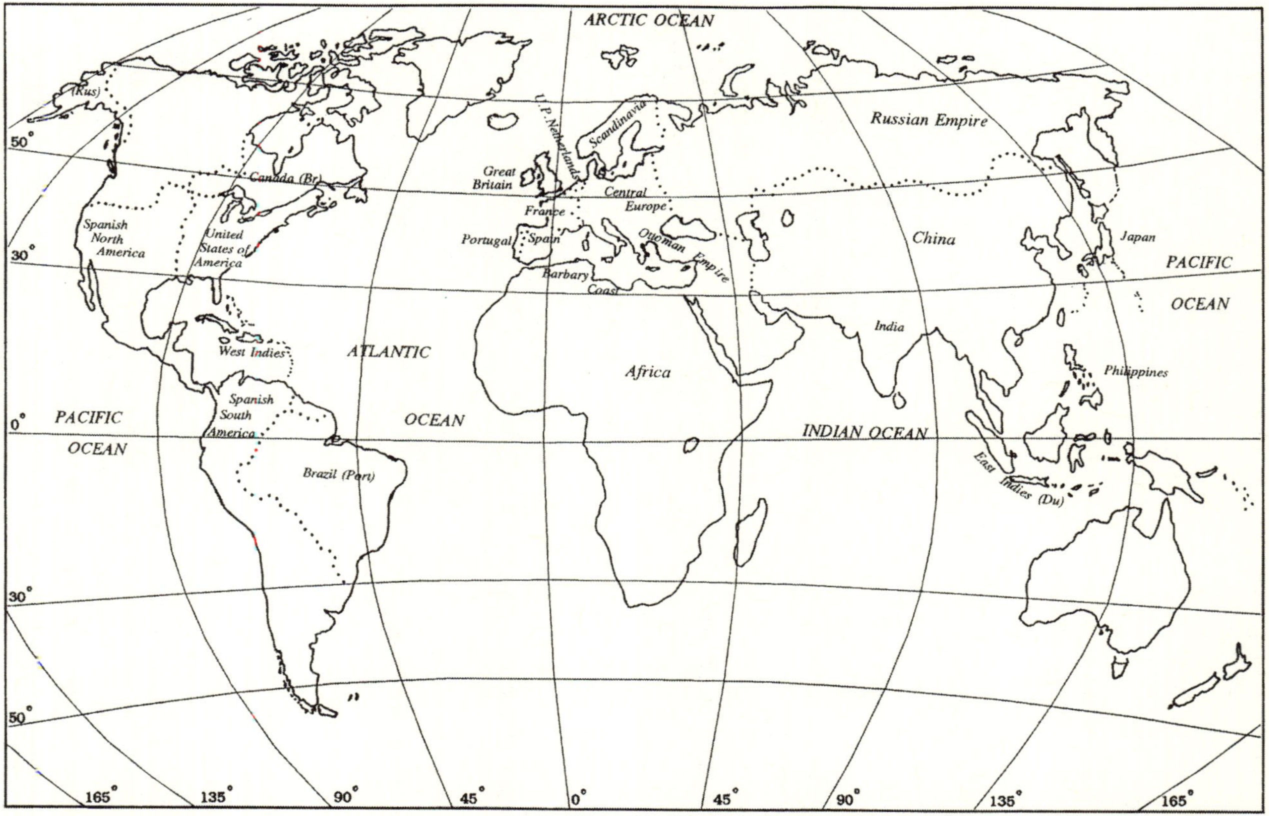

Map 1. The world circa 1789. Drawn by R. L. Craig.

Historical Overview

The French Revolution erupted in 1789, and by 1793 France had declared war on Britain and other European powers. Hostilities extended to French and British possessions in the New World and to the seas around the West Indies, as each nation strove to capture the other's naval ships and merchantmen as prizes (map 2). In November 1793, the British ships *Penelope* and *Iphigenia*, commanded by Captains B. S. Rowley and Patrick Sinclair, respectively, captured the French frigate *L'Inconstante*, one of the principal ships protecting France's interests in Saint-Domingue.[3] Captain Joseph Riouffe, along with other *L'Inconstante* officers and seamen, was mortally wounded in the engagement.

Following its seizure, the British sailed the prize to Jamaica and sold the vessel into His Majesty's Service as HMS *Convert*, under the command of Captain John Lawford. As a British ship of war, the frigate *Convert* was to escort and protect a produce-laden convoy of fifty-five merchantmen on their winter journey across the Atlantic to ports in England, Ireland, and Scotland; three vessels bound for America would join them. Ironically, the greatest danger was not to be the French, for on 8 February 1794 the *Convert*, together with nine ships of the fleet, wrecked on the perilous eastern reefs of Grand Cayman (map 3).

The inhabitants of Grand Cayman helped rescue survivors but had little to offer the shipwrecked mariners. The island's population numbered fewer than one thousand people and was still suffering from a lack of provisions caused by a hurricane the previous October. Representatives of the Caymanian people begged Lawford to remove the surviving crew members as soon as possible. Captain Lawford, the officers of the *Convert*, and thirty of Lawford's best seamen stayed to salvage what they could from the frigate while the remainder of the ship's complement was sent off on other vessels in the convoy. Aware that the loss of His Majesty's ship and nine merchantmen would adversely affect the security and commerce of Britain and her colonies, Lawford dutifully sent letters back to Jamaica and on to Europe, informing his superiors of the disaster. Meanwhile, he camped with his men in tents on the beach opposite the wreck site and began a salvage attempt. After receiving news of the shipwrecks, Commodore John Ford sent Captain Francis Roberts in HMS *Success* to Grand Cayman to assist in the salvage. At the end of March, the *Success* transported Lawford, his officers, and the remaining crew back to Jamaica. Before Captains Lawford and Roberts left Grand Cayman, they signed an agreement with Robert Knowles Clarke and William Bodden Sr., two prominent Caymanians, giving them permission to continue the salvage of the *Convert* frig-

Map 2. The Caribbean circa 1793. Drawn by R. L. Craig, after map by R. Wilkinson, 1794, Cayman Islands National Archive.

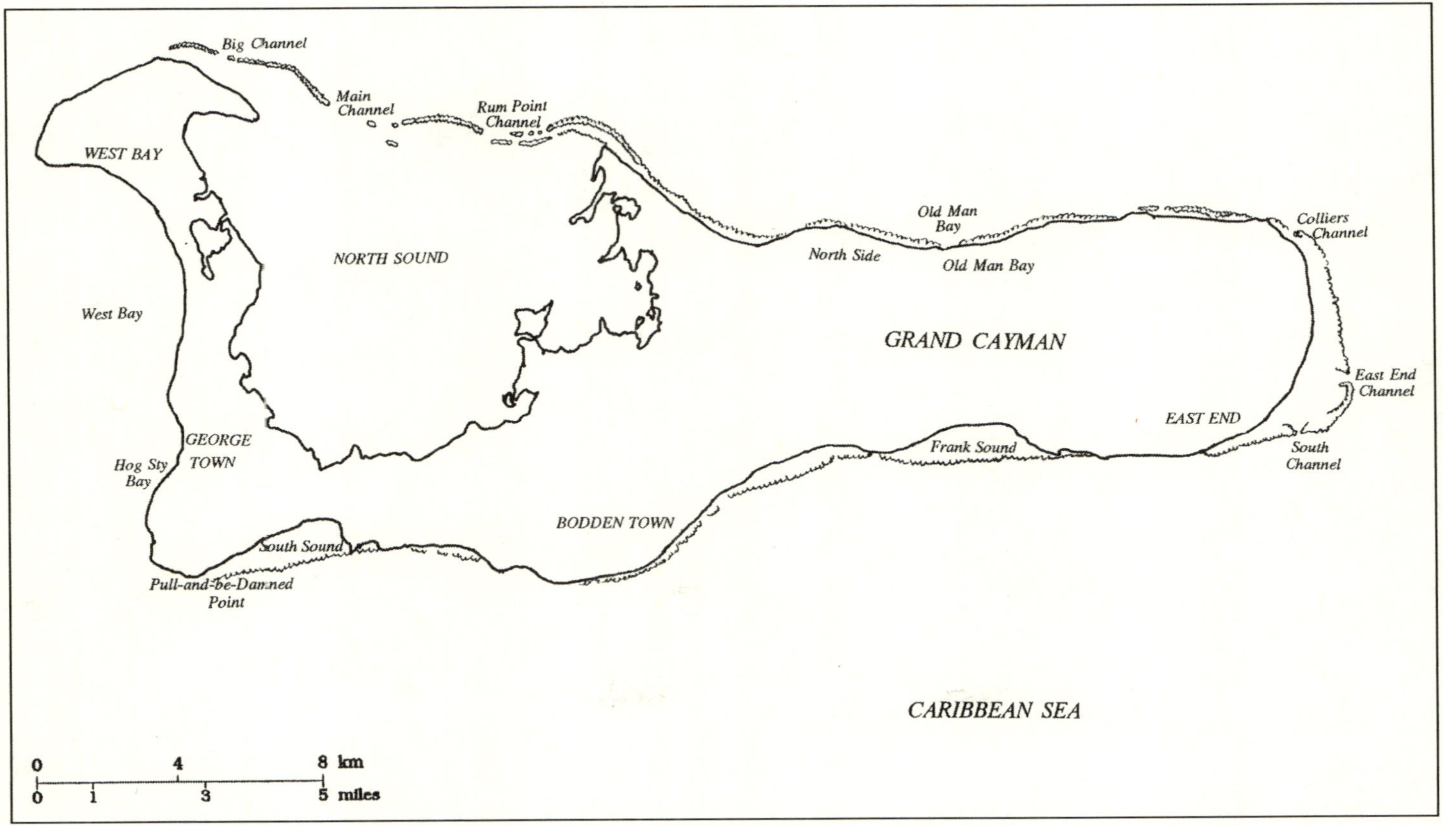

Map 3. Grand Cayman. Drawn by R. L. Craig.

ate and promising compensation. No documents have yet been found that reveal how much of the authorized salvage Clarke and Bodden carried out.

All the captains who survived the wrecking, along with the small crews of the merchantmen, would have stayed to salvage merchandise and ship's equipment from their vessels. Attempts to rescue the cargoes were mostly unsuccessful, however, because the ships broke apart quickly and because they carried perishable goods, including rum, cotton, sugar, and wood.

On his return to Jamaica, Captain Lawford faced a court-martial over the loss of the *Convert*. After hearing evidence that included testimony from Captain Lawford, First Lieutenant Joseph Bradby Bogue, Second Lieutenant William Earnshaw, Master Thomas Popplewell, Master's Mate James Hutchins, and Midshipman Colin Campbell, all of the *Convert*, and from Master Richard Davy of the *Success*, the court recommended acquittal.

Sometime after 1794, interest in further salvage of the wrecks waned, and people forgot their locations. The story of the Wreck of the Ten Sail, however, continued to be told and is still told in the Cayman Islands, more than two hundred years after the event. Not surprisingly, the tale has come down to the present generation in colorful versions.

Discovery of Documentary Accounts and Archaeological Evidence

Until 1979 little archival research had been conducted on the Wreck of the Ten Sail. Two Cayman Islands histories, one by Commissioner George Hirst, published in 1910, and the other (based closely on Hirst's) by Neville Williams, published in 1970, contain brief and inaccurate descriptions of the event.[4] Even the name of the naval escort, given as HMS *Cordelia*, and the date, given as 1788, are incorrect. The accounts are based largely on an oral narrative told to Commissioner Hirst before 1910, by a man whose grandfather was alive when the shipwrecks occurred.

While the Caymanian's story is valuable as a traditional version, there are also surviving eighteenth-century accounts in archives in Europe and the Caribbean. Roger Smith, director of an archaeological survey conducted by the Institute of Nautical Archaeology (INA) in 1979 and 1980, and the present author, in her research in the 1990s, discovered primary documents describing the disaster. These records provide details about the shipwrecks, the victims, and the islanders who responded, and are cited in the present work and in Smith's book *The Maritime Heritage of the Cayman Islands*.[5]

The 1980 INA survey also found archaeological evidence of the shipwrecks,[6] and a few years later, Indiana University's Department of Physical Education Scuba Research and Development Group carried out additional underwater survey work at East End. All of the survey findings are discussed in detail in chapter 8.

Historical Significance of the Wreck of the Ten Sail

Researchers investigated various aspects of the Wreck of the Ten Sail during the 1980s, but none of the studies focused exclusively on the ships, the people, and the wreck itself. When examined as a whole, the information the various surveys gathered indicated that the disaster was more significant than researchers had hitherto assumed. Defining its place in Caymanian, Caribbean, and European history and providing as accurate and complete an account of the event as possible, as well as locating sites and recovering and conserving samples of the artifacts lying under the sea, became the focus of the research that led to this book. I recorded and studied the rich oral accounts of Caymanians; located valuable supporting primary documents in archives in the United Kingdom, Jamaica, and France; and, with a dedicated team of volunteers, discovered tangible evidence of the disaster on the reefs of East End. These three forms of history have been woven together to create *Cayman's 1794 Wreck of the Ten Sail.*

While we know from the start how many of the historical events played out on the world stage and in the Caribbean, this book introduces specific ships, actions, and shipwrecks of two rivaling European countries; the people who lived, sailed, and experienced the shifting world of the late eighteenth-century; and those who have kept the stories alive. With the tension and drama of a Shakespearean play, this account allows readers to empathize with real historical figures as their history, Caymanian history, Caribbean history, and world history unfold.

Complete research notes for the present volume are available for scrutiny by interested readers at the Cayman Islands National Archive. *Our Islands' Past*, volume 2, a joint publication of the CINA and Cayman Free Press, was published in 1994 to commemorate the bicentenary of the Wreck of the Ten Sail and to increase awareness among the Caymanian public, particularly students, of the importance of local history. The introduction provides a comprehensive summary of the Wreck of the Ten Sail, and, among other original documents, it contains the full transcript of Captain Lawford's court-martial. These works have inspired lively articles in history books and tourist publications.

Oral History and Folklore

Between 1990 and 1993, I interviewed older Caymanians and studied narratives that were recorded a decade earlier in the Cayman Islands about the

Wreck of the Ten Sail. My original intent was to seek oral histories that would facilitate archival and archaeological work. While clues to history and archaeology emerged, the real discovery was that rich and culturally valuable folklore surrounds the eighteenth-century episode. Thus, I documented narratives of the Wreck of the Ten Sail to provide a background to remembrances and surviving tales. These stories demonstrate the lasting effect of the shipwrecks on the people of the Cayman Islands.

Archival Research

Archival research revealed specific details about the ships and people associated with the Wreck of the Ten Sail as well as about the broader history and significance of the late eighteenth-century era. Research trips in 1991 and 1993 to the Public Record Office and the National Maritime Museum in London revealed eighteenth-century documents that pertain to the capture of *L'Inconstante* and the frigate's wrecking as HMS *Convert.* These repositories also hold key data about the merchant ships as well as naval and biographical details about the *Convert*'s captain, John Lawford. Lloyd's Register of Shipping provides contemporary published information about the merchantmen in both *Lloyd's Register* and *Lloyd's List*, and the College of Arms and Whitehall Library have data on Lawford. Through phone calls, letters, and a 1992 visit to Jamaica, High Court of Vice Admiralty records regarding the prize, *L'Inconstante*, and the subsequent sale of the vessel and ship's stores came to light in the Jamaica Archives in Spanish Town, and eighteenth-century periodical data was found in the National Library at the Institute of Jamaica in Kingston. Copies of vital documents were obtained through correspondence with individuals at three archives in France: the Archives de France in Paris, the Service Historique de la Marine in Château de Vincennes, and the Archives du Port de Rochefort in Rochefort, where *L'Inconstante* was built. Communication with Jean Boudriot, a renowned expert on the history of French shipbuilding, and with David H. Roberts, who has translated from French to English several of the works of Boudriot, was extremely beneficial. Many other people assisted in accessing rare sources, which were available in diverse repositories.

Examples of original documents that were examined for the archival research include British Admiralty and French Navy correspondence, other official correspondence, Jamaica Vice Admiralty Court records regarding prize ships, and information gleaned from transcriptions of prisoners' statements and interrogations, captain's letters, court-martial proceedings, ships' logs, muster rolls, port and dockyard records, registers of ships, eighteenth-century periodicals, prize-ship inventories, shipwreck salvage accounts, and drafts of ships. These documents provide historical data that illuminate the epoch, reference the construction of the French frigate, describe the British capture of the prize, and clarify events surrounding the multiple shipwreck disaster. They also contain information about equipment, stores, and the wrecking that facilitates the archaeology.

Archaeology

Tangible evidence disclosed through archaeology can provide a physical link with the past and substantiate, dispute, or clarify much of the written historical record. Therefore, under the auspices of the Cayman Islands National Museum, a team of avocational archaeology volunteers and I embarked on an investigation to locate HMS *Convert* and nine ships of the frigate's convoy. Following a background search on land, for previously salvaged cannons, the team carried out an underwater survey of the eastern reefs of Grand Cayman in the summer and fall of 1991. The research focused primarily on important sites thought to be associated with the Wreck of the Ten Sail. It thereby laid foundations for the in situ protection of these resources and for selective programs of survey, excavation, recovery, and interpretation in the future. Results of the investigation encouraged the National Museum to further develop a growing inventory of Cayman Islands shipwreck sites over the following decades, to create a maritime heritage partnership, and to advocate for protective legislation and creation of a conservation laboratory, including the capability to process wetsite artifacts. Once the Cayman Islands establishes such a permanent facility, finds from the islands' shipwrecks can be treated and stabilized for research, curation, interpretation, and exhibition by the National Museum and its partners.

Acknowledgments

I extend my sincere appreciation to all the people and organizations who contributed to the research, writing, and publication of this book and the work that preceded it. During the twenty-nine years that have passed since this research began, many of the individuals have died, and so whether they are now present in person or memory, I owe a debt of gratitude and special thanks to the following: University of Alabama Press editor in chief Dan Waterman, Kelly Finefrock-Creed, and the UAP team for acquisition, editorial support, and seeing this book through to publication; copyeditor Dawn Hall and indexer Susan G. Harris; and UAP's Maritime Currents: History and Archaeology series editor Gene Smith for unwavering belief in the manuscript and determination to see it in print.

To my mentors at Texas A&M University: George F. Bass, for his guidance, encouragement, and faith in me from the beginning right up to publication of this book; Kevin J. Crisman, for generously sharing his seafaring knowledge; Sylvia A. Grider, for expanding my anthropological horizons into folklore; Donny L. Hamilton, for years of practical archaeology instruction and for Port Royal; Harry J. Shafer, for a solid foundation in archaeological methods and theory; and David A. Brooks, for oceanographic insight and contributions.

Also at Texas A&M University: J. Richard Steffy, Frederick van Doorninck Jr., and Fred Hocker, for teaching me about ships; Vaughn M. Bryant Jr. and the students, faculty, and staff of the Department of Anthropology and the Nautical Archaeology Program; the College of Liberal Arts; and Donald Dyal, Terry Bridges, and Shawn Carlson of Special Collections of the Sterling C. Evans Library.

In the Cayman Islands: the Cayman Islands National Museum, museum board, and Portfolio of Culture for their support, and National Museum emeritus director Anita Ebanks and the staff, especially present and former curatorial members Debra Barnes-Tábora, Brian Watler Jr., Shenice

McField, Michael Hislop, Bill Tennent, and Mary Peever, for their encouragement and assistance; Philip Pedley, former director of the Cayman Islands National Archive, for archival guidance and significant additional help, and the CINA staff, including director Kimlon Lawrence, Tammi Seltzer, Charisse Morrison, and Tricia Bodden; Roger Craig, past CINA director and preservation head, for the dedicated and detailed preparation of maps, illustrations, and photographs; the Cayman Islands government, for support and permission to conduct archaeological work on the seabed; underwater survey crew members Jeanne Masters, Helene Schindler, Arthur Schindler, Mike Guderian, Dennis Denton, and Keith Neale, Patrick Rogers, and Cebert McLaughlin previously of Tortuga Divers; Pat Smith, Earl Smith, Kendal Massias, Dawson Whittaker, Brian Butler, Tom Isaacs, Dale Banks, Adrian Briggs, Kent Eldemire, and the National Trust for the Cayman Islands, for providing information about and access to cannons previously recovered from the French Cannon Site; the staff of the Department of Environment (former Natural Resources Unit), especially director Gina Ebanks-Petrie, Scott Slaybaugh, and Tim Austin, for professional support; Suzette Ebanks and Lennon Christian (formerly) of Government Information Services; the Department of Tourism; the Currency Board who authorized the Royal Mint to strike a 200th anniversary commemorative coin; the Postal Service who created a special stamp issue in 1994; the Visual Arts Society who held an art competition won by John Doak in 1994; Duncan McCleod, George Sparling, Monica Gore, William Keegan, Anne Stokes, Reed Toomey, Bruce Craig, Don Scott, Theresa Grundy, Michael Grundy, Sue Gibb, Robin Gibb, James Gibb, Andy Gibb, Lynda Parsons, Simon Boxall, Sonya Donnelly, and Michelle Coles, for their keen participation in archaeological research and documentation through the years; Morritts Tortuga Club, Atlantis Research Submersibles, the Department of Environment, and Ocean Frontiers, for equipment and offshore support services; Heather McLaughlin, Arthurlyn Pedley, Vernicia Watler, Phoebe Watler Spence, Marshall Watler, Mary Antoinette Wood Levy, Edison Jackson, Weddy Connolly, and the National Archive Oral History Program (former Cayman Islands Memory Bank), for oral history research and support; Claudette Upton, for her essential guidance and copyediting skills in 2007 toward preparation of the manuscript; and Bill Mailer, Annick Tacq-Lietaer, Bernard Lietaer, Geraldine Duckworth, Anton Duckworth, Sue Adams, Charles Adams, Darryl Myers, Michael Alberga, Christine Rosesmythe, Stuart Mailer, Carmen Conolly, Alvin McLaughlin, Steve Broadbelt, Arden McLean, Darrel Rankine, Bob Williams, June Williams, and William H. White.

In France: Jean Boudriot and his translator David H. Roberts; Marc

Fardet and Christian Carrière of the Archives du Port de Rochefort; Pierre Waksman and le contre-amiral Kessler of the Ministère de la Défense Service Historique de la Marine; and Gérard Ermisse and Florence Clavaud of the Archives Nationales, Archives de France.

In the United Kingdom: Queen Elizabeth II and Prince Philip who, in February 1994, held the interest to visit the *200th Anniversary Wreck of the Ten Sail* exhibit at the Cayman Islands National Museum and opened the Wreck of the Ten Sail Park at East End; author David R. MacGregor; David Lyon, Ian MacKenzie, David Taylor, Karen Peart, Keith Percival, David Topliss, Stuart Bligh, Andrew Tullis, and other staff of the National Maritime Museum; Paul Johnson and Nick Forbes of the National Archives (former Public Record Office); Alan Borthwick of the Scottish Record Office; R. H. Searle and Bridget Spiers of Whitehall Library; Melvyn Barnes and D. T. Barriskill of the Guildhall Library; Barbara Jones of Lloyd's Register of Shipping; P. L. Dickinson of the College of Arms; J. S. Davis of the Kent Family History Society; Patricia Rowsby and L. Richardson of the Kent County Archives; Janice Burr of Conway Maritime Press; the staff of the British Library; L. S. Lawford; and Clive Lawford.

In Jamaica: Elizabeth Williams and the staff of the Jamaica Archives, John A. Aarons and the staff of the National Library of Jamaica, and Dorrick Gray and colleagues at the Jamaica National Heritage Trust.

In the United States: Roger Smith, K. C. Smith, the Institute of Nautical Archaeology, and the 1980 Cayman Islands Project field crew (Dennis, Bob, Steve, Denise, Pilar, Ricardo, and Pat), for an introduction to shipwrecks of the Cayman Islands; Charles Beeker and Indiana University, for sharing data gathered during their investigations; Donald Keith of Ships of Discovery, for conservation guidance; Keith Moorehead of the National Geographic Society; Keith L. Seitter of the American Meteorological Society; Julie A. Hedlund of the American Geophysical Union; Della Scott-Ireton, Amanda Evans, and Bert Ho, for recent maritime fieldwork assistance; and Stephen R. Bilicki, John Broadwater, Daniel Lenihan, Robert L. Molinari, and Robert F. Marx.

J. Philip Dering of the Palynology Laboratory and Wayne Ahr of the Department of Geology, Texas A&M University, and Michael Savarese, Charles Vitaliano, Clifford Ambers, and Rebecca Robinson of the Department of Geological Sciences, Indiana University, provided specialized analysis of archaeological materials. The yacht *Platinum* generously provided photographic helicopter flights.

I also thank Andrew Griffin, for his professional archival advice and insightful editorial comments on the manuscript; Claudia LeDoux, for her wisdom and for facilitating communications throughout this endeavor;

Suzie Lidstone, Clyde Reese, Becky Jobling, and Mike Fitzgerald, for their timely assistance; Ingrid Fulda, Henry Fulda, Hera Konstantinou and Joe Cozzi, for sharing their homes during my research; Dennis Denton, my husband, for excellent photography, skilled assistance in the field, digitalization of the book's illustrations, patience, and support of this project; my parents Marvin and Jean Leshikar; and the many others, whose interest and support have facilitated and enhanced this project.

Cayman's 1794
Wreck of the Ten Sail

I

Ship Ashore!

Lost, but Not Forgotten

The Cayman Islands have a long tradition of word-of-mouth communication and storytelling—even today, news travels as fast "on the marl road" as on the internet. Thus, when embarking on this shipwreck investigation into the Wreck of the Ten Sail, it was natural for me to search out some of the "older heads" to see if there might be a hint of surviving collective island memory to enhance a historical and archaeological study of this two-hundred-year-old shipwreck disaster. I found people eager to sit down with me to share surviving tales of the shipwrecks—these older individuals loved a visit and so did I. The colorful folklore they recalled illuminates the fact that the Wreck of the Ten Sail was a significant event in Cayman Islands history, attained a strong local value in Caymanian society, and lives today as the foremost of Cayman's many wrecking tales. While the stories may be inconsistent with the historical and archaeological record, they do reveal seeds of truth that miraculously survived the centuries by oral tradition.

In his *Notes on the History of the Cayman Islands*, published in 1910, Commissioner George Hirst recorded what might be the first written account of the Wreck of the Ten Sail from the Caymanian point of view. Hirst reported the story in the words of R. Tulloh Coe, who had learned it from his grandfather. The grandfather had witnessed the wrecking, or at least had lived on Grand Cayman when it occurred, and had assisted the shipwreck victims. Over a century after the Wreck of the Ten Sail, Coe told Commissioner Hirst:

> In the month of November, in the eighties of the eighteenth century a fleet of laden Jamaica merchantmen under convoy of His Majesty's ship "*Cordelia*" struck on the East End of this island at nine o'clock in the evening. Earlier in the evening the Commodore told the sailing master, Popplewell, if he did not alter his course he would be ashore

> on the East End of Grand Cayman before daylight. Popplewell replied that his course would take him twenty miles to the North of Cayman. When the "*Cordelia*" struck she fired for the fleet to keep off, and the other captains mistaking this signal for an order to close in did so, with the result that one after another they all struck before they found out their mistake. In the morning they found the other ships were off South West Point. The Commodore sent for them and put on board what was saved which was only one ship's cargo out of the ten which went ashore. No lives were lost with the exception of one captain and his wife, who instead of standing by his vessel took to a raft. The other vessels proceeded to England with the crews and what had been saved. A heavy North-east wind was blowing, and the Cayman canoes being, at that time, very small dare not venture out to the reef; but the Caymanians performed many heroic acts in saving life. It is said that for these acts a Bill was passed in the British Parliament not to impress Caymanians in the time of war. This wreck is known locally as the "wreck of the ten sail."
>
> . . . Popplewell was removed from the Navy List and became captain of a Jamaica vessel trading with Cayman. My father sold many a canoe load of turtle to him afterwards. He told my father that if he was tried in Heaven, Earth or Hell his conscience was clear as he made sure the course he was steering that eventful night would have taken him twenty miles North and East of the East-end of Grand Cayman.

Others told Commissioner Hirst that the presence of cannons on the Gun Bay reef indicated that an old fort had once stood there. He regarded this concept as impractical and improbable, however, and noted that Mr. Coe's story "tells us clearly how those guns got there, for it was exactly on this spot the 'wreck of the ten sail' took place."[1] Hirst recognized the true archaeological and historical value of the shipwreck site.

By the early twentieth century, the names of His Majesty's ship *Convert* and those of the nine merchantmen of the warship's convoy had been lost in the oral tradition. The vessels had been renamed for their collective end, the Wreck of the Ten Sail. The Royal Navy escort, identified as *Cordelia*, may have been another of His Majesty's ships that perhaps had visited Grand Cayman in the intervening period. The name most accurately remembered is that of Popplewell, the sailing master on *Convert*. This man probably continued his relationship with Grand Cayman as master of a trading ship, as Coe told Hirst; this would explain why his name survives in the Caymanian story.

It's not important that the name of the naval escort, the precise date of the episode, and other details are not exact in Coe's version of the Wreck of the Ten Sail. It is, in fact, remarkable that more than 115 years after the historical event occurred, its description retains so many factual elements and only slightly altered details. Coe's narrative reveals that in the late eighteenth century, nine laden merchantmen from Jamaica and their escort, one of His Majesty's ships, wrecked on Grand Cayman's East End in the dark. The commander of the naval escort discussed with the sailing master the course of the vessel in relation to the island of Grand Cayman. Through some misjudgment, a calamitous wrecking occurred. An interesting and inaccurate twist to the tale is that the Royal Navy vessel struck the reef ahead of the nine merchantmen; these vessels mistook her signal warning the fleet to keep off as a signal to close in, and thus also wrecked. It is true that other ships in the convoy waited nearby and, at the naval commander's request, took aboard ships' crews for the passage to England. Little of the merchant vessels' cargoes were saved, and few lives were lost. The captain of a wrecked merchant ship, and perhaps his wife, perished; in proper seafaring fashion, the tale blames the merchant captain's death on his not standing by his ship. There was a strong northeast wind blowing, which made rescue efforts difficult, but Caymanians heroically assisted in saving the shipwreck victims. Hirst found no documentary evidence to corroborate Coe's point about exemption of Caymanians from impressment in time of war. It is possible, though, that the captains of Royal Navy vessels on the Jamaica station recognized the benefit of leaving mariners on sparsely settled Grand Cayman rather than pressing them into His Majesty's ships. These Caymanian seamen had a reputation for providing timely assistance and relief when British ships or vessels called for water and provisions, or when they wrecked there.

In 1970, sixty years after the publication of George Hirst's *Notes on the History of the Cayman Islands*, the Cayman Islands government published *A History of the Cayman Islands* by Neville Williams. This brief book is based largely on Hirst's published works but also includes some original research. Regarding the Wreck of the Ten Sail, however, Williams summarized Hirst's account as related by R. Tulloh Coe, writing that the event occurred in November 1788. He pointed out that some versions make the lead ship HMS *Cordelia*, a British man-of-war, but he remarked that there was no HMS *Cordelia* in commission for another twenty years. Williams also highlighted additional stories that had sprung up around the shipwreck incident, including the tale that a British prince was on board the warship. Williams wrote that Prince William Henry, Duke of Clarence (the future King William IV, "the Sailor King") served in the Royal Navy and in 1788 commanded a frigate on the Jamaica station, but that his ship was in port when the wreck (supposedly) occurred. Related to this legend are two versions of reward bestowed on Caymanians. Both maintain that George III, the prince's father, was so impressed with the courage of the East Enders in saving lives that he made special concessions to the people of Cayman. In one story King George III decreed that Caymanians would be free from conscription in time of war, and in another account the British Parliament passed a bill to forever free Caymanians from taxation. Williams found no historical documents to substantiate these legends.[2] In fact, the idea that Caymanians were granted freedom from conscription seems to be a modernization of Coe's earlier narrative, as told to Hirst, that Caymanians were exempted from impressment in wartime.

For three decades Neville Williams's book was the only published history of the Cayman Islands and was therefore considered authoritative.[3] It was widely read by both Caymanians and visitors and was used in Caymanian schools. It relates the history that until the 1990s—with the research for this book—was generally accepted in Cayman as fact, including the description of the Wreck of the Ten Sail.

Oral Accounts

George Hirst and Neville Williams wrote their descriptions of the Wreck of the Ten Sail because the story survived through the generations. Fortunately in the 1990s, when I began my research, there were still older Caymanians living who remembered tales their parents and grandparents had told them. While some versions are closer to historical fact than others, we cannot judge them as right or wrong by scholarly criteria. Each tale has its own unique merit and the right to be told. Furthermore, folklore provided valuable clues and insight into archival and archaeological research during the Wreck of the Ten Sail Project.

Under the auspices of the Cayman Islands Memory Bank, I had the opportunity to interview Caymanian elders. The program, operated by the Cayman Islands National Archive and today known as the Oral History Program, gathers and preserves historical information through tape-recorded interviews; the tapes and transcribed narratives are made available for research and educational purposes and may be published.[4] I asked each informant to describe the Wreck of the Ten Sail and then posed a series of questions to trace the origin of that particular story and elicit what details each person knew about the Wreck of the Ten Sail and its aftermath.

I interviewed Phoebe Watler Spence on 14 November 1990, in her home overlooking the East End reef at Gun Bay.[5] Miss Phoebe was born in

1907 so was eighty-three at the time. She figured that from the age of four she could remember tales of shipwrecks told to her by her father, William James Watler (the first policeman of the eastern district). Miss Phoebe looked out to sea and began to speak about the story related by the "natives." She said that in the eighteenth century there was a lack of communication with the outside world, and there were no lights to direct ships at East End. The natives were often short of groceries, cloth, and building materials for houses. Thus, as soon as a ship's light was spotted on the horizon, the natives would go out and walk the beach or ride a donkey, carrying a lantern, to lure ships in the wrong direction. As the vessel sailed toward the light (believing it to be another ship) it would "get on" the reef. The East Enders would go out in the morning in their boats and gather what they could off the ships, such as foodstuffs, clothes, and lumber. In fact, East Enders built many houses from the lumber salvaged off these shipwrecks. It was not until 1908 that there was a light at East End—a ship's mast on which Miss Phoebe's father hoisted a lantern each night.

Miss Phoebe told the story of the Wreck of the Ten Sail that she remembered from childhood. There were ten ships loaded with cannons and guns that started from Port Royal, Jamaica. Steering in a westerly direction, they struck the reef on the eastern end of Grand Cayman. The leading ship in the convoy got on the reef and fired flashing lights and cannons, trying to warn the others not to follow. These ships, thinking it was a pirate attack, followed in the same direction, and all lodged on the reef, one right after the other. In the morning, the people saw all of the wrecks lined up on the reef, so went out in their boats and rescued the survivors. Miss Phoebe explained that they put them in the little houses they had along the beach, their homes, and helped them. And from this act, she concluded, "they say the King said this was so great that they exempt all Caymanians from taxes."

When asked whether she had any ancestors who had lived at East End when the Wreck of the Ten Sail occurred, Miss Phoebe said that her great-grandfather, William James Watler, was one of the first settlers. She believed that he had lived at the eastern end of Grand Cayman in the eighteenth century. In answer to further questions, she replied that she did not know of any survivors from the shipwrecks who stayed on the island or who moved into East End. Her father, however, had told her that the ships were ammunition ships loaded with cannons and guns, and she had never heard that there were merchant ships in the convoy. The ships were dark-looking, nothing fancy, just ships that went to war; they were English ships, with the English government. She had never heard the names of any of the vessels; they were just called the Wreck of the Ten Sails. Most of the cannons and guns from the wrecks remained around the island until World War II, when islanders salvaged the ships for iron. Other informants agreed that cannons from the sea contributed to England's war effort. Miss Phoebe said that neighbors Earl and Pat Smith mounted one of the cannons from the Wreck of the Ten Sail in their front yard at Gun Bay. In times past cannons were mounted up on Gun Bluff next to the makeshift lighthouse erected in 1908. Although Miss Phoebe had never heard how many people in all were on the wrecked ships, she understood that just one sailor had died; she did not know the dead sailor's name, but she understood that there was a sailor buried up around Collier's (north of Gun Bay). She included clues helpful to archaeology when she said that in more recent years people had found lumber, ship's parts, dishes, bottles, and bricks on the reef, but no gold. She pointed out that East Channel and South Channel had been widened or dredged around the 1950s (see map 3), and that the East End lagoon is shallower now than it was in earlier times. In the first part of the twentieth century, when East End was an official port of clearance, ships (probably schooners) would enter the lagoon through the Eastern Channel.

Toward the end of the interview, Miss Phoebe read aloud a poem that she had written called "The Wrecks of Cayman," which is reproduced here from her typewritten copy.

Grand Cayman, one of the smallest
And most beautiful of the Caribbean,
It's surrounded by coral reef
Which has brought sailors, soldiers and pirates much grief.

Cayman was hardly on the map,
There were no lights warning sailors of that.
We have tales of pirates, on sea,
But there were stories of pirates to be,
Walking the beach with lanterns in hand,
Changing the ship course at their command.

They were not looking for silver or gold
They just wanted food, cloth and lumber to store.
For these ships were loaded with cargo,
Rice, sugar, corn meal, beans and tobacco.

And so it was that the ship steered in the wrong direction,
So when the ship struck reef,
This roused a question?

I'm sure I saw a light
But now it has gone from my sight.
Said the Captain to the old man at the wheel,
"You must have been asleep, I feel.
What school have you been to, I'd like to hear."
"S'a I've been to dam fool school aw fear,
But au got out and leave you there."

By this time the natives were coming aboard,
Taking every thing they could never afford,
Food, clothing, lumber and such,
"Oh," said the Captain, "don't take too much.
Why don't you try to save us first."

And so we have ships on the coral reef,
The most popular to my belief,
Was the wreck of the Ten Sails.

This did not happen by burning shore lights,
The leading ship struck reef, fired cannon and flashed light.
Trying to warn the others of their plight.

The others in the convoy, fearing pirates attack,
Were bold, brave sailors and would not turn back.

They were trained in any case to do their best,
So they came in aid of the rest.
As birds of a feather, all in one nest.

No food for the natives, only cannons and guns,
But they came to their rescue,
In catboats and canoes.

How many sailors were there,
I cannot say,
But they were lodged in thatch huts along the bay.

Only one life was lost of all
This is a great story to recall,
And has left on our mind
That our Cayman sailors are some of the greatest
That sail the brine.

And the good they have done
Comes down to all people as one.

The King said, "For this from tax you're all free."
Then all Caymanians went on a spree.

For years these ships remain on the reef high and dry,
This always draw the attention of the passers-by.

And what an attraction for the visitors who come
For all the wrecks they have heard of
Was sunk in the Main.

On 4 January 1991, I interviewed Marshall Watler, also an East End resident.[6] He was in failing health and almost deaf at the time. Marshall Watler was born in 1905 and died in 1991. When I asked about the shipwreck, he assured me that he was not so old that he remembered it, but he could tell me something about it. Although a little confusing, his narrative is colorful. He wasn't sure, but thought the "Ten Sail" left from England, and came to the Cayman Islands in search of pirate ships. There were ten of them, enough to sink all the pirate ships they could find. The pirate ships were big wooden, flat-bottom ships, so they couldn't run and tack to keep them off. He said, "So, when they known that they was in on the reef, to the southeast here, they couldn't tack her, see. So that of course put them right up on the reef. And . . . she fired a cannon and . . . [alerted] the other nine . . . they run ashore and they fire much cannon, let them know they was in distress. . . . And then they named them the Ten Sail because they was sailing boats." Mr. Watler continued, saying that these were not battleships but rather sailing ships, and that half of them were French and others old pirates, and Spanish ships too. He closed the narrative by stating, "Wasn't all of one type ship, but all different ships because they was searching for gold. Some of them found gold and sink the other ships and all that."

Mr. Watler went on to say that his ancestors were Irish, and that the Irish were great pirates. It is intriguing that both he and Miss Phoebe mentioned pirates. Mr. Watler's curious mention of French ships may be related to his having been an informant in the 1980s, during archaeological projects at East End, by which time archaeologists knew that French cannons were present on one shipwreck site; otherwise, the folklore rings true about a historical French connection. According to Mr. Watler, some of the shipwreck victims had left the island and others had stayed. He also knew about twelve "pirates' cannons" that lay side by side at Sand Key, just north of East Channel. He mentioned that Earl Smith, an expatriate East End resident, had two cannons in his front yard, one English and one French. He also told me that he had found Spanish olive jars in the East Channel area, that he had told other people about them, and that some of those people had also found such jars. We know that in addition to the Spanish, other nationalities used these late-style Spanish olive jars during the late eighteenth century.

On 4 January 1991, I interviewed Edison Jackson of Bodden Town, who was born in 1910.[7] Edison Jackson was knowledgeable about shipwrecks, especially those in the Bodden Town area, and named and described several. He knew less about the Wreck of the Ten Sail, which he described as "all just an old story," but he acknowledged that the wrecks had occurred. He had heard the "old people" speak of it. They told him that the first ship went aground and fired a warning shot. The others thought that the vessel was in battle or in distress and instead of keeping off, piled in on the first wrecked ship. They were naval ships and all the people on board were saved. He hadn't been told that any of the shipwreck victims stayed on Grand Cayman, but he felt that naturally they had. Mr. Jackson also reported cannons in the sea at Gun Bay, though much had been removed from the wrecks at East End, and he said that some people had found ceramic jars (Spanish olive jars).

Mary Antoinette Wood Levy of Bodden Town, born in 1888—and at the time of the interview the oldest person living in the Cayman Islands—was interviewed on 24 January 1991 (she died later that year).[8] Miss Netty, as she was locally known, said that the Wreck of the Ten Sail, when ten merchant ships wrecked on the reef one after the other, had occurred on the northeast end of Grand Cayman. She had never seen the wrecks, but she had known people from the north side of the island who had seen them. She recalled from the stories they had told her: "Well, it seems like the ships leave port to go south, but they missed the trail and come north. And that brought them to come to Grand Cayman on the east, coming round on the east from up here going right round they got ashore, one after the other, ten of them. . . . All the people survived. Some run off and hide away in North Side bushes . . . some of their ancestors is alive now."

Miss Netty had some difficulty remembering but said that among the names of people who were descended from survivors of the Wreck of the Ten Sail were Solomon, Whittaker, Old Bob Farkey Bodden from the North Side, who could make turtle nets, Old Bald Head Bodden, whose daughter married in George Town, and Craddock Ebanks. She recalled that the Whittakers were the firemen on board who did the coal work. When asked about salvage of the vessels, Miss Netty said that although some of the sailors stayed in Grand Cayman, the ships got off the reef. This was the story told to her by her grandfather, Louden Wood. She had never heard the specific names of the ships, only that they were called the Ten Sail. The "old folks" had not told her the type of merchandise that the ships carried. She said that out on the Gun Bay reef at a place called "Old Rob" is a piece of old ship from the Wreck of the Ten Sail. Her reference seems to be to an area on the south side of the East End Channel. Archaeology reveals that there are three or four mid to late nineteenth-century wrecks in the area, which would account for her observing ship wreckage there as a child. She said that there were no people living at East End when the Wreck of the Ten Sail occurred. Miss Netty worried that she was wandering a bit and reminded me that she was over a hundred years old and was telling stories from her childhood.

The stories these Caymanians told have elements that tie them to the historical account of the Wreck of the Ten Sail, but all include other incongruous details. They exemplify the types of stories and tales remembered by elder Caymanians in the 1990s. New research questions emerged from the interviews regarding locations of shipwreck sites, repeated salvage of wrecks (contemporary, World War II, and more recent), types of artifacts recovered (cannons, ceramic jars, dishes, bottles, bricks, ship parts, and lumber), and the possibility that survivors of the Wreck of the Ten Sail took up residence in Grand Cayman. That possibility cannot be confirmed without genealogical research, but survivors of other shipwrecks are known to have settled in the Cayman Islands. Surprisingly, none of the oral accounts mention the hardships Caymanians were facing following the hurricane of October 1793, and the islanders' request that the survivors of the wrecks leave the island. It is possible, of course, that more recent hurricanes, such as the one that occurred in 1932 with great loss of life, superseded narratives of earlier storms.

Other narratives concerning the Wreck of the Ten Sail were collected earlier, in 1982–83, by Anita Ebanks of the Cayman Islands National Museum. The original tapes and backup copies of these tape-recorded interviews with older Caymanians (mostly East Enders) are now held by the Cayman Islands National Archive in the Oral History Program (former Memory Bank).[9] They have a decade's advantage over the later recordings. Many of the interviewees died during the intervening decade, and those still living in 1990–91 had been younger when they were first interviewed. The tapes used for transcription are one or two generations away from the original and are, in some cases, difficult to understand. Following are the narratives—quoted or paraphrased—told in response to questions Ms. Ebanks posed in her interviews.

Barrett Welcome had heard tales of the Wreck of the Ten Sail from his father and older sister. He said that his grandfather (or great-grandfather—he used the terms interchangeably) was the "coxswain" of the first ship that struck the reef, and he explained that in those days the captain of a ship was called the coxswain. The name of the ship was *The Leader*, and it wrecked and was lost with nine other ships. He said that his great-grandfather, James Leslie Welcome, born of an Irish father and an African mother, was the captain and navigating officer of *The Leader* of the Ten Sail who willfully put them ashore on Grand Cayman. Mr. Welcome did not explain why his ancestor intentionally wrecked the ships; nonetheless, there are other tales told of such actions. There is a popular narrative about a ship called *Geneva Kathleen*, which wrecked on the North Side at the East End of Grand Cayman in 1930. It is said that the cargo vessel was loaded with lumber from Mobile, Alabama, and that her Caymanian captain purposely put the ship ashore. *Geneva Kathleen* was subsequently salvaged, and many houses in the districts of North Side and East End were built from the lumber that she carried.

Mr. Welcome explained that there were fifty-two ships, and Captain Joseph Martin, the commander of the whole fleet, planned to put all of them on shore, but only ten actually wrecked. The ships were bound to Alabama from Africa. Two brothers, one a captain and the other "on the deck," decided to put the ships ashore. The ten ships were landed along the beach from Old Isaacs Point down to the "head of the ironshore down there." The people from the wrecks went down to Bodden Town, Northward, and Lower Valley to settle because there was no settlement in East End. Years later, Mr. Welcome's grandfather walked the beach up to Colliers and settled there. At that time he told Old Man Martin (presumably the commander of the convoy) that he was going to settle on the northeast point of the island, but that if he needed him he could call. Only one sailor was killed off the ship, and he was probably buried somewhere in East End. A lot of the people went down into the Pedro bush and stayed there. Some of the white people, some of the seamen, left on the other ships. Captain Martin and twenty or twenty-five men from *The Leader* stayed on Grand Cayman. The first ship struck the reef at three o'clock in the morning and started firing cannons. One ship was in trouble, and the rest of them piled in on him to help him get out of trouble. That is how he (the commander) trapped the ten of them. He planned to get fifty-two ships on the reef, but the wind dropped and slowed him down. The first ship hit the reef at ten o'clock that night, and he hit at three o'clock in the morning, but by six in the morning the others could see what was happening and they hauled off. The passengers practically had to save themselves. They saved most of their stuff, but since East End was not settled, most of it went down the other way. Mr. Welcome's grandfather went up to Colliers with about twenty or twenty-five people to start a settlement and came back in a few weeks' time to get the others. *The Leader* was a square-rigged barkentine and carried a crew of twenty to forty men. Barrett Welcome's grandfather was the navigating officer. Martin could not navigate and his original navigator got killed, so he picked up Welcome in the Canary Islands. He was twenty-two when he got on the ship. He was never a slave; he was a shipwright and a captain.

At the time of her interview, Ethellen Jackson was one hundred years old. She reported that she used to hear about the Wreck of the Ten Sail but she couldn't remember much about it. She remembered plenty of wrecks striking at East End in her lifetime. When the people saw a wreck on the reef they would call out, "Wreck ashore!" They would all go see the ship, and then the men would go out to the wreck in their canoes while the women made breakfast and carried the food to their husbands and sons. Regarding the Wreck of the Ten Sail, she had heard her parents say that a man from the wrecks was buried at East End, but she was not old enough to remember.

William Allen McLaughlin was born in 1895 and was eighty-eight when he was interviewed. His grandfather had told him that the Wreck of the Ten Sail happened in the time when warships and cargo ships had to be convoyed. Mentioning the cannon shot, he said, "The convoy is coming and one ship got ashore and she fired off a cannon. And then instead of taking it that they were in distress and firing . . . the whole fleet took it that they had been attacked by pirates or something of the kind and so they closed in . . . and didn't find out how it was in error until ten was ashore." When the wrecking occurred, the weather was not too bad, but a northeaster was "blowing heavy." The people from East End who were there on the island saved the people on the ships. William McLaughlin could not recall the names of the ships or how many were in the convoy, but he remembered seeing remains of the warship when he was a boy. When he was ten he went to school at Gun Bay, and at low tide he could see cannons in the bay. During World War II a number of these cannons were taken from Gun Bay to George Town to be sent off for the war effort. He didn't know if any of the shipwreck victims stayed on the island or whether the ships were salvaged at the time. When asked whether there were tricky currents in the area, he remarked, "After a south wind, heavy south wind, and then coming onto a north wind, the current is always very strong. It pulls a boat as they coming down, they come in sight. It pulls them right up towards the point of the reef."

William Warren Conolly, born in 1920, was one of the youngest people that Anita Ebanks interviewed. He had learned the story of the Wreck of the Ten Sail from his grandmother, Adelyn McCoy, who was born in 1857. He told the interviewer that Mrs. McCoy had a very good memory and an ability to relate things correctly. She had witnessed a number of shipwrecks on the reef during her lifetime, but someone else had told the story of the Wreck of the Ten Sail to her. Conolly's recollection of her narrative was that there was a convoy of ships traveling and a leader in the convoy. He said, "And if danger was approaching—that means if they were being attacked by a pirate ship or anything—then they would fire a gun and alert the other ships." Referencing the cannon shot, he explained that when the first ship ran on the reef, a gun was fired. The others mistook the warning "as being some danger from a pirate vessel or vessels . . . and they closed in. And eventually all ten of them went on the reef. This is what she told me."

Mr. Conolly did not recall his grandmother mentioning that lives were lost. He pointed out that although he had heard some people tell a story about a prince or duke being on board, there was nothing in her story like that. He had not heard about people saving things off the wrecks, but he imagined that they did because "ship wrecking" was customary in those days. He did not know the names of the ships. He said that along the beaches and reefs of Gun Bay there are numerous cannons, but that many other ships also wrecked there, so he couldn't be certain whether they came from this squadron of ships or from other single ships that hit the reef. It was difficult to determine how the cannons, lined up and buried in the seabed, adjacent to the beach, got to shore from the reef, which is about a mile away. There are two known locations offshore where cannons positioned side by side are buried in sand at East End. English cannons have been recovered from a site adjacent to shore at Gun Bay, and French ones from a sandbar just inside the reef north of East Channel.

Mr. Conolly speculated that perhaps the whole side of a ship had floated in during a hurricane and settled. He hadn't seen the cannons when he was a child because they were buried in the sand and not exposed. He remembered, however, that in 1940, during World War II, three or four of the cannons were recovered and sent to England for scrap metal. He was one of several young men who, under the direction of Donald McLean, dug them up, pried them out, and maneuvered them from the beach with the help of Inspector Watler's truck.

The description of the Wreck of the Ten Sail that Phoebe Watler Spence gave Anita Ebanks in 1982 was essentially the same narrative, with a few minor variations, that she told me in 1990. In the earlier narrative, however, she described the convoy as merchant ships instead of warships. Additional details recorded in 1982 suggest that among the items salvaged from the shipwrecks were iron furnaces, cannons, and cooking pots as well as materials to build houses. In 1982 she said that some of the shipwreck victims settled in Bodden Town or other districts, but not in East End. She also commented that when the wrecks occurred the weather must have been good.

Another woman (Katy Rochelle Wood?) was eighty when she was interviewed.[10] She said that she did not remember very much about the Wreck of the Ten Sail, but that *Ridgefield* (a Liberty ship that ran aground in 1962) was "riding on the *Ten Sail* anchor." She explained that when the *Ten Sail* struck she dropped an anchor (apparently she thought that the Ten Sail was the name of a single ship) and later *Ridgefield* struck on the *Ten Sail* anchor. In fact, the wreck of *Ridgefield* is located on the south side of East Channel at East End, near several nineteenth-century wrecks and atop at least one.

This narrator said that people were living at East End when the Wreck of the Ten Sail occurred. She knew that there was a sailor buried in the graveyard but was not certain whether he was from the *Ten Sail.* There was a marker on the grave with no writing on it, and when it fell down she picked it up. She remarked that her father always said that it was the sailor's head post. The grave is located at the north end of the Gun Bay cemetery.

Nina Watler Conolly, Miss Phoebe's sister, was born in 1903. She remembered hearing her father say that in the days of piracy, ships traveled in convoy. There were "ten ships going and ten more taking care of what were going in case pirate attack come. So when they strike the reef, when a pirate had attacked them, they would shoot a lot of gun to let them know to hurry get to them." But, in this case, "when they got ashore on this point of reef out here they shoot a lot of gun and the other ships that was taking care of them, coming behind, they speed up. But they had shoot the gun because they had got ashore on the reef, to know they had need help. And when the ten come behind all ten of them got ashore, along with what was that they had strike." She concluded, saying, "The whole Gun Bay was nothing but guns along the shore. And all of there now you can go and get guns."

She agreed that perhaps Gun Bay got its name from all the cannons located there. She did not think any lives had been lost in the Wreck of the Ten Sail. She believed that Caymanian men had helped rescue some of the shipwreck victims in big canoes. Miss Nina did not know the names of any of the ships. She was unsure whether items had been saved from the vessels, but assumed that they had. Her father had a gun that she said was sold only some years ago. It was located on the beach and was said to be from the Ten Sail. She remarked that an American (Earl Smith) took two or three guns from the Ten Sail. She hadn't heard that any of the shipwreck victims from the episode stayed on the island but supposed that they had because a number of foreigners who came ashore from various shipwrecks never left the island. She said that when a cesspool was dug in 1979, some bones were found. She believed they were bones of a dead sailor from the shipwrecks.

Mary Antoinette Wood Levy was ninety-four when Anita Ebanks interviewed her in 1982. Her narrative was similar to what she told me in 1991 but was more detailed. In her story, "the Ten Sail left Jamaica, coming to the West Indies of Cayman . . . one got ashore and . . . made a report and the other nine that was behind thought that . . . she had something happening on board her. . . . And by giving report that she was ashore, the next one came to her for aid and she got ashore, and the next seven came to her and she got ashore, till all ten got ashore, leaving now in this island some of the crew of the first one that got ashore." In her tale, some sailors did not go back to their ships. She exclaimed, "It's a Miller, he's from the Ten Sail. It's an Ebanks, he's from the Ten Sail. It's a Whittaker, he's from this Ten Sail crew that came ashore here in North Side that didn't went back boat. . . . You understanding me now? Now their generation is here now. It is one girl that is married to one fellow in George Town, to Miss Gladys Ebanks. . . . That is one of the Ten Sail only daughter . . . grandfather told us the stories off and on till we had learnt it almost by heart."

Miss Netty suggested that the weather was stormy when the wrecks occurred. She also gave the names of some of the ships as *Dean*, *Romanoff*, *Skudland*, *El Rica*, and *Florence*. These may be the names of other vessels that subsequently went aground in Grand Cayman. Some of these vessels managed to get off the reef.

Miss Netty said that the people from the wrecks who stayed on Grand Cayman went to North Side; to the previously mentioned names she added Bodden and Chisholm. She noted that the Bodden daughter married in this island. Miss Netty said that one of the wrecks left a bolt of satin that the people from the North Side saved. Her grandfather received a couple of yards of that satin, or velvet, because he was one of those who boarded the ships when they came ashore. No one was harmed in the shipwrecks, as the people from East End and North Side went out and saved them in canoes. She noted that a piece of one of the wrecks is still there off Rogers Wreck. There were no slaves, women, or children on the Wreck of the Ten Sail, but a prince was aboard the first ship that struck, the *Dean*. Miss Netty concluded that Caymanians got their freedom from being impressed for any wars because they had done their duty in saving the Ten Sail crew. Miss Netty and her grandfather were good storytellers. Their narrative weaves many Cayman Islands shipwrecks as well as imagination into the Wreck of the Ten Sail.

Retired schoolteacher Doris Wood was seventy-six when her interview took place. She said that according to the older folks, the Wreck of the Ten Sail took place in 1791. At the time there were no people living at East End. She understood that when the event took place, the first ship struck off Corkers Reef at the lower end of the bay (at the south end of the East End reef). It was during the pirate age and King Edward III wanted to free the seas of piracy. He had gathered a convoy of twenty-five or thirty ships to go out. There were no lights at that time on the island, and one of the ships came ashore at Corkers Reef. Miss Doris narrated, “She gave a distress signal. She blew a trumpet that she was having trouble and they thought it said come on these pirate ships. And they all ten made for her, and they keep coming from different angles. They . . . kept getting ashore until they all got ashore between Corkers Reef and Gun Bay. By morning there were ten of the ships ashore.” In her tale, people were not living at East End at that time, but news spread and people arrived from Bodden Town. She remarked, “Slavery is on, the slave boys and slave ships, slave people they came then to their rescue. And I understand that it was, it was a duke among them. I didn't hear of any prince. I hear it was a duke. . . . Everyone was saved. . . . They took time and not a soul never got killed.” She proudly stated, “And for that reason King George made a subscription, an inscription that nobody from Cayman would ever be forced to go to war. On a cause of the kindness that these people that took 'em, different ones in their homes and lodged them till some of them could go back to England. Now that is really fact. . . . Some could get back to England and some decided to stay here.” Miss Doris revealed that Captain William Martin was on the flagship and clarified that “she struck on Corkers reef. . . . And that's where the first one struck and they keep striking further up until they got in Gun Bay, ten of these ships. As I understand it six of them got off, six stayed here. Four got off.”

Miss Doris suggested that the weather was choppy when the wrecking occurred and that people in canoes helped those from the wrecks. She said that the names of two of the ships were *Caradosa*, Captain William Martin's vessel, and *Gwendolyn Warren*. She pointed out that the event had happened a long time before she was born and before her grandma was born; the story was what Miss Doris's grandmother had learned from her grandmother. According to the story, the people from Savannah know about the wrecks because the Ten Sail people went to Newlands and built a house. When questioned about the names of people from the ships, Miss Doris said that one of the sailors from the Ten Sail took up with Sarah McCoy from Bodden Town and that she lived with him and had a child by him. He and other sailors went back to England to collect their money and then returned to Cayman because they liked it so much. In the meantime Sarah McCoy took up with another man, and when the sailor returned she wouldn't have anything to do with him. Miss Doris sang a song that she said was sung about Jimmy Little Fool from the Ten Sail:

Kick him out, kick him out the door.
Kick Jimmy Little Fool, kick him out the door.

She's my darling Sarah McCoy,
Tell her I say I come again.
You see my darling Sarah McCoy,
You can tell her I say I come again.

Kick him out, kick him out the door.
She, she kick him out, kick him out the door.
Kick him out, kick him out the door.

Miss Doris emphasized that the song was made about the Ten Sail people and that they "were here!" She also said that Captain William Martin and the Masons were from the Ten Sail. Captain Martin's wife was called Maybee, and his granddaughter Betsey married Lee Christian.

The event that traveled the 1794 version of "the marl road," and known by oral tradition as the Wreck of the Ten Sail, lives on in the folklore of the Cayman Islands. This suggests that the historical episode attained a significant local value in Caymanian society. It persists in narratives passed along for over two centuries that were told to the children, who became the elders; older Caymanians still tell a variety of stories about the event. Admittedly, the tales are frequently inconsistent with the historical and archaeological record; historical accuracy, however, is not characteristic of folklore. All of the narratives add insight into the lasting effect of the shipwreck episode, and shipwrecks in general, on the local population.

2

Hazard, Landmark, Food

A Hidden Mountain

Within a few decades of Columbus's first voyage to the New World, European seafarers learned that following prevailing wind and ocean currents facilitated navigation to and from the Americas; these rotated in a clockwise direction in the North Atlantic Basin (map 4).[1] It was also discovered that within the Caribbean the prevailing sea and air currents flowed east to west, making it easy to enter the Caribbean between the Lesser Antilles but very difficult to exit by that route. Although ships could depart from the Caribbean Sea through the Windward, Mona, and Anegada Passages in the Greater Antilles, the favored route was the Leeward Passage, in which ships exited through the Yucatán Channel, entered the Gulf Stream in the Gulf of Mexico, and followed the currents through the Straits of Florida out into the Atlantic for the return passage to Europe.[2]

The Cayman Islands emerge abruptly—peaks of a hidden mountain—in the western Caribbean Sea. The three small islands are located amid the Greater Antilles (Cuba, Jamaica, Hispaniola, and Puerto Rico) along the path of the Leeward Passage (see map 2). They are more isolated geographically than most West Indian islands, but their position on the important sailing route ensured that, from the earliest days of New World exploration and discovery, seafarers knew of them. Grand Cayman, the largest and westernmost island, is about 300 km south of Cuba and 280 km north-northwest of Jamaica. It is 35 km long and 6 km to 14 km wide and reaches a maximum elevation of approximately 20 m above sea level.[3] Cayman Brac is 19.5 km long and 3.2 km wide; it rises from sea level at the southwest tip to about 43 m above sea level at the northeastern end. Little Cayman is the smallest and least elevated of the Caymans with a length of 16 km, a width of 3 km, and a maximum height of 10 m above sea level. The geology of the three Cayman Islands, situated on the Cayman Ridge that forms the southern margin of the North American Plate, has been the subject of intensive recent research.[4]

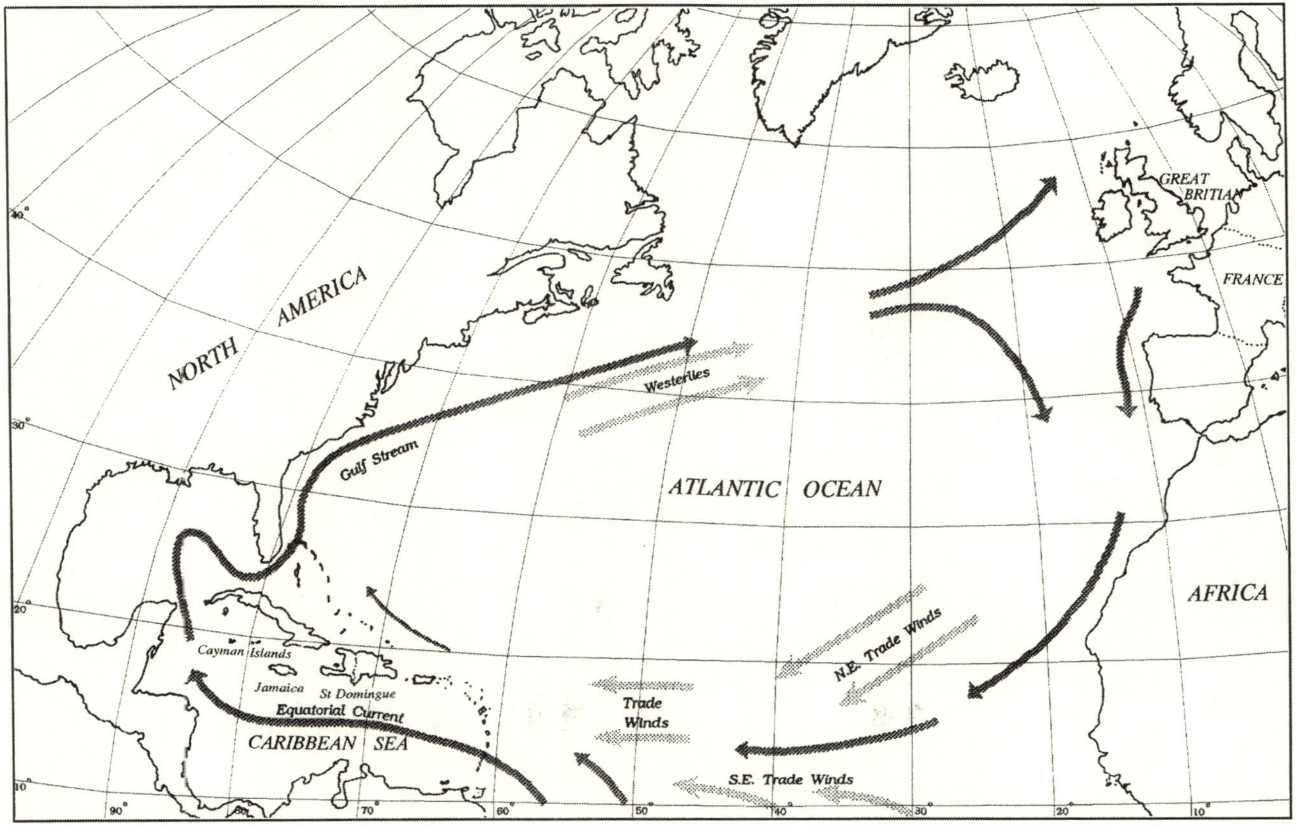

Map 4. North Atlantic Basin winds and ocean currents. Drawn by R. L. Craig.

Histories are available, including a comprehensive history of the Cayman Islands published in 2003; a few years earlier, the University Press of Florida published Roger Smith's book focusing on the islands' maritime heritage.[5] Earlier, shorter histories still provide valuable insights.[6] To provide a historical context for the Cayman Islands and the nature and situation of the people who lived there and responded to the Wreck of the Ten Sail, among other maritime disasters, here is a brief overview with emphasis on the late eighteenth century.

The Fifteenth through Eighteenth Centuries

The Cayman Islands entered the annals of recorded history on 10 May 1503, when Columbus, probably passing between Cayman Brac and Little Cayman through waters teeming with innumerable turtles, named the islands Las Tortugas.[7] Although Columbus did not make landfall in the Caymans, knowledge of their presence spread. From the early sixteenth century on they began to appear in approximately correct geographical positions, although under several different names, on maps drawn by European cartographers.[8]

Spaniards used the Cayman Islands as navigational landmarks and to some extent as provisioning grounds for turtle meat to supply their ships in the sixteenth and early seventeenth centuries, but they stopped short of settlement. It was the Dutch, French, and English seafarers, the challengers to Spain's monopolistic empire, who fully recognized the exceptional value of Cayman's turtle fisheries, and from the sixteenth century forward they regularly exploited the islands' resources in order to replenish their ships' stores.[9]

English navigator Francis Drake landed on Grand Cayman while en route from Cartagena to Cuba during his West Indian voyage of 1585–86. He recorded the island as being uninhabited, and although Drake and his followers could find no water—there are no rivers, and they apparently did not dig for groundwater—they captured turtles and other marine and land animals for provisions. They noted that Grand Cayman had desert and wilderness and that it was full of woods, which they set on fire when they departed.[10] Not only Englishmen but also many Dutch and French seafarers wrote of their sixteenth- and early seventeenth-century visits to the Cayman Islands. And the Dutch West Indiaman *Dolphijn* wrecked on Cayman's shores in 1630.[11]

The English likely established fishing settlements in the Cayman Islands soon after Cromwell's army occupied Jamaica in 1655. Less than 125 years later, while completing the first hydrographic survey of Grand Cayman in

1773, George Gauld noted that Grand Cayman "was originally settled by one of Oliver Cromwell's soldiers, named Bodden, who had been at the taking of Jamaica," and that his grandson Isaac Bodden, over seventy years of age in 1773, remembered when only five families lived on the island.[12] Twenty-nine years later, while taking a census of Grand Cayman in 1802, Edward Corbet heard two versions of how the island was originally settled: while some people told him that the first occupants were pirates, others testified that a person by the name of Bodden from Cromwell's disbanded army in Jamaica was the original settler.[13] About thirty years after Corbet's visit, American settler Nathaniel Glover asserted—without benefit of documentation—that the original settlers were two soldiers from the Cromwellian army whose names were Walter and Bowden, and that they first came to Cayman in about 1658 to catch turtles.[14]

It is clear that during the early days of the Restoration period in England, the Cayman Islands were considered to be English territories. Thomas Windsor, the newly appointed governor of Jamaica, received instructions in 1662 from the English government to take charge of the Cayman Islands among other small islands near or adjacent to Jamaica. Authorities encouraged Windsor to give land grants to individuals and to raise forts on these islands, but neither step appears to have been taken in the seventeenth century in the Cayman Islands.[15] Although the English secured a permanent foothold in the Caymans, an obscure Spanish document suggests that the French also had a settlement on one of the islands in the mid-seventeenth century.[16] Archaeological evidence points to the north coast of Grand Cayman as its possible location.

Certainly, by the late 1660s, the English had founded a village or semi-permanent turtling station on Little Cayman, but this settlement of approximately twenty houses was sacked and destroyed in 1669 by Manuel Rivero Pardal, who held a reprisal commission from the Spanish Crown for revenge on English interests, particularly on the English privateer Captain Henry Morgan, who had recently attacked Porto Bello in Panama.[17] By the Treaty of Madrid, ratified in 1670, Spain and England finally agreed to revoke all reprisals worldwide. Spain also agreed to recognize England's right to the colonies that it then occupied in the West Indies, including Jamaica and the associated territories, which encompassed the Cayman Islands.[18]

It is possible that the Cayman Islands lost some of their occupants in 1671. Thomas Lynch, governor of Jamaica, and members of the governing council offered amnesty to all people who had previously lived in Jamaica and who feared punishment for past irregular actions, but who now lived in Cayman and other more distant places.[19] The governor and council possibly considered the Cayman Islands too remote for protection and encouraged a more intensive occupation of Jamaica in order to establish a stronger English presence on that island and thereby secure a permanent base in the Greater Antilles. Just how the amnesty affected the population of the Cayman Islands is not apparent. However, between the destruction of the turtle fishing village on Little Cayman and the amnesty, people did not establish permanent settlements there or on Cayman Brac until the 1830s.[20] Grand Cayman's greater size likely offered increased protection from invasion and outside interference and better asylum for fugitives, army deserters, and others who needed it.[21]

Into the eighteenth century, all three Cayman Islands served as seasonal fishing grounds and for provisioning passing ships. Although they were used primarily by the English from Jamaica, in 1686 the English government gave the French permission to fish for turtle on the Caymans, which led to a complaint from the British inhabitants of Jamaica some fifty years later.[22] The Cayman Islands also were used to some extent by pirates; tradition further suggests that in the first half of the eighteenth century the islands served as a rendezvous for buccaneers, if not as an actual base for their operations. Daniel Defoe's wildly popular 1724 *General History of the Pyrates* includes tales that Edward Teach (Blackbeard), Edward Low, George Lowther, John Evans, and other pirates had adventures in the Caymans.[23] That piracy was a problem in the area is apparent in the fate of one British navy ship on the Jamaica station. On patrol for pirates in 1715, HMS *Jamaica*, Captain Francis Knighton, was dismasted west of Jamaica in a storm; after being towed to Grand Cayman to be refitted with a new mast, it ran up on the reefs.[24] And pirates George Bradley and Thomas Anstis wrecked *Morning Star* on Grand Cayman in 1722, "through intolerable neglect."[25]

Immigrants from Jamaica who brought slaves, and shipwrecked seamen who decided to take up residence, increased the population of Grand Cayman.[26] Although settlers may have made their homes on the large island in the seventeenth century, the earliest recorded land grants issued in Jamaica include one dated 1734, followed by several dated 1741–42.[27] In the second half of the eighteenth century numerous other people, including many of British descent, took up residence on Grand Cayman; their names are still evident in Cayman's twentieth-century population.[28] In 1773, George Gauld recorded thirty-nine families living on Grand Cayman, consisting of at least two hundred white people and more than two hundred blacks and mulattoes. The island was subordinate to Jamaica, and population growth often could be attributed to shipwrecked mariners who chose to remain there and to people who sought asylum from debt in Jamaica. Both mariners and asylum seekers married into the local population and became settlers.[29] Cayman imported a small number of slaves from Jamaica throughout the eighteenth century; it is said that when *Nelly*, a slave ship bound for Jamaica, was wrecked in Cayman in 1781, some of the slaves were sold on the island to pay salvage expenses.[30] Documentary evidence in support of this event has yet to come to light.

As the population grew, new villages emerged, including those shown on the British Admiralty chart of the island produced from the survey conducted by George Gauld. Several hand-drawn versions of the map dated 1773 exist.[31] The first printed version appeared in 1790 (map 5).[32] It depicts Old Isaacs on the east end, Bodden Town on the south side, the Hogsties on the western shore, and Arnold's on the north side of Grand Cayman; these early settlements survive today as East End, Bodden Town, George Town, and North Side / Old Man Bay. By the end of the eighteenth century, Grand Cayman's population numbered almost one thousand residents.

Throughout the 1700s, the Cayman Islands had seaborne commercial ties and loose political connections with the parent colony of Jamaica; Jamaican merchants capitalized on the Caymanian resources of hardwoods and turtles.[33] In 1773 half a dozen sloops and schooners from Grand Cayman turtled and traded with Jamaica, chiefly exporting cotton and turtles.[34] Although surviving documentation of eighteenth-century seaborne trade between Jamaica and Grand Cayman is scarce, existing records suggest that there was regular sailing between the two islands in the last quarter of the eighteenth century. By the close of the century ten or more vessels per year were involved in the trade, several of them owned by Caymanians.[35] In 1793, residents built one 60-ton vessel, *Two Friends*, and perhaps another vessel.[36] Although the people of Grand Cayman lived relatively insular lives, they received news and commodities from the outside world through their commercial ties to Britain's leading West Indian colony, through opportunistic trading with merchantmen sailing past the islands on Leeward Passage voyages from Jamaica to Britain, and through occasional visits from British warships that called at the island for water and provisions while patrolling the western Caribbean.[37]

Circumstances and dangers that affected Jamaica likely had parallel effects on Cayman during the European wars that extended to the Caribbean in the first three-quarters of the eighteenth century. The taking of prize ships between opponents was common in West Indian waters in the last quarter of the century, during the American War of Independence. British ships and colonies faced threats from American privateers as well as from French, Spanish, and Dutch warships and armed merchantmen, loosing several territories and numerous ships. However, the British also captured prizes, which supplemented Britain's naval and merchant fleets as

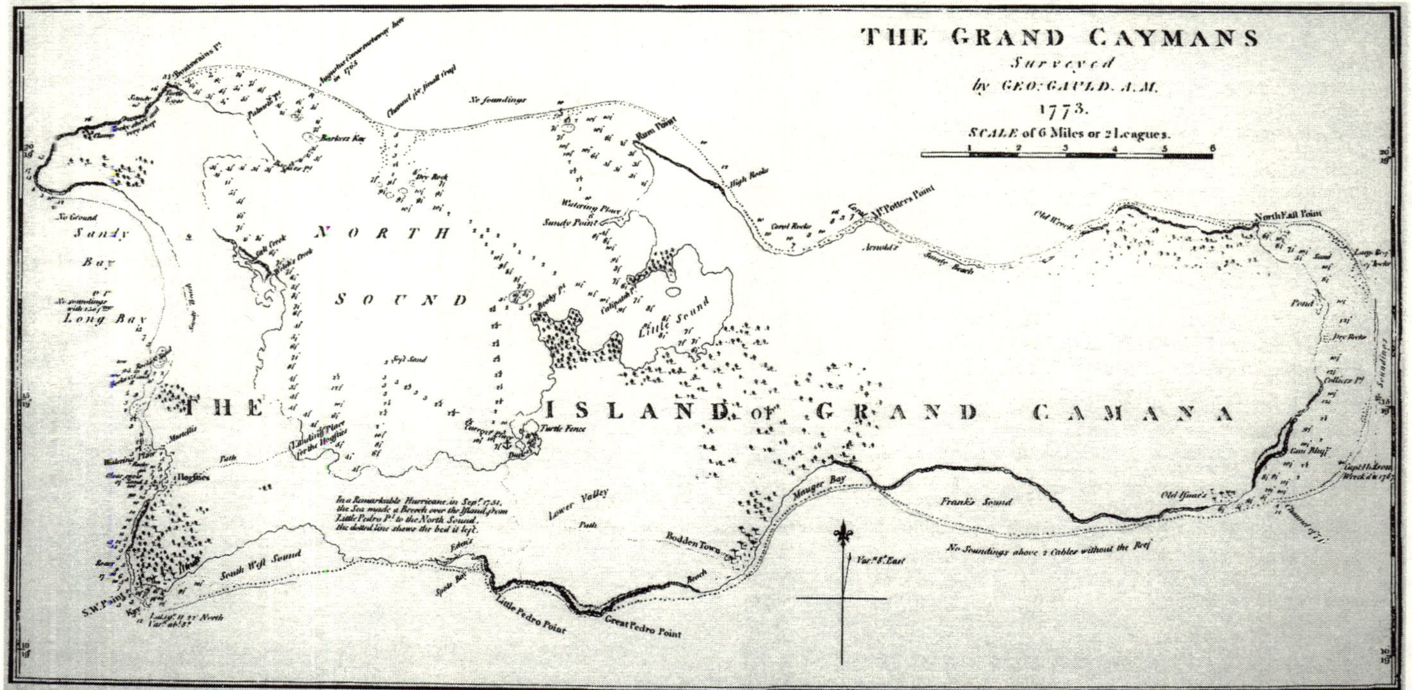

Map 5. British Admiralty chart of Grand Cayman, printed 1790, produced from a 1773 survey conducted by George Gauld. Courtesy of the Public Record Office, Kew.

well as the merchant and fishing fleets of island dependencies like Jamaica and her territories.[38]

While not primary targets for invasion in the American War of Independence, the Cayman Islands were relatively accessible victims for the Spanish in Cuba. The Spaniards launched an attack on Grand Cayman that caused much damage, but they did not attempt to secure and occupy the island.[39] Two decades later, in 1802, Caymanians described the event to Edward Corbet; while the Spaniards had not invaded the island during the most recent war (the French revolutionary wars), they attacked and destroyed their small fort at George Town during the previous war, the American War of Independence.[40]

Edward Corbet's Description of Grand Cayman

Fewer than one thousand people resided on Grand Cayman when the Wreck of the Ten Sail occurred on the windward coast on 8 February 1794; 933 people lived there in 1802, when Edward Corbet took the first official census at the close of the French revolutionary wars, but before the outbreak of the Napoleonic Wars in 1803. In his report, Corbet penned that resident on Grand Cayman were 309 whites, 73 free people of color, 6 free Negroes, and 545 slaves.[41]

Governor Nugent of Jamaica sent Corbet to the Cayman Islands in the summer of 1802 to assess the condition of the islands, their inhabitants, and their defenses.[42] Thus, his report reflects the state of Grand Cayman soon after HMS *Convert* and nine ships of the Royal Navy frigate's merchant convoy wrecked.

He maintained that of the three islands, only Grand Cayman was inhabited, with land there held by possession rather than by grant. The eleven settlements included East End, Frank Sound, Bodden Town, Little Pedro, Spotts, Prospect, South West Sound, George Town, West Bay, Boatswains Bay, and North Side. Corbet listed the inhabitants and noted that most of the (white) settlers were connected by marriage and that most had been born in Cayman.

The largest settlements were at Bodden Town, well protected by a reef through which only canoes and other small vessels could pass, and George Town, located at the western end of Grand Cayman adjacent to a large bay called Sandy Bay. Corbet emphasized that the island's coasts were relatively inaccessible except at Sandy Bay and the channels of the North Sound. Small vessels drawing less than nine feet of water could navigate the North Sound, whereas the harbor at George Town—secure from all but a westward wind and praised for value as a good anchorage—could accommo-

Figure 1. Historic stepwell cut into the Ironshore. Photograph by M. E. Leshikar-Denton.

date much larger ships. In fact, it was the only harbor in the island where large ships could safely anchor. Corbet pointed out that passing ships could obtain very good water and reasonably priced provisions at George Town. In 2003, archaeologists and volunteers discovered several old stepwells that were exposed during construction for a new shopping center on the waterfront. They excavated one particularly early and unique well, which developers preserved and incorporated into Bayshore Mall (figure 1). When cleaned up, the well yielded potable water—as it must have done for centuries. In the late nineteenth century, for yet unknown reasons, people filled the well with debris and covered it, thus preserving it. This well contributed to Cayman's fresh water supply in the 1700–1800s, so perhaps even Corbet tasted it.

Corbet conveyed that Grand Cayman's inhabitants chose their own militia officers, never having received any commissions through the British government system. Nonetheless, other documents show that William Bodden Sr. received a commission from the government in Jamaica to serve as captain in Cayman's militia.[43] Perhaps eighty people on the island could muster to bear arms. There were two small forts, one at George Town with three 4- or 6-pounder cannons, and one on the south side of the island at Prospect, several miles west of Bodden Town, with four guns. Several late eighteenth-century British 6-pounder cannons, thought to be from the two forts, survive today. One is in the National Museum Collection, and one is at Pedro St. James Historic Site.

The inhabitants referred to the laws of Jamaica as they knew or understood them, but generally submitted proposed new measures to the island inhabitants as a whole for their consideration before adoption. Three of five magistrates under a January 1798 commission from Lord Balcarres, a former governor of Jamaica, continued to act in that capacity. The chief magistrate was William Bodden Sr. Two others who had received commissions had since died and the posts had not been filled.

Corbet quantified that the island had eight or nine seagoing vessels of 20 to 50 tons that were used to fish turtle around Grand Cayman and especially off the coast of Cuba, but also around Little Cayman and Cayman Brac in the summer season. The Caymanians brought live turtles back to Grand Cayman, kept them in the sea in "crawls," and later sold the creatures to passing ships sailing on the Leeward Passage to Europe or America.

Corbet learned that about a third of the island could be cultivated and that Caymanians grew cotton, coffee, plantains, yams, sugarcane, corn, and other ground provisions. They raised coconut trees, especially around the coast. Residents estimated a production of about 30 tons of cotton per year, which they sent to Jamaican ports in exchange for needed supplies. The islanders carried on most of this commerce with Montego Bay, the closest Jamaican port. In addition to turtles, Cayman's livestock consisted primarily of pigs and poultry as well as a few head of cattle.

And so, when Edward Corbet visited Grand Cayman in 1802 he found a small, relatively self-sufficient populace whose members made a living by fishing for turtle, cultivating produce, and trading in these commodities. Although the Caymanians ventured to sea in their own craft to fish and to carry on commerce with Jamaica, they conducted a large part of their business from their shores with passing seafarers because of the island's favorable location along the Leeward Passage. Corbet advised Governor Nugent, in terms of British government interest in the Cayman Islands, "that altho' these islands from their limited extent and also soil, cannot become a very valuable appendage of the Government they are to a certain degree a useful one—Lying in the track of vessels going from hence to Europe by the Leeward passage in the event of shipwreck upon them which is not infrequent, the Settlers have afforded great relief to the Sufferers, and have been instrumental in saving many lives which otherwise would have been lost." He concluded that "in time of war Sandy Bay has been found extremely convenient to such of His Majesty's ships of war as have been cruising to leeward, being there able to procure, if they happen to require it, when returning a supply of water and of certain species of Provisions upon reasonable terms." Clearly, Corbet did not regard the Cayman Islands to be essential to Britain's West Indian interests, but because of their geographical locations and the helpful inhabitants, he considered them of value.

The late eighteenth-century era was a time of revolution and warfare within and among European nations and their dependencies, and the conflicts—often involving colonialism as well as ideals of human rights and independence—extended to the Americas and West Indies. Countries were born, colonies were lost and gained, ships were seized from the enemy or were captured by the enemy, and even shipwrecks affected the competitors. These years of crisis ultimately resulted in great changes in Europe, North America, and the West Indies. The European wars that extended to the Caribbean must have facilitated the growth of the Cayman Islands by stimulating communication and commerce between Britain and her colonies; by this time even the smallest British territories were not isolated from the wider world community.

3

L'Inconstante

A Place in the Navy

Dynamics and technologies of the late eighteenth century set the scene for a dramatic history that unfolds with a ship that belonged to two rivaling European powers—the frigate *L'Inconstante* was built by France but captured by Great Britain and renamed HMS *Convert*. The warship wrecked on the East End reefs of Grand Cayman on 8 February 1794.

Looking back in time, the Seven Years' War had largely destroyed the French fleet, and at its close, France embarked on a massive program of naval expansion and re-equipment.[1] It created new scientific academies of naval architecture and established a network of modern dockyards. The country reserved its best timber resources to create a new French navy.[2] French naval scholar Jean Boudriot has stated that French naval architecture reached its pinnacle at about the time of the American War of Independence and that the era marked the last time that French naval strength equaled that of England.[3] If true, the warships of the 1780s represented the shipbuilding achievements of France at the height of French naval design.

During this time King Louis XVI ordered the construction of *L'Inconstante*, a 12-pounder frigate laid down in 1789.[4] Renamed *Convert*, the warship wrecked under British flag in the 1794 Wreck of the Ten Sail, with archaeological remains surviving today in the Cayman Islands. To acquaint this book's wide audience with the frigate's place among the late eighteenth-century warships of France and Britain, and to gain an appreciation for the primary sources relating to her construction, the following is a look at the anatomy of both navies.

Ships and Navies

Between 1793 and 1815, spanning the revolutionary wars and the Napoleonic Wars, Great Britain and France engaged in virtually continuous struggle, in the last major wars fought by sailing navies.[5] It was the era in which heavily armed wooden sailing ships reached their zenith as weapons, particularly when organized in great lines of battle at sea. On the eve of the French Revolution, Great Britain and France had the world's supreme fighting navies, and France had many of the world's finest ships. But the 1789 revolution resulted in social, economic, and military upheavals that adversely affected the substance and organization of the French Navy, leaving it ill prepared for war in 1793. The British navy was perhaps never more ready for action.[6]

During the European conflicts of the late eighteenth century, each nation made use of ships captured from the naval and merchant fleets of its enemies, as had been the wartime practice for hundreds of years. These powers shared common shipbuilding technologies, which made it possible to assimilate foreign ships of comparable design and purpose into their own navies.[7] The French, however, did not rely heavily on the influence of foreign vessels for the design of their own ships[8] but depended almost exclusively on French shipwrights who had received formal training at the special schools of Paris.[9] Conversely, the British frequently sought knowledge about foreign ships and used the information to enhance their own shipbuilding efforts.[10] They conducted espionage and employed foreign designers (including several notable royalist French shipwrights, after the eruption of the French Revolution) but obtained their primary intelligence from captured French, Dutch, Spanish, Danish, and American ships. They made and sometimes directly copied drafts of these vessels, making extensive use of French prize ships to significantly improve hull design throughout the second half of the eighteenth century. They also developed important technologies and designs, among which was the use of copper sheathing to increase speed and reduce hull maintenance for wooden ships, a practice that became widely adopted for naval and merchant vessels, including those of France.[11]

Each country built its ships for its own purposes. French ships were often more lightly constructed than their British counterparts because speed was essential to carry out timely expeditions in specific campaigns, whereas British ships were more powerfully built for overall strength to achieve dominance and control of the seas—vital needs for an island nation.[12]

French Ships

During the 1780s and throughout the revolutionary and Napoleonic wars, the French Navy comprised a variety of vessels. Two-decker and three-decker warships that were large and strong enough to form part of the line of battle in major fleet actions were called ships of the line. An admiral usually commanded the largest, a three-decker of 110 or 120 guns, with its primary ordnance supported on three separate, unbroken decks, and additional guns on the forecastle and quarterdeck. Such ships had thicker and higher sides than two-deckers and carried more guns than any other vessels in the French Navy, qualities that were advantageous for close combat, but that made them less stable when sailing on the water than their smaller counterparts.

The standard two-deckers carried either eighty or seventy-four guns, the main ordnance being located on two continuous decks with secondary guns on the forecastle and quarterdeck. The eighty-gun ship with larger timbers carried heavier armament than the ship of seventy-four guns, but the seventy-four-gun ship became widely recognized for its balance of heavy broadside weight and good sailing ability.[13] It carried 36-pounder cannons (that is, guns firing 36-pound iron shot) on the gundeck, 18-pounder cannons on the upper deck, and 8-pounder cannons on the forecastle and quarterdeck.[14] According to Boudriot, the seventy-four-gun ship "formed the backbone of the fleets, and thus the maritime power of nations."[15]

Weak for the line of battle, and ceasing to be built shortly after the American War of Independence, the two-decker sixty-four-gun ship still remained in the French Navy at the close of the eighteenth century. The fifty-gun ship, another two-decker, had also become obsolete, as it was too small for the line of battle.[16]

The French designed the medium-sized 8-, 12-, and 18-pounder frigates for speed, using them chiefly for reconnaissance missions, for patrolling cruises, and as convoy escorts. The numerical designation indicated the size of the ordnance mounted on the gundeck. Frigates carried their primary ordnance on a single unbroken gundeck and the secondary armament on the forecastle and quarterdeck. The 8-pounder became obsolete by the 1780s, with the 12-pounder, including *L'Inconstante*, considered the ideal size up until the revolutionary wars. The more powerful 18-pounder frigate became the standard by the Napoleonic Wars.[17]

A French corvette was any vessel smaller than a frigate. The sloop of war carried only a single tier of guns on its open main deck. The next class included lightly armed two-masted craft, smaller than the ship-rigged vessels already mentioned (which carried three masts and square sails), and identified by rig as snows, brigs, and schooners; cutters or luggers composed vessels with a single mast. Other naval craft included gunboats, storeships, and transports.[18] At the outbreak of the revolutionary wars in 1792, the French Navy had 241 ships and vessels, including eighty-three ships of the line and seventy-seven frigates.[19]

British Ships

French, Spanish, and Dutch involvement in the American War of Independence severely challenged Britain's naval strength and superiority in the conflict. In response, Britain began a substantial shipbuilding program that reached fruition after the war ended in 1783, but which prepared Britain for the French revolutionary wars.[20]

At the start of the British involvement in the conflicts in 1793, the Royal Navy consisted of 498 ships and vessels.[21] For the vessels that carried at least twenty guns, Britain had developed a classification scheme of six "rates." They revised the scale for ships built after 1792, but the navy was made up of ships built both before and after that date.[22] The British used the system to define the number of officers assigned to each type of ship as well as their pay scales; the rating system also suggested the size of a ship and its role or function.

Ships of the line included first-, second-, and third-rate ships; the fourth-rate ship, officially considered within this class, had largely become obsolete by 1793. First-rate ships carried a hundred or more guns, with the primary ordnance located on three unbroken decks and the secondary artillery on the forecastle and quarterdeck. Commanded by an admiral and carrying his staff, a first-rate ship mounted guns that ranged from 42- or 32-pounders to 12-pounders. Second-rate ships carried from ninety to ninety-eight guns, usually ranging from 32-pounders to 12-pounders, on three decks. Third-rate ships compared somewhat to the French two-deckers of eighty, seventy-four, and sixty-four guns and mounted ordnance that varied from 32-pounders to 6-pounders. Like its French counterpart, the British seventy-four-gun ship embodied the perfect balance of good sailing ability, broadside strength, and seaworthiness.

The fourth-rate two-deckers mounted between fifty and sixty guns ranging from 24-pounders to 6-pounders, but the Royal Navy had few of these vessels. Fifth-rate ships consisted of frigates of between thirty-two and forty guns and essentially outdated forty-four-gun two-deckers, mounting ordnance that ranged from 18-pounders to 6-pounders.[23] Frigates served as reconnaissance vessels for the fleet and as cruisers, convoy escorts, and commerce raiders. They carried significant firepower and yet were fast enough to evade larger enemies; these ships sailed on independent missions and often fought single-ship actions against foreign frigates and privateers.[24] Sixth-rates, the largest usually being twenty-eight-gun frigates, and the smallest rated vessels, mounted between twenty and thirty guns. Unrated vessels included ship-rigged sloops with three masts and square sails as well as small craft identified by rig or purpose as brigs, schooners, cutters, transports, bomb vessels, and gunboats.[25]

Clearly, with few pronounced variations between French and British ships of the period in hull design, rigging, and armament, captured ships could be readily assimilated into the victor's fleet.

The 12-Pounder Frigate

L'Inconstante, a French 12-pounder frigate mounting forty guns, was one of the medium-sized warships designed for speed and used to escort convoys, patrol, and conduct reconnaissance missions.[26] The ship was constructed at Rochefort, one of France's three great royal dockyards where most of the French Navy's warships were built. The other principal dockyards were at Brest and Toulon, and warships were produced at L'Orient (map 6). Frigates, corvettes, and smaller craft also were built in the ports of Bayonne, Bordeaux, Marseille, Nantes, Le Havre, Saint-Malo, and Dunkirk.[27] Located up the River Charente and adjacent to the anchorages of Aix and Basque roads, protected by the islands of Ré and Oléron, Rochefort served as a principal base on the Atlantic coast of France. Established by Jean-Baptiste Colbert in the late seventeenth century, Rochefort exhibited one of Europe's few planned dockyard towns with complete facilities.[28]

During the seventeenth and early eighteenth centuries, the term *frégate* was used in France to describe several types of armed vessels, one a small two-decked ship and another the *frégate légères*, which in 1660 carried eight to sixteen 3- to 4-pounder cannons on a single deck, covered at both ends with a small forecastle and a quarterdeck.[29] Boudriot suggests that the *frégate moderne* that emerged in the mid-eighteenth century descended from the *frégate légères*. In some aspects, the prototype of the *frégate moderne* was *La Médée*, built in 1741, which supported its primary ordnance of twenty-six 8-pounder cannons on a single deck and also had a small forecastle and a quarterdeck. The 12-pounder frigate was an adaptation of the 8-pounder vessel, but it carried heavier ordnance, which made it stronger and more forceful. The first such frigate to be constructed was *L'Hermione*, which was built in the dockyards of Rochefort in 1748 by the noted shipwright Morineau. The 8-pounder frigate was built until about 1774, and the 12-pounder frigate until 1798, when the more powerful 18-pounder frigate superseded it.[30]

In the fifty years between 1748 and 1798, France built more than one hundred 12-pounder frigates, including twenty-one at Rochefort and others at Toulon, Saint-Malo, Le Havre, Brest, L'Orient, Nantes, Bordeaux,

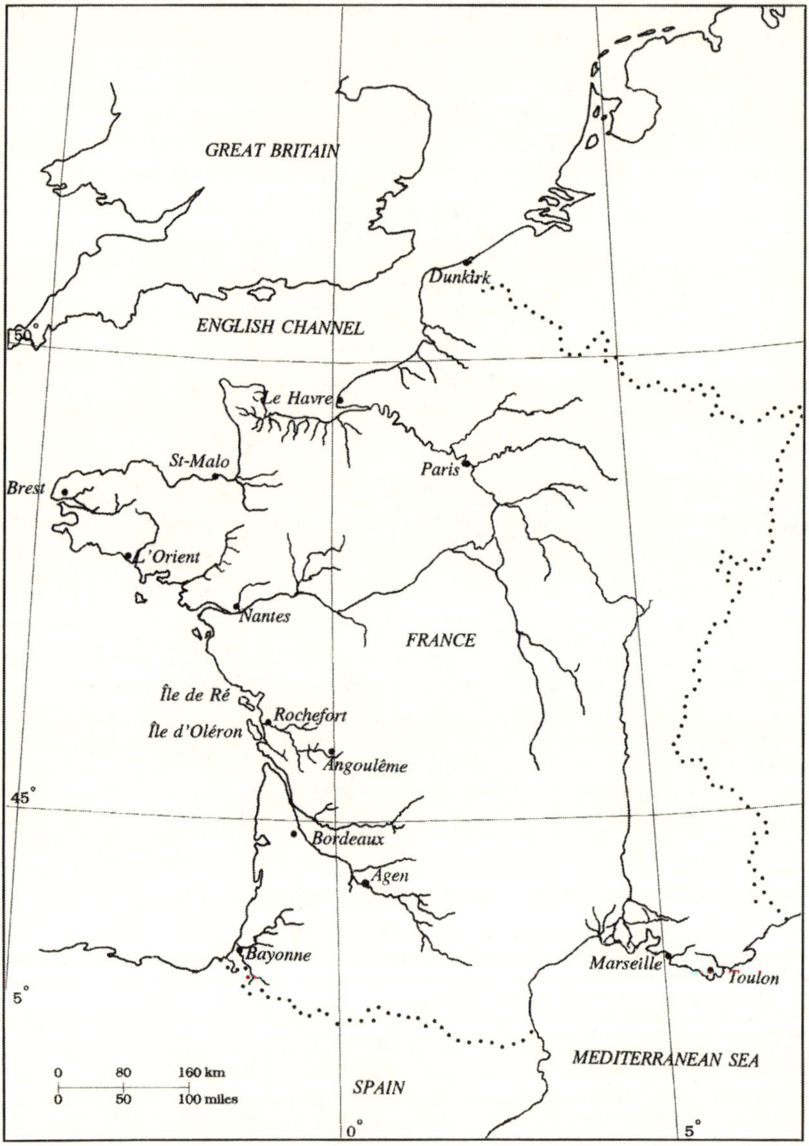

Map 6. Late eighteenth-century France. Drawn by R. L. Craig.

and Bayonne.[31] Frigate construction occurred in clusters, especially around times of war. France built twenty-three frigates in the period before, during, and after the Seven Years' War (1756–63). French shipbuilders constructed most at the conclusion of the conflict, suggesting that they recognized their superiority over the more common 8-pounder vessels during the war. There was a lull in construction in the years between 1768 and 1776, but during the American War of Independence, forty-five 12-pounder frigates were built. In the postwar period between 1784 and 1786, nine others were laid down in the dockyards.

L'Inconstante was among nine frigates placed under construction between 1788 and 1790, the volatile era preceding, during, and immediately after the 1789 revolution in France. Yet in 1791 and 1792, France did not lay down any frigates. During the early years of the revolutionary wars, from 1793 to 1795, they started fourteen 12-pounders in the dockyards. The building of the last four 12-pounder frigates by the French Navy began in 1797 and 1798, several years before the conclusion of the French revolutionary wars in 1802. The 12-pounder frigate had proved its worth in the Seven Years' War and was highly celebrated in the American War of Independence. In 1786 there were still forty of these vessels in the French Navy, compared with only twenty of the newer 18-pounders. Nonetheless, the more powerful 18-pounder gained preeminence during the French revolutionary wars and became the standard frigate of the Napoleonic Wars.[32]

Although built to drafts designed by at least twenty-one different shipwrights, during the second half of the eighteenth century, 12-pounder frigates changed relatively little and most shared common attributes.[33] The primary differences between frigates were in the underwater lines.[34] Therefore, although no representations of *L'Inconstante* have been found, engravings by Pierre Ozanne of 12-pounder frigates of the late 1770s and 1780s accurately depict the sails, rigging, and above-the-waterline features of French 12-pounder frigates (figure 2).[35]

According to naval scholars Jean Boudriot and David H. Roberts, *L'Inconstante* was built according to a design prepared by Jean Denis Chevillard, who was called the Younger to differentiate him from his older brother Henri Chevillard (the Elder). Born on 9 October 1738, Chevillard the Younger became an eminent designer-shipwright who designed and built superb ships for the French Navy. His career began in July 1755 when he entered the navy as *elève-constructeur* (student shipwright). Promoted in May 1757, he became *sous-constructeur* (assistant). In April 1765, after the introduction of the Regulations of 1765, his title became *sous-ingénieur-constructeur* (under-shipwright). The following year he achieved the title of *ingénieur-constructeur-ordinaire* (ordinary assistant). In July 1781 he be-

Figure 2. Frigate seen from abeam, close-hauled with sheets to port. Engraving by P. Ozanne. Courtesy of Jean Boudriot.

came *ingénieur-constructeur en chef* (master shipwright) at the Rochefort Dockyard, a post that he held from 1781 to 1786 and again from 1792 to 1795, when he retired. Chevillard the Younger died on 31 March 1804.[36]

A number of ships were constructed at the Rochefort dockyard according to the designs of Chevillard the Younger, and it is believed that eight of nine 12-pounder frigates whose construction began between 1777 and 1789 were fashioned according to identical drafts, with the following principal dimensions: length 136 *pieds* (44.2 m), breadth 34.6 *pieds* (11.24 m), and depth in hold 17.6 *pieds* (5.72 m).[37] Plans for *L'Inconstante* are lost or destroyed, though drafts for several sister ships survive in various French and British archives.[38]

Construction of *La Gracieuse* began in 1785 and of *L'Inconstante* in 1789. The similar dimensions between the two vessels suggest their construction according to the same draft by Chevillard the Younger. Like the plans of *L'Inconstante*, however, the original drafts for *La Gracieuse* are lost or do not survive.[39] Subsequently, the British captured *La Gracieuse*, renamed *L'Unité*, during the Revolution of 1796 in France. The lines taken off the frigate by the Royal Navy are preserved in the National Maritime Museum at Greenwich, London (figures 3–5).[40] Thus, it can be assumed that *L'Inconstante* conformed largely to the same plans as *L'Unité*, ex-*Gracieuse*. Additional details of construction for *La Gracieuse*, notably the spar dimensions, survive in the Rochefort Archives, and presumably these also apply for *L'Inconstante*. These documents mention the excellent sailing characteristics of *La Gracieuse*. The frigate could achieve noteworthy speeds of up to fourteen knots in strong winds—and it is likely that *L'Inconstante* could do the same.[41]

Of the eight sister 12-pounder frigates designed by Chevillard the Younger, the British captured several, while others were shipwrecked. Five had careers in the French Navy of less than five years, from the date they were placed under construction to the date they were struck from the navy list. The remaining three served France for between ten and fifteen years.[42] *La Charmante* and *La Junon*, both built at Rochefort during the American War of Independence, experienced campaigns in the West Indies during their short careers. Each served France well in the conflict and each was involved in captures of British ships, but both frigates met untimely ends as shipwrecks. *La Charmante* wrecked in Europe in March 1780 while en route from L'Orient to Brest; she was cast up on the rocks of the Chaussée de Sein in a strong wind, with the loss of many of her crew. *La Junon* was wrecked on 11 October 1780 in the West Indies when she was hurled up on the coast of the island of Saint Vincent in a hurricane, but her crew was saved.[43] *L'Inconstante* was captured by the British in 1793 and in 1794 was wrecked in the Cayman Islands, and the British captured *L'Unité*, ex-*Gracieuse*, in 1796. The other four 12-pounder frigates built to Chevillard the Younger's design were struck off the French Navy list in the following years: *La Tourtereau* in 1787; *L'Atalante* in 1797; *La Fraternité* in 1802; and *L'Hélène* in 1793.[44]

Construction and Outfitting

In 1788 and 1789, directions were given for seven 12-pounder frigates to be built in the Royal Dockyards of France, including *L'Hélène* and *L'Inconstante* at Rochefort, to the drafts of Chevillard the Younger.[45] In 1791 and 1792 no additional 12-pounder frigates were requested, probably due in part to France's unsettled political and social state.

L'Inconstante's story begins only four months before the start of the French Revolution. Archival sources reveal a brief and fragmented but nonetheless fascinating account of the progress of the frigate's construction at Rochefort. The following, in near chronological order, is informa-

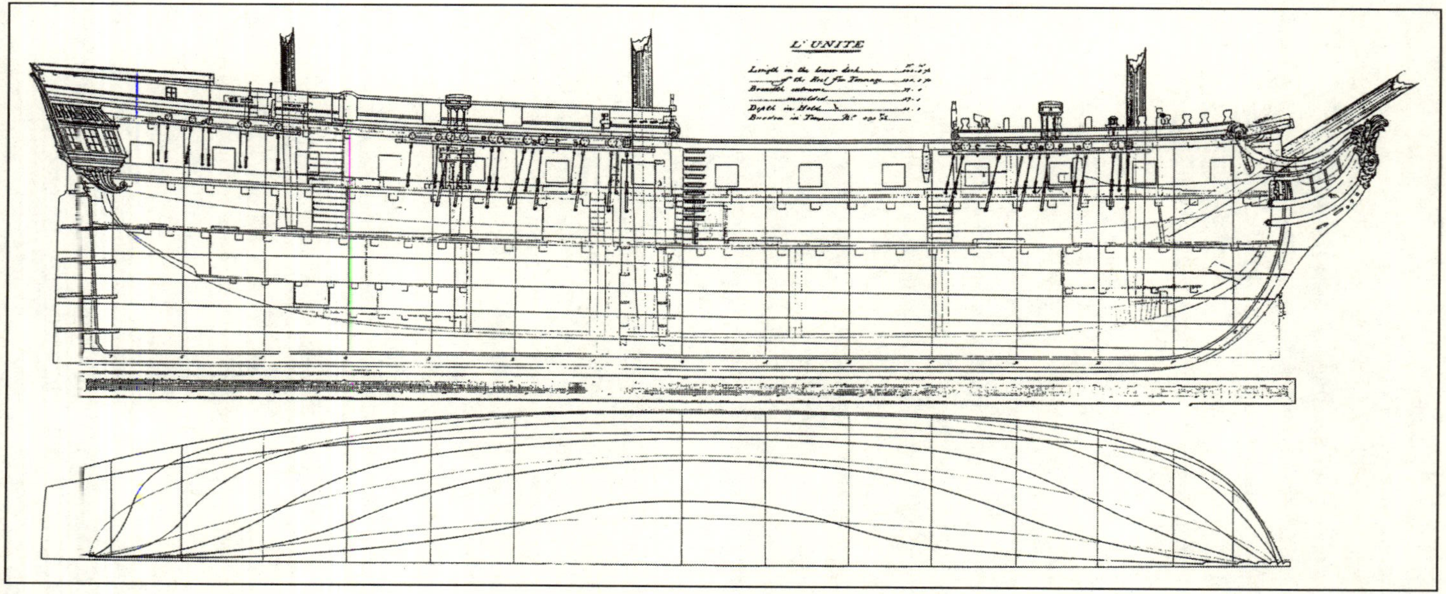

Figure 3. *L'Unité*, profile, as taken. Courtesy of the National Maritime Museum, London.

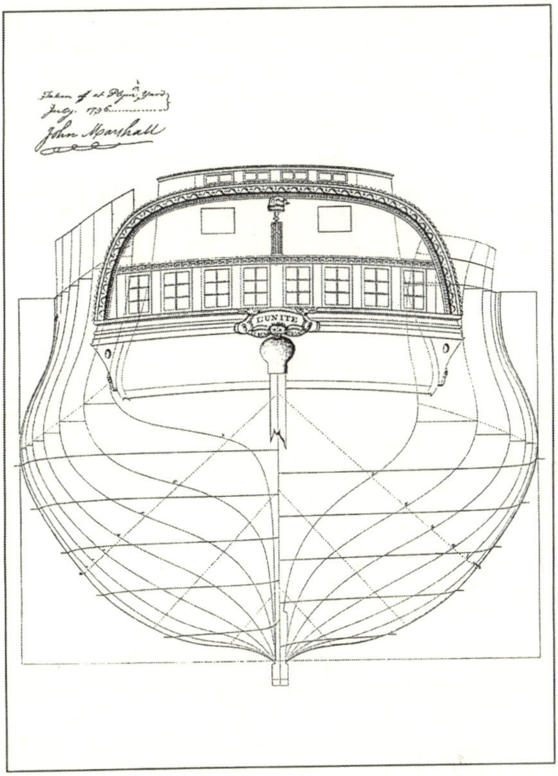

Figure 4. *L'Unité*, stern, as taken. Courtesy of the National Maritime Museum, London.

tion that provides insight into the workings of the dockyard and the building of the frigate.[46]

L'Inconstante was first referred to by name in early 1789. According to instructions in a letter of 14 March 1789 from M. le Comte de La Luzerne (of the central navy administration in Versailles) to MM. le Comte de Vaudreuil and de La Grandville (principals at Rochefort), two 12-pounder frigates that had been ordered were to be called *L'Hélène* and *L'Inconstante*, by order of King Louis XVI (figure 6).[47]

Rochefort operated in an organized fashion. Workers took inventories periodically to assess quantities of supplies and equipment on hand in the warehouses and on ships in the port, and to determine what items shipwrights required to complete the numerous building and repair projects that were undertaken simultaneously. One such summary of the articles needed to complete and equip the ships under construction and repair at the dockyard, compared with the existing items in the Magasin Général,

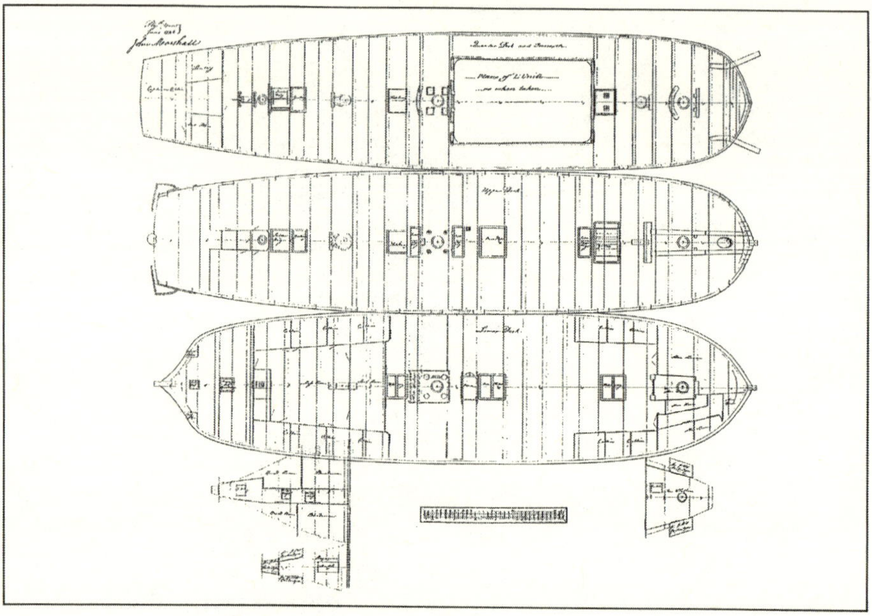

Figure 5. *L'Unité*, decks, as taken. Courtesy of the National Maritime Museum, London.

was taken on 1 May 1789, shortly before *L'Inconstante* was laid down. The inventory revealed that at that time there were more shortages than excesses in the list of specific commodities, which included copper sheathing, copper nails for sheathing, bars of copper, launches and smaller boats, masts and spars, canvas for sails, cordage, anchors, and barrels.[48]

The earliest clue to the actual commencement of work on *L'Inconstante* was found in a letter sent to La Grandville from La Luzerne dated 16 May 1789. In the dispatch, La Luzerne confirmed that an estimate of labor costs for the first phase of the construction of *L'Inconstante* had been reviewed by the Naval Council and found to be reasonable for the king's interests. La Luzerne had therefore put his approval on it and the work could go forward.[49]

A significant document from Rochefort, dated 26 June 1789 and titled "Diréction des constructions," described the state of the *plancons* and *barrots* necessary for the ships under construction and in drydock or maintenance at the port. It seems that the first phase of building *L'Inconstante* proceeded without delay, because the timbers ordered for the frigate included beams for the deck, the orlop deck, the forecastle, and the quarterdeck. For the decks and orlop decks of *L'Inconstante* and *L'Hélène*, 128 beams of 28 to 34 *pieds* by 10 and 11 *pounces* were required (there are 12 *pounces* [2.71 cm] to

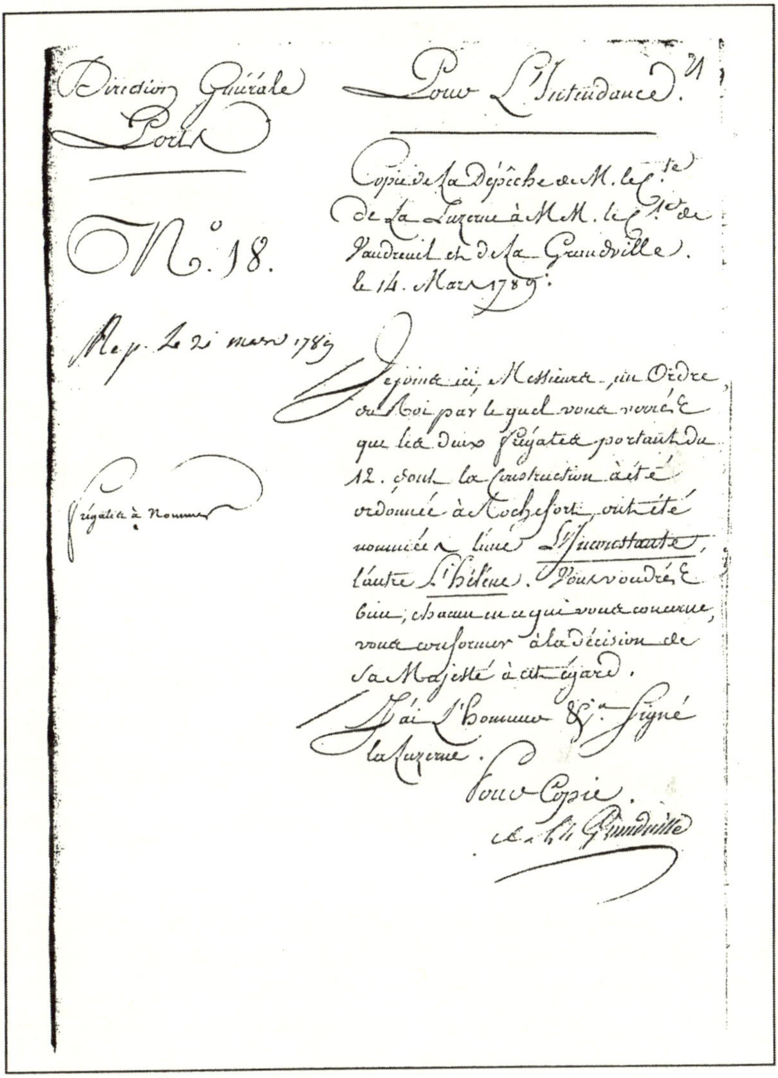
Direction Générale Port

Pour L'Intendance.

N°. 18.

Copie de la Dépêche de M. le Cte de la Luzerne à MM. le Cte de Vaudreuil et de la Grandville. le 14. Mars 1789.

Reçu le 21 mars 1789

Frégates à nommer

Je joins ici, Messieurs, un Ordre du Roi par lequel vous verrez que les deux frégates portant du 12. dont la construction a été ordonnée à Rochefort, ont été nommées l'une L'Inconstante, l'autre L'Hélène. Vous voudrez bien, chacun en ce qui vous concerne, vous conformer à la décision de Sa Majesté à cet égard.

J'ai l'honneur &ca. Signé La Luzerne.

Pour Copie.

de la Grandville

Figure 6. Order of King Louis XVI naming *L'Inconstante* and *L'Hélène*. Courtesy of the Archives du Port de Rochefort, Rochefort.

1 French *pied* [32.5 cm]). Presumably, sixty-four such beams went to each vessel. Sixty beams of another variety, perhaps the ledges that extended between the main beams, were to be provided for the forecastles and quarterdecks of the two 12-pounder frigates. These were to be 26 to 31 *pieds* long by 9 *pounces* wide and 9 *pounces* thick, and, presumably, thirty were needed for each vessel.

Although work on *L'Inconstante* must have been underway by this time, it appears that *L'Hélène* had not yet been placed under construction; the "Diréction" shows that four pieces of timber for the ship's keel were still required. These were to be 32 to 36 *pieds* long by 16 and 14 *pounces*, and it can be assumed that the keel requirements of the sister ship *L'Inconstante* had been the same. Rochefort dockyard was a busy place: the 12-pounder frigate *Embuscade* also was under construction there, and three ships of the line were being built or repaired.[50]

In mid-July, Paris experienced the storming of the Bastille. Undoubtedly conditions at the Rochefort dockyard were affected by the subsequent turmoil and confusion throughout France, and work on *L'Inconstante* and *L'Hélène*, among other vessels, was delayed. Four months after the Bastille incident, a copy of a letter of 21 November 1789 sent from La Luzerne to de Vaudreuil and de Bellefontaine circulated at the dockyard. It stated that the king had recently ordered a report on the state of French naval forces. After consulting the Naval Council, the king had decided that only two seventy-four-gun ships would be built at Rochefort dockyard during 1790, because two other ships and the frigates *L'Inconstante* and *L'Hélène* needed to be completed. The frigates were behind schedule, and the king and Naval Council wanted them launched in 1790. The dispatch maintained that the scheduled work was sufficient to keep all the workers at the dockyard employed, because they would also repair other ships. La Luzerne expressed concern about the budget, as it was the same as the 1789 budget. Also, a portion of the 1790 funds would go toward half the cost of building two *flûtes* that would be launched near Bayonne in 1791.[51] Although the authorities attempted to present an image of stability, it is not surprising that there was a sense of insecurity in the dockyard town of Rochefort.

Correspondence of 25 September 1789 mentioned ballast of stone and iron. There were only two providers of iron ballast for Rochefort, M. la Pouge and M. Butet, who should be requested to make timelier deliveries because they currently were not fulfilling their commitments.[52] A document dated 10 January 1790 specified the amount of iron ballast considered necessary for various ships according to the Regulations of 28 January 1787. The 12-pounder frigates not outfitted with masts and other equipment each needed four hundred tons, and those equipped for sea required 110 tons of pig iron.[53]

No specific reference to the second phase of *L'Inconstante*'s construction has been found. In a letter dated 26 March 1790 from La Luzerne to de Vaudreuil and La Grandville, La Luzerne confirmed that he had given the Naval Council their letter of 20 February and La Grandville's letter of 6 December concerning allocation of labor for the third stage of the frigate's construction. Because a recent tariff had resulted in the reduction of allocated funds, the Council of Rochefort wondered whether workers would receive their full daily pay and wanted authorization to ensure that the salaries would be paid, but the Naval Council was unsympathetic to this request. La Luzerne instructed La Grandville to postpone work on the frigate *L'Inconstante* until further notice.[54]

Subsequently, in a letter to La Grandville, written in Paris and dated 23 April 1790, La Luzerne acknowledged La Grandville's recent correspondence. La Grandville managed to get the labor for the third part of the construction of *L'Inconstante*, but in order to keep to the conditions of the contract, he reduced the number of workers. The fact that La Luzerne's correspondence now was from Paris rather than from Versailles underscores the movement of revolutionary France away from the monarchy.[55]

In a 30 April 1790 letter to La Grandville, La Luzerne acknowledged La Grandville's letters that had come before the Naval Council: one concerned the allocation of labor for the fourth stage of the construction of *L'Inconstante* and another, the labor for the second stage of *L'Hélène*. La Luzerne informed La Grandville that both projects were accepted.[56]

A journal the Commandant de la Marine at Rochefort kept about activities at the port in 1790 revealed that there was a request for copper in bars, nails, and sheets. There was specific mention that 560 ten-*pounce* copper nails were being acquired for *L'Inconstante*. The entry for 11 September recorded that the frigate was launched on 9 September 1790. The shipwright who directed her construction was mentioned by name. The Commandant wrote that, notwithstanding a scarcity of funds, a gratuity should be given to *Sous-ingénieur-constructeur* St. Pennevert, who had directed the building of the frigate, and to *Mt-charpentier* Dubois, who had worked under St. Pennevert, because the work had been well executed. It is not known whether Chevillard the Younger was actually involved in the construction—the designer of a ship was not always in charge of the actual building of the vessel.[57] The entry for 11 December revealed that one side of the hull of *L'Inconstante* had been sheathed in copper and that the other side was still to be completed.[58]

An inventory of the quantity of ballast present in the ships and the warehouses of Rochefort was requested in a letter of 28 December 1790.[59] The report of 10 January 1791 indicated that eight 12-pounder frigates required a total of 880 tons. *L'Inconstante* was among these frigates and would have been supplied with 110 tons of iron ballast.[60]

In 1791 *L'Inconstante* was furnished with masts, sails, and rigging and the hull fitted out with equipment and necessities. On 3 December 1791, Alexandre Joseph Riouffe, soon promoted to Capitaine de Vaisseau, re-

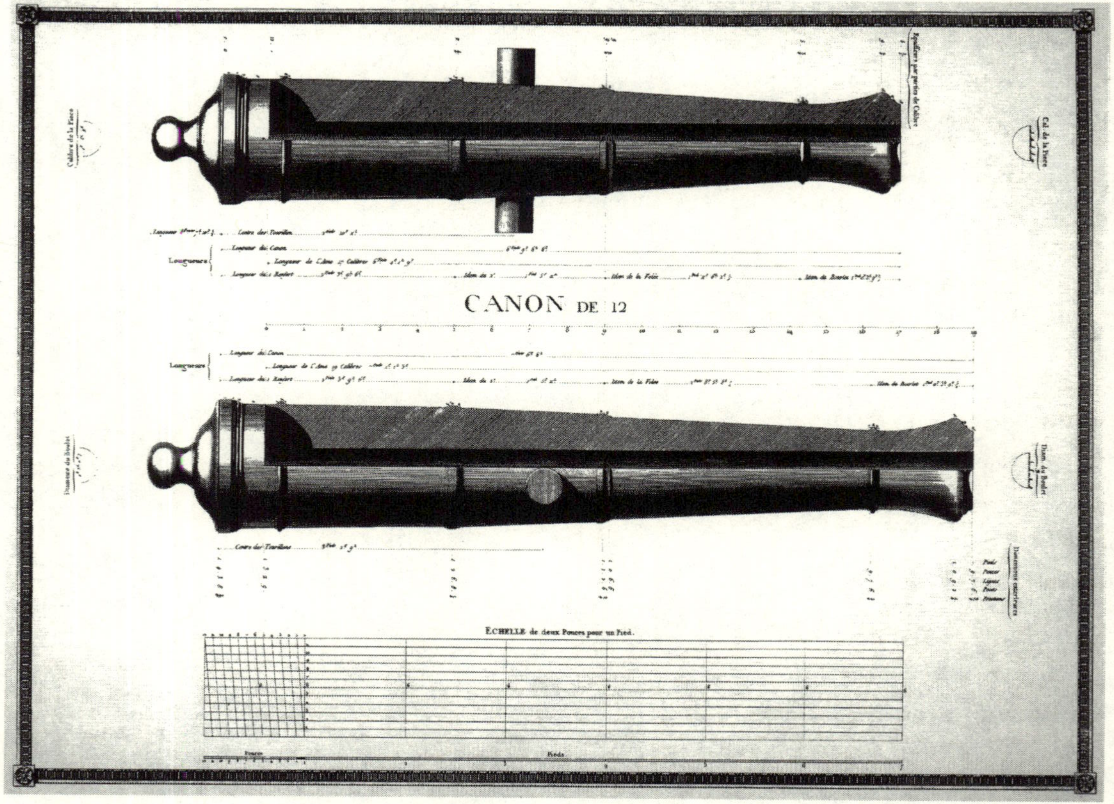

Figure 7. Twelve-pounder cannons to the Regulations of 1778–79. *L'Inconstante* carried long pattern cannons as in the lower illustration. Courtesy of Jean Boudriot.

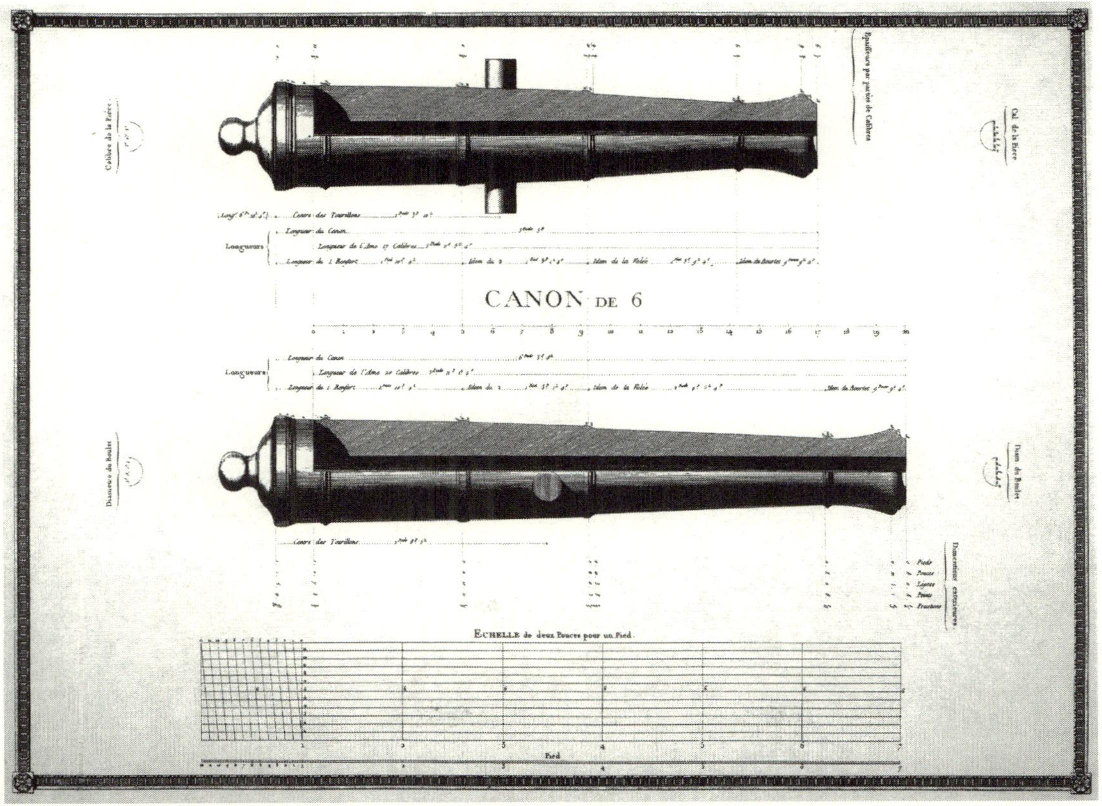

Figure 8. Six-pounder cannons to the Regulations of 1778–79. Courtesy of Jean Boudriot.

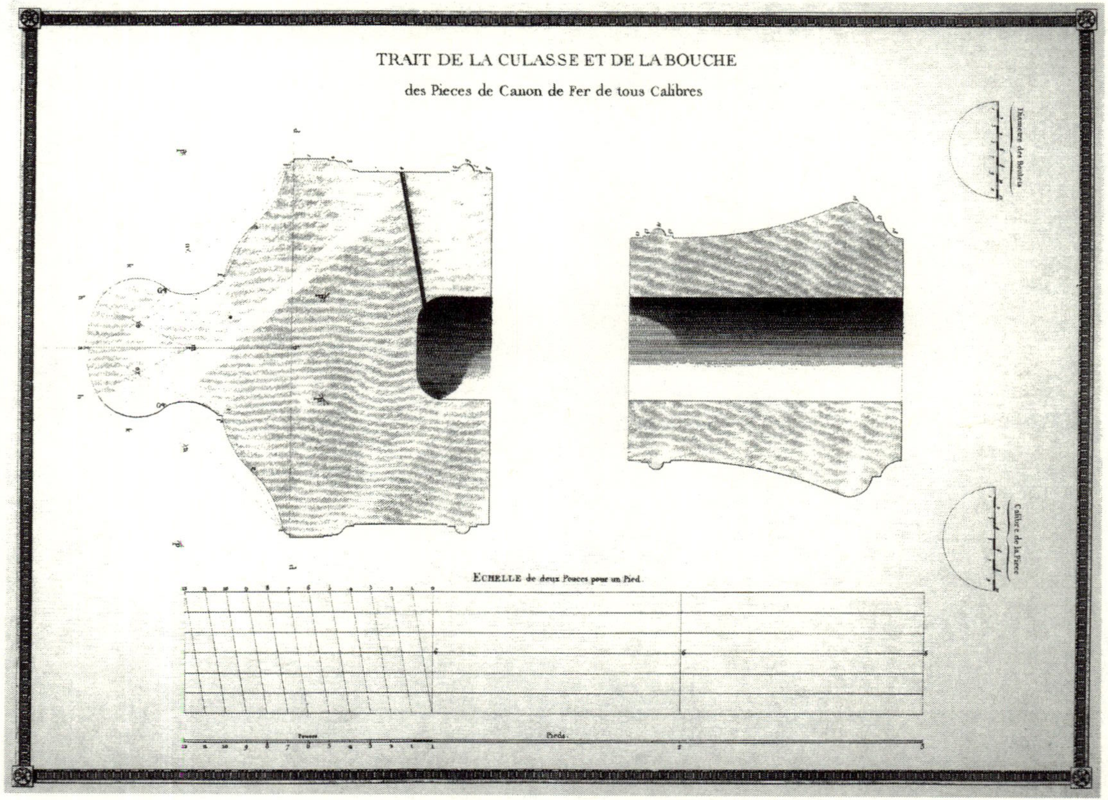

Figure 9. Details of the breech and muzzle of iron cannons of all calibers to the Regulations of 1778–79. Courtesy of Jean Boudriot.

ceived his orders to command the frigate, and under his authority the vessel was further equipped. *L'Inconstante* was intended to carry forty guns, but her ordnance consisted of only twenty-six 12-pounder cannons and six 6-pounders.[61] In theory, the frigate was armed with guns cast according to the Regulations of 1786, but archaeological finds described in chapter 8 suggest that her gundeck armament was made up of 12-pounder cannons cast according to the French Navy's former Regulations of 1778–79 (figures 7–9).[62] They were long-pattern cannons with a defined overall length of 2.413 m (from the face of the muzzle to the back of the base ring), but the lengths varied up to 3 cm owing to casting variances in guns made before 1786. Whether the frigate's secondary armament of 6-pounders was of the 1786 or 1778–79 pattern has not been ascertained. Although *L'Inconstante* was launched in 1790, her primary ordnance consisted of a slightly older-style gun—probably because of shortages at the ordnance stores in Rochefort.[63] The theory is supported by a letter of 13 June 1789 from La Luzerne to de Vaudreuil and La Grandville that was circulated at the Rochefort dockyard. It expressed concern that a recent inventory of the state of ordnance for ships in the harbor and under construction at Rochefort had not been accurate and did not show the actual deficit, and it ordered a reexamination of the situation for a more exact accounting.[64] Use of the older-style cannons probably made little difference in the overall firepower of *L'Inconstante.*

By January 1792, *L'Inconstante* was prepared to embark on her first campaign. It was to be a tour of duty in France's important West Indian colony, Saint-Domingue. And it was to begin with a winter passage across the Atlantic.

4

France's Saint-Domingue Campaign

The Best and the Worst of Times

Before France declared war on Great Britain, resulting in the capture of the frigate that became the *Convert*—France was embroiled in the French Revolution. Events that occurred in the mother country during and after 1789 affected the French colony of Saint-Domingue, where the revolution took on a profound meaning. Once the world's most productive sugar producer, the colony experienced civil upheavals rooted in social inequality among its inhabitants.

A decree issued by the French National Assembly on 15 May 1791 gave mulattoes the hope of achieving the same status as the white population. It ruled that mulattoes born of free parents were to have social and political rights. The white planters of Saint-Domingue were opposed to this decree—indeed, to any form of intrusion on their social, economic, and political advantages. Thus, when news of the decision reached the Caribbean colony, white planters refused to abide by it, the governor would not enforce it, and some whites discussed the possibility of seceding from France. In response, the mulattoes demanded their rights and were preparing to take up arms when, in August 1791, a rebellion by Saint-Domingue's most disadvantaged body of inhabitants, the immense slave population, overwhelmed the colony. It was a time of shifting alliances, confusion, and bloodshed. In the ensuing revolts, thousands of people on all sides were brutally killed and hundreds of plantations devastated. Finally, in September, the desperate whites called a truce, under the terms of the truce mulattoes were awarded equal status with whites.

Decisions and events in revolutionary France reflected the shifting state of French governmental affairs. Communications between France and Saint-Domingue frequently took months. Before word of the August slave revolt reached France, the French National Assembly had repealed its 15 May decree, and on 24 September 1791 had replaced it with a resolution to let colonial assemblies make legislation regarding slaves and mulattoes in each colony. Subsequently, the colonial whites of Saint-Domingue abandoned their truce and rebellion erupted again.[1]

In November, about the time that news arrived in France of the August slave revolt in Saint-Domingue, a small expedition was ordered to be sent to the unstable colony. *L'Inconstante* was among the vessels commissioned for this duty. Although there are gaps in the narrative, archival sources provide significant details about preparation of the frigate for the voyage and her later presence in the French West Indies.

Captain Joseph Riouffe and the Expedition for Saint-Domingue

On 3 December 1791, Alexandre Joseph Riouffe, Major de Vaisseau, received orders to command the frigate *L'Inconstante* on an expedition to Saint-Domingue. On 1 January 1792, during the first days of the campaign, he was promoted to Capitaine de Vaisseau de la troisième classe, and on 1 January 1793, while on service in the West Indies, he became Capitaine de Vaisseau de la première classe. Riouffe entered the French Navy in 1765, and about the time of the American War of Independence achieved the rank of Lieutenant de Vaisseau et de Port. During the war he served as lieutenant on two ships of the line from Brest, *Le Diadême* (1778) and *Le Vengeuse* (1778–81), and as second captain on a frigate from Rochefort, *L'Andromaque* (1782–83). In 1784 Lieutenant Riouffe commanded his first vessel, a frigate named *La Flore*. During the following years of peace he was not commissioned into another ship, but in November 1786 he secured the rank of Sous Directeur de Port et Major de Vaisseau at Rochefort. It was not until the serious insurrection of 1791 in Saint-Domingue that he received orders for his next command.[2]

Although Joseph Riouffe became the captain of *L'Inconstante*, he was not the first person selected to command the frigate. In a letter of 17 November 1791, Minister of the Navy de Bertrand informed de Vaudreuil and Charlot at Rochefort that, according to a deposition made by the king for the expedition to Saint-Domingue, Major de Vaisseau Villeblanche from the Department of Brest had been appointed to the command of the frigate *L'Inconstante* and Sous Lieutenant de Vaisseau Guillotin to the *gabarre* (transport ship) *La Lionne*. These officers had been given orders and advised of their destination and were to be joined by another frigate, *La Néréïde*.[3] It is not clear why Villeblanche did not take command of *L'Inconstante*, but Riouffe had served in 1782–83 as second captain on the frigate *L'Andromaque* under an officer named Villeblanche, perhaps the same man.[4]

On 17 November 1791 an abstract of the crew requirements for three vessels, including the frigates *L'Inconstante* and *La Néréïde*, was prepared at

Rochefort,[5] probably in response to directions given in a 16 November letter that the frigates should be fitted out *en flûte* (as troop transports rather than fighting ships) for the expedition to Saint-Domingue. A day later these orders were revised according to directions given in correspondence, also dated 17 November 1791, from de Bertrand to officials at Rochefort. The latter dispatch stated that the three French Navy vessels, accompanied by a merchantman, were to make the expedition to Saint-Domingue, and that they were to transport a battalion of troops from Agen. Although the two frigates were originally to be equipped *en flûte*, based on information received from the colony, the king had decided that *L'Inconstante* would take all of her artillery and would be fitted out on peace terms and not *en flûte*. The change meant that the frigate would carry a larger crew and fewer troops. More of the 250 passengers included in the expedition would have to be spread throughout the other three vessels.[6] News had perhaps just reached France of the massive slave revolt and the ensuing violence that had disrupted Saint-Domingue in late August and September. The armament and crew complement for *L'Inconstante* had therefore been modified; a larger number of naval personnel would be dispatched to the troubled colony, and the frigate would be battle ready in the West Indies.

Preparations for the expedition to Saint-Domingue were quickly underway. According to a letter of 27 November 1791, three supply officers by the names of Gaudin, Mayon, and de St. Pierre received assignments to *La Néréïde*, *L'Inconstante*, and *La Lionne*.[7]

On 3 December 1791, de Bertrand wrote to de Vaudreuil and Charlot of the last disposition for the embarkment of the Agenois Battalion, which was to be distributed aboard the frigates *L'Inconstante* and *La Néréïde*. The minister of the navy remarked that the owner of *Le Meulan*, a merchant ship employed for the expedition to help transport the battalion, was charging an exorbitant price, but that because of the dramatic circumstances of the moment and the fact that the vessel was the only seaworthy ship available, an arrangement to use it had been made and it could be ready to sail with the frigates. De Bertrand sent official instructions for Major de Vaisseau Riouffe of *L'Inconstante* and asked de Vaudreuil to advise Riouffe not to lose a moment in getting the ships ready for the expedition.[8]

Another clue to the urgency of the intended mission and its purpose, to restore order, is suggested by the large quantity of small arms and ammunition that was to be transported to Saint-Domingue. A letter of 8 December 1791 from de Bertrand in Paris to Charlot in Rochefort approved 5,000 *fusils* (muskets), 15,000 *cartouches* of the same caliber, 3,600 *balles* of the same caliber, and 2,100 sabers (300 with lion's heads) to be taken from the arsenals of Rochefort.[9]

Clearly, the safeguarding of French interests in Saint-Domingue was important to the home government. A letter of 17 December 1791 from the minister of the navy to Charlot authorizing the passage of a civilian to Saint-Domingue illustrates this. Since the man sought to make the Atlantic crossing so that he could protect his home—and thereby French concerns—in the colony, de Bertrand allowed his passage at the cost of the state.[10]

The journal of remarks about port affairs that the Commandant de la Marine at Rochefort kept provides details about the final preparations and the departure of the expedition for Saint-Domingue. In the entry for 13 December 1791, the writer noted that he had made his inspections aboard *L'Inconstante* and *La Néréïde*, but that bad weather had delayed the frigates' departure down the River Charente. On 24 December they had descended the river and were anchored in the port des Basques. Reference was also made to the troops who were to board the frigates and to the merchant ship *Le Meulan*, which would sail with the naval vessels.

On 27 December it was recorded that during the night of 23 December, the wind from the west and northwest had been so violent that the two anchored frigates had dragged their anchors and been damaged, and *L'Inconstante* had suffered injury to her bow. A shipwright sent aboard to assess the damage had determined that the repairs could be done on site in the anchorage. Attempts were made to accelerate them, but the continuing storm intervened. On 2 January 1792 the commandant wrote that repairs were going well on *L'Inconstante* and that he hoped that they would be completed within the week. He also remarked that if the winds became favorable, the two frigates and *Le Meulan* could sail in eight days. On 9 January the troops, numbering about six hundred, were being boarded on *L'Inconstante, La Néréïde*, and *Le Meulan*. It was thought that the three ships might leave that day because the weather was calm. The comments of 14 January noted that the three vessels sailed on 13 January 1792 from the anchorage of the Isle d'Aix, by favorable winds, for the island of Saint-Domingue. Before the departure, the troops on *Le Meulan* had become insubordinate because of overcrowding, and so the commandant had given new orders to take fifty men off that vessel and put them aboard the two frigates. These troops seemed unreliable to him, and he speculated that they would probably be ill suited to establishing order in Saint-Domingue.

According to the 4 February journal entry, *La Néréïde* aborted her voyage and returned to Rochefort. Apparently, on 13 January the frigate had been forced to detach from the other two ships; after encountering violent winds and being pounded by heavy seas the crew had been forced to cut off the mizzenmast. The commandant wrote that the ship would be repaired and sent out again as soon as possible and that he had not heard from *L'Inconstante* or *Le Meulan*.[11]

But the winter crossing of the Atlantic was not to be. *L'Inconstante* also received substantial damage and sailed back to France.[12] The frigate arrived at Port Louis near L'Orient on 7 February 1792, and on 10 February was taken to L'Orient for repairs. It was not until spring that *L'Inconstante* once again sailed for the West Indies.[13]

Naval Service in Saint-Domingue

The frigate *L'Inconstante* finally sailed for Saint-Domingue on 12 April 1792.[14] It is likely that Captain Riouffe carried news of the famous decree of 4 April 1792, whereby the new Legislative Assembly in France conferred on free Negroes and mulattoes in the French colonies political rights equal to those of whites.[15] No doubt he was aware that his mission would be difficult, and that recent events in France, including the decrees concerning the colonies, would further fuel the civil unrest that was occurring in Saint-Domingue. However, Captain Riouffe could not have anticipated the profound changes that soon were to envelop not only France and Saint-Domingue but also the West Indies, Europe, and the world.

The French Revolution had occurred in 1789, but in April 1792 France was still officially ruled by a limited monarchy. However, extremist revolutionaries were now in power in a new legislative assembly, and during these difficult times radical changes occurred with little warning. Only eight days after *L'Inconstante* set sail for the West Indies, France declared war on Austria, igniting the French revolutionary wars. Dynamic forces, including massive civil uprisings in France in August 1792, soon led to the total abolition of the French monarchy and establishment of the first French Republic by the end of September. Several months later, in January 1793, Louis XVI would be executed as a traitor. These events marked the onset of the Reign of Terror in France.

Between February and March 1793, the new French Republic declared war on Great Britain, the United Provinces of the Netherlands, and Spain, leaving Saint-Domingue and all the French West Indies in imminent danger of attack from British, Dutch, and Spanish naval forces.[16] During the frenzied Reign of Terror between 1793 and 1794, the French Republicans turned on all real and suspected traitors and, in a single blow, annihilated almost all of the country's pre-revolutionary naval officers, who had traditionally been noblemen. Many of these officers, as members of the aristocracy, would be executed on the guillotine, while others would flee into

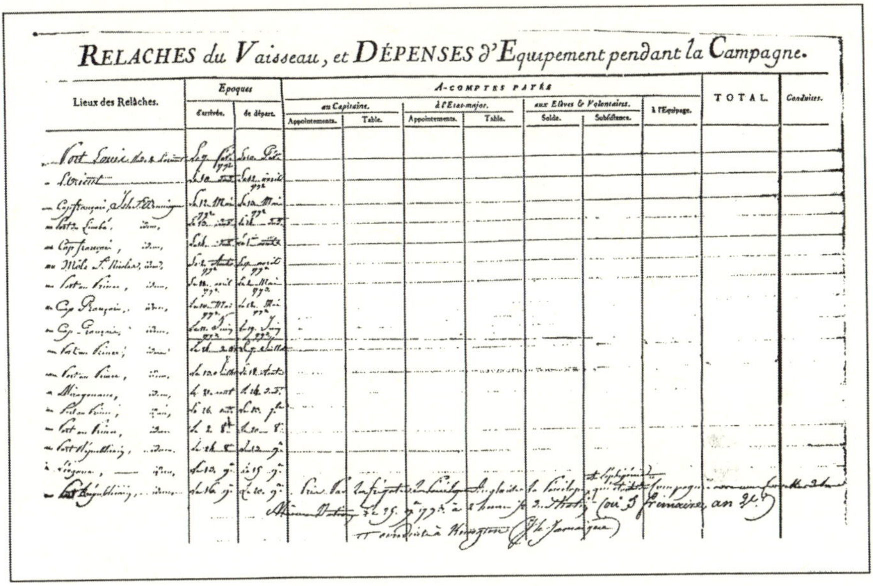

Figure 10. *Rôle de bord* extract detailing *L'Inconstante* ports of call during the Saint-Domingue campaign. Courtesy of the Archives du Port de Rochefort, Rochefort.

exile; only later, under the Directory, would the error of this policy be realized and attempts be made to restore order to the French Navy.[17] If Captain Riouffe had not been sent to Saint-Domingue before these tragic events occurred, he might have suffered the fate of his fellow officers. Nonetheless, his situation in the West Indies was to be exceedingly difficult and his lot almost as unfortunate.

The unpredictable situations in Saint-Domingue and France probably resulted in a longer West Indian tour of duty for *L'Inconstante* than had previously been the case for French naval vessels. Instead of returning to Europe after a six- or seven-month campaign, the frigate remained in the revolutionary colony for more than a year and a half, at the end of which the British captured her. The dates and destinations of the vessel's voyages are recorded in the ship's *rôle de bord*, which today is housed in the Archives du Port de Rochefort (figure 10).[18] Although the purposes of the passages and details about them are not specified, most of the absences from various ports are of relatively short duration. The pattern typifies the French tradition of using ships for certain naval tasks rather than for offensive patrolling missions to maintain control of the seas—a common practice in the Royal Navy of Great Britain.[19]

L'Inconstante arrived at Cap Français on the north coast of Saint-Domingue on 12 May 1792, a month after her departure from L'Orient (map 7). Considered by many to be the Paris of the Antilles, Cap Français was one of the two largest towns (the other was the official capital, Port-au-Prince); its population numbered approximately twenty thousand.[20] At the time the entire colony had about 544,000 inhabitants, not counting troops and sailors.[21] On 13 May the frigate sailed to nearby Port du Limbé, from which she returned the following day to Cap Français, where she remained for two and a half months. On 1 August the vessel sailed for Le Môle St. Nicolas, a town of perhaps 250 houses that has been referred to as the Gibraltar of the Caribbean Sea, presumably because of its strategic location adjacent to the Windward Passage.[22] The frigate arrived at Le Môle St. Nicolas on 2 August 1792 and remained there for eight and a half months, until mid-April 1793. During this lengthy period, terrifying events took place in both France and Saint-Domingue.

Although civil uprisings had overwhelmed France in August 1792 and eventually resulted in the abolition of the monarchy and the establishment of the French Republic in September, word of these events did not reach Saint-Domingue until October.[23] In mid-July, just before the upheaval, three new government commissioners, Messrs. Sonthonax, Polverel, and Ailhaud, accompanied by four thousand national guards and two thousand troops of the line in fifteen ships, sailed for Saint-Domingue.[24] Sent by the Assembly, the commissioners and the support forces arrived at Cap Français in mid-September. The commissioners had orders to enforce the decree of 4 April 1792 that conferred political rights on free Negroes and mulattoes. Among other responsibilities, they were to establish peace and order and to identify, arrest, and send to France the authors of troubles in the colony.[25]

Immediately after the arrival of the commissioners, the island's governor, M. Blanchelande, was taken prisoner and sent to France. Fundamental problems remained, however. The commissioners were revolutionaries and the national guard were civilians of the revolution, while the troops and their commanding officers were still soldiers and officers of the king. Once news of the August events in France reached Saint-Domingue in October, the colony became absolutely divided and experienced a general state of terror. Those who chose to be royalists sided with the new governor, M. Desparbes, who was general and commander in chief of the deposed king's forces, while revolutionaries aligned themselves with Sonthonax. The mulattoes supported Sonthonax, who emerged as victor. Desparbes, royalist leaders, and others who opposed the commissioners were arrested and sent to France,[26] where many of them were executed. In Saint-Domingue the

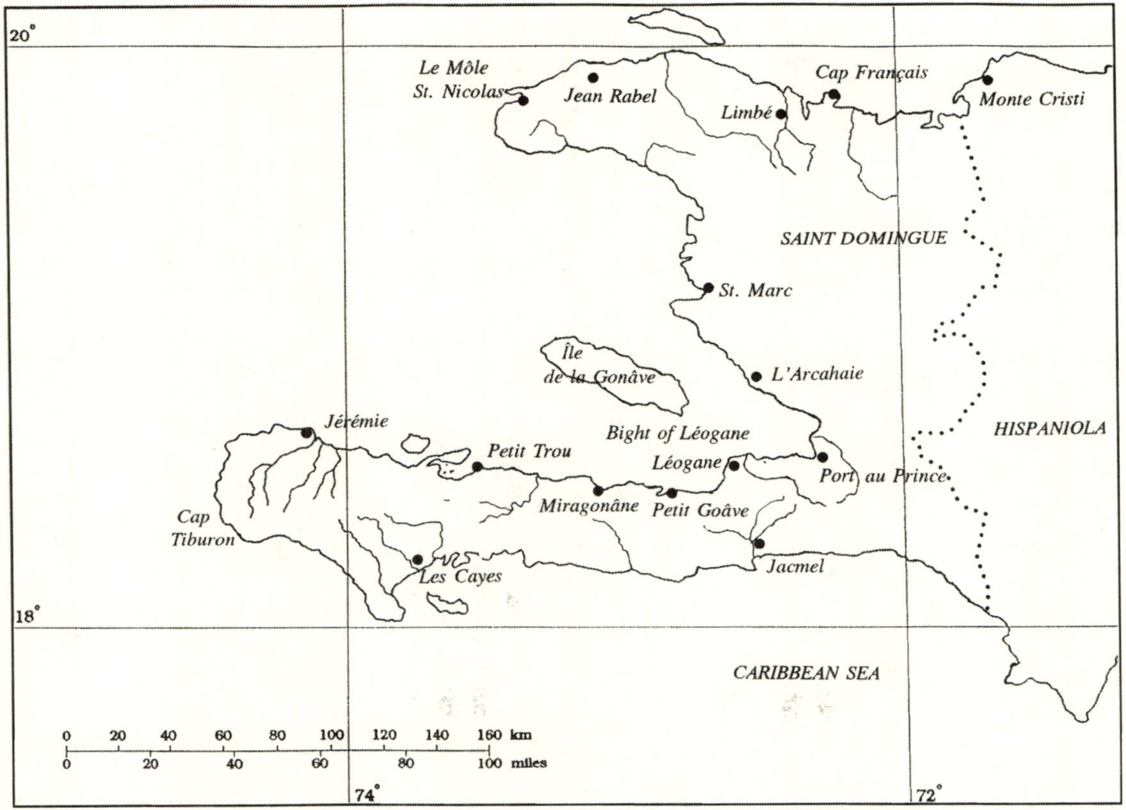

Map 7. Eighteenth-century Saint-Domingue. Drawn by R. L. Craig.

commissioners disagreed among themselves and expelled Ailhaud, leaving Sonthonax and Polverel in complete control of the colony by early 1793.[27]

On 23 September 1792, shortly before discord erupted in Saint-Domingue, an account was given to the National Convention of the state of the French Navy under the newly established republic. The minister of the navy told the convention that the navy had recently been disorganized and that there had been rebellion among some of the officers of the ancien régime. He assured them that there had been a reorganization of administrators at the ports and that the national navy included many excellent seamen who were devoted to the support of liberty and capable of defending the flag of the republic. He stated that reinforcements had been sent to the fleets in the Mediterranean and to the colonies, and that there was unity and harmony among the ships' crews, who had all sworn to support liberty and equality. Addressing the National Convention, the minister minimized the troubles in the French Caribbean: "The situation of our Western Colonies becomes every day less critical since the arrival of ships and troops; and above all, since the decree which permanently establishes the political relation of their inhabitants." He assured the convention that the French Republic maintained its rights in Saint-Domingue with a fleet of four ships of the line, four frigates, one corvette, three packets, and four *flûtes*, and that a force of eight thousand troops carried out their decrees. He pointed out, however, that while he would have liked to report on the good citizenship of the colonial ships' officers, he did not yet know their sentiments.[28]

Given the shifting political situation in the months after the arrival of the government commissioners in Saint-Domingue, it is no wonder that *L'Inconstante* remained quietly in port at Le Môle St. Nicolas. During this period, slanderous statements against Captain Riouffe were circulating back home in Rochefort. Officials of the municipality of Le Môle, however, in an attempt to quell these unfounded assertions, made an impartial public statement that was read on board *L'Inconstante* on 28 January 1793. Subsequently, the document was signed by eighty-six of the people aboard, comprising all those who could write, and it was generally approved by all. Along with additional statements, the content of the speech was entered into records of a session of the municipality of Le Môle on 29 January. The address affirmed that Captain Riouffe and the officers of *L'Inconstante* had conducted themselves irreproachably and had shown courage and patriotism in their actions and operations in Saint-Domingue during the nine months that they had been stationed in the colony. The city officials expressed indignation at the authors of false and defamatory rumors against the conduct of Captain Riouffe that were known to be widespread at Rochefort. They maintained that since 2 August 1792 the frigate had been stationed in their port and that during her time there the crew had professed considerable patriotism. Riouffe and the officers of *L'Inconstante* were said to support the doctrine of the French Revolution and to keep the crew obedient to the law and respectful of authority. The officials said that the citizens of Le Môle St. Nicolas had confidence in Captain Riouffe and the officers of *L'Inconstante*, who had guarded the town in perilous times. They stated that their declaration was addressed to the crew of the frigate as testimony to the civic virtues that characterized their leader, that the petition would be sent to the municipality of Rochefort to destroy the injurious rumors that were in circulation there regarding the conduct of Captain Riouffe, and that a copy would be deposited in the archives of the municipality of Le Môle St. Nicolas.[29]

Attacks on the loyalty and character of high-ranking naval officers suspected of having links to nobility were common during the Reign of Terror in France, and it is easy to appreciate the uncertainties that must have flooded Captain Riouffe's mind. But in early 1793, when France declared war on Great Britain, the United Provinces of the Netherlands, and Spain, Riouffe must have known that the greatest threat to his ship was at hand. Foreign enemies, particularly the British, would soon be on the horizon, and the role of *L'Inconstante* and the rest of the French fleet clearly would be to defend the merchant shipping and the coasts of Saint-Domingue.

News that France had declared war on Great Britain reached Jamaica on 29 March 1793, and immediately the British seized all of the French merchant ships in the harbor at Kingston.[30] Soon Royal Navy vessels patrolled the waters near Saint-Domingue to seek intelligence and to disrupt the colony's shipping, and also to protect British trade and communications bound for Jamaica in the Windward Passage (see map 2). They took numerous small French merchantmen as prizes. On 16 April 1793, HMS *Penelope* captured *Le Goelan*, a 290-ton corvette of twelve guns, bearing the colors of the French Republic, and her ninety-man crew, commanded by Lieutenant Leisseguese.[31]

Perhaps in response to news of *Le Goelan*'s seizure in the Bight of Léogane, *L'Inconstante* sailed south to those waters (see map 7). On 17 April the frigate departed from Le Môle St. Nicolas; she arrived the next day at Port-au-Prince, a city of about 14,700 people including fewer than three thousand whites, four thousand mulattoes, and eight thousand slaves.[32] The frigate remained in Port-au-Prince for two weeks, until 2 May. She then sailed north and on 10 May arrived at Cap Français. On 18 May, after a week at Cap Français, *L'Inconstante* sailed again, but she returned to the same port three and a half weeks later, on 11 June 1793.

On the basis of naval intelligence obtained by Captain Rowley of HMS

Penelope from a small boat that he captured, the British knew that on about 30 May the *Jupiter* and the frigates *Concorde*, *Fine*, and *L'Inconstante* were absent from Cap Français because they had gone to gather a convoy from Aux Cayes.[33] The *Oole* and the frigate *Surveillante* were with a convoy at Cap Français, and the seventy-four-gun ship *America* remained at Port-au-Prince.[34] Around this time the British lost HMS *Hyæna*, of twenty-four guns, to *La Concorde*, of forty guns, while under orders to protect the trade bound to Jamaica and to annoy the enemy in the seas between Cap Tiburon and Altavella.[35]

During May, while the French Republic's commissioners were away from Cap Français to quiet an insurrection in Port-au-Prince and Jacmel, a new governor, M. Galbaud, arrived in Cap Français with orders to put Saint-Domingue in a state of defense, since war had been declared on Britain and the Netherlands. The governor was well received in the town but was later dismissed from office by the commissioners, who returned to Cap Français in June. The assembly in France, fearing planter disloyalty to the new republic, had issued a decree that colonial governors could not own estates in the colonies they governed, and Galbaud owned a plantation in Saint-Domingue. Galbaud resisted his dismissal from office and managed to enlist the support of about 1,200 men, including the Cap Français militia and seamen in the harbor. The commissioners opposed him and called on the slaves, promising them emancipation. Beginning on 21 June, three thousand slaves descended on Cap Français. During the ensuing massacre, the colonial whites, including the ex-governor, retreated to the sea, seeking protection aboard ships in the harbor. Thousands of refugees sailed from Saint-Domingue to other islands and to North America, never to return to the island, and some of the principal planters openly renounced allegiance to France and turned to Britain. Cap Français was largely burned and pillaged, and even the commissioners temporarily sought protection aboard a ship of the line in the harbor.[36]

It is not known what role, if any, *L'Inconstante* played in these dramatic events. The frigate was in port at Cap Français between 11 and 19 June, but she had sailed before the carnage of 21 June and the subsequent exodus of refugees.

L'Inconstante's movements for the following months are known. On 24 June she arrived in Port-au-Prince and remained for two weeks. On 7 July the frigate embarked on a one-week cruise and then on 13 July returned to Port-au-Prince, where she stayed for about a month. On 18 August she left Port-au-Prince again and on 21 August arrived at Miragonâne, where she remained until 24 August. On that date she sailed from Miragonâne and arrived in Port-au-Prince on 26 August. *L'Inconstante* was in the harbor there for about a month, until 23 September 1793.

French planters, wishing to maintain their way of life, had since 1789 made gestures toward transferring their allegiance to Britain, but Britain had not wanted to openly violate her peace with France. Nonetheless, unofficial communications with Saint-Domingue planters had taken place, and once France declared war on Britain, it was inevitable that the British would attempt to secure the lucrative colony. On 9 September 1793 a force of almost nine hundred British troops, accompanied by Commodore Ford aboard the fifty-gun HMS *Europa*, the frigates *Iphigenia* and *Hermione*, the sloop of war *Goelan* (now in British service), and the schooners *Mosquito*, *Flying Fish*, and *Spitfire*, embarked on a campaign from Jamaica. The frigate *Penelope* had previously sailed for Saint-Domingue.[37] The British arrived at Jérémie on 19 September; as had been previously arranged, the town surrendered. On 22 September they occupied the fortress and harbor at Le Môle St. Nicolas, but the town remained hostile. During the campaign, the British captured *La Convention Nationale*, a ten-gun schooner of the French Republic.[38] By the end of 1793, Jean Rabel, St. Marc, L'Arcahaie, Boucassin, and Léogane had surrendered on the same terms as Jérémie, and the British controlled navigation in the Bight of Léogane. By June 1794 Port-au-Prince was taken.[39]

On 23 September 1793 *L'Inconstante* left the harbor of Port-au-Prince, probably on hearing news of the British occupation of Jérémie and Le Môle St. Nicolas. The frigate returned to Port-au-Prince on 2 October and remained there until 20 October, when she sailed again. An officer of *L'Inconstante* later made a declaration in which he criticized Captain Riouffe for his lack of action against the British on 20 and 22 October. He testified that on 20 October the frigate was about one league distant from nine corsairs but that Riouffe had fired a cannon shot to facilitate their escape. He maintained that on 22 October, while they were escorting a convoy from Petit Goâve to Port Republicain (apparently a new revolutionary name used for Port-au-Prince), an English corvette came before La Gonâve to capture some of the merchantmen. Riouffe, he declared, decided to chase it only because rumors were circulating on board, and when he did pursue the vessel, it was after tacking twice to give it time to see *L'Inconstante* broadside, thus giving the enemy time, and the impetus, to escape.[40]

The frigate arrived in Port Republicain on 24 October and remained there for several weeks. On 13 November *L'Inconstante* sailed for and arrived in Léogane, an important town in the West Province, consisting of between three hundred and four hundred houses.[41] The frigate left Léogane on 15 November and arrived the following day in Port Republicain, where she remained for several days. On 20 November she sailed from Port Republicain to convoy two sloops loaded with provisions bound for Petit Trou; there, a French woman escaping the troubles in St. Domingue came aboard as a passenger.[42]

On the return voyage of *L'Inconstante* from Petit Trou to Port-au-Prince, His Majesty's ships *Penelope* and *Iphigenia* captured the frigate, which had served France in Saint-Domingue for almost nineteen months. Captain Riouffe and other French officers and seamen were mortally wounded in the engagement, on 25 November 1793.[43] *L'Inconstante*, the prize, would become a Royal Navy ship.

5
The Prize
A Ship by Another Name

Eighteenth-century Britain and France acquired, maintained, and defended colonies in the West Indies by naval strength. The British kept permanent squadrons in Jamaica and in the Leeward Islands, and in times of peace these squadrons protected the colonies and the seaborne merchant trade. During wartime they provided convoy protection for British ships and cruised to defend Britain's commerce; they attacked their enemy's trade and captured or destroyed their naval forces.[1]

Declarations of war were generally not bad news for Royal Navy officers. The lure of prize money for the seizure of enemy merchantmen and warships was, in fact, a great inducement for a naval career, as prize money was largely a wartime phenomenon.[2] The Cruiser and Convoys Act of 1708 had established a system for convoy defense and protection of trade; it contained clauses that became the basis of prize law for the remainder of the eighteenth century. The act provided that almost all prize money went to the captors of enemy ships, and outlined when prize-taking could begin and how it should be regulated.

At the onset of each war, seizure of prizes commenced with a royal proclamation. Once a vessel was captured, certain procedures had to be followed, and the question of whether it actually belonged to the enemy had to be adjudicated. Either the High Court of Admiralty in London handled this or a Vice Admiralty Court located elsewhere in Britain or in the colonies. The prize had to go through the process of condemnation. When the procedure was completed, prize money was awarded and distributed among the officers and crews of the vessels that had achieved the capture, and those that were in sight when the enemy surrendered. Flag officers, such as admirals and their junior flags, also received a percentage of the value of prizes taken by the ships and vessels under their command.

Merchantmen, the most tempting vessels to seize, often carried valuable cargoes and were less dangerous to contest than ships of war. Captured warships, however, attracted promotions, and head money of five pounds per member of the enemy's crew was payable for both warships and privateers. Furthermore, a foreign navy vessel itself might be sold to the Admiralty, at a good price.[3]

The history of the French *L'Inconstante* and British *Convert* bridges an era of international peace and war in the eighteenth-century Caribbean. The story unfolds in fascinating historical details captured in this narrative.

Commodore John Ford's Squadron in Jamaica

When Commodore John Ford, aboard His Majesty's fifty-gun ship *Europa*, reached Jamaica on 3 January 1793 to command the squadron stationed there, Great Britain and France were still at peace. In his first letter to the Admiralty, dated 13 January, he reported that the colony was in a tranquil state. On his arrival he had met up with the frigates *Triton* and *Penelope* and the sloops *Hound*, *Falcon*, and *Serpent*, off the east end of Jamaica, and had ordered them into Port Royal Harbour; there he found the frigate *Proserpine*, the twenty-four gun *Hyæna*, and the sloop *Helena* (figure 11). The next day, when the cutter *Advice* arrived, Commodore Ford gathered his squadron. After consulting with the governor and council, he ordered the vessels on official service missions in the Caribbean.

Serpent was to cruise the Bahamas and Turks Islands and look into Cap Français on her return voyage. *Penelope*, commanded by Captain Bartholomew Samuel Rowley, was to sail to Cap Français to deliver documents from the lieutenant governor of Jamaica: for the payment of a demand that the French colonial government had acknowledged was due, for damages done by rebellious Negroes who had been landed in the Bay of Honduras, and for costs incurred for conveying them back to the cape. He was also to cautiously make observations on the French naval and military forces that were present at Cap Français. *Proserpine*, *Hyæna*, *Falcon*, and *Advice* were to cruise for six weeks to protect the commerce and internal tranquility of Jamaica, while *Triton* and *Helena* were to remain at Port Royal with *Europa*.[4] *Hound*, commanded by John Lawford since 1790, in the English Channel and in the West Indies,[5] was to carry four months' provisions for duty in the Bay of Honduras at the British settlements located there. That voyage was delayed, however, because the lieutenant governor of Jamaica had received a request from the secretary of state in Britain that a proper officer be sent to meet the Spanish commissary to inquire into and settle disputes between British settlers and Spaniards in the Bay of Honduras. He thought perhaps Ford himself should go. In due course, Lieutenant Governor Adam Williamson appointed Commander Lawford as commissary for His Britannic Majesty, so *Hound* would sail for Honduras in February on the diplomatic

Figure 11. Port Royal and Kingston Harbours in the 1700s. From Edward Long, *The History of Jamaica* (London: Printed for T. Lowndes, 1774), vol. 2, plate 10, facing p. 139. Courtesy of the Cayman Islands National Archive. The original image from the copperplate engraving was reversed and has been corrected.

mission.[6] Later in January, HMS *Providence*, Captain William Bligh, and the brig *Assistant*, Lieutenant N. Portlock, arrived from the South Seas and joined Commodore Ford's squadron.[7]

Shortly before *Hound*'s departure, on 24 January, *Hyæna*, Captain William Hargood, was almost lost on a reef east of Port Antonio, Jamaica. The combined efforts of the ship's company, Captain Lawford and his crew from *Hound*, and a merchant ship captain by the name of Goodwin saved the vessel.[8]

Revolutionary France declared war on Great Britain on 1 February 1793. Subsequently, arriving by the packet *Cumberland* on 29 March, John Ford received orders from the Admiralty dated 8 and 9 February to complete the complements of the ships of the squadron under his command and "to seize or Destroy all Ships or Vessels belonging to the subjects of France." French prizes taken immediately in the Port of Kingston included five schooners and three sloops of between thirty-five and sixty-five tons. Without hesitation, the commodore had the naval storekeeper purchase a fast-sailing sixty-ton schooner, which he named *Spitfire*, to "gain Intelligence of the Enemy's Force and Movements at Port-au-Prince and Cape Francois, or other important Purposes."[9] He also detained *Providence* and *Assistant*, which he had intended to send home at the beginning of April with botanical plants for His Majesty's Garden at Kew, because the vessels were not fitted for war. They would, instead, escort the homeward-bound merchantmen across the Atlantic, once he appointed a convoy.

In all likelihood, Ford's officers welcomed the news of war. The West Indies was an excellent post for prize-taking. The commodore mobilized *Europa* with the rest of the squadron, excluding *Hound*. He transferred his pennant to *Providence*, which, along with the brig *Assistant*, remained at Port Royal.[10] Between 29 March and 14 April 1793 he dispatched the fleet on courier, reconnaissance, and intelligence-seeking duties. He sent *Serpent*, Captain Richard Lee, to the Bahamas and Turks Islands with news that war had commenced with France, after which she was to cruise in the passages to inform and protect ships from North America that were bound for Jamaica. The others were on services around Saint-Domingue: *Europa*, Captain George Gregory, *Hyæna*, Captain William Hargood, *Penelope*, Captain Bartholomew Samuel Rowley, and *Proserpine*, Captain James Alms, were to protect the Jamaica-bound trade and to annoy the enemy; *Europa* was also to support and guard the British cruisers, and her captain was to direct actions of *Fly*, Captain William Brown; *Advice*, Lieutenant Edward Tyrrell, and *Spitfire*, Lieutenant John Perkins, were to look into Port-au-Prince and Cap Français to learn the force of the enemy and to seek intelligence on their intentions. Within two weeks the group captured a hundred-ton brig, two sloops, and three schooners.[11]

Away from the main action, *Hound* was still on services in the Bay of Honduras. On 11 April 1793, Captain Lawford received news of Britain's state of war with France. Commodore Ford had sent him orders to complete the complement of his sloop and to seize all French ships and vessels that he might encounter.[12]

Word arrived in Jamaica that on 8 April a French frigate, *L'Ambuscade*, had arrived off the coast of the United States.[13] The frigate was said to be completely blocking the harbor at Charleston (presumably the British ships therein, since the United States and France were not at war) and had taken several British prizes. Privateers under French commissions and colors were fitting out in the American port. The missive expressed hope for help from Jamaica to clear the coast of the frigate because there were many British merchantmen in the harbors of Charleston, Savannah, and Wilmington.[14] In contrast to the overt actions by France against British ships in American waters, the French Navy in Saint-Domingue faced the colony's civil disorder and defended its shores.

During the following months Commodore Ford's squadron continued activities near Saint-Domingue: cruising in the area to protect trade bound to Jamaica, seeking information on attitudes and events in the French colony, observing French naval and military forces, harassing the merchant trade, and capturing prizes. Around 12 June, His Majesty's ships *Proserpine*, *Providence*, *Assistant*, and *Fly* sailed from Jamaica with a convoy of 155 merchantmen bound to ports in Britain, and three additional vessels headed for America. *Providence* and *Assistant* were also to meet British merchant ships from Honduras, expected to join the fleet off Cape Antonio (map 8). In June the schooner *Mosquito*, Lieutenant John Fenton, joined Ford's forces. In July additions to the squadron included the frigate *Hermione*, Captain John Hills, and the fifteen-ton schooner *Flying Fish*, Lieutenant James Prevost, a former prize to *Mosquito*.[15]

Between 29 March and 11 July, the British fleet in Jamaica seized at least fifty-eight merchant prizes of between 8 and 250 tons, one packet, and the French Republic's 290-ton corvette, *Le Goelan*. Although some of the merchantmen were in ballast, many were laden with valuable cargoes including lumber, sugar, coffee, tobacco, wine, cotton, salt, flour, cacao, oil, dry goods, linen, earthenware, soap, and candles; a few carried slaves.[16] *Penelope* captured *Le Goelan*, Lieutenant Leisseguese, on 16 April in the Bight of Léogane. Ford deemed the prize to be a fine and fast-sailing vessel, so had the vessel purchased by the naval storekeeper and classified as a sloop of war to mount fourteen short 9-pounders and to carry a crew of ninety men. Her captain was to be Thomas Wolley, former first lieutenant of *Europa*.[17] The British lost HMS *Hyæna*, William Hargood, to the French in May.[18]

Another loss to Ford's squadron occurred in Honduras. The schooner *Advice*, Lieutenant Tyrrell, which had replaced the decommissioned cutter *Advice*, was wrecked there on 1 June 1793, but the vessel's crew was saved. Her commander was under orders to deliver dispatches to magistrates of the district and to Captain Lawford concerning the planned 12 June sailing of the convoy from Jamaica. Although Lawford's orders via *Advice* were to escort the merchant ships from Honduras to join the convoy from Jamaica, he was unable to do so. He did not want to leave the British settlements undefended, and, after the loss of the schooner, Lieutenant Tyrrell could not relieve him of that duty. Lawford informed the masters of the merchant ships in Honduras of the convoy, but only six vessels could be ready to sail in time to meet the fleet. He sent the names of these merchantmen to the senior officer, Captain Rowley, along with news of the shipwreck as his reason for not being able to join them.[19] After assisting in the salvage of *Advice*, Captain Lawford sent her commander, the officers, and the crew back to Jamaica in a merchant ship and remained in Honduras with *Hound*.[20]

His Majesty's seventy-four-gun vessels *Hannibal*, Captain John Colpoys, and *Hector*, Captain George Montague, arrived in July, but both sailed with

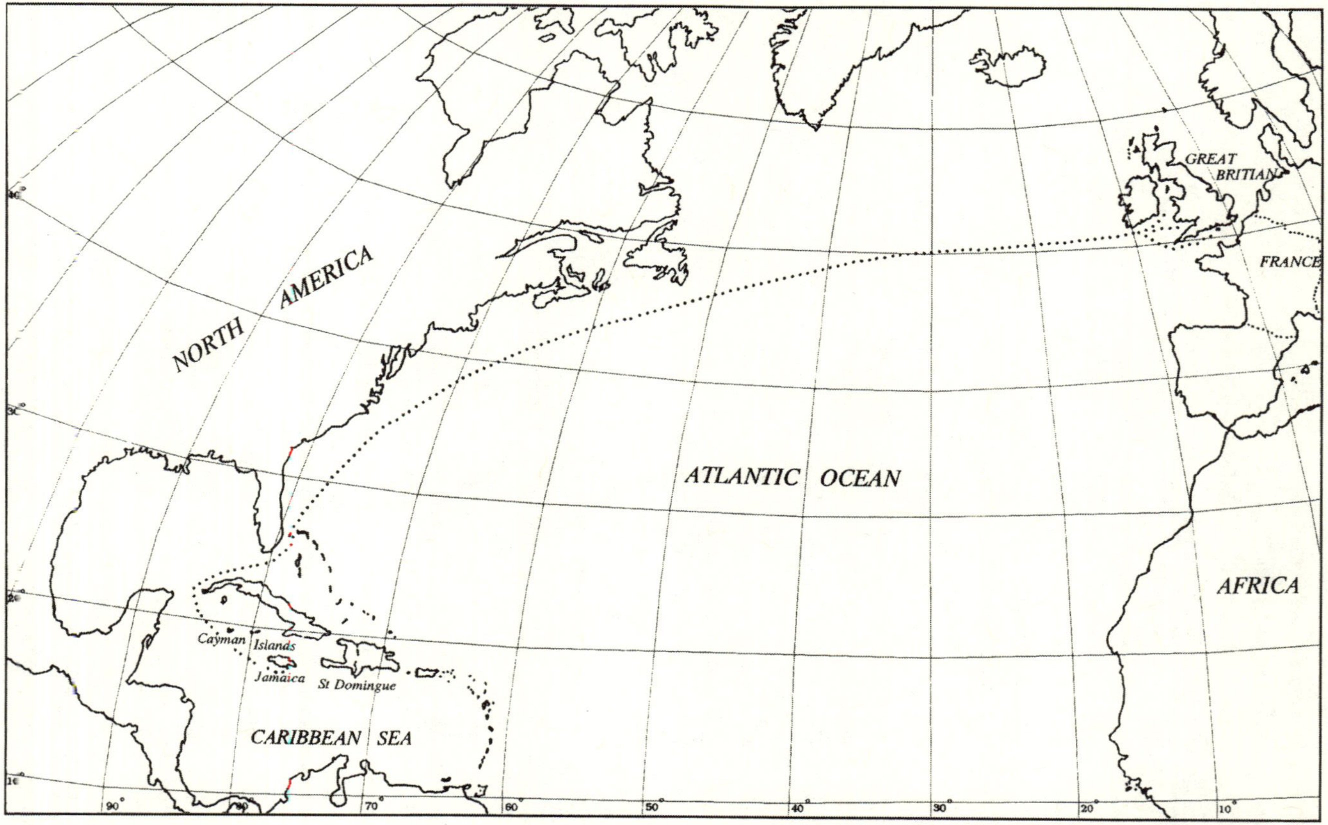

Map 8. Route of His Majesty's ships and their merchant convoys from Jamaica to various British ports. Drawn by R. L. Craig.

convoys from Jamaica by the end of the month. Together they escorted almost one hundred merchantmen bound for ports in Britain, Canada, and America. Aware of the presence of French forces near the United States, Commodore Ford ordered *Europa* to accompany the convoy until it was clear of the US coast.[21] As news, and perhaps as a warning to those merchantmen who did not seek convoy protection, an excerpt from a letter written by a passenger on a captured British merchant ship appeared in the Marine Intelligence section of the *Royal Gazette*, a weekly government publication in Jamaica. The Liverpool-bound *Golden Age*, which left Jamaica in August, fell in with the July convoy off the US coast, but then left it. *French Citizen*, a privateer from Bordeaux, captured the ship in the mid-Atlantic and took her into Wilmington, on the Delaware River, in the United States.[22]

According to the Disposition of the Squadron dated 11 August, *Hound* was serving in the Bay of Honduras; *Europa* was accompanying the July convoy and afterward was to cruise in the Caicos Islands; *Flying Fish* was seeing the packet through the Windward Passage and then was to cruise off the Caicos Islands; and *Spitfire, Hermione*, and *Penelope* were stationed near Saint-Domingue. Commodore Ford was aboard *Goelan* at Port Royal, and *Mosquito* was refitting there.[23]

By the following month the frigate *Iphigenia*, Captain Patrick Sinclair, had joined the forces in Jamaica. The Disposition of the Squadron dated 8 September reveals that *Hound* was still in Honduras, *Penelope* was cruising near Saint-Domingue, and on 9 September *Europa*, with Commodore Ford on board, along with *Iphigenia*, *Hermione*, *Goelan*, *Mosquito*, *Flying Fish*, and *Spitfire* were to sail with troops on an expedition against French Saint-Domingue (see figure 11).[24] The British secured the town of Jérémie on 19 September and the harbor and fortress at Le Môle St. Nicolas by 22 September 1793. During the September campaign they captured *La Convention Nationale*, a schooner bearing the colors of the French Republic.[25]

In November the frigate *Alligator*, Captain William Affleck, and the schooner *Marie Antoinette*, a recent capture, now commanded by Lieutenant John Perkins, formerly of *Spitfire*, became part of the squadron. Lieutenant Maitland now commanded the *Spitfire*. Commodore John Ford's British forces based in Jamaica now included one fifty-gun ship, four frigates, two sloops of war, and four schooners.

In a letter of 24 November, Commodore Ford informed the Admiralty that the ports of Jérémie and Le Môle St. Nicolas, with their dependencies, remained under British possession and that the French had not troubled them at either location. On 7 November, Ford had returned to Jamaica from Le Môle St. Nicolas for provisions, leaving the frigates and some of the small craft of the squadron to protect the British posts in Saint-Domingue. According to entries in the Disposition of the Squadron for 24 November, *Penelope*, *Hermione*, *Alligator*, and *Flying Fish* were at or near Le Môle St. Nicolas to protect the garrison; *Iphigenia*, *Spitfire*, and *Mosquito* were in the vicinity of Jérémie for its protection; and the sloop *Goelan* was in the Bahama Islands. *Europa*, *Hound*, and *Marie Antoinette* were refitting at Port Royal.[26] *Hound* had arrived in Jamaica from the Bay of Honduras on Sunday, 17 November, having completed more than eight months of service there.[27]

John Lawford missed the lucrative prize-seeking opportunities that his fellow officers pursued in Saint-Domingue during *Hound*'s service in Honduras. He dutifully carried out his mission as British commissary in the Bay of Honduras with propriety. He gained the respect of the governor of Yucatán and the Spanish commissary as well as that of Lieutenant Governor Adam Williamson and Commodore John Ford in Jamaica. On 13 December 1793, the lieutenant governor wrote a letter of commendation about John Lawford to Henry Dundas, secretary of state for war. The letter contained twenty-nine enclosures, consisting of Lawford's correspondence with Spanish officials in Honduras and with Williamson himself in Jamaica, detailing occurrences and the decisions made during the eight-month tour of duty.[28] He also directed Lawford to give him an accounting of his expenses while stationed in Honduras. In a letter of 20 December 1793, after listing all of the general expenses incurred on the duty, Lawford expressed reluctance to provide an opinion regarding compensation for his "Personal trouble on this Service." Instead, he deferred to the lieutenant governor to "submit it entirely to the Consideration of His Majesty's Ministers, trusting that they will be pleased to recollect my having been employed upon this detached Service, at a Period when my situation on the Station had every prospect of being in a very high degree advantageous." Williamson wrote a cover letter for Lawford's itemization and on 16 January sent it to the secretary of state for war.[29] In a letter of 6 March 1794 to the lieutenant governor, Dundas wrote, "The Conduct of Captain Lawford, during his Visitation at Honduras, seems to have been exceedingly proper. . . . I am of opinion that 25 Shillings a day, during Captain Lawford's absence on the Visitation, exclusive of his Expenses, is a proper allowance to him for that Service."[30]

The Capture of *L'Inconstante*

The British captured or destroyed at least 143 French frigates, including privateers and national ships, during the French revolutionary wars. These vessels made up a large percentage of the frigates in the Royal Navy. Some were relegated to harbor service, but others were extremely successful and were copied, including *Hébé*, *Pomone*, *Belle-Poule*, *Magicienne*, and *Impérieuse*.[31] Had HMS *Convert*, ex-*Inconstante*, not been lost shortly after her capture, she probably would have been copied too.

British Accounts

In late November 1793, when much of the Jamaica squadron was in Saint-Domingue protecting Britain's newly acquired possessions at Jérémie and Le Môle St. Nicolas, the *Royal Gazette* in Jamaica published in its Marine Intelligence section that "a forty-gun frigate, an armed brig, and a sloop, chiefly manned with brigands, are lying at Port-au-Prince, but not in a condition for service."[32] The French 12-pounder frigate *L'Inconstante* had been in Port-au-Prince for much of the previous five months and certainly was there during most of November.[33] As the British perceived it, *L'Inconstante* and Commander Joseph Riouffe had not escaped the ill effects of upheavals in Saint-Domingue. Among the frigate's crew of officers and seamen there were undoubtedly both cloaked royalist sentiments and open revolutionary views, and also considerable uncertainty.

On declaration of war, Captain Rowley of HMS *Penelope* cruised the waters of Saint-Domingue seeking intelligence and seizing French ships. He must have earned quite a reputation for prize-taking; in the previous eight months his frigate had been responsible for a large percentage of the captures Commodore Ford's squadron achieved, including the sloop of war *Goelan*. In those eight months he had also become familiar with events in the French colony. In late November, while under orders to protect the harbor and garrison at Le Môle St. Nicolas, he received an intelligence report that sparked his interest. In his letter of 30 November 1793 to Commodore Ford, Captain Rowley described the capture of *L'Inconstante* (map 9).[34] On 20 November, he sailed from Le Môle St. Nicolas after receiving intelligence that *L'Inconstante* was expected to leave Port-au-Prince to convoy a large armed merchantman. The next day he fell in with *Iphigenia*, Captain Sinclair, and gave orders to keep company. While en route to Port-au-Prince, he was informed from Léogane that *L'Inconstante* had sailed with two small vessels for Petit Trou and was daily expected back. He immediately made sail with the intention to take or destroy the frigate in the harbor, "but on the Night of the 25th we had the good fortune to fall in with her, and after exchanging a few Broad Sides she struck her Colours to the Frigates." He reported one man killed and seven wounded aboard *Penelope*, including Midshipman John Allen. *L'Inconstante*, he continued, had six killed, including the first lieutenant and the captain, and twenty men wounded, three of whom later died. He praised the gallant be-

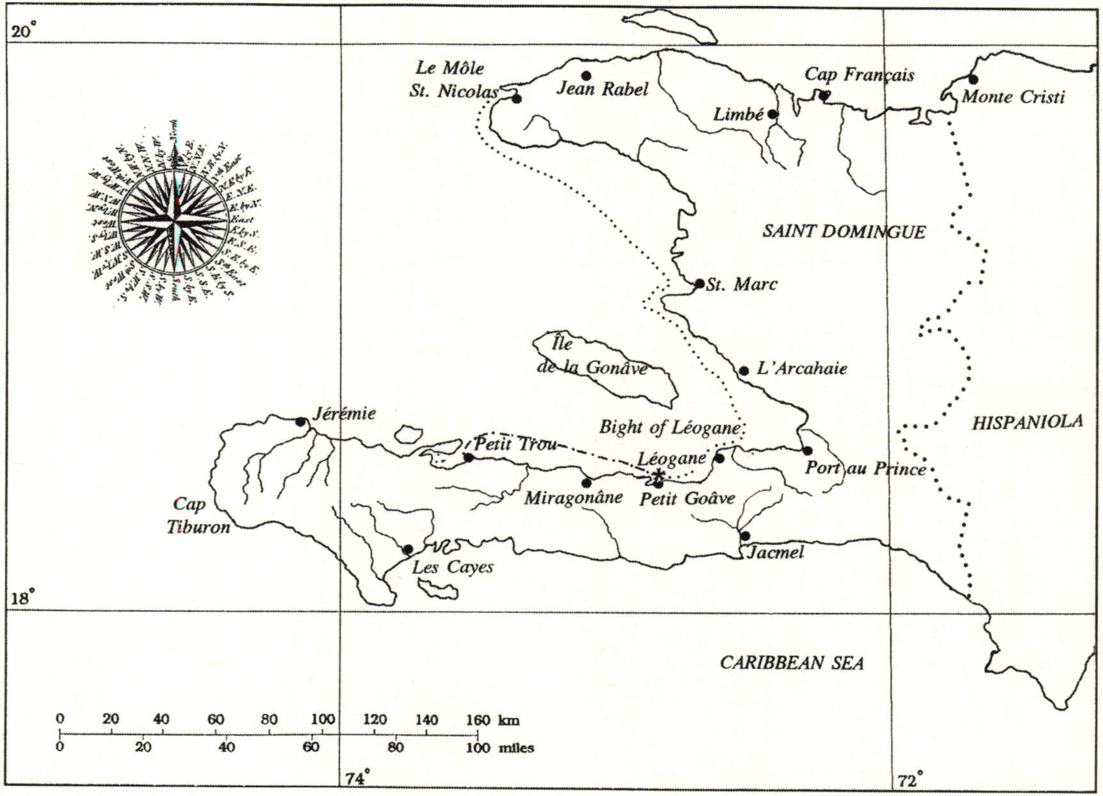

Map 9. Simplified route of the British frigates from Le Môle St. Nicolas to *L'Inconstante* capture site. Drawn by R. L. Craig.

havior of Lieutenant Malcolm, and the Officers and Ship's Company, and proudly suggested that "had either of His Majesty's Frigates been Single, they would have been equally fortunate in capturing her." He concluded by adding that "Captain Sinclair's very favorable report of the Conduct of his Officers & Ship's Company, is such as does them the greatest honor."

The master's log of *Penelope*, kept by John Douglas, includes a more detailed narrative of the search for and seizure of *L'Inconstante*. It reveals the courses sailed and the calculated actions performed by the British frigates (figure 12).[35] On 23 November 1793 *Penelope* was cruising in company with *Iphigenia* and the schooner *Flying Fish*. There were light breezes and the weather was clear. The three vessels ran into Saint-Marc's Bay, where they saw at anchor two large merchant ships, a brig, and several schooners and sloops flying French national colors, along with two US and two Danish vessels. Boats from shore approached *Penelope* twice, coming alongside.[36] The British vessels left Saint-Marc's Bay, and the frigates parted company with *Flying Fish*, sailing on a southward course toward Port-au-Prince. Later they encountered another vessel and fired a shot to bring it to. An officer from *Penelope* in the jolly boat approached the unidentified ship, finding it to be *America* from Le Môle St. Nicolas, bound for Port-au-Prince in ballast. Several hours later, while at sea and in anticipation of meeting *L'Inconstante*, *Penelope* "exercised her great guns and small arms." *Iphigenia* remained in company.

During the following day, the frigates observed an American brig standing into Léogane, where several small vessels were already at anchor. They sailed on, but later hove to for a boat that was approaching them from Léogane, with news for Captain Rowley that *L'Inconstante* had sailed to Petit Trou and was soon expected back in Port-au-Prince.

On Monday, 25 November 1793, according to Master Douglas's log, there were light breezes, the weather was clear, and the frigates were cruising west of Léogane. Two sailing ships appeared to the westward, and subsequently the British boarded a fishing boat from Guanaja. In the moonlit hours, a light southeast breeze sprang up. At one o'clock in the morning, *Penelope* sighted another sail to the westward, and orders passed to clear the ship for action. By one thirty *Penelope* was alongside the French national frigate *L'Inconstante*, bound from Petit Trou to Port-au-Prince. *Penelope* fired several broadsides into the hull of the French ship, which returned the fire. Presently, *Iphigenia* came up on the starboard quarter of the 12-pounder frigate. At two, *L'Inconstante* surrendered. *Penelope* hoisted out her boats, and for the following two hours they were used to shift French prisoners and man the prize; half of the prisoners were put on board *Iphigenia*, and two midshipmen and thirty seamen were sent from *Penelope* to the captured

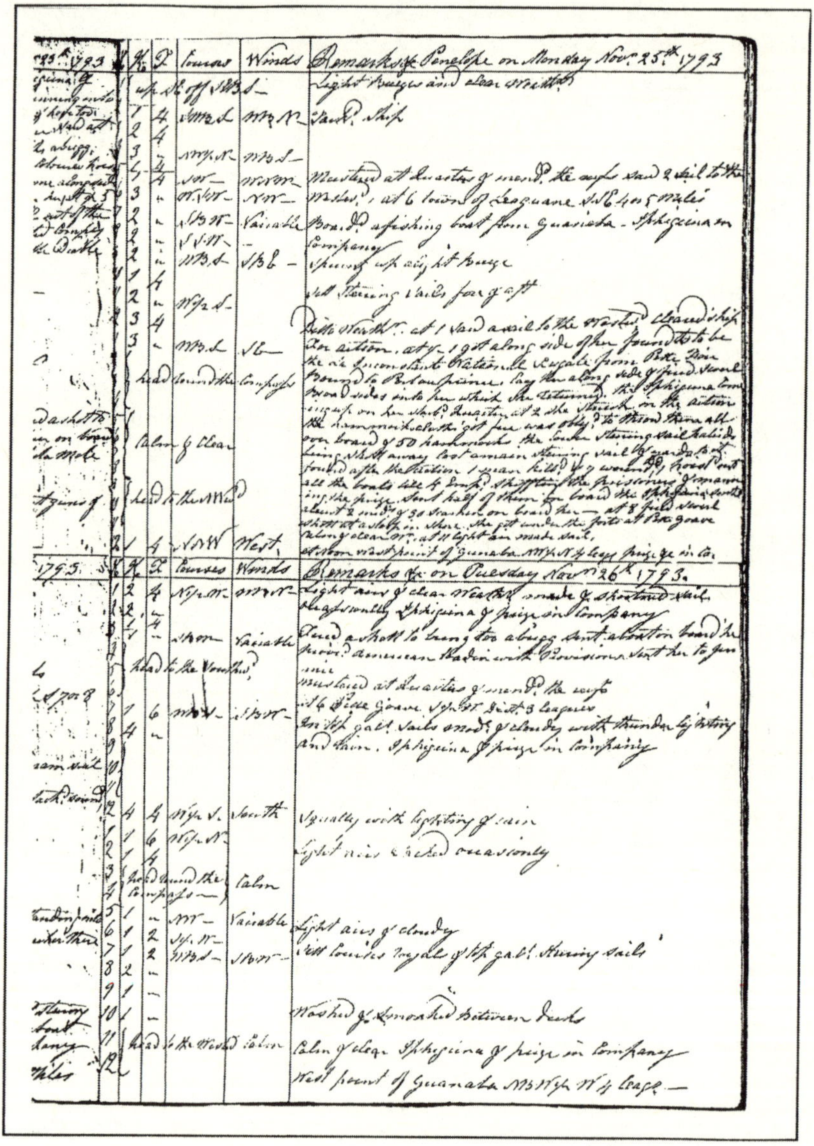

Figure 12. Excerpt from HMS *Penelope* master's log, including 25–26 November 1793. Courtesy of the Public Record Office, Kew.

frigate. Losses suffered by *Penelope* during the engagement were one man killed and seven wounded; the losses on board *Iphigenia* and *L'Inconstante* were not listed in the master's log of *Penelope*. There was minor damage on board *Penelope*: fifty hammock cloths that caught fire had been thrown overboard, the lower steering-sail halyards had been shot away, and a main steering sail with its yards had been lost. At eight in the morning *Penelope* fired shots at a sloop, which took refuge under the forts at Petit Goâve.

On 26 November *Penelope*, *Iphigenia*, and *L'Inconstante* sailed in company on a slow westward course in intermittently clear and squally weather. The following day they reached Jérémie, where they encountered His Majesty's schooner *Spitfire*, commanded by Lieutenant Maitland. Subsequently Captain Rowley sent *Spitfire* north to Le Môle St. Nicolas with news of the capture of *L'Inconstante*. On 28 November the three frigates made sail out of Jérémie Bay and set a course for Jamaica.

On Saturday, 30 November, *Penelope* arrived in Port Royal Harbour, where *Europa* and *Hound* were at anchor; *Iphigenia* and *L'Inconstante* arrived later. On 2 December, eighty of *Penelope*'s men boarded the prize to unbend her sails. Also on this day HMS *Success*, Captain Francis Roberts, and *Magicienne*, Captain George Martin, arrived with the convoy from Great Britain. By the master's log for 3 December 1793, the prize had been commissioned and her name had been changed to *Convert*; twenty men from *Penelope* were sent on board the frigate to assist in warping her alongside the wharf. Meanwhile, *Penelope* headed off on another cruise.[37]

A personal letter sent from Jérémie on 27 November 1793 and received in London on 27 January 1794 also refers to the captured *L'Inconstante* and provides insight into the early British perception of the events that were affecting their standing in Saint-Domingue.[38] The writer expressed optimism in the probability that "Port au Prince & all the Country to the Westward being in our possession speedily increases every day." He explained that "the people of Colour & the Whites in the Neighborhood of St. Marc have United & are now taking the field against the Commissioners whose only hope seems now to be in the Slaves whom they have universally declared free, almost all the Whites that can escape from Port au Prince & that neighborhood are flying to us & implore our protection, & a few more Regiments which we are told we may hourly expect from England will I am persuaded do the business." A key development the writer felt was that "the *Inconstante* french frigate of 40 Guns the only Vessel of Force the Democratic party had in the bite [*sic*] of Leogane is now off this Harbour a Prize to the *Penelope* and *Iphigenia* Frigates she was taken Two days ago after a short engagement."

On 1 December 1793 John Lawford, formerly of the sloop *Hound*, was

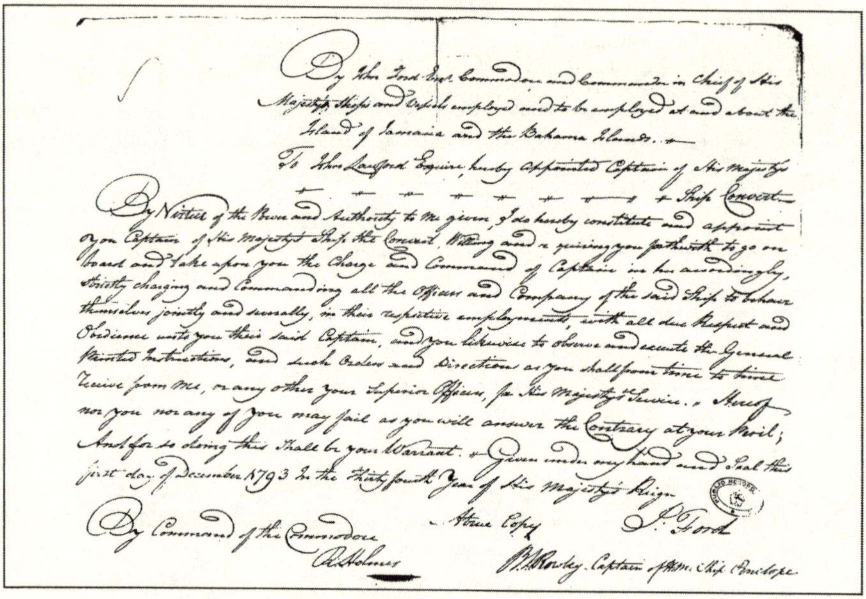
By John Ford Esq. Commodore and Commander in Chief of His Majesty's Ships and Vessels employed and to be employed at and about the Island of Jamaica and the Bahama Islands.

To John Lawford Esquire, hereby appointed Captain of His Majesty's Ship Convert.

By Virtue of the Power and Authority to me given, I do hereby constitute and appoint you Captain of His Majesty's Ship the Convert, Willing and requiring you forthwith to go on board and take upon you the Charge and Command of Captain in her accordingly, strictly charging and commanding all the Officers and Company of the said Ship to behave themselves jointly and severally, in their respective employments, with all due Respect and Obedience unto you their said Captain, and you likewise to observe and execute the General Printed Instructions, and such Orders and Directions as you shall from time to time receive from me, or any other your Superior Officer, for His Majesty's Service. Hereof nor you nor any of you may fail as you will answer the Contrary at your Peril; And for so doing this shall be your Warrant. Given under my hand and Seal this first day of December 1793 In the Thirty fourth Year of His Majesty's Reign.

J. Ford

By Command of the Commodore
R. Holmes

A true Copy
B. Rowley. Captain of H.M. Ship Penelope

Figure 13. Captain John Lawford's commission into HMS *Convert*, 1 December 1793. Courtesy of the Public Record Office, Kew.

promoted to the rank of post captain aboard the Royal Navy's newest acquisition, the fifth-rate frigate *Convert*. Thomas Surridge replaced him on *Hound* (figure 13).[39]

On 7 December 1793, John Ford wrote to the Admiralty about the prize *L'Inconstante*, enclosing a copy of Captain Rowley's letter of 30 November to him that described the incident.[40] The commodore remarked, "I shall add (in Justice to the commendable Zeal, Activity and Enterprise of those Officers on all occasions, the high Condition and Discipline of their Ships) that, in my Opinion, either of them alone would have accomplished what fell to their United Efforts." He praised the qualities of the frigate and explained his reasoning for giving her command to John Lawford: "As this *Inconstant*, is a very fine Ship, about Two Years and a Half old, and reported by Survey a very fit Ship in all Respects for His Majesty's Service . . . I have . . . as an Encouragement to Service, and the Practice of other Officers on similar Occasions, commissioned her accordingly . . . by Name the *Convert*, there being already an *Inconstant* in His Majesty's Navy."

Commodore Ford's List of the Squadron for 7 December 1793 reveals that on that date, in addition to the fifty-gun ship *Europa*, there were seven frigates, two sloops of war, and four schooners under his command in Jamaica. *Penelope*, *Hermione*, *Magicienne*, *Alligator*, and *Flying Fish* were protecting British interests at and in the vicinity of Le Môle St. Nicolas. *Mosquito* and *Spitfire* were protecting Jérémie, and *Goelan* was in the Bahamas. *Europa*, *Success*, *Iphigenia*, *Convert*, *Hound*, and *Marie Antoinette* were in Port Royal Harbour; *Convert* was discharging her stores alongside the wharf.[41]

The *Royal Gazette* also published details about the seizure of *L'Inconstante*. Although the prize arrived in Port Royal on 30 November, the periodical printed, in the issue for the week 23 to 30 November, a brief paragraph about the capture, but *Iphigenia* was not mentioned, and the description of casualties was incorrect. The following issue included Captain Rowley's 30 November letter to Commodore Ford to report the incident more accurately to the public. News that the frigate had been renamed *Convert* and her command given to Captain Lawford appeared in the *Gazette* when the paper reported how "the well-directed fire of musquetry from the *Iphigenia* frigate" quickly decimated the crew of *L'Inconstante*; *L'Inconstante*'s commander was wounded in the right arm, necessitating amputation.[42]

Thus, British accounts of the capture of *L'Inconstante* show that the short engagement went according to Captain Rowley's plan. British losses were low and French casualties were high. Commodore Ford praised the achievement, as the prize itself was a fine warship that he acquired and commissioned for Royal Navy service as *Convert*. The new ship gave the commodore an opportunity to promote deserving officers on the Jamaica station, among whom was John Lawford, who had distinguished himself during service in the Bay of Honduras.

French Accounts

There are also French accounts of the taking of *L'Inconstante*. In Jamaica two of the frigate's officers gave brief testimonies, which were translated during the interrogation and recorded in English.[43] In 1794 French authorities were provided with declarations from the commander of *Le Goelan*, a prisoner in Jamaica since the seizure of his corvette in April 1793, and from a naval officer who had been on board *L'Inconstante*; both men criticized the frigate's captain for his actions during her capture.[44] Others recorded an opposing viewpoint in documents regarding Captain Riouffe and his widow, Hypolite Valliet Riouffe, in her quest to clear her husband's name and to secure a pension for her family based on his many years of service in the French Navy.[45]

Second Lieutenant Augustin de Boyery and Boatswain Joseph Goy, French prisoners from *L'Inconstante*, were interrogated in the proceedings for the captured prize in the High Court of Vice Admiralty in Jamaica. The officers testified that *L'Inconstante* held a commission as a French ship of war, granted by Louis XVI, late king of France. Her commander had been Jean Riouffe, who also carried a commission from the late king, and whose wife and family resided in France. Boyery had met Captain Riouffe several years before, and Goy had known him for more than thirty years.[46] The second lieutenant had encountered *L'Inconstante* in Saint-Domingue and had been on board her for eleven months, while the boatswain had first seen her four years before at Rochefort. Both men testified that no person on board had any holdings in the frigate. According to Boyery her crew was made up of about 250 people who had come aboard at different times in different ports, and her ordnance comprised twenty-six 12-pounders, six 6-pounders, and two swivels. Goy said the crew numbered 240 and that there were four swivels.

The second lieutenant testified that on 20 November 1793, *L'Inconstante* had sailed from Port-au-Prince to Petit Trou to convoy two sloops laden with provisions, and that a French woman escaping the troubles in Saint-Domingue (mentioned previously) had come on board there. On the return voyage the frigate had been steering her course for Port-au-Prince when she fell in with and was seized by *Penelope* and *Iphigenia*. The frigate, sailing under French national colors, was taken in the Bight of Léogane at about three in the morning on Monday, 25 November 1793. Second Lieutenant Boyery said that many guns had been fired by *Penelope* and several by *L'Inconstante*. He had been stationed between decks during the engagement, so he did not know whether *Iphigenia* had discharged any guns, but he stated that she was with *Penelope* and that no other ships had been in sight at the time. Boyery also affirmed that the ship's commission and muster roll were on the frigate at the time of capture; he did not know of any other papers being on board, and none were destroyed. The boatswain's testimony largely paralleled Boyery's, although he recalled that both British ships had fired guns when the French frigate resisted capture, and he thought that the female passenger, named Poitier, had come on board at Port-au-Prince.[47]

On his return to France by prisoner exchange, Lieutenant Leissegues, former commander of the captured *Goelan*, made a declaration on 27 June 1794, circulated at Brest, concerning the fate of the frigate *L'Inconstante*.[48] He stated that the frigate *L'Inconstante*, commanded by Captain Riouffe, had surrendered at the first volley from the English frigate, and that Captain Riouffe had fired only six cannon shots. He said that both the port and starboard batteries had been encumbered by the *bittures* laid with the cannons by Riouffe's orders; the *bittures* consisted of anchor cable brought up on the gundeck and laid down in a serpentine manner to run out freely when anchoring. Leissegues testified that the second captain had been killed and the captain and the third in command had been wounded; two officers were not wounded, Citizens Ouinet and Boisguere.[49] This was the report of the incident made to him in Jamaica by Citizen Morice, *Aspirant* (midshipman) aboard *L'Inconstante*.[50]

In July 1794, Officier de Marine (naval officer) Ouinet arrived in France. The testimony this zealous officer gave was critical of his captain, but his own performance remains questionable.[51] Ouinet's narrative is based on his description of events surrounding the day of combat between *L'Inconstante* and *Penelope* and *Iphigenia*, followed by his report of his imprisonment in Jamaica and return voyage to France.

According to Ouinet, *L'Inconstante* had left Port Republicain (Port-au-Prince) between Tuesday and Wednesday, 19 and 20 November 1793, to escort two small vessels, a *golete* and a *bateaux* full of provisions to Petit Trou.[52] On Friday, 22 November, the three vessels reached their destination, and the frigate, having completed her mission, sailed again for the return trip to Port-au-Prince (see map 9). On the evening of Sunday, 24 November, and the early morning of Monday, 25 November, the French vessel was passing Petit Goâve when, at one o'clock, Soldat de la Marine (marine) La Font, on the forecastle, sighted two ships ahead. He went to the stern to give the news to Ouinet, who immediately went to the forecastle to see for himself. Ouinet saw the two vessels coming toward them but could not discern what types of ships they were because they were partially hidden by land. He immediately went to the captain's quarters to report that there were two ships ahead. When the captain asked what vessels they were, Ouinet responded that he had been unable to identify them. A moment later, the captain appeared on the deck and, on sighting the vessels, stated that they were American ships; he went back to his room and returned with his spyglass, but still insisted that both ships were American. Lieutenant La Bourt, who was second captain on board the frigate, pointed out to Riouffe that the ships seemed very large for American ships, yet Captain Riouffe was unconvinced.

In the meantime, the two ships approached rapidly before a good land wind from the east-southeast, which was common in the area, and *L'Inconstante* was picking up a little wind from the west. In his testimony, Ouinet emphasized that it didn't matter whether the ships were North American or not, because as they approached under full sail the battery remained unprepared.

Finally, the captain gave Officer Ouinet the order to silently assemble the crew on deck, with no bell. Ouinet immediately ordered the Maître de Quart (watch boatswain) to awaken and have the crew prepare for combat; shortly, the captain's order came for everyone to go to his station. At the captain's command, Ouinet had the sails adjusted to change the course away from Île de La Gonâve toward the coast of Saint-Domingue. They felt the wind from the east and simultaneously were almost becalmed. The time was 1:20 a.m.

Ouinet turned the watch over to M. Tourneur, Officier de Manoeuvre (navigator) in combat, and went to his own station in the forward battery. When he arrived he was astonished to find that the port and starboard batteries were not prepared, despite the fact that Officer Boyery was present. It took some time to stow the *bittures*, but eventually everything was ready and everyone was at his station.

Ouinet asked the cheffe des pièces (gun captain) if he had everything he needed for the cannons, including ammunition, to which he replied *no*. Ouinet sent men, and eventually went himself, to retrieve the ammunition, but the *maître canonnier* (gunner's mate) would not release it without the captain's orders. Ouinet stated that he would take the responsibility, believing that in such circumstances an officer of the battery had the authority to give orders for the delivery of all items needed for the cannons. Finally he went directly to the captain, who allowed the release of small quantities of ammunition—only two boxes for each cannon. Everyone was at his post and the battery was prepared.

At one-thirty the two approaching ships were but a single gunshot away, and Riouffe still maintained that they were American. Ouinet, in telling the story, emphasized that the captain should not have made the mistake because the vessels were clearly warships. Riouffe had Officier Marignie (naval officer?) Vinette call out to ask the ships who they were, and simultaneously *L'Inconstante* raised the French flag and pennant. One of the approaching ships answered that they were English frigates, *Penelope* and *Iphigenia*. They raised their flags while demanding the surrender of *L'Inconstante*; in the moonlight, it was easy to distinguish the English colors.

On hearing the answer, Captain Riouffe ordered a change of course to secure a tailwind, presumably to outrun them, and commanded that the crew put up the studding sails. Later, in his declaration regarding the capture, Ouinet severely criticized his captain for these actions, stressing that *L'Inconstante* was becalmed while *Penelope* and *Iphigenia* still had the breeze with them. He maintained that, in consequence, Riouffe had taken the most disadvantageous position possible. He felt that if they had sailed their original course, the English ships would have been forced to let them pass, and they could have used their entire battery on the enemy. As it was, they could fire only the port cannons between the stern and the mainmast.

Although the enemy frigates were at port and starboard, the ship at starboard had not closed within firing range, Ouinet asserted. At 1:36 a.m. Lieutenant La Bourt suggested to him that he ask for three or four cannons at starboard, since they were taken at both sides, and asked him if he was ready. Ouinet was ready, except he had little help, so La Bourt promised to send him men from the guns on the forecastle, but they never arrived.

The English frigates observed *L'Inconstante*'s maneuver, and at only a pistol's distance away, the ship on port, *Penelope*, opened fire. The other frigate, *Iphigenia*, which was behind at starboard, immediately followed suit. The French frigate fired back at port, but, as her unfavorable position prevented her from using the starboard cannons, her return fire was weak.

Ouinet lamented that at the first cannon shot fired aboard, many of the combat lanterns fell, and several people left their posts and went below deck. He castigated Riouffe for his lack of bravery, maintaining that his actions were discouraging the unhappy, homesick crew. He testified that when the first shots were fired at *L'Inconstante*, Captain Riouffe shouted to lower the flag and surrender. Lieutenant La Bourt instantly headed for the stern but was killed by debris falling from the damaged mainmast. Ouinet interjected that he had since been told that La Bourt had gone to discover the motive for surrender—which he, Ouinet, still could not figure out, as they had not been in distress and only a few people were removed from combat.

Ouinet reported that the shooting had ceased for a moment when *Iphigenia* appeared at starboard. Not knowing that they had surrendered, he ordered the starboard *canonnier* (gunner) to fire, which he immediately did. When the English frigate was fired on, she instantly discharged a volley that seriously wounded Captain Riouffe, leaving him motionless. At the same moment, *quartier-maître* (quartermaster) Simon came to Ouinet and told him to hold fire because both the captain and the lieutenant had surrendered. The time was a few minutes past two.

Although firing had just begun on the starboard side, Ouinet ordered it stopped. He stated that before he knew they had surrendered, he had seen lights that made him think they were being boarded. Subsequently, he had gone on deck and had seen the lowered flag, the injured captain, and the enemy boarding *L'Inconstante*. The English asked for the captain and then, when they learned of his injuries, for the commanding officer. Second Lieutenant Augustin de Boyery came forward and surrendered his sword; they took him aboard the frigate *Penelope*. Officer Ouinet stayed on the prize with almost eighty men while the rest of the crew was transported to the two English frigates. Those who stayed on board took care of the sick and the wounded until their arrival in Jamaica, but there apparently was no linen for bandages.

Ouinet presented statistics concerning the engagement. He stated that the English frigates each had a crew of 120 men and that both were armed with twenty-six 12-pounder cannons and six 6-pounders.[53] *L'Inconstante* had a crew of 245 men and, although she was pierced for forty-four guns, carried the same armament as the English frigates.[54] He maintained that the French ship had fired, at most, fifteen cannon shots, and that, although the gun captain of the three cannons under his control at starboard had wanted to continue firing, Ouinet had pointed out that only a few men remained at their stations. Others were already aboard the English launches.[55]

There were eight French dead, including Captain Riouffe, who died in Jamaica after three progressive amputations of his arm, and Lieutenant La Bourt. Eight others were wounded but survived.

According to Ouinet, *Penelope* and *Iphigenia* escorted *L'Inconstante* to Jamaica. They arrived on Saturday, 30 November, and by Sunday the crew, including the wounded, were on land. Ouinet remained on board the frigate until Tuesday, 2 December, with the surgeon; he was responsible for removing all of his own possessions as well as those belonging to Captain Riouffe and the late Lieutenant La Bourt.[56]

Although Ouinet was a prisoner of the British, he, like most officers, was paroled and therefore enjoyed limited freedom in Jamaica until he was returned to France by prisoner exchange. In contrast, most of the crew were securely imprisoned, and when he visited them they complained of poor conditions and bad food. Ouinet said he had gone to see the commissary on behalf of the prisoners but was ignored. On 7 December when he and the surgeon of *L'Inconstante*, along with twenty-nine other people, were taken to Spanish Town, he spoke to the governor about the problem, and the governor seemed sympathetic. Subsequently, however, the prisoners were treated even worse; the guards robbed them, and when they complained they were shot in their cells.[57] Ouinet claimed that villains visited and upset the prisoners, told them lies about the position of France, and tried to get them to take service with Great Britain. When they refused, they were often shot on the pretext that there was an uprising. Ouinet believed that the villains gave the British troops money to commit the atrocities. Eventually, Ouinet secured parole from the governor for five men, but the commissary refused to release them and would no longer let him into the prison.

Ouinet said that eight days after their arrival in Jamaica, Captain Riouffe died, and a few days after his death, while they were in Spanish Town, the surgeon was taken away, allegedly to be sent to London. Ouinet wanted to know the motive for the action and was told that the governor had ordered it and that he would be told nothing else. He wrote to Second Lieutenant Boyery, who said he did not know the reason but that he had seen paperwork suggesting that the surgeon was sent to London as a partisan of the Civil Commissary of Sonthonax (in Saint-Domingue). At this point Ouinet alluded to hearsay that Captain Riouffe might have been responsible. He testified that the surgeon from *Goelan*, who was also a paroled prisoner, knew Dr. Renal, and that Dr. Renal had told him that the surgeon from *L'Inconstante* had been in the prison at Port Royal.[58] Captain Riouffe, in his dying moments, had asked Dr. Renal if his surgeon had been the cause of his death. He suspected that the man had purposely operated badly, out of vengeance. Riouffe had asked, for mercy's sake, that the surgeon be imprisoned until the end of the war.[59]

Ouinet left Jamaica on 7 May 1794 aboard a *parlementaire*, a neutral ship used to transport prisoners under exchange, with a British captain bound for Saint-Malo, and about two hundred other French prisoners. Four of the prisoners jumped ship before leaving the harbor at Port Royal. Ouinet related that the remaining prisoners refused to accept a white flag on the *parlementaire* and insisted on making a national flag from several seamen's turbans. They encountered two French corsairs in the Windward Passage. After tiring of the prisoners' complaints, Ouinet persuaded the captain to give them one pound of bread rather than the allotted four ounces and said that he would be reimbursed in France. Three men died during the Atlantic crossing, but the captain would not provide anything in which to wrap their bodies. On approaching France, the prisoners wanted to head for the nearest port. They persuaded the captain to take them to Nantes rather than Saint-Malo, but they encountered a British convoy of more than one hundred merchantmen, escorted by two ships of the line and three frigates, and were boarded by an officer from one of the naval ships. The captain of the *parlementaire* complained that the French prisoners had taken over his ship; Ouinet was called on to explain his actions and was told that he deserved to be sent to London. They were ordered to proceed to Saint-Malo and were told to leave the commands to the captain. The convoy departed. In his account, Ouinet interjected that although they were told that the fleet was bound for India, he believed it was headed for Jamaica, because when he had left the island the British had been waiting for a large convoy that would enable them to take over the whole of Saint-Domingue. The *parlementaire* encountered a pirate ship carrying people of various nationalities, which left them to pursue two Dutch ships. At this point they were short of food, and when they neared France, Ouinet forced the captain to sail into the closest anchorage. They arrived at Camaret to the south of Brest on 12 July 1794 (see map 6).

The following day, Ouinet was sent to Brest, where he secured permission for their ship to enter the anchorage there. He spoke to French officials about his journey and gave them intelligence information about the Jamaica-bound convoy, about a Europe-bound convoy that left Jamaica shortly after their departure, and about encountering the pirate ship.

Ouinet's narrative ends here, but at the bottom of the final page of his declaration he added some further observations about Captain Riouffe. He declared that the capture of *L'Inconstante* was not the first time that Riouffe had performed badly, and he listed several instances. He stated that on 20 October the French frigate had been about a league's distance from nine corsairs, and the captain had fired a cannon shot to facilitate their escape. Next he attributed to Riouffe their loss of a chance on 22 October to take as prize an English corvette; the Royal Navy vessel arrived near Île de la Gonâve to capture prizes from a French convoy being escorted by *L'Inconstante* from Petit Goâve to Port Republicain (see map 7). Ouinet maintained that Captain Riouffe decided to chase the corvette only because there were rumors about Riouffe circulating among the crew, many of whom were refusing to work for him. The corvette remained broadside, too, under English colors, but *L'Inconstante* tacked twice to give it time to see her broadside before giving chase.

There is another source of information regarding Captain Joseph Alexandre Riouffe and *L'Inconstante.* This is a series of certified documents regarding his personal history, which were compiled as supporting evidence for a claim by his widow, Hypolite Valliet Riouffe, for a commissioned officer's pension based on her husband's more than twenty-eight years of service in the French Navy.[60] These documents add detail to events surrounding the taking of *L'Inconstante* and provide insight into the revolutionary period and the character of Captain Riouffe and his family.[61]

Among the documents are a chronology of Riouffe's career in the French Navy, a listing of all the vessels on which he served, and the positions that he held on board each, including his commission into *L'Inconstante.* There is an excerpt from his death notice that reveals not only that the captain's left arm was amputated but also that in the battle with the English frigates he was also seriously wounded in the lower abdomen and the left eye, which he subsequently lost; he died two weeks later in Jamaica on 9 December. Although Captain Riouffe's exact age is not revealed, since he began his naval career in 1765 he was probably about forty when he died.

Joseph Riouffe fils (Joseph Marie Hypolite Riouffe, born on 27 March

1782), the young son of the captain, had embarked with his father on board the frigate as a *mousse* (ship's boy) on 3 December 1791 and had been aboard for nearly two years when *L'Inconstante* was captured. The boy was subsequently held as a prisoner of war in Jamaica. He wrote a letter to his mother from Kingston, dated 31 March 1794, that was taken to France aboard a *parlementaire* bound for Saint-Malo. In it he consoled his mother, telling her that he was well and that M. Boyery was a good friend, teacher, and counselor to him; he sent her "a million kisses."

Hypolite Valliet Riouffe was born on 18 February 1756 and thus was thirty-seven years old when her husband died. Captain Riouffe and his wife also had two daughters, Marie Josephine Hypolite and Marie Sophie Hypolite, who were nine and four respectively when their father was killed. They did not escape the discord of the period, for the records show that Madame Riouffe was arrested before the capture of *L'Inconstante.* On 27 October 1793, members of the Comité de Surveillance Révolutionaire of the District of Rochefort came to the family home, sealed the writing desk, and confiscated various papers and letters. They separated Mme Riouffe from her daughters and imprisoned her, on the pretext that the family was related to foreigners and nobility, and under the suspicion that her husband had emigrated. In a letter of 31 July 1794 to the Commission de la Marine, the widow demanded her freedom. She declared that her husband had been a brave naval officer who had died in service to the French Republic, and she asked for a pension for her young children and herself based on Captain Riouffe's lengthy service. In a meeting on 29 October 1794, the Comité de Surveillance granted Mme Riouffe provisional freedom.

The widow secured the assistance of M. Blutel, the Representative of the People in the ports of La Rochelle, Rochefort, Bordeaux, Bayonne, and adjacent Ports, who filed a statement on her behalf dated 12 January 1795, along with supporting documentation. Representative Blutel wrote that he had seen the widow's petition, which declared that she was a mother who had been inhumanely separated from her children and detained for a year under vague pretexts. She was devastated to learn that her husband had died from grave and numerous wounds received on board *L'Inconstante*, the frigate that he commanded. He stated that the widow asked for a pension, to which she had a right, and for temporary assistance to keep the children from suffering. Blutel had seen a certificate from the Bureau des Armemens that affirmed that Joseph Riouffe had died from wounds received in combat against two English frigates, and that the second captain had been killed at his side. He had seen a certificate from the Municipality of Rochefort that the widow had only 400 *livres* income and was the mother of three children. He had seen a certificate from the head of the Bureaux Civils de la Marine at Rochefort confirming that she had not received any provisional aid from the pension accorded her for her husband's service. Blutel stated that because Captain Riouffe had died while serving the republic, he had authorized the maritime agent at Rochefort to pay Widow Riouffe a provisional sum of 800 *livres* from the pension she would be entitled to receive under the terms of the Decree of the National Convention, the governing body of the French Republic. Blutel concluded that various pieces relative to her claim were being forwarded to the Comité de Secours of the National Convention.

The supporting documentation included official papers regarding Captain Riouffe and his son, the imprisonment and innocence of Mme Riouffe, testimonials that the family was not considered nobility, and certificates proving that the children were legitimate. Also sent were excerpts from personal letters that Joseph Riouffe had written to his wife from Saint-Domingue, which revealed his temperance, loyalty, and devotion to his family and to France. He wrote tender words regarding his wife and children. He wanted peace, union, and order and to be of service to his country; he hoped that all would end well. Blutel also forwarded an extract from a public address given by the citizens of Le Môle St. Nicolas on 28 January 1793 on board *L'Inconstante*, and signed and accepted by the crew, regarding the patriotism exhibited by Captain Riouffe in Saint-Domingue to the appropriate officials.

Mme Riouffe sent a detailed and moving letter to the Comité de Marine on 17 January 1795, in which she requested a pension for a widow and three children, aged five, ten, and twelve, the eldest of whom was a prisoner in Jamaica. The letter effectively sums up both Riouffe's patriotism and his family's situation.

Mme. Riouffe wrote that she had been unjustly imprisoned at Brouage, a victim of passions unleashed at the beginning of the revolution, to the detriment of her three children, under false accusations of fanaticism, suspicious correspondence, and family ties to nobility and foreigners. She lamented that secret enemies and exaggerated patriotism were not the purpose of the revolution, which should have been beneficial to all instead of causing misery, and that, once slandered, it was difficult to prove one's innocence.

But justice had emerged. She had proven that she was not a fanatic, that her beliefs (protected by law and the Rights of Man) and actions had never troubled public order, that she had no suspicious correspondence, and that her three brothers remained employed and attached to the revolution. Among her possessions had been found only family papers and some perfectly innocent letters from her husband. Ultimately, the Comité de Surveillance had determined, through personal testimonies from six respected people, that neither she nor her husband had foreign relatives or ties to nobility, though her husband's first cousin had married a man who had gone to Russia in the first year of the revolution and stayed there.

Mme Riouffe wrote warmly of her marriage, saying that she and her husband had been happily united. She maintained that they had associated with everyone, and her associations had not changed since before the revolution; they had shared what they possessed, had considered their children and their domestic helpers as friends, and they had enjoyed bringing happiness to all who surrounded them.

She wrote that before she was freed, she had had to absorb not only the cruel reality of her husband's death but also the malevolence of those who sought to dishonor him in the last moments of his life. She said she would leave it to the campaign journals to justify his behavior but stressed that one error was not a crime, and she swore adamantly that he was incapable of betraying his country. She pointed out that he would be in Russia with his in-law if he hadn't favored the revolution. On the contrary, he had always refused invitations of that kind, and when the reorganization of the navy released him from his attachment to the port, he not only solicited employment but also sacrificed his only son, then age ten, to his country. The boy was still in Jamaica, not having been exchanged along with other prisoners because he had contracted smallpox.

Mme Riouffe insisted that her husband had served the cause of liberty in Saint-Domingue, especially at Le Môle St. Nicolas. She explained that *L'Inconstante* had been surprised and attacked at two o'clock in the morning by superior forces that he thought were neutral ships. He had received mortal wounds in the abdomen, had his arm severed, and eventually lost his left eye after it was damaged by shot; his second captain was killed. She claimed that her husband had been accused of betrayal by treasonous, malevolent men who had escaped from Saint-Domingue and found themselves on board as part of the crew. She suggested that it would not be the first time that the dead had been used to justify the actions of the living. Mme Riouffe believed that her husband had done his duty and that *L'Inconstante* had been forced to surrender; Captain Riouffe died at his post, at arms, as a consequence of grave wounds. She speculated that even if his wrongdoings had been real, he had been punished sufficiently. And she asked whether, even if she was still believed guilty of the offenses for which she had been imprisoned, it would be fair to punish her children. The widow concluded that she could not even provide them with bare necessities. She commended herself to the national munificence, stating that she and the children were victims of the misfortunes of war who trusted that the Comité de Marine would apply the pension law and give them what they so desperately needed.

Apparently, Mme Riouffe was successful in clearing her husband's name. Under the terms of the National Convention's decree of 4 September 1795 regarding widows of citizens who died in defense of their country, she was awarded a certificate for a pension, signed by the Commissaire des Secours Publics in the name of the National Convention and dated 2 November 1795. The document indicates that she would receive the maximum annual award of 1,500 *livres* for herself and 750 *livres* for each of her children until they reached the age of twelve. Payment of the funds commenced with the date of Captain Riouffe's death on 9 December 1793 (though she had to struggle with the authorities to receive installments throughout the succeeding years).

The High Court of Vice Admiralty

On Saturday, 30 November 1793, *L'Inconstante* and His Majesty's frigates *Penelope* and *Iphigenia* arrived in Port Royal Harbour from Saint-Domingue. On Sunday, 1 December, Commodore Ford commissioned the prize as *Convert* under the command of Captain John Lawford. During the following days men from *Penelope* assisted in unbending the frigate's sails and warping her alongside the wharf.[62] In a letter to the Admiralty on 7 December, John Ford wrote of the capture of the French prize, reporting that she was a fine ship that had been found fit for His Majesty's Service; the commodore had ordered the assessment on 30 November and planned to send the report by the next packet.[63] (See appendix A for a complete transcript of the inventory and appraisement of the sails, rigging, ordnance, and stores from *L'Inconstante* that were acquired for His Majesty's Service.) He informed the Admiralty of the commission of the prize and the promotion of John Lawford to be her commander. In the 7 December listing of the disposition of the squadron, John Ford wrote that *Convert* was at Port Royal discharging her stores.[64]

Although Commodore Ford lost no time in acquiring *L'Inconstante* for the Royal Navy and commissioning her as HMS *Convert*, the ship still had to go through the formal legal process of condemnation in an Admiralty Court. This was standard procedure because some ships and vessels sailed under false colors. All French prizes—warships and merchantmen alike—had to be proved to have belonged to France.[65] The case of the French frigate *L'Inconstante* was adjudicated in the High Court of Vice Admiralty in Jamaica. Records regarding the litigation survive today in the Jamaica Archives.[66]

Two of the surviving French officers from *L'Inconstante*, Second Lieutenant Augustin de Boyery and Boatswain Joseph Goy, were produced, sworn, and examined as part of the Vice Admiralty Court proceedings on 2 December and 4 December 1793, respectively. A synopsis of their largely parallel testimonies was presented earlier in this chapter. Of particular relevance to the prize court, they attested that there were about 240 or 250 people on board the frigate, which had a commission as a French ship of war from the late king of France; that the ship sailed under French national colors; that no person on board had any interest or share in the ship or sustained any loss from her capture; that the ship's commission and muster roll, but no other papers, were on board; and that *Penelope* and *Iphigenia* were the only other ships in sight at the time *L'Inconstante* was taken.

On 5 December 1793 copies of a monition (appendix B) were publicly posted in the towns of St. Jago de La Vega (Spanish Town), Kingston, and Port Royal, where they remained on display for three days. The official legal notice was intended to notify people of the capture of *L'Inconstante* and order them to appear before the judge in St. Jago de la Vega on the morning of 10 December if they had proof of any just claim, right, title, or interest in the vessel. If they failed to appear or to show such documents they forfeited their rights, and the judge would pronounce the vessel to be a just and lawful prize to Bartholomew Samuel Rowley and Patrick Sinclair and their "officers, seamen, marines and Mariners."

Also on 5 December, Advocate General George Ricketts, at the relation of B. S. Rowley and Patrick Sinclair, instituted a suit against *L'Inconstante* by a libel, a formal written declaration filed in the Court of Vice Admiralty (appendix B). *L'Inconstante* was proved to have belonged to the wartime enemy, France, and so was subsequently condemned on 3 January 1794.

The Jamaica Archives contains another document titled "Sales of Vessel & Stores of the Frigate *L'Inconstant* [*sic*] Prize to His Majesty's Ships *Penelope* and *Iphigenia*" (figure 14).[67] On 1 August 1794 Benjamin Waterhouse, acting as agent for the relators, was sworn in and stated that the document as presented was a just and true account of the sale of *L'Inconstante*, condemned in the Court of Vice Admiralty in Jamaica. The document is divided into two registers: the right column, dated 25 January 1794, is a tabulation of the funds received for the sale of the frigate and her stores, while the left column, dated 26 May 1794, is an account of payments made from the proceeds of the sale.

Under the Prize Law in effect in 1794, prize money was awarded and distributed among the officers and crews of all Royal Navy vessels involved in the capture of an enemy ship and those that were in sight at the time of surrender. Since *Penelope* and *Iphigenia* were the only British ships in

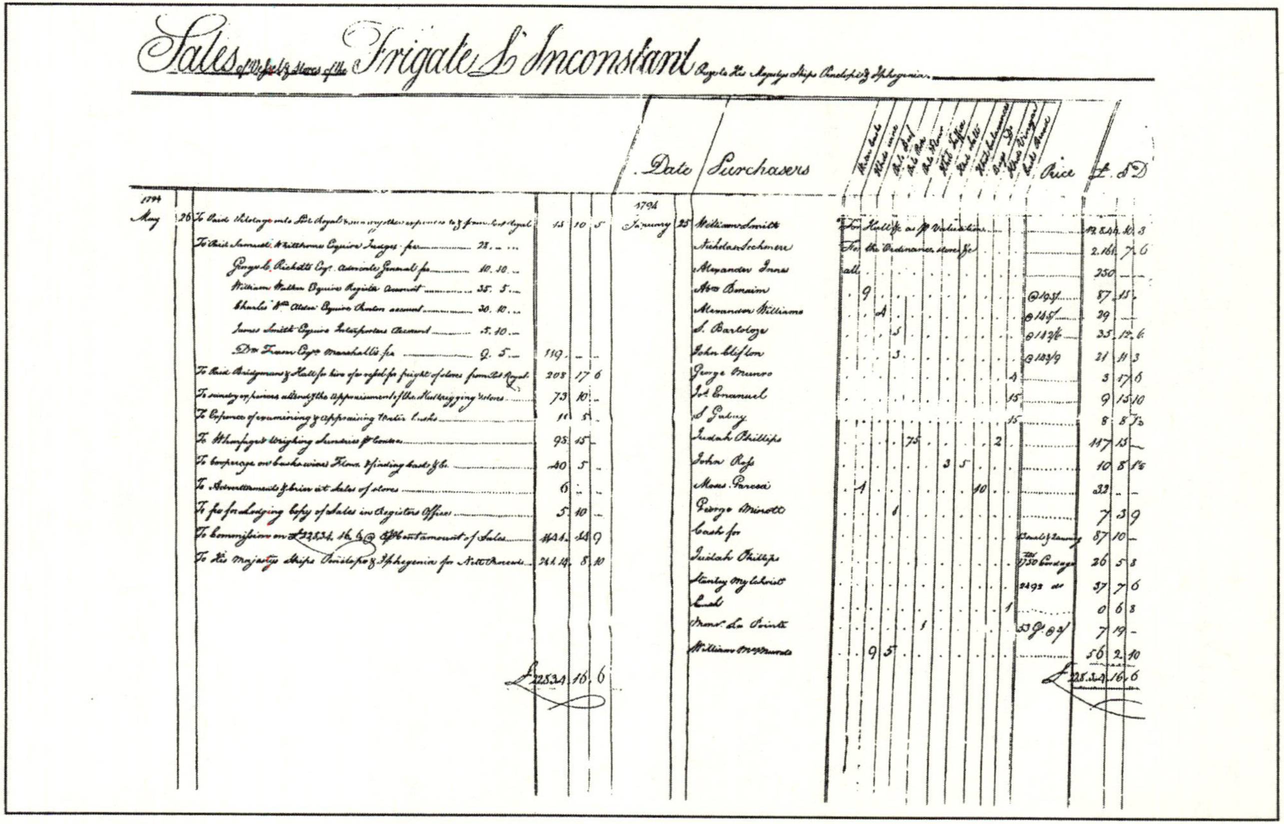

Figure 14. Sales of the vessel and stores of the frigate *L'Inconstante*. Courtesy of the Jamaica Archives, Spanish Town.

view when *L'Inconstante* was seized, they received the net prize money of £21,114.8s.10d from the sale of the frigate. It is likely that this sum was supplemented by head money of £5 per member of the crew of the captured French frigate, totaling approximately £1,225 for the complement of 245 men on board *L'Inconstante*. Consequently, about £22,339 would have been disbursed to the officers and men of the two frigates according to a standard formula based on rank.[68]

6

Great Britain's *Convert* Convoy

Duty versus Profit

In 1792 more than sixteen thousand merchant vessels, totaling 1.5 million tons, were engaged in shipping in Great Britain and her overseas colonies; these commercial interests had significant political influence. The Royal Navy depended on the British merchant marine for timber, naval stores, provisions, and troop transports and was paid from tax funds that merchant shipping generated. In turn, the Royal Navy protected the seaborne trade.[1]

When war broke out, it significantly affected British commerce. Enemy ships and privateers posed a constant danger to merchant shipping. Owners faced rising costs and diminishing manpower to sail their vessels, and insurance rates spiraled. The Royal Navy therefore provided naval escorts to guard the merchant fleets. While this service safeguarded the merchants' interests, convoys were time consuming to organize and, once underway, dependent on the speed of the slowest sailing vessel. And the greatest annoyance, to the masters of merchantmen, was the Royal Navy's practice of impressing trained seamen from their ships.[2]

Preparation for the Winter Convoy

From the time that Commodore Ford received news of war with France on 29 March 1793, he appointed periodic convoy protection for homeward-bound merchant fleets from the West Indies. The *Proserpine* convoy sailed from Jamaica around 12 June with 158 merchantmen, accompanied by *Providence* and *Assistant*, which were also to meet the ships from Honduras en route, to escort them to Britain.[3] In late July, *Hector* and *Hannibal*, with separate convoys, left Jamaica with a total of almost one hundred vessels.[4] But six months passed before Commodore Ford spared another of His Majesty's ships to escort the merchant trade to Europe.

The Jamaica squadron was small in the first year of Britain's war with France, and Ford was unable to appoint more frequent convoy protection for British merchantmen, particularly to and from outlying areas. The Assembly of Jamaica, on 12 November, expressed concern that the commander in chief of His Majesty's ships would not have the power to grant a convoy for the homeward-bound winter fleet, much less provide protection for British vessels bound to and from America for staves, lumber, and other provisions.[5] By the end of November, however, the capture of *L'Inconstante* provided the commodore with another frigate, which he purchased for the Admiralty and prepared to lead the winter convoy.

On 1 December 1793, *L'Inconstante* was renamed *Convert*, and her command was given to Captain John Lawford, former commander of the sloop *Hound*. (See appendix C for a biographical sketch of John Lawford.) Admiralty regulations specified the ship's complement and the number of commissioned and warrant officers, petty officers, servants, artisans, and marines that should be on board, but they did not specify the makeup of the balance of the crew. A fortunate captain would be able to muster a significant percentage of able seamen, but most had to settle for a number of ordinary seamen and landmen as well.[6] Admiralty regulations also provided that John Lawford, as captain of the newly commissioned frigate, was responsible for finding the ship's crew—though he would be afforded some assistance.[7]

Commodore Ford promoted several officers for their services on the Jamaica station. *Convert*'s four commissioned officers and most of the warrant officers received assignments from other Royal Navy ships. (See appendix D for an extract of data from the muster table of HMS *Convert*.) *Convert*'s muster table reveals that on 1 December 1793 commissions were granted to First Lieutenant Joseph Bradby Bogue and Second Lieutenant William Earnshaw; John Scott (purser), George Innes (gunner), Joseph Blease (cook), and John Doran (surgeon's first mate) were appointed to their posts by warrant. In the following two days additional warrants were issued to William Porter (surgeon), Thomas Popplewell (master), Roger Kirby (boatswain), and William Cruise (carpenter). On 10 December John Allen, a former midshipman on *Penelope* who had been wounded in the taking of *L'Inconstante*, was commissioned as third lieutenant of *Convert*. Two of the warrant officers, George Innes and William Cruise, died before the end of December. Innes was replaced by William Dixon (gunner), who was appointed by warrant on 2 January 1794, but apparently no fully qualified replacement was found for the post of carpenter.[8] These men constituted all the commissioned and warrant officers assigned to *Convert*.

By Commodore Ford's order, *Convert*'s complement was to be 220 men in addition to the twenty-nine marines who were also assigned to her. At the end of the first eighteen days of her commission, there were ninety-one crew members listed in the muster table. Among these men were the captain, nine captain's servants (most of whom were young men who planned to become officers), and two "widow's men" (fictitious seamen whose pay went into a general pension fund for widows and dependents of officers killed in action).[9] Also included were the three lieutenants and their respective three servants as well as seven warrant officers and their ten servants. Fifteen men were appointed by list (presumably identified by John Lawford) from *Hound*, Captain Lawford's former command, and one came as a volunteer; eleven of these sixteen men were ranked as petty officers, and the other five were rated able seamen. The purser's steward also came from *Hound*. One midshipman was listed from Port Royal, and one able seaman was assigned from *Penelope*. The remaining thirty-seven crew were able seamen who signed on as volunteers, five of whom were given petty officer assignments.[10]

The bounty of £5 each that was paid to new recruits on joining the navy surely encouraged the initial enlistment of volunteers. Yet in fact, when news of war with France had first arrived in Jamaica, many seamen had fled into the countryside. To counter this resistance to navy service, Commodore Ford had issued a Proclamation for Bounty, as given in England, in order to lure them into Royal Navy service.[11] From the time he commissioned *Convert*, however, Ford knew that additional measures would be required to complete the frigate's complement.

The offer of bounty enticed some seamen, but life in the socially stratified navy was hard and hazardous. Volunteers did not fill His Majesty's ships. The Royal Navy, therefore, relied heavily on impressment; this was a form of conscription for naval service that theoretically applied only to professional seamen, for warships needed trained men. It was unpopular for many reasons, not the least of which was the indefinite term of service that the navy required.[12]

On 2 December 1793, Commodore Ford wrote a letter to Lieutenant Governor Williamson, and the next day Williamson brought it before the Council of Jamaica. Ford presented the fact that he had commissioned *L'Inconstante* for His Majesty's Service, but had little expectation of "raising a sufficient number of seamen to man her without having recourse to an Impress." He requested Williamson to obtain an Order of Council "to the extent of two hundred and fifty men as absolutely necessary to her Complement, and the present exigency of the Squadron."[13] The board consented to impressing 250 men because they considered it "emergent and necessary" for the protection of the island and its trade. Citing "An Act for the better Encouragement of the Trade of His Majesty's Sugar Colonies in America," the commodore and all the captains and commanders of His Majesty's ships of war on the Jamaica station were provided with "Concurrence Approbation and Consent to Impress throughout this Island and the several Ports thereof for the term of six weeks from the date hereof, Mariners and Seamen to serve on board His Majesty's said Squadron." The impressment was not to exceed 250 men, or more than one man out of seven from on board any one merchant ship. Impressments on shore required attendance by a constable, and such men were required to be carried before a magistrate to insure that only marines or seamen be impressed.[14] Captain Lawford was issued a press warrant, as was usual, that authorized him to appoint lieutenants to impress seamen to complete the complement of *Convert*.[15]

On 7 December 1793, the Marine Intelligence section of the *Royal Gazette* reported, "We understand that a convoy will sail for Great Britain about the third week in January."[16] The issue of 28 December showed that "a smart impress took place on Sunday evening in this town, and near fifty seamen were procured for the *Convert* frigate."[17] *Convert*'s muster table enlarges this report, for between 21 and 24 December, entries for 106 additional names appear: a midshipman assigned from *Alligator*, six able seamen from *Penelope*, a captain's servant from Port Royal, and ninety-eight able seamen (fourteen "prest men" and eighty-four volunteers).[18] The majority of these new recruits appear as volunteers, but it is probable that the impressment prompted their enlistment. The "press gang" could take seamen afloat as well as ashore, a task made easier in the harbor at Kingston, filled with merchant ships. When the officer in charge of impressment boarded a merchantman, he was required to gather the crew together and offer them a bounty if they volunteered for navy service; he was also obliged to tell them that if they did not volunteer they were liable to be impressed in any case.[19]

Between 31 December and 8 January, entries in the muster table increased from 197 to 281.[20] Although the number of entries was now well above *Convert*'s specified crew allotment, *Convert* had not actually exceeded her complement. Some men had died, others had jumped ship, and several had been legally discharged. There was a high degree of mortality on board, a situation that would plague the Jamaica squadron in the following months.[21] In fact, before *Convert* sailed, thirty-one of her mustered crew had been "discharged dead," including a gunner, a carpenter, a carpenter's servant, two captain's servants, a master's servant, and twenty-five able seamen. Twelve men had been discharged for legitimate reasons, including one midshipman (to *Success*), two gunner's servants, two carpenter's servants, one purser's servant, and six able seamen (two impressed). An additional thirty-one men had "run" (deserted), including thirteen who had been impressed into service and eighteen volunteers. Only one person formally listed as prest remained on board for *Convert*'s voyage.[22]

Convert's first commission was to provide convoy escort for a fleet of merchantmen from Jamaica to Britain. In his letter of 22 January 1794, Commodore Ford informed the secretary of the Admiralty that "in consequence of a Requisition of the Merchants and Planters of Jamaica, through General Williamson, for a Convoy to be appointed to sail with the Trade of that Island, I have directed Captain Lawford of the *Convert* to proceed through the Gulf of Florida to England with such Ships as may be ready to sail on the 20th instant, and to proceed agreeable to the extract of the Orders No.1, herewith enclosed."[23]

On 5 January Commodore Ford had given Captain Lawford instructions regarding organization of the convoy, the intended sailing route, and the protection of the fleet from the privateers and naval ships of France. He began, "Whereas the Principal Merchants and Planters of Jamaica have applied to me by means of Governor Williamson, for a Convoy to be appointed to Sail with the Homeward Bound Trade about the Middle of this Month. You are therefore hereby required and Directed to be at Bluefields Bay on that Island, with His Majestys Ship under your Command, by the 18th Instant." Lawford was to take the merchant ships that were ready to sail from the Port of Kingston with him, and to take under his protection ships that were assembled at Bluefields. He was ordered to "put to Sea with them and His Majestys Ship under your Command on the 20th Instant, proceeding (through the Gulf of Florida) off Cape Clear in Ireland, if the Wind and Weather will admit thereof, but if the Contrary or if you should receive Intelligence that a Superior force of the Enemy is Cruising in the Vicinity thereof, you are then left at Discretion to act according to the exigency of the Moment for His Majestys Service and the Protection of the Convoy."

On making land, Lawford was to give directions when he judged expedient "for the Masters of such Vessels as may be bound up St. Georges Channel, to repair without loss of time to the Ports to which they are respectively destined; and proceed with His Majestys Ship under your Command and such part of the Convoy as may be bound so far to the Eastward, to the Downs, giving the Secretary of the Admiralty an Account of your arrival & proceedings, and . . . permitting the Masters of the Ships and Vessels bound to any of the Western Ports, to repair thither, as you arrive off them respectively."

Captain Lawford was to be "very attentive to the Ships and Vessels under your Care, Keeping them together by every means in Your power, and giving their Masters such Orders and Directions as you judge will be most conducive to that end; and on no account or pretence whatever to leave them, but to accommodate your Progress to that of the worst Sailing Ship among them; and in Case (not withstanding these precautions) any of them shall part Company with you, or disobey your Commands, you are to transmit to the Admiralty a list of their Names; with the Circumstances attending such separation or Disobedience."[24]

On 11 January 1794, the Marine Intelligence section of the *Royal Gazette* reported, "It is intended that the *Convert*, Capt. Lawford, shall sail on the 18th for Bluefields, and from thence the 20th, with the convoy for England; but there is some doubt whether Capt. Lawford can be ready exactly at the time."[25] Lawford was having difficulty completing the complement of his ship.

On 12 January, in the absence of Commodore Ford, who was aboard *Europa* in Saint-Domingue, Captain Francis Roberts of *Success*, the senior officer present in Jamaica, wrote to Lieutenant Governor Adam Williamson regarding the difficulty Captain Lawford was experiencing in securing sailors for *Convert*. This was due in part to "the obstructions to this service on the part of the officers and seamen of various privateers and armed merchant ships." The *Convert* was still fifty men short of her complement, so Roberts requested that the powers of the warrant be extended "until the above mentioned number is completed."[26]

At a meeting of the Council of Jamaica on 20 January, the lieutenant governor laid Captain Roberts's letter before the board. The council granted an extension of the warrant for the impressment of fifty seamen to man *Convert* and other exigencies of the Jamaica squadron for a period of six weeks, under the previously outlined restrictions.[27] Ten additional crew were enlisted for *Convert* before she sailed, so the impressment undoubtedly helped fill shortages in other of His Majesty's ships.[28]

On 18 January, the *Royal Gazette* reported, "In consequence of an application to the Commander in Chief, the departure of the Convoy has been postponed for a few days."[29] Captain Lawford, writing from the *Convert* in Port Royal Harbour on 21 January, informed Commodore Ford about the two-week delay. He explained that with great assistance from Captain Roberts *Convert* would have been ready to sail according to Ford's orders. He officially communicated this news "to the Merchants of Kingston through the Custos of that Parish. A Meeting of the Planters and Merchants was called in consequence, the result of which was a petition to the Lieutenant Governor, praying that the Sailing of the Convoy might be put off 'till the 3rd of February, this General Williamson thought proper to acquiesce in, and wrote to Captain Roberts, and myself on the occasion, sig-

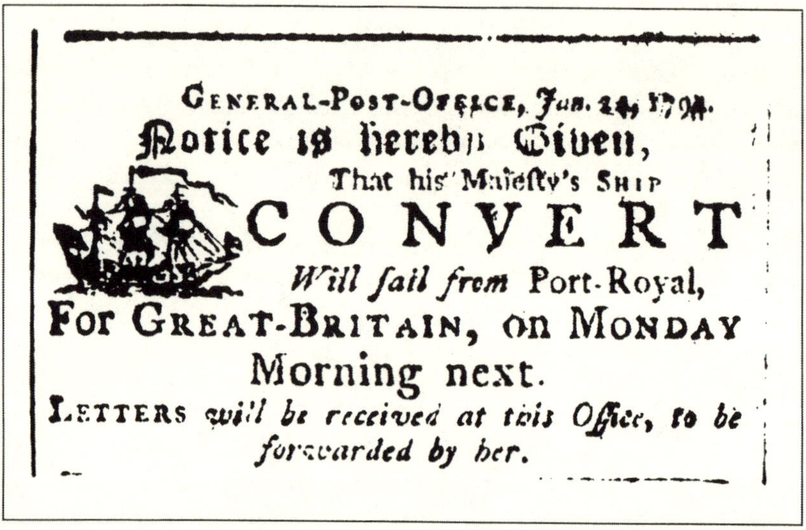

General-Post-Office, Jan. 24, 1794.
Notice is hereby Given,
That his Majesty's Ship
CONVERT
Will sail from Port-Royal,
For Great-Britain, on Monday
Morning next.
Letters will be received at this Office, to be
forwarded by her.

Figure 15. General Post Office notice regarding HMS *Convert*, published in the *Royal Gazette* 16, no. 4 (18–25 January 1794), Jamaica. Courtesy of the Public Record Office, Kew.

nifying that he should take the earliest opportunity of informing you of it accordingly, by forwarding a Dispatch to you by the way of Jeremie."[30] Commodore Ford, after the fact, informed the Admiralty of the delay in a letter sent from Saint-Domingue on 5 February.[31]

The *Royal Gazette* published a General Post Office notice on Saturday, 25 January, advertising that *Convert* would sail on "Monday morning next," that is, on 3 February (figure 15). The frigate would carry letters to Britain.[32]

On that same Saturday, a detachment of twenty-nine marines arrived aboard *Convert* from Port Royal: eight sergeants, ten corporals, four drummers, and seven privates. The muster table describes them as "Non-Commissioned Officers & Privates borne for whole allowance of all Species per order of Captain Lawford."[33] There were no commissioned officers listed among the marines, although it was usual for such detachments aboard a frigate to be commanded by a first lieutenant (on smaller vessels marines were commonly commanded by a sergeant).[34] Personnel shortages in Jamaica in the early years of war with France may have contributed to *Convert*'s lack of a commissioned marine officer aboard.

In addition to *Convert*'s crew and marines, there were other groups of people on board for the warship's voyage to Britain. The muster table identifies thirty-one "Supernumeraries Borne for Victuals only." These were passengers who received meals but were not paid crew members.[35] Nonetheless, three men in this category had positions aboard ship (one pilot, one able seaman, and one master at arms). The pilot who came on board on 1 December 1793 was discharged before *Convert* sailed, and two men died. Thus, the frigate bore twenty-eight supernumeraries for her passage; they had embarked between 14 and 28 January, and most of them were invalids. They included two men from the Port Royal Hospital, four from *Success*, Lieutenant Brice from *Hermione*, seven men from *Europa*, three each from *Penelope*, *Iphigenia*, and *Mosquito*, two from *Alligator*, and one each from *Convert*, *Spitfire*, and *Flying Fish*.

Convert's muster table also listed "a Prisoner and Eight Invalids belonging to the 1st Regt. Royals, & 62nd Regt. of Foot & Royal Artillery, Victualled at 2/3ds allowance of all Species of Provisions per order of Captain Lawford." The French prisoner had been sent by Admiral Sir John Jervis, via a packet from Barbados to Jamaica, to be taken to England. He had come on board on 26 January; the others embarked two days later.

No entries appear in the crew list of the *Convert* between 8 and 26 January, but between 26 and 28 January the frigate took on three more volunteers. Among them were an able seaman and an ordinary seaman (the only one on *Convert*) as well as a second able seaman from *Mosquito* who was appointed to the carpenter's crew on 2 February.[36]

The Marine Intelligence section of the *Royal Gazette* of 1 February reported, "His Majesty's Ship *Convert*, Capt. Lawford, sailed for Bluefields on Tuesday morning. Col. Amherst of the 10th regiment and Captain Thomson of the Royal Artillery are passengers in her for England."[37] *Convert*'s muster table lists neither Colonel Amherst nor Captain Thomson as being on board the frigate, but other evidence suggests that Amherst was on board either *Convert* or one of her merchant convoy for the passage to Europe.[38]

The Merchantmen

In 1792 Britain boasted the greatest merchant shipping fleet in the world, with at least 16,079 vessels totaling 1.5 million tons, manned by some 118,286 seamen. In 1796, out of 15,996 registered vessels, there were only 157 of over five hundred tons, while there were more than 11,000 vessels of under one hundred tons. In other words, merchantmen were relatively small.[39]

The merchant trade involved both coastal shipping at home and overseas commerce, primarily with British colonies; the trans-Atlantic trade with the West Indies was one of the most profitable routes. Merchantmen

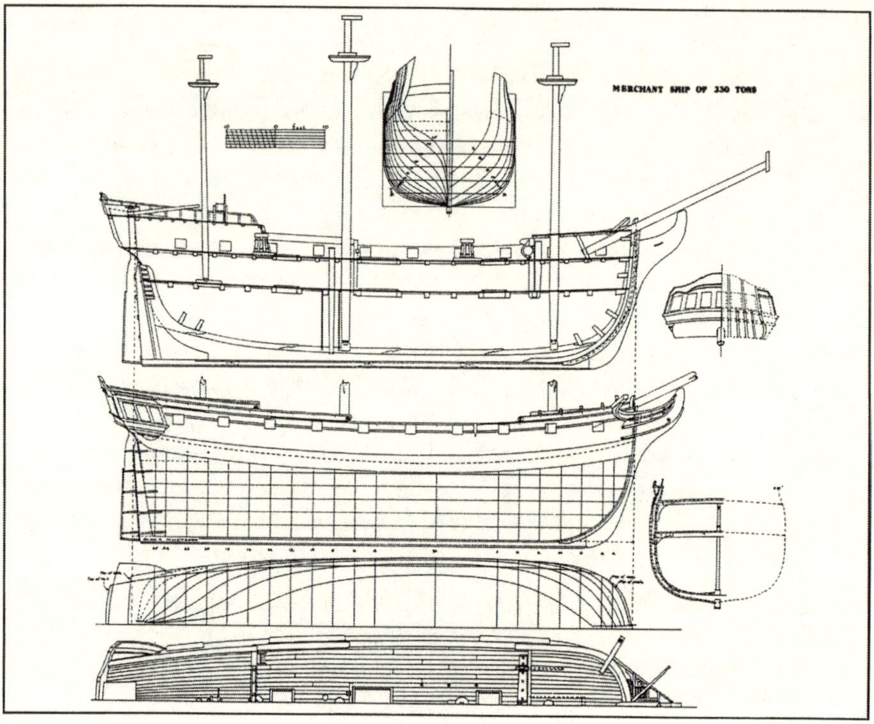

Figure 16. Merchant ship of 330 tons. Plate 122 from David R. MacGregor, *Merchant Sailing Ships, 1775–1815* (London: Conway Maritime Press, 1985). Courtesy of David R. MacGregor.

used for the overseas traffic were built and rigged according to the same fundamental principles as warships, but they generally had more square midship sections and bluff bows.[40] So, many seagoing merchantmen were full-bodied, slow sailers. In fact, David MacGregor, a leading historian on merchant sail, notes that British merchants' reliance on the convoy system in wartime frequently prompted them to forgo speed in order to maximize cargo space in the hulls of their ships. There were, however, well-armed, fast-sailing merchant ships built to outsail the slow convoys and thereby capture commercial markets.[41]

Lavery suggests that the square rig was the preferred rig of larger merchantmen, and vessels of over 250 tons usually were rigged as "ships." A ship was a three-masted vessel carrying square sails. Vessels of between 80 and 250 tons were frequently rigged as brigs.[42] The two principal types of merchantmen that departed Jamaica for Britain with the *Convert* convoy were ships and brigs; there were also a couple of snows. At least one schooner was bound for North America.[43]

A typical vessel used in the West Indies trade is found in David MacGregor's illustration of a merchant ship of 330 tons, which is based largely on plans in David Steel's 1805 work *The Shipwright's Vade-Mecum* (figure 16). Also depicted is the sail plan of a merchant ship of 330 tons, which MacGregor reconstructed from late eighteenth- and early nineteenth-century sources (figure 17).[44]

William Falconer, in his *Universal Dictionary of the Marine*, first published in 1769, describes a brig as follows:

> Brig, or Brigantine, a merchant-ship with two masts. This term is not universally confined to vessels of a particular construction, or which are masted and rigged in a method different from all others. It is variously applied, by the mariners of different European nations, to a peculiar sort of vessel of their own marine.
>
> Amongst English seamen, this vessel is distinguished by having her main-sail set nearly in the plane of her keel; whereas the main-sails of larger ships are hung athwart, or at right angles with the ship's length, and fastened to a yard which hangs parallel to the deck: but in a brig, the foremost edge of the main-sail is fastened in different places to hoops which encircle the main-mast, and slide up and down it as the sail is hoisted or lowered: it is extended by a *gaff* above, and by a boom below.[45]

A typical brig of the late eighteenth century was the collier brig of 170 tons, redrawn by David MacGregor from David Steel's 1805 work *Elements and Practice of Naval Architecture* (figure 18). The sail plan was reconstructed by MacGregor from late eighteenth- and early nineteenth-century sources (figure 19).[46]

The snow was usually the largest type of two-masted vessel, similar in many respects to the brig. According to MacGregor, however, "the snow was fully square-rigged on both masts, with the addition of a boomless gaff trysail which hoisted on its own trysail mast. This mast was stepped on the deck and terminated at the after end of the main top, and the sail was hooped to this mast."[47] In the late eighteenth century, the schooner rig also was carried primarily on two-masted vessels. Different nations had varying practices regarding the exclusive use of fore-and-aft sails or the addition of square sails on schooners.[48]

In December 1793 and January 1794, before *Convert*'s departure from Jamaica, advertisements appeared in the *Royal Gazette* for ten ships and one brig that would constitute part of the convoy.[49] Among the ships publicized were *Britannia*, Master Daniel Martin, and *Lion*, Master Thomas King,

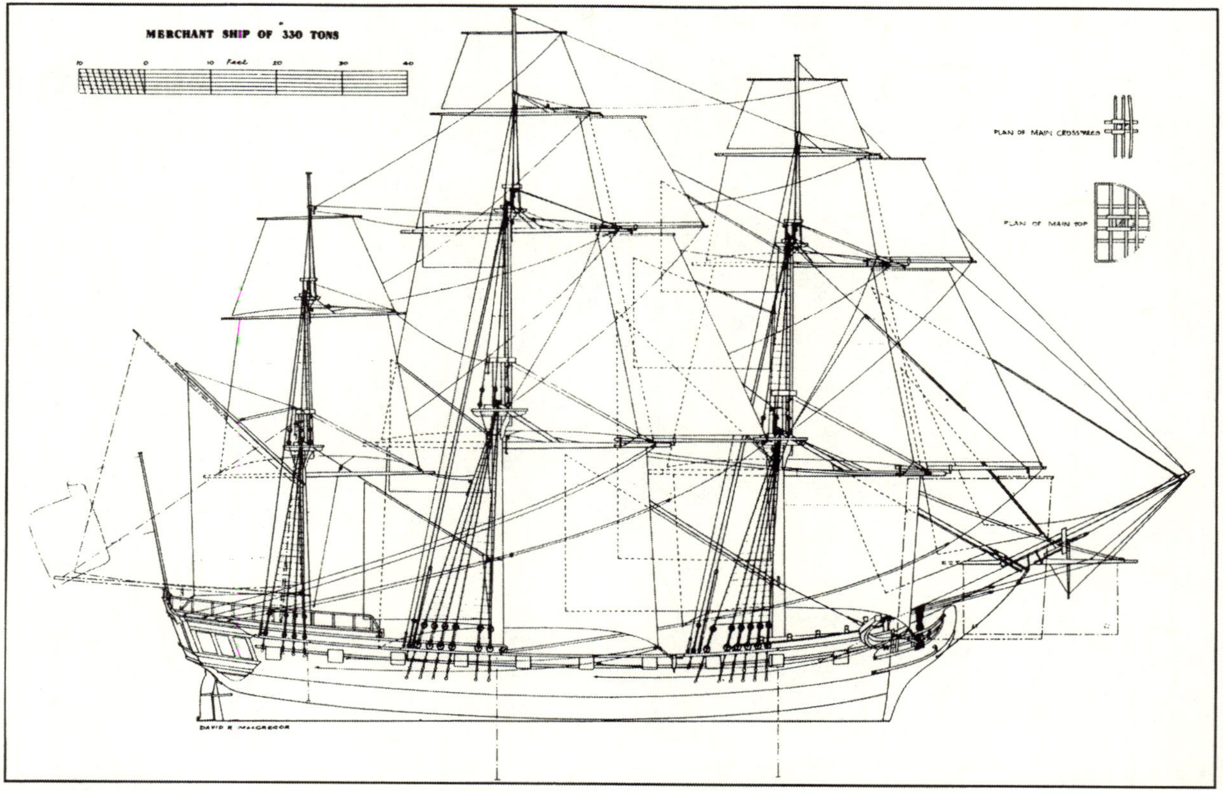

Figure 17. Sail plan of a merchant ship of 330 tons. Plate 126 from MacGregor, *Merchant Sailing Ships, 1775–1815*. Courtesy of David R. MacGregor.

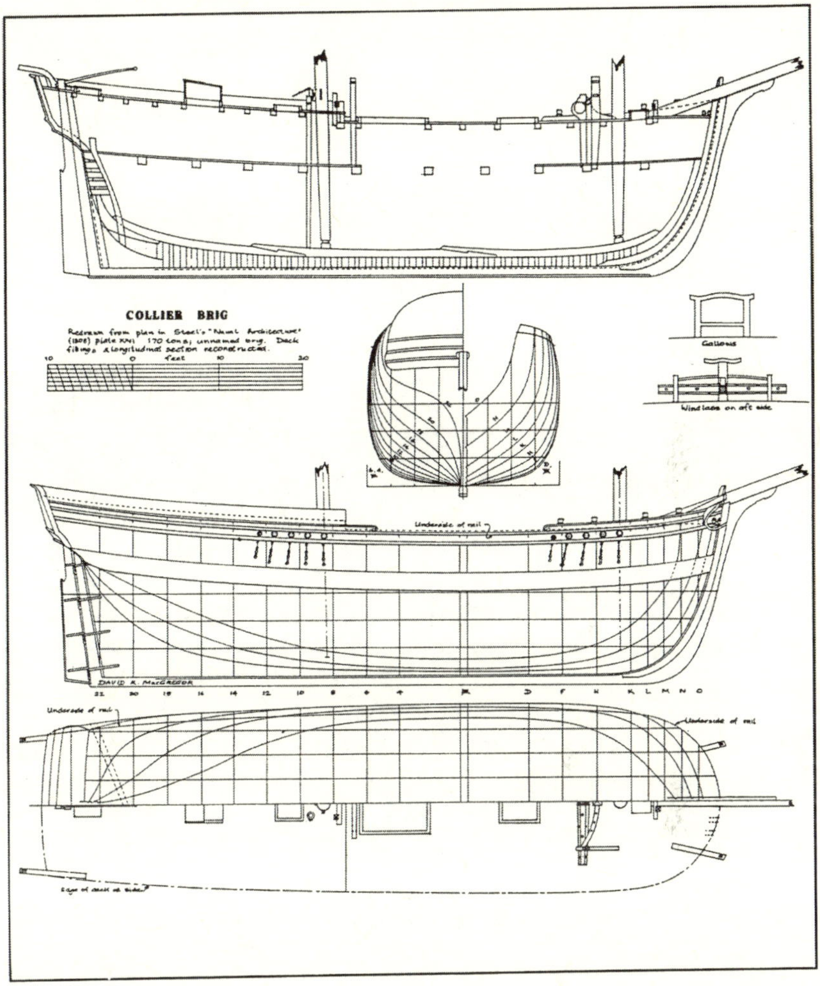

Figure 18. Collier brig of 170 tons. Plate 158 from MacGregor, *Merchant Sailing Ships, 1775–1815*. Courtesy of David R. MacGregor.

bound for London (figure 20). According to MacGregor, it was common practice for foreign-going merchantmen to take on passengers as well as cargo when space allowed.[50] *Cowley*, Master Richard George, armed with twelve 6-pounders, would transport cargo and travelers from the Kingston area to Saint Ann's Bay or on to Britain, and would also load goods and passengers outward to London from Saint Ann's Bay.

The copper-sheathed ships *Lord Charlemont*, Captain Pinder, mounting fourteen 6-pounders, *Cyclops*, Captain Patrick Fairweather, and *Alice*,

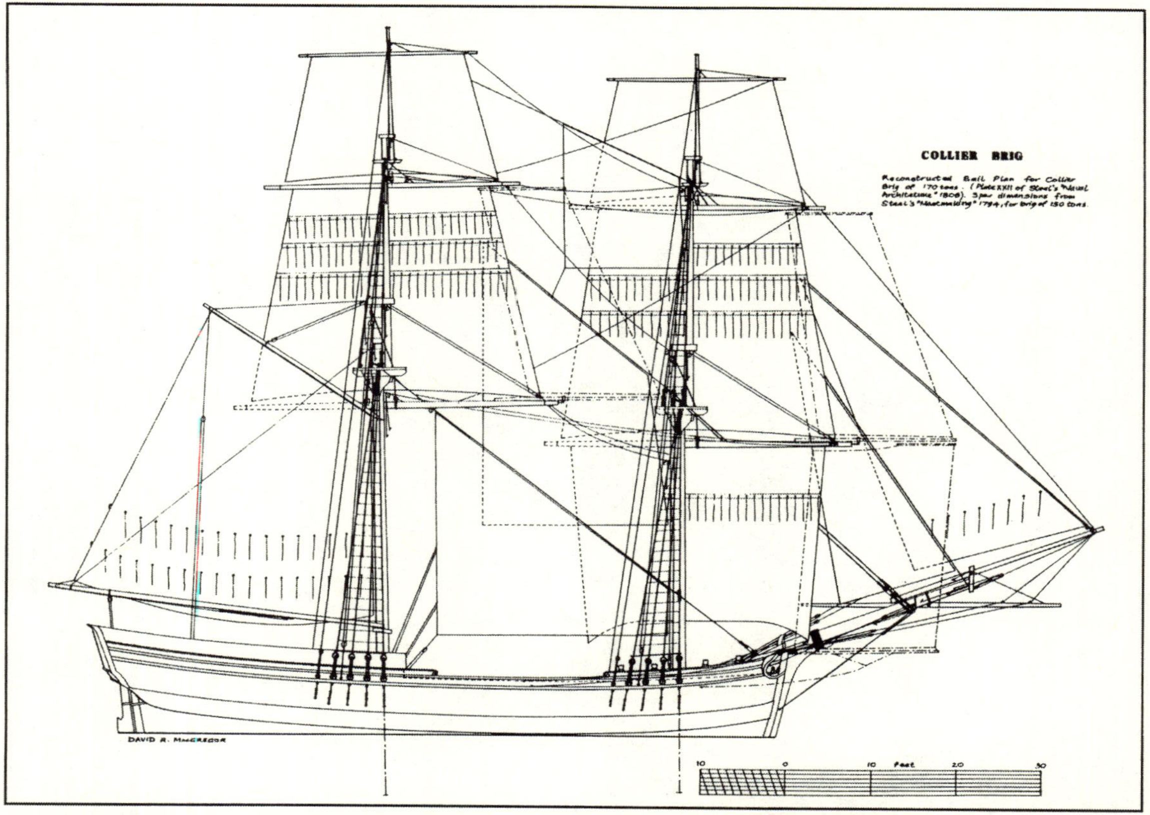

Figure 19. Sail plan of a collier brig of 170 tons. Plate 163 from MacGregor, *Merchant Sailing Ships, 1775–1815*. Courtesy of David R. MacGregor.

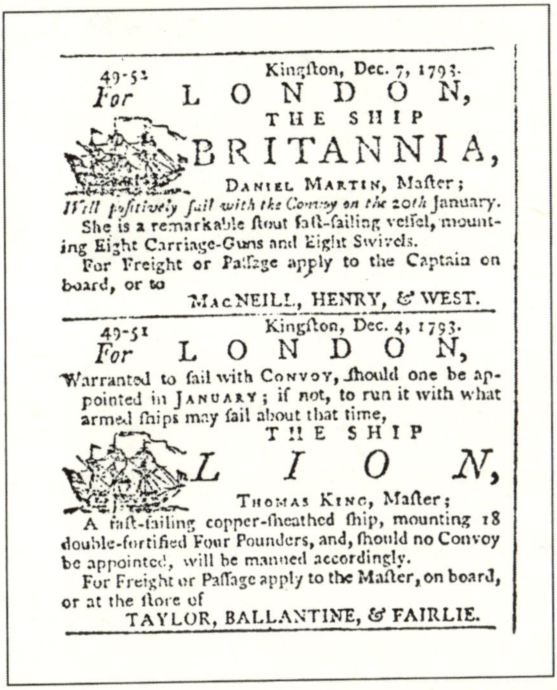

49-52 Kingſton, Dec. 7, 1793.

For LONDON,

THE SHIP

BRITANNIA,

DANIEL MARTIN, Maſter;

Will poſitively ſail with the Convoy on the 20th January.

She is a remarkable ſtout faſt-ſailing veſſel, mounting Eight Carriage-Guns and Eight Swivels.

For Freight or Paſſage apply to the Captain on board, or to

MACNEILL, HENRY, & WEST.

49-51 Kingſton, Dec. 4, 1793.

For LONDON,

Warranted to ſail with CONVOY, ſhould one be appointed in JANUARY; if not, to run it with what armed ſhips may ſail about that time,

THE SHIP

LION,

THOMAS KING, Maſter;

A faſt-ſailing copper-ſheathed ſhip, mounting 18 double-fortified Four Pounders, and, ſhould no Convoy be appointed, will be manned accordingly.

For Freight or Paſſage apply to the Maſter, on board, or at the ſtore of

TAYLOR, BALLANTINE, & FAIRLIE.

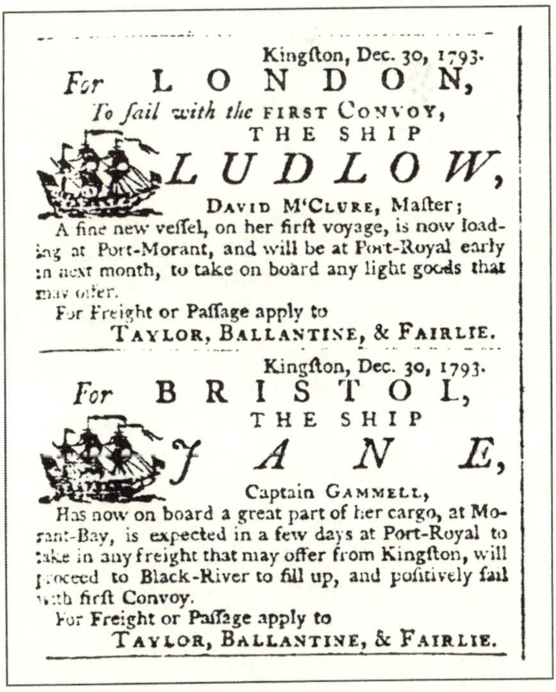

Kingſton, Dec. 30, 1793.

For LONDON,

To ſail with the FIRST CONVOY,

THE SHIP

LUDLOW,

DAVID M'CLURE, Maſter;

A fine new veſſel, on her firſt voyage, is now loading at Port-Morant, and will be at Port-Royal early in next month, to take on board any light goods that may offer.

For Freight or Paſſage apply to

TAYLOR, BALLANTINE, & FAIRLIE.

Kingſton, Dec. 30, 1793.

For BRISTOL,

THE SHIP

JANE,

Captain GAMMELL,

Has now on board a great part of her cargo, at Morant-Bay, is expected in a few days at Port-Royal to take in any freight that may offer from Kingſton, will proceed to Black-River to fill up, and poſitively ſail with firſt Convoy.

For Freight or Paſſage apply to

TAYLOR, BALLANTINE, & FAIRLIE.

Figure 20. Advertisements for the ships *Britannia*, *Lion*, *Ludlow*, and *Jane*. From *Royal Gazette* (Jamaica) 15, no. 50 (7–14 December 1793), courtesy of the National Library of Jamaica, Kingston, and *Royal Gazette* (Jamaica) 16, no. 1 (28 December 1793–4 January 1794), courtesy of the Public Record Office, Kew.

Master Brian Smith, each defended by six carriage guns, were headed for Liverpool.[51] Sailing to the same port, *Moorhall*, Master Samuel Nicholson, carried "ten double-fortified Four Pounders, with Small Arms, and men answerable," while the brig *Betsey*, Master Richard Kent, mounted ten 6-pounder carriage guns.

Traveling to London, the new, fast-sailing, and coppered *Martha*, Captain Robert Brown, boasted twelve 9-pounders. Also bound for London with the first convoy was *Ludlow*, Master David McClure: "A fine new vessel, on her first voyage." *Jane*, Captain Gammell, was destined for the port of Bristol.[52] The advertisements for *Ludlow* and *Jane* are the only ones that fail to mention weaponry. The nine armed merchantmen were probably among the most self-sufficient and fastest sailing ships in the convoy.

The Departure from Jamaica

On Tuesday, 28 January, *Convert* sailed from Kingston Harbour for Bluefields Bay on the southwest coast of Jamaica (map 10). The frigate was to collect her convoy there and ready it for the passage to Great Britain. There are two lists of vessels that sailed from Port Royal, printed respectively in the 1 February and 8 February Marine Intelligence section of the *Royal Gazette* (figure 21). These lists reveal that, besides *Convert*, twenty-eight merchantmen departed Kingston for Bluefields and various British ports between 28 January and 3 February. Among these merchant vessels were nineteen three-masted square-rigged ships, eight brigs, and one snow. There were also three merchantmen bound for America (two brigs and a schooner).[53] *Jane*, Captain Gammell, had previously sailed for Bluefields on 22 January.[54] Although *Convert*'s list of the convoy has not survived, it is likely that all thirty-two merchant ships joined the convoy. (See appendix E for a reconstructed list of *Convert*'s convoy.)

On 4 February 1794, the brig *Eagle*, Master Manning, bound for Charleston, and the Schooner *Hope*, Master O'Neil, bound for Halifax, sailed from Port Royal.[55] Since they departed a day after the official date on which the convoy was scheduled to sail from Jamaica, they presumably did not intend to join the fleet, though they probably intended to accompany it unofficially.

According to the orders that Captain Lawford had received from Commodore Ford, he assembled the merchantmen that had rendezvoused at Bluefields Bay with the intention of sailing on Monday, 3 February 1794. Lawford contended, however, that "light Westerly winds and Calms prevailing, rendered it impossible for the Heavy Merchant Ships to Clear the Bay before the morning of the 5th." When he did get underway, "at Day

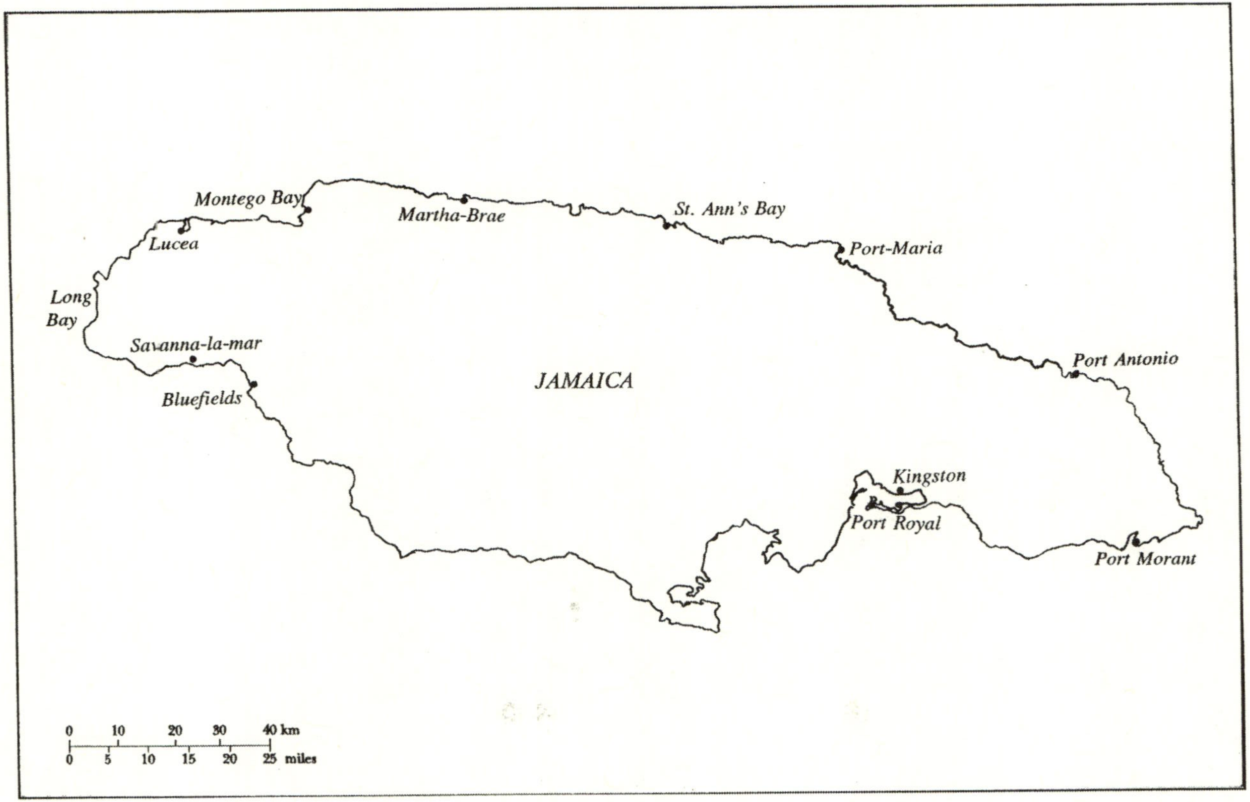

Map 10. Ports of eighteenth-century Jamaica. Drawn by R .L. Craig, after map by Bryan Edwards, 1794, Cayman Islands National Archive.

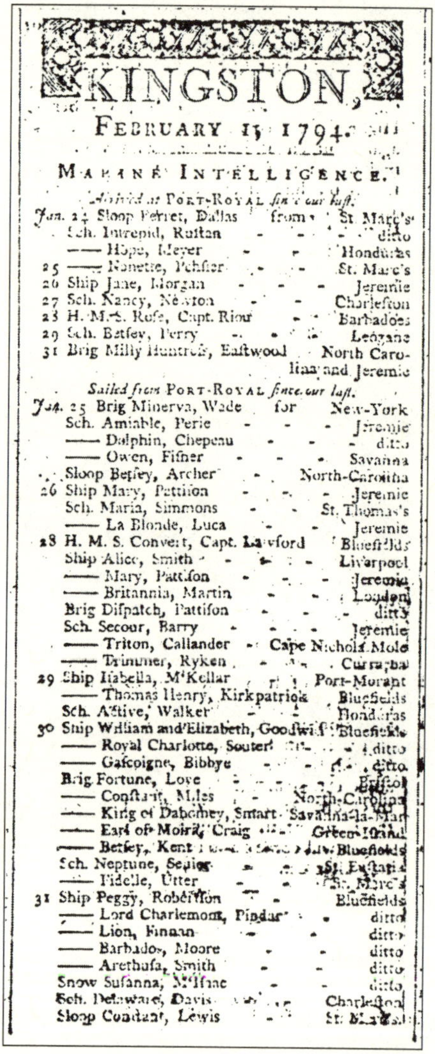

KINGSTON,

FEBRUARY 1, 1794.

MARINE INTELLIGENCE.

Arrived at PORT-ROYAL *ſince our laſt.*

Jan. 24	Sloop Ferret, Dallas	from	St. Marc's
	Sch. Intrepid, Ruſtan		ditto
	—— Hope, Meyer		Honduras
25	—— Nanette, Peltier		St. Marc's
26	Ship Jane, Morgan		Jeremie
27	Sch. Nancy, Newton		Charleſton
28	H. M. S. Roſe, Capt. Riou		Barbadoes
29	Sch. Betſey, Perry		Leogane
31	Brig Milly Huntreſs, Eaſtwood		North Carolina and Jeremie

Sailed from PORT-ROYAL *ſince our laſt.*

Jan. 25	Brig Minerva, Wade	for	New-York
	Sch. Aminble, Perie		Jeremie
	—— Dolphin, Chepeau		ditto
	—— Owen, Fiſher		Savanna
	Sloop Betſey, Archer		North-Carolina
26	Ship Mary, Pettiſon		Jeremie
	Sch. Maria, Simmons		St. Thomas's
	—— La Blonde, Luca		Jeremie
28	H. M. S. Convert, Capt. Lawford		Bluefields
	Ship Alice, Smith		Liverpool
	—— Mary, Pattiſon		Jeremie
	—— Britannia, Martin		London
	Brig Diſpatch, Pattiſon		ditto
	Sch. Secour, Barry		Jeremie
	—— Triton, Callander		Cape Nichola Mole
	—— Trimmer, Ryken		Curracoa
29	Ship Iſabella, M'Kellar		Port-Morant
	—— Thomas Henry, Kirkpatrick		Bluefields
	Sch. Active, Walker		Honduras
30	Ship William and Elizabeth, Goodwin		Bluefields
	—— Royal Charlotte, Souter		ditto
	—— Gaſcoigne, Bibbye		ditto
	Brig Fortune, Love		Briſtol
	—— Conſtant, Miles		North-Carolina
	—— King of Dahomey, Smart		Savanna-la-Mar
	—— Earl of Moira, Craig		Green Iſland
	—— Betſey, Kent		Bluefields
	Sch. Neptune, Sepiez		St. Euſtatia
	—— Fidelle, Utter		St. Marc's
31	Ship Peggy, Robertſon		Bluefields
	—— Lord Charlemont, Pindar		ditto
	—— Lion, Finnan		ditto
	—— Barbados, Moore		ditto
	—— Arethuſa, Smith		ditto
	Snow Suſanna, M'Iſaac		ditto
	Sch. Delaware, Davis		Charleſton
	Sloop Conſtant, Lewis		St. Marc's

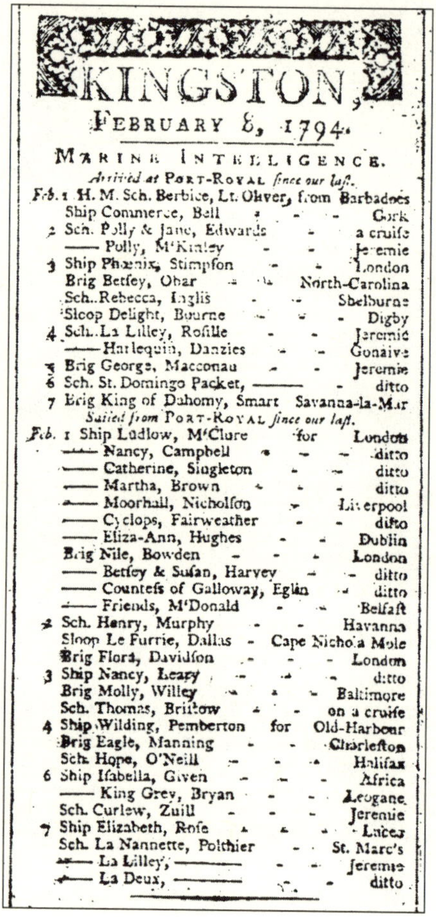

KINGSTON,

FEBRUARY 8, 1794.

MARINE INTELLIGENCE.

Arrived at PORT-ROYAL *ſince our laſt.*

Feb. 1	H. M. Sch. Berbice, Lt. Oliver,	from	Barbadoes
	Ship Commerce, Bell		Cork
2	Sch. Polly & Jane, Edwards		a cruiſe
	—— Polly, M'Kinley		Jeremie
3	Ship Phœnix, Stimpſon		London
	Brig Betſey, Obar		North-Carolina
	Sch. Rebecca, Inglis		Shelburne
	Sloop Delight, Bourne		Digby
4	Sch. La Lilley, Roſille		Jeremie
	—— Harlequin, Danzies		Gonaive
5	Brig George, Macconau		Jeremie
6	Sch. St. Domingo Packet, ——		ditto
7	Brig King of Dahomy, Smart		Savanna-la-Mar

Sailed from PORT-ROYAL *ſince our laſt.*

Feb. 1	Ship Ludlow, M'Clure	for	London
	—— Nancy, Campbell		ditto
	—— Catherine, Singleton		ditto
	—— Martha, Brown		ditto
	—— Moorhall, Nicholſon		Liverpool
	—— Cyclops, Fairweather		ditto
	—— Eliza-Ann, Hughes		Dublin
	Brig Nile, Bowden		London
	—— Betſey & Suſan, Harvey		ditto
	—— Counteſs of Galloway, Eglin		ditto
	—— Friends, M'Donald		Belfaſt
2	Sch. Henry, Murphy		Havanna
	Sloop Le Furrie, Dallas		Cape Nichola Mole
	Brig Flora, Davidſon		London
3	Ship Nancy, Leary		ditto
	Brig Molly, Willey		Baltimore
	Sch. Thomas, Briſtow		on a cruiſe
4	Ship Wilding, Pemberton	for	Old-Harbour
	Brig Eagle, Manning		Charleſton
	Sch. Hope, O'Neill		Halifax
6	Ship Iſabella, Given		Africa
	—— King Grey, Bryan		Leogane
	Sch. Curlew, Zuill		Jeremie
7	Ship Elizabeth, Roſe		Lucea
	Sch. La Nannette, Poltier		St. Marc's
	—— La Lilley, ——		Jeremie
	—— La Deux, ——		ditto

Figure 21. *Left*, a list of ships that arrived at or sailed from Port Royal, published in the *Royal Gazette* (Jamaica) 16, no. 5 (25 January–1 February 1794). *Right*, a list of ships that arrived at or sailed from Port Royal, published in the *Royal Gazette* (Jamaica) 16, no. 6 (1–8 February 1794). Both courtesy of the Public Record Office, Kew.

light, with about Thirty Two Sail and brought too off Long Bay in the Afternoon," he gave the signals to the ships that joined from the North-side.[56] On gathering at a specified rendezvous, it was standard procedure for the master of each merchant ship seeking convoy protection to send a boat to the naval escort for a copy of the official instructions. These directions detailed various signals used for communication among the ships during the passage.[57]

A witness reported on *Convert*'s departure from Bluefields Bay on 5 February 1794. A note sent from Montego Bay, dated 8 February, appeared in the *Royal Gazette*: "We are informed from Savanna-la-Mar, that the fleet under convoy of his Majesty's Ship *Convert*, Capt. Lawford, numbering about 40, sailed on Wednesday last, and at sun-set were nearly out of sight."[58] They had sailed to Long Bay, off the west end of Jamaica near Negril, to meet the ships from ports on the north coast of the island that had been gathering at Lucea to join the convoy. Reports from Montego Bay in the *Royal Gazette* suggest that the following six vessels called at, or sailed past, Montego Bay to Lucea to assemble and rendezvous with the convoy for Europe: the ships *Nereus*, Master McIver, from Port-Maria, *Fanny*, Master Withall, from Saint Ann's, and *Alfred*, Master Bryan, and *Hawke*, Master Hill, both from Martha-Brae; and the snows *Sarah*, Master Potter, from Bucknor's Bay, and *Diana*, Master Thompson, from Martha-Brae.[59] According to an advertisement in the *Gazette*, it is also likely that the ship *Cowley*, Master George, sailed from Saint Ann's Bay to join the *Convert* convoy.[60]

Commodore Ford assumed that the *Convert* convoy had departed from Jamaica on 3 February, and in correspondence sent two days later from Saint-Domingue, he informed the Admiralty that the *Convert* was "On her Passage to England with the Convoy" (figure 22). At that time, the Commodore, aboard *Europa*, was preparing to return to Jamaica where two of His Majesty's schooners were refitting, but eleven vessels under his command remained in Saint-Domingue to promote British interests there. Ford's list of the squadron on 5 February suggests that the sixty-four-gun ship *Sceptre* had joined his forces and that there remained on the Jamaica station one fifty-gun ship (*Europa*), six frigates (*Penelope*, *Hermione*, *Iphigenia*, *Alligator*, *Magicienne*, and *Success*), two sloops (*Hound* and *Goelan*), and four schooners (*Spitfire*, *Mosquito*, *Flying Fish*, and *Marie Antoinette*).[61]

On the evening of 5 February, *Convert* and the merchant convoy lay to in Long Bay off the west end of Jamaica. Earlier that day, before *Convert* had sailed, John Lister, one of *Convert*'s able seaman, had deserted at Bluefields anchorage. The muster table suggests that Lister was the only deserter who managed to wait long enough to receive his £5 volunteering bounty

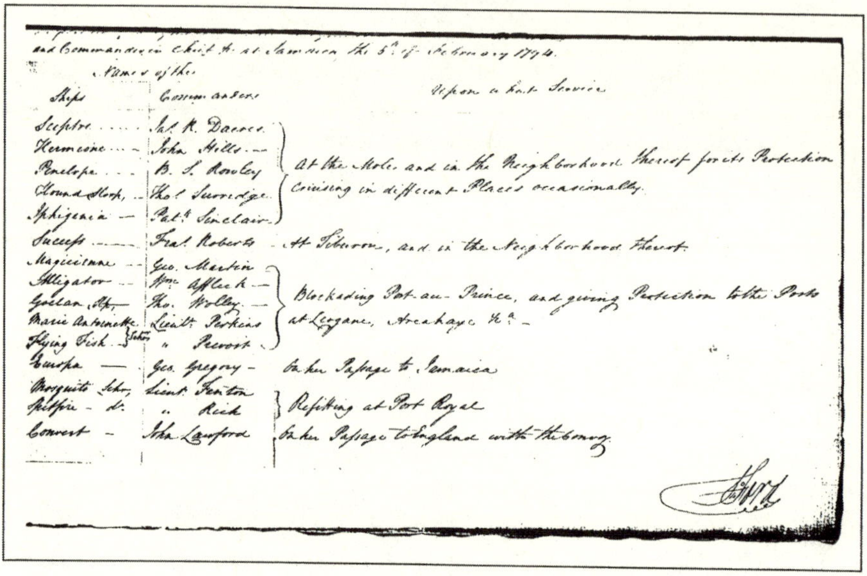
and Commander in Chief &c at Jamaica the 5th of February 1794.

Names of the Ships	Commanders	Upon what Service
Sceptre	Jas. R. Dacres	At the Mole, and in the Neighborhood thereof for its Protection cruising in different Places occasionally.
Hermione	John Hills	
Penelope	B. S. Rowley	
Hound sloop	Thos. Surridge	
Iphigenia	Patk. Sinclair	
Success	Fras. Roberts	At Tiburon, and in the Neighborhood thereof
Magicienne	Geo. Martin	Blockading Port-au-Prince, and giving Protection to the Ports at Leogane, Arcahaye &c.
Alligator	Wm. Affleck	
Goelan Sp.	Tho. Wolley	
Marie Antoinette	Lieut. Perkins	
Flying Fish Schr.	" Prevost	
Europa	Geo. Gregory	On her Passage to Jamaica
Mosquito Schr.	Lieut. Tonton	Refitting at Port Royal
Spitfire do.	" Reid	
Convert	Jno. Lawford	On her Passage to England with the Convoy

Figure 22. Commodore Ford's list of the disposition of the Jamaica Squadron on 5 February 1794. Courtesy of the Public Record Office, Kew.

before he ran. The muster table also reveals that, on 6 February, *Convert* acquired seven additional able seamen, all volunteers, in an attempt to complete her complement. These men, very likely arriving on board the convoy vessels from the north side ports, may have been offered the choice of a £5 bounty or impressment, though payment of the bounty was not recorded.

The muster table registered 283 people to be on board *Convert*, including 217 officers and crew, twenty-nine marines, twenty-eight supernumeraries, one prisoner, and eight invalids.[62] There were actually 281 people listed to be on board, because the two widow's men were fictitious. The issue of the *Royal Gazette* dated 25 January to 1 February reported that Colonel Amherst and Captain Thomson were on board *Convert* for the voyage, but they are not mentioned in the muster table.[63] If these two military officers were on board, the ship, in fact, carried 283 souls. On Thursday morning, 6 February 1794, Captain Lawford wrote, the *Convert* "bore away, having Fifty Five Sail of square rigged vessels Bound to Europe, and three Schooners to Different Ports in America."[64]

7

The Wreck of the Ten Sail

Breakers Ahead, Close to Us!

It must have been trying to be the Royal Navy officer in charge of and accountable for the safety of a merchant convoy. Although legal restrictions applied to merchantmen under convoy, their masters often disobeyed signals and orders. Some disregarded cannon shots; others deserted the formation without giving notice, particularly on nearing the destination, for it could be lucrative to reach port ahead of the fleet.[1] A case in point is that of the *Hector* convoy, which sailed between 22 July and 4 October 1793. At the end of the voyage, Captain George Montague furnished the Admiralty with a document in which he wrote this final note: "The Above is the list of the Trade who sailed from Jamaica under Convoy of His Majestys Ship *Hector* under my Command. The Disobedience of the Masters of the Merchantmen in General to my Signals not only retarded our Passage but very frequently placed them out of my Protection."[2] While masters of merchantmen faced little repercussion for disobeying directions, the captain of a convoy escort who neglected his convoy was subject to penalty.[3]

The Voyage

On Thursday, 6 February 1794, the *Convert* convoy sailed westward from Long Bay. According to Commodore Ford's orders of 5 January, Captain Lawford aimed to sail the Leeward Passage. *Convert* would lead the fleet through the Yucatán Channel and the Florida Straits, and then follow the Gulf Stream across the Atlantic to Britain (see map 8). The convoy was to proceed to Cape Clear in Ireland, and on sighting land Lawford was to direct the masters of vessels bound up Saint George's Channel to proceed directly to those ports (map 11). *Convert* was to escort the remainder of the merchantmen through the English Channel to the Downs, an important anchorage near Dover, Deal, and Ramsgate, where on arrival Captain Lawford was to make his report of the voyage to the secretary of the Admiralty. Along the way he was to permit the ships under his command to call

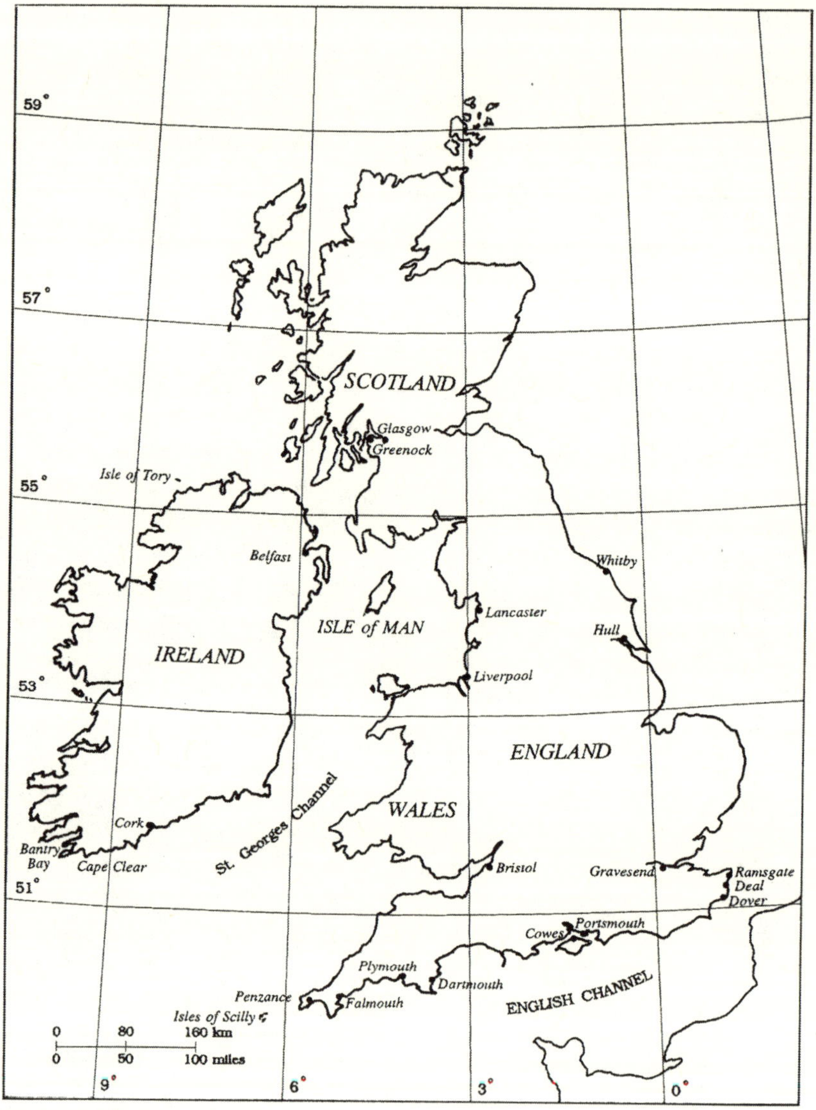

Map 11. Referenced ports of the British Isles. Drawn by R. L. Craig.

at their respective ports. Commodore Ford directed Captain Lawford to be attentive to all the vessels in his care and to pace the voyage at the speed of the worst sailing ship among them. But if any of the merchantmen disobeyed orders or parted the convoy without notice, he was to make a report of their conduct to the Admiralty.[4]

Captain Lawford later commented on the circumstances of the *Convert* convoy after departing from Long Bay:

> On Friday noon the 7th Instant the Master, with three Assistants, with two Sextants and two Quadrants, found by Observation the Lattitude to be 18°, 47′ North and from the Course Steer'd, and the Distance run from the West end of Jamaica, we considered that the East end of the Island of Grand Cayman, bore N.W. 1/2 N. 18 Leagues Distant, the Convoy had been lying too for several hours to give Assistance to a Schooner in Distress, and after getting the Observation (the goodness of which there could be no doubt) we bore away and Steer'd W.N.W; at 1 p.m. I made Sail ahead of the Convoy in order to make the Land before Dark, but a Gun being fired astern about 3 oClock I conceived it my Duty, (knowing that several of the Ships were in bad Condition) to stand back into the Fleet to give all the Assistance in my power; I accordingly Wore Ship, and found that the Signal of Distress was made by the same Schooner that had delayed me in the morning, this Circumstance having prevented me from prosecuting my original intention of making the Land before Dark, I steer'd West from Six to twelve oClock, making a run of nine or Ten Leagues, which by our Reckoning carried us to the Westward of the Grand Cayman, and Seven Leagues to the Southward: at 12 oClock the Master, who then became officer of the Watch upon Deck, representing to me that from the Prevalence of the Northerly Winds, it might be necessary to haul more to the Northward to ensure the making Cape Corientes, and deeming ourselves perfectly Clear of the Grand Caymans, I directed him to steer W.N.W., the Convoy being at this time well Collected and not one Ship ahead; the *Convert* had at this time (as well as during the greater part of the time) her Sails all furl'd and Yards braced aback, owing to her very great Superiority in point of Sailing.[5]

The Wrecking

In his letter of 20 February 1794, Captain Lawford regretfully informed the commodore and commander in chief of the Jamaica squadron that "his Majesty's Ship *Convert* was unfortunately Wreck'd, together with Nine Sail of Merchantmen under my Convoy, on the Reefs of the East end of the Grand Cayman on the morning of 8th Instant; but it is some Alleviation of this misfortune to be enabled to add, that from the most Strenuous exertions on our part, and the timely assistance rendered by the Few Inhabitants (by all the means in their power) few Lives were lost."[6]

Captain Lawford described to Commodore Ford the disaster that had occurred in the early morning hours of 8 February (map 12).[7] He recounted that "about 3 oClock the Master came down and inform'd me that one of the Ships to Leeward had fired two Guns, on which conceiving it to be a Signal of Distress, I directed him to make Sail and run down to her; on my getting on Deck instantly after this, I found that the Guns had been fired by a Ship ahead, and that several Ships of the Convoy had run ahead since 12 oClock." He continued, saying, "I had not been on Deck a Minute before some of the Men on the Topsail Yard called out, 'Breakers ahead Close to us,' I immediately (as the Breakers appeared in every direction and I could not tell from the Darkness of the Night to what extent they might run,) deemed it most expedient to make the Signal for the Convoy to disperse and do the best for their own Safety that their own judgement could suggest." Of his own predicament Lawford informed that "as the Topsails were now sheeted home, the *Convert* would have certainly cleared the Breakers, if a Ship ahead had not unfortunately fallen on Board us, and before it was possible to extricate ourselves we got so near the Reefs, that all hopes of Clearing them vanished and she in a few moments struck, and very soon after Bilged."

Captain Lawford believed that the disobedient merchantmen who had sailed ahead of *Convert* after midnight were responsible for causing the misfortune to occur. He advised Commodore Ford that "had the Ships of the Convoy kept their stations and attended to Signals, which I am sorry to say was not the Case generally with the far greater part, this misfortune could not have happened." He maintained that "however the Current might have set us to the Northward of our Course; or from whatever Cause any error might have arisen in the reckoning, had the Ship I commanded been the leader without any intervening Object being between her and the Breakers, they must have been observed in time enough to have warned the Ships astern of their Danger." He judged that "the worst that could possibly have happened which I do not Conceive could be the Case, would have been the loss of the *Convert*." He had since learned that "the Ship that fired the Guns was on Shore before she fired, and that Five or Six others were on Shore before her."[8]

At daylight, Captain Lawford observed the other ill-fated ships of the convoy and endeavored to save *Convert*'s crew. In describing his actions to the commodore, he lamented that "the dawning of the Day presented a most Melancholy scene, seven Ships and two Brigs on the same Reef with the *Convert*, a very heavy sea running and the Wind blowing directly on the Shore; from the bad appearance of the Weather the Merchant Ships would not venture near enough to us to give any effectual assistance, and the Ships on Shore could not assist each other." Lawford "immediately ordered out the Boats to provide as far as possible for the safety of the Ships Company." Reporting further actions taken, he stated that "the Masts were Cut away,

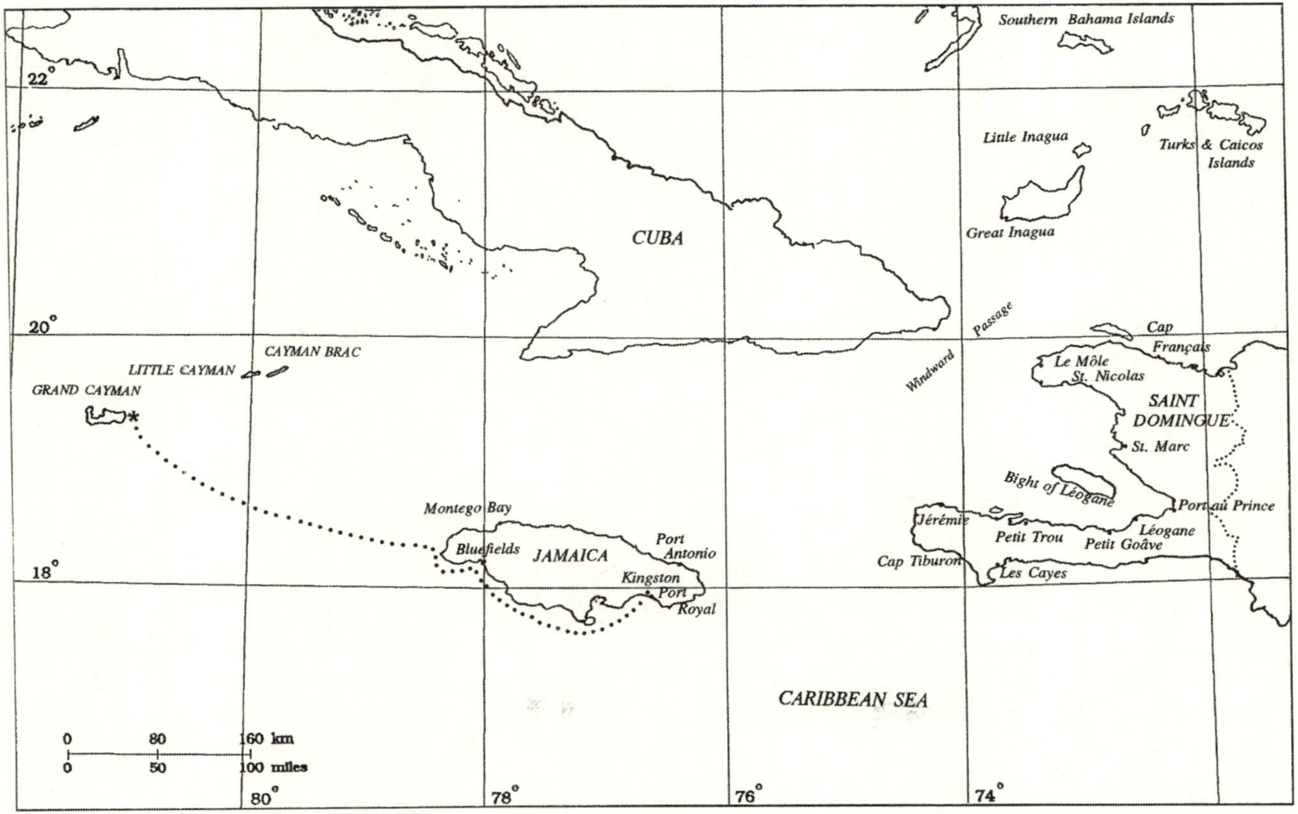

Map 12. Route of the *Convert* convoy from Jamaica to Grand Cayman, where ten ships of the fleet were wrecked. Drawn by R. L. Craig.

and by unremitting exertions untill Night, the whole of the Ships Company (excepting about Twenty who, has [*sic*] the Weather seemed to moderate, preferr'd staying on Board to the risque of getting on Shore) were put on Board two or three Vessels that appeared at a great Distance in the offing, or were put on the reef by means of rafts, &c. and taken up by Canoes."[9]

Although bad weather had not caused the Wreck of the Ten Sail, strong winds and rough seas hindered rescue efforts. Each ship had no choice but to provide for its own passengers and crew with little assistance from the others. Lawford had *Convert*'s masts cut away. Launching the ship's boats he attempted to carry more than 280 people to safety; most were removed on the day *Convert* wrecked. They were transported to merchantmen that hovered in the distance, or were landed on the reef, to be assisted by Caymanians in canoes who waited on the leeward side.

In describing his management of the rescue operation John Lawford informed Commodore Ford that on Sunday morning he had "prevailed on a Canoe to go to the few remaining Ships in the Offing with a Letter to the Commanders of them to desire them either to Anchor at the Hogsties or lay off and on there to receive the men saved from the Different Ships." He had thoroughly investigated and found that "on the Affidavits of the Principal Inhabitants, it would be impossible to subsist for any time on this little Island, which suffered most severely from a Hurricane in October last." As for the remaining convoy, Lawford reported, "The greater part had bore away to the Westward before they could receive this Intimation, and only Nine of the remainder thought proper to pay any regard to it."[10]

And so, Lawford appointed a rendezvous for the remaining merchantmen at the Hogsties (as George Town, situated on Hog Sty Bay, was known in the late eighteenth century) on the west end of Grand Cayman (see map 5).[11] Captain Lawford's letter of 9 February to the "Commanders of the Merchant Ships and Vessels off the Island of Grand Cayman" stated, "I beg to acquaint You that the Officers and Crew of the *Convert* and the Merchant Vessels lately Wrecked on the reefs to the Eastward of this Island are in the greatest distress, not being able from the very great Surf to save any Provisions or any other necessary Convenience." He expressed that he "must therefore desire of You, Either to anchor at the Hogsties, or lay off and on there ready to take the People on board as soon as it is possible to get them over, it being impracticable to embark them from this part of the Island whilst the Sea is so great."[12]

In a petition dated 12 February, signed by eight principal inhabitants of Grand Cayman, the Caymanians testified to Captain Lawford that they could not provide subsistence for the shipwreck survivors. They implored Captain Lawford to quickly remove the ships' crews from the island (fig-

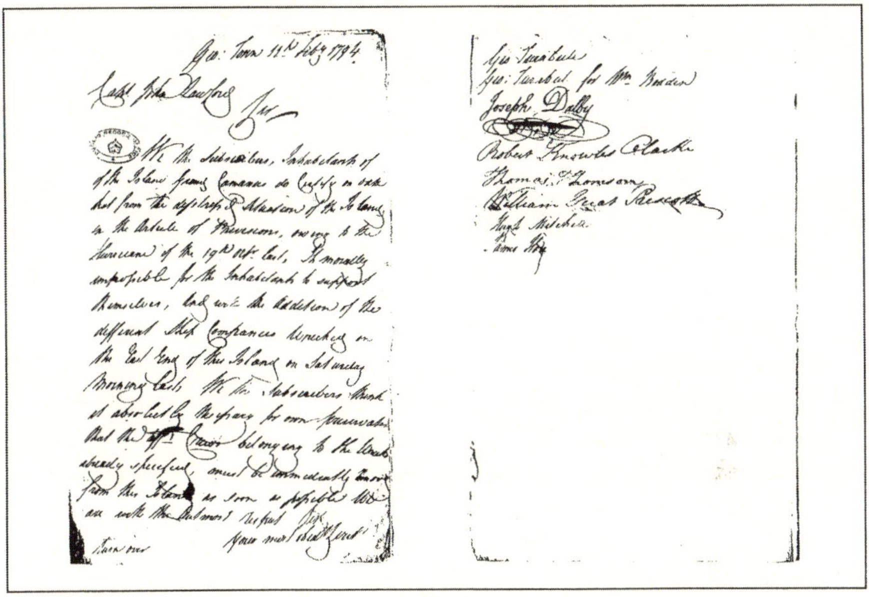

Figure 23. Petition from the principal inhabitants of Grand Cayman to Captain Lawford. Courtesy of the Public Record Office, Kew.

ure 23): "We the Subscribers, Inhabitants of of [*sic*] the Island Grand Camanas do Certify on oath that from the distressed Situation of the Island, in the Article of Provisions, owing to the Hurricane of the 19th Octr. last, Its morally impossible for the Inhabitants to support themselves, And with the Addition of the different Ship Companies Wrecked on the East End of this Island on Saturday Morning last, We the Subscribers think it absolutely Necessary for [our] own preservation, that the diff. Crews belonging to the Wrecks already specified, must be immediately removed from this Island as soon as possible."[13] The *Royal Gazette* had, in fact, published a letter in its Marine Intelligence section on 21 December 1793 that supports the Caymanians' account of their depressed situation. In a report from Montego Bay dated 14 December 1793, which arrived via a schooner from Grand Cayman, the *Gazette* reported "an account that the severe gale which was experienced here on the 21st of October, was very destructive at that island on the 20th and 21st. The West end of the island was overflowed by the sea, and several houses washed away. At Boatswain's Bay, every house was destroyed . . . and such was the violence of the tempest, that the cocoanut trees were torn out by the roots." Furthermore, the paper maintained "that the inhabitants are in great distress for provisions, from this calamity, and look up to Jamaica for relief. A schooner, belonging to Mess. Clark and Bodden, of that island, was lost in the gale, and two men drowned."[14]

At least three merchant vessels provided relief to the Cayman Islands, but it is unclear whether they were Cayman or Jamaica-owned vessels. According to the *Royal Gazette*, on 25 November 1793 the sloop *Sea-Flower*, Master Taylor, arrived in Port Royal from Grand Cayman, and on 11 December she left Jamaica for Cayman (see map 12). The account also suggests that a schooner arrived in Montego Bay from Grand Cayman on about 10 December. A week later, on 18 December, the sloop *Industry*, Master Wright, sailed from Port Royal for Grand Cayman. Between 18 December 1793 and 28 February 1794, the *Royal Gazette* did not report any further ship traffic between Jamaica and the Cayman Islands.[15]

From George Town, on 13 February 1794, Captain Lawford wrote to the masters of nine merchantmen who answered his request for assistance and who sailed their vessels to the rendezvous: the ships *Louisa*, *Alfred*, *Llandovery*, *Nancy*, *Barbados*, and *Jane*; and the brigs *Betsey and Susan*, *Countess of Galloway*, and *Mars* (figure 24). After explaining the islanders' situation, he asked them to "receive as many of the above mentioned Seamen on Board the Vessels You respectively command as You can possibly accommodate." On arrival in England they were to "deliver them to the Commanding Officer on the Impress-Service at Any of the Ports or on Board of Any of His Majesty's Ships of War that You may fall in with, sending regular lists & taking Receipts; and transmitting at the same time to the Lords Commissioners of the Admiralty An Account of the Expenses of Victualling &c. during the Passage."[16]

In his 20 February report, John Lawford let Commodore Ford know that he had distributed as many men as possible among the merchantmen and had given each of the masters a letter addressed to the governor of Havana, requesting his assistance.[17] "It is with infinite Concern I have to inform Your Excellency that on the 8th Instant H.B.M. Ship the *Convert* convoying the Jamaica Fleet was unfortunately wrecked on the East End of this Island," he penned to the Spanish governor on 13 February. He continued with news that the *Convert*'s crew were fortunately saved, but that the inhabitants of the Caymans did not have the capacity to provide them with provisions. So, he had embarked them "on board of the Merchant Ships who are now proceeding on this Voyage to Europe without Convoy." He expressed the expectation that "under these circumstances induced by the good understanding which subsists between our respective Courts I take the liberty of recommending to the protection of Your Excellency Such Ships of the Convoy as may be under the necessity of revict-

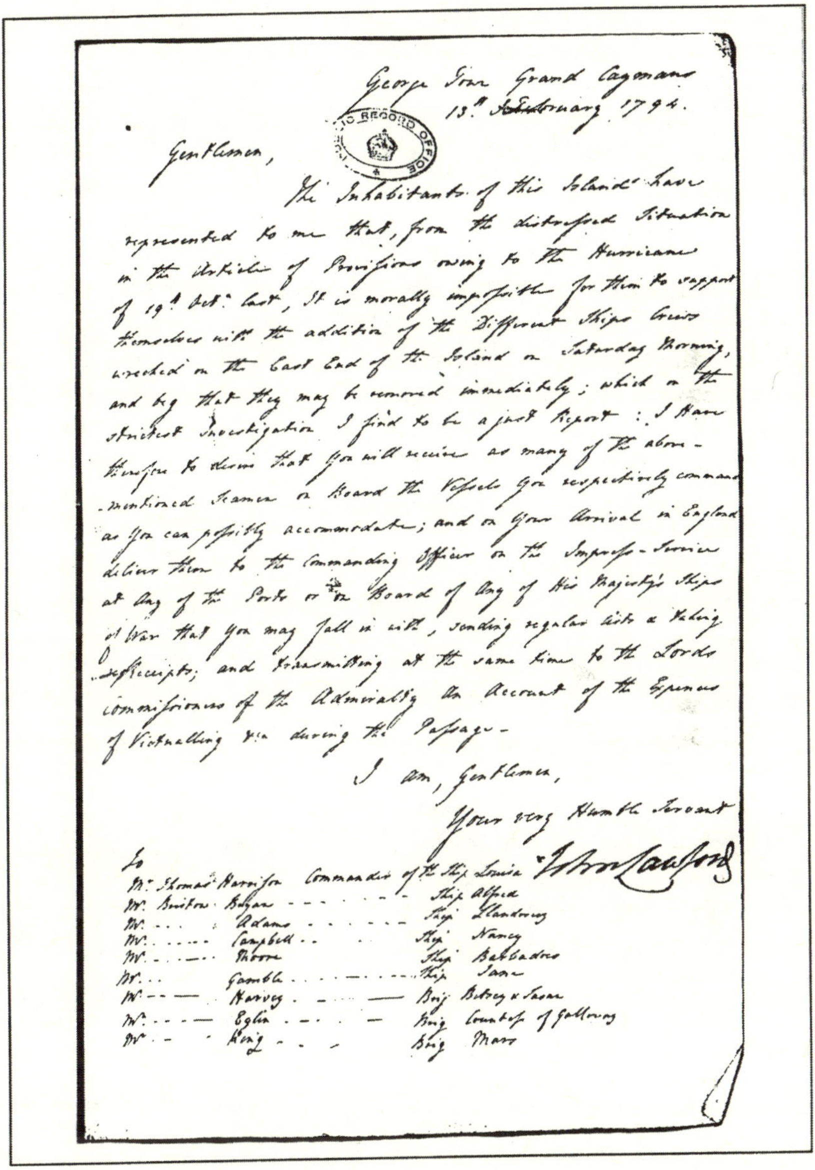

George Town Grand Caymanas
13th February 1794.

Gentlemen,

The Inhabitants of this Island have represented to me that, from the distressed Situation in the Article of Provisions owing to the Hurricane of 19th Octr last, It is morally impossible for them to support themselves with the addition of the Different Ships Crews wrecked on the East End of the Island on Saturday Morning, and beg that they may be removed immediately; which on the strictest Investigation I find to be a just Report: I have therefore to desire that you will receive as many of the above-mentioned Seamen on Board the Vessels you respectively command as you can possibly accommodate; and on your Arrival in England deliver them to the Commanding Officer on the Impress-Service at Any of the Ports or on Board of Any of His Majesty's Ships of War that you may fall in with, sending regular lists & taking their Receipts; and transmitting at the same time to the Lords Commissioners of the Admiralty An Account of the Expences of Victualling &ca during the Passage -

I am, Gentlemen,

Your very Humble Servant

John Lawford

To
Mr. Thomas Harrison Commander of the Ship Louisa
Mr. Britton Bryan - - - Ship Alfred
Mr. - - Adams - - - Ship Llandovery
Mr. - - Campbell - - Ship Nancy
Mr. - - Moore Ship Barbadoes
Mr. - - Gamble - - - Ship Jane
Mr. - - Harvey - - Brig Betsey & Susan
Mr. - - Eglin - - Brig Countess of Galloway
Mr. - - King - - Brig Mars

Figure 24. Letter from Captain Lawford to the masters of the merchantmen. Courtesy of the Public Record Office, Kew.

ualing at the Havannah." Lawford closed his appeal, recognizing that "the Humanity of the Spanish Nation and more particularly the Character of Your Excellency leave no room to doubt of Your Excellencys Willingness to afford every Assistance to Your Friends and Allies."[18]

Among the passengers taken on board one of the merchant ships was Lieutenant Brice, former first lieutenant of His Majesty's frigate *Hermione*, who was returning to England for the recovery of his health. Lieutenant Brice had been on board *Convert* when she wrecked. Captain Lawford charged him with the responsibility of delivering a dispatch regarding the shipwrecks to the Admiralty.[19]

John Lawford's letter of 20 February informed Commodore Ford that until he received his commands he would remain on Grand Cayman with all of his officers and about thirty chosen seamen, to salvage *Convert*'s stores when the weather improved; he would accomplish this with the assistance of the islanders' small craft. Once a vessel could be organized, with the help of *Convert*'s carpenters, Lawford would send First Lieutenant Bogue to Jamaica with the rest of the seamen and with news of the loss of *Convert* and nine of her convoy. Captain Lawford referred the commodore to Lieutenant Bogue for further details regarding the shipwrecks. He sent John Ford copies of the letters exchanged in Grand Cayman as well as his best accounting of *Convert*'s company. Lawford could not, however, send a list of the convoy because it had been lost in the shipwreck, along with his other papers.

In relating the circumstances of those who remained in Grand Cayman for the salvage of *Convert*, Lawford described that they were at present "hutted and under Tents in the best manner possible opposite the Wreck which is about Two Miles from the Shore." Regarding their unfavorable situation, "very few Articles has been practicable to get on Shore, except two Puncheons of Rum and some few Casks of Provisions, the Bread is totally spoiled and the miserable situation of this Island precludes us from being furnished with anything of the Bread Kind." In reviewing *Convert*'s situation, it was impossible for him to judge what might be saved, "being on a Reef to the Eastward of the Island of Course a Weatherly one, and such a Distance from the Land and Very Shoal water within it." His only suggestion at present was, "if the service would admit of it, to request that a Ship of War be dispatched with such relief as you may judge (from the Circumstances above related) proper." Lawford thought that by the time such relief could reach Cayman, that "we shall be enabled to Determine if any thing of consequence is likely to be saved and what Kind of Vessel may be proper to send here to receive it, or, if it appears that nothing material was to be saved, we might return in her to Jamaica." He assured Ford that "in the meantime you may depend that every exertion on my part and that of my Officers and Men, shall be particularly manifested."[20]

Captain Lawford regretfully concluded his missive to Commodore Ford, "Truly convinced of the Magnitude of this Calamity and Knowing its evil influence on the Commerce of my Country in whose service I have pass'd my Life." Woefully, Lawford acknowledged his "Distress of mind would be insupportable were I not supported by a Consciousness of having done my Duty and the utmost my judgment could dictate, and of having never spared myself in this or any other Instance, in point of exertion and Vigilance."[21]

The schooner *Rachel and Elizabeth*, Master Parsons, arrived in Jamaica from Grand Cayman on Friday, 28 February 1794, according to the list of ship arrivals at Port Royal published in the *Royal Gazette*. It is probable that the vessel actually arrived the previous evening with First Lieutenant Bogue of *Convert* aboard. The Marine Intelligence section of the *Gazette*, dated 1 March 1794, reported:

> Thursday night arrived from the Grand Caymanas, Lieutenant Bogue, of his Majesty's Ship *Convert*, with the melancholy intelligence of the loss of that frigate, with nine vessels of the fleet under her convoy, on the North-east end of that island, about three o'clock in the morning of Saturday the 8th ultimo, five days after they left Bluefields.
>
> The names of the merchant vessels lost are the *William and Elizabeth*, Goodwin; *Moorhall*, Nicholson; *Ludlow*, McLure; *Britannia*, Martin; *Richard*, Hughes; *Nancy*, Leary; *Eagle*, Ainsworth; *Sally*, Watson; and *Fortune*, Love.
>
> Captain Martin of the *Britannia*, and five seamen belonging to the *Convert*, perished in the confusion; but we have not heard of any other lives being lost.
>
> The remainder of the fleet proceeded on their voyage, on the 13th, and it was supposed would rendezvous at the Havanna. The passengers and crews of those that were lost were distributed amongst the fleet. The crew of the *Convert* are encamped until a vessel can be sent for them.
>
> We have not heard this accident accounted for; but it appears, that by the *Convert*'s reckoning they ought to have been five leagues distant from the island when they struck; and the loss of so many vessels is said to be owing to those who went ashore first not firing any signals of distress.
>
> The greater part of the rum, cotton, and wood will be saved; of the heavy produce in the lower tiers there can be little hope.
>
> The mail, which was on board the *Convert*, has been saved, and is

now at the Coffee-House of Messrs. Wights, where, on application, the letters will be delivered.[22]

Once news of the shipwrecks reached Jamaica, numerous merchantmen departed Port Royal for the Cayman Islands. The schooner *May-Flower*, Master Kidd, and the sloop *Marlborough*, Master Ball, sailed on 3 March, and the schooner *Little Ann*, Master Smith, the following day. On 7 March the sloop *Alert*, Master Hay, set sail.[23] On 9 March the brig *Mary*, Master Nicholson, was Cayman-bound, and on 13 March the brig *Tamerlane*, Master Gilbert, left Jamaica for Grand Cayman.[24]

On 8 March, the *Royal Gazette* published an extract of a letter sent from Grand Cayman. Although not identified, the writer was a literate man of some stature who stood by Captain Lawford throughout the shipwreck ordeal. On 13 February he embarked for Britain in one of the nine merchant ships that gathered at George Town to receive survivors. Although it appears that the letter writer was aboard *Convert* when she wrecked, he refers to some people as having been on his ship who do not appear in *Convert*'s muster table. It is probable that the writer was Captain Thomson. Captain Thomson of the Royal Artillery and Colonel Amherst of the 10th Regiment do not appear in *Convert*'s muster table, but they were reported by the *Royal Gazette* to be passengers on the naval escort.[25] Maybe the author was First Lieutenant Brice of the *Hermione*. Captain Lawford entrusted Lieutenant Brice with the dispatch for the Admiralty explaining the shipwreck incident.[26] The letter is quoted in full, for it recounts in clear detail the Wreck of the Ten Sail:

> Before this can reach you, you will probably have heard of our misfortune in being shipwrecked, on the reefs at the east-end of the Grand Caymanas, on the night between the 7th and 8th inst. with nine sail of ships and brigs. Some error in our reckoning, arising from I know not what cause, and the set of current running strongly to the northward, occasioned this heavy disaster. We struck about half-past three o'clock in the morning, very dark: It being soon found that all efforts to get off were ineffectual, the three masts were cut away by five o'clock, and the ship lay tolerably easy till day-light, when we had the melancholy view of nine other vessels in a similar predicament. A heavy sea was running, and the surf beating violently over the reef, which was about an hundred yards from us, and two miles from the shore. The first use made of the boats was to send off the ladies, women, and children, to some ships that appeared at a great distance in the offing, but which could not, from the heavy weather, approach

with safety a lee shore; the invalid soldiers and sailors, with the men of the 20th regiment, and Colonel Amherst, were, with great difficulty and danger, sent off in the boats; this employed the time until any further communication with the ships became impossible.

It was now time to devise other modes of safety: the day was fast wearing away, and a gale of wind would have terminated our disasters: about the middle of the day the ship fell down very much, and the sea frequently made a complete breach over her; the cells [*sic*] of the lee ports were on a level with the water, which had a free passage through every part of her; recourse was therefore had to rafts, in order to land the men, if possible, on the reef, on the inside of which several canoes were ready to give assistance. The sharp coral rocks cut every rope that was sent ashore, and the reverberation of the water from the reefs made it highly dangerous to approach it; the stoutest swimmers found it a most hazardous attempt. About six o'clock, Captain Lawford, (with whom I had staid, in the hope of supporting him amid this scene of distress, and calming the agony of his mind) myself, the purser, the old French prisoner, and my servant, and about ten sailors, got into the barge, with an intention to stand out to sea, and to sail toward the West end of the island, a distance of ten leagues; the master, some petty officers, and about 20 men, preferred staying on board all night, to the risque of getting ashore; all the other men, except those, the few with Captain Lawford, and about 13 that were to accompany us in the pinnace, had been got ashore, or drowned in the attempt. The barge pushed off from the lee side of the ship; but before we could get round the stern, being obstructed by the wreck of the Main and mizen masts floating by her side, a tremendous succession of waves came in so rapidly that the boat's head could not be got to the sea, and she was filled in a moment.

Our only chance of safety now, was in preventing the boat's oversetting; three dreadful seas struck us, and a fourth providentially and unexpectedly carried us over the reef, when the people in the canoes seized us, and prevented our being carried back by the reflux.

It were superfluous to attempt enlarging on this circumstance; the mind of every man will suggest to him the horrors of our situation. Individual, personal feelings were absorbed in the great scene of surrounding misery.

Some small part of the vessels cargoes may be saved; about eight men, (so far as we know) including the Master of the *Britannia*, were drowned; several sick persons have died.

Our situation, on arriving at the miserable hovels of the few inhabitants, was only one degree better than that we had escaped from; no dry clothes, no meat, drink, or bedding were held out to us; what they had not they could not bestow.

Lady Emilia Cooke was saved in an open boat, and taken on board one of the ships without a change of clothes; Mr. Mellifont, from our ship, saved two trunks; poor Mrs. Smith, the builder's widow, saved only one small box containing about [£90].

On Sunday the sea ran very high, but towards the evening the remainder of the men were brought from the ship, and a raft made, which brought some baggage; on Monday the weather moderated, and several articles were got ashore. Captain Lawford and his officers have saved some of their things, but are great sufferers. Nearly the whole of my books, letters, and papers, &c. are ruined, as are my clothes; the bedding, and most other articles are totally lost.

On Tuesday morning, Capt. Lawford, another officer, myself, and a guide, set off for the west end of the island, over the most execrable road imaginable; for three miles were hot burning sands, and sharp-pointed coral rocks, that would have foiled the attempts of the most dexterous animal to pass them without injury. About Wednesday noon, we reached the west end (George-Town) commonly called the Hogsties; and I this day embark again for Europe on board the *Louisa*, where already are Lady Cook, Capt. Drinkwater, and Mr. Burrell of the 62nd. We propose stopping at the Havanna for provisions, having a number of shipwrecked sailors on board, for whom no supply can be obtained here.

The ships that are here, and will sail in company this evening, are the *Louisa*, *Llandovery*, *Alfred*, *Nancy*, *Barbados*, and *Jane*; brigs *Betsey and Susan*, *Mars*, and *Countess of Galway* [*sic*]:—Bryan, in the *Alfred*, to act as Commodore.[27]

The Salvage of HMS *Convert*

Commodore John Ford received news of the wreck of *Convert* on 13 March 1794 and sent Captain Francis Roberts in *Success* to Grand Cayman. The commodore apprised the secretary of the Admiralty by way of a 3 April letter, in which he recounted that "on the 13th Ulto. on my way from St. Domingo to this Port I received a Letter from Captain Lawford of His Majesty's Ship *Convert* dated Feby. 20th, containing an Account of the Loss of that Ship, together with Nine Sail of Merchant Ships under his Convoy on the Island of Grand Cayman on the 8th of that Month." Since the detail of the misfortune was related in Captain Lawford's letter, he enclosed a copy for the Admiralty's reference, and "immediately dispatched His Majesty's

Ship *Success* to that Island, in order to save whatever might be possible from the Wreck, as well as to receive on board such of the Officers and Crew as remained there and conduct them to Jamaica."[28]

The logbooks of Captain Roberts and Master Richard Davy of *Success* have survived. These sources provide largely parallel descriptions of the frigate's mission to Grand Cayman.[29] On the day that Commodore Ford learned of the shipwreck incident, *Success*, on service in Saint-Domingue, was at anchor in Tiburon Bay. The frigate had been moored there since 8 March, and her crew had been employed replenishing the vessel with water and wood from shore, stowing the after holds, and repairing the rigging of the fore and main yards. At 8:00 a.m. the commodore, aboard *Europa*, arrived in the offing and at eight thirty signaled for *Success* to come within hail. By eleven thirty the frigate had weighed anchor and made sail. By noon Cape Tiburon was northwest by west five or six miles, and the commodore was southwest by west three or four leagues.[30] On 14 March Captain Roberts's log records that "came on board Mr. Bogue, 1st Lieutenant of His Majestys Ship *Convert* with the account of her being lost on the Grand Caymains [*sic*], stood out to join the Commodore."

Success sailed westward from Cape Tiburon, sighting first the northeast end of Jamaica and, by noon, Saint Ann's Bay. On 15 March the frigate continued along the north coast of Jamaica, sighting Montego Point and then crossing open seas toward the Cayman Islands. Captain Roberts's and Master Davy's logs for 16 March remark that on their passage they spoke to a brig that had been out six days, sailing from Grand Cayman for Jamaica. At nine in the morning they sighted Grand Cayman bearing west by north, and at ten they hove to and made the signal for a pilot to come out to them. Roberts noted that *Convert* was west-southwest about two and a half miles, whereas Davy recorded a distance of two miles. By 11:30 a.m. *Convert*'s pilot came on board, and at noon *Success* bore away for the Hogsties on the west end of Grand Cayman. On 17 March the frigate came to anchor in George's Bay (Hog Sty Bay) in seven fathoms of water and remained there for several days.[31]

Captain Lawford and his officers and seamen had been encamped in tents on the beach at the east end of Grand Cayman since 8 February. For almost six weeks they had conducted salvage operations on *Convert*. Lawford prepared and later transmitted an account of the stores saved from the frigate and additional related papers to Commodore Ford (figure 25).[32] (See appendix F for a list of the salvaged items.)

The recovered goods were transported back to Jamaica, but relatively few of *Convert*'s stores and none of her primary guns were retrieved by *Convert*'s men. Therefore, before leaving Grand Cayman, Captains Roberts and Lawford signed agreements with two prominent Caymanians. The Royal

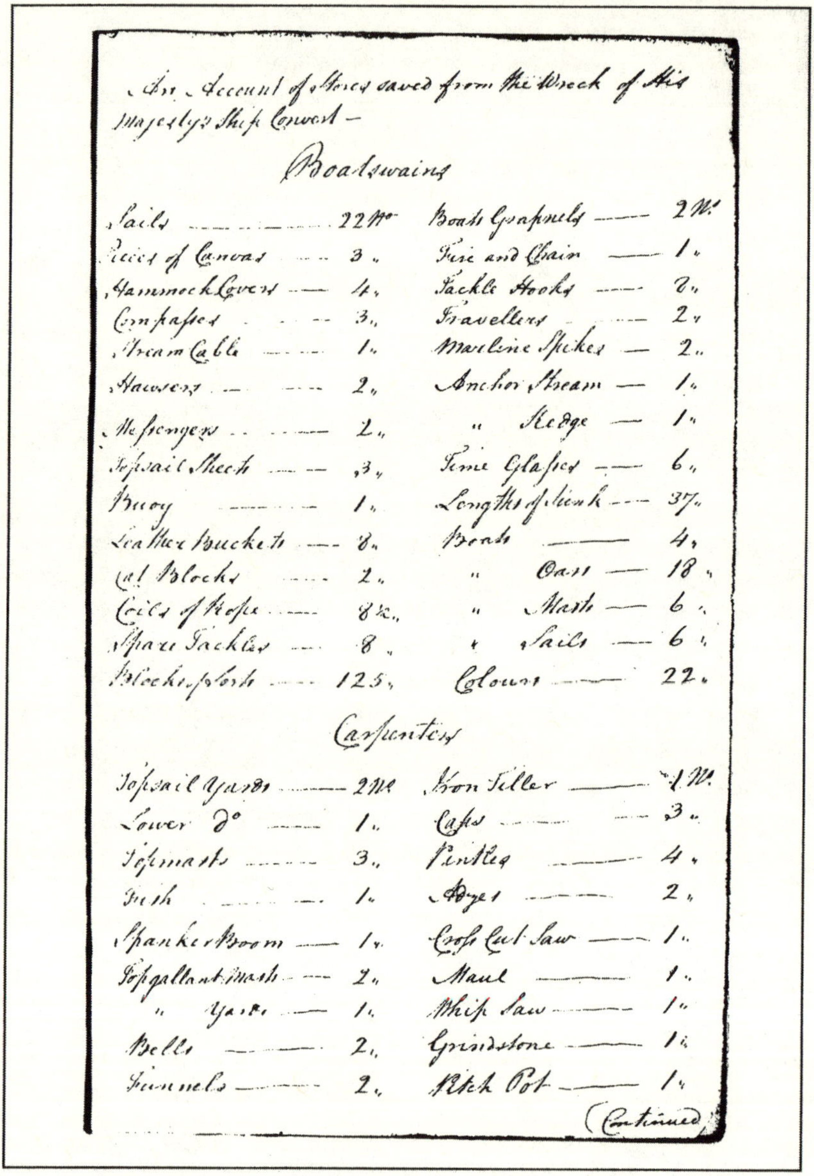

An Account of Stores saved from the Wreck of His Majesty's Ship Convert –

Boatswains

Sails	22 No.	Boats Grapnels	2 No.
Pieces of Canvas	3 "	Fire and Chain	1 "
Hammock Covers	4 "	Tackle Hooks	2 "
Compasses	3 "	Travellers	2 "
Stream Cable	1 "	Marline Spikes	2 "
Hawsers	2 "	Anchor Stream	1 "
Messengers	2 "	" Kedge	1 "
Topsail Sheets	3 "	Time Glasses	6 "
Buoy	1 "	Lengths of Hawk	37 "
Leather Buckets	8 "	Boats	4 "
Cat Blocks	2 "	" Oars	18 "
Coils of Rope	8½ "	" Masts	6 "
Spare Tackles	8 "	" Sails	6 "
Blocks of Sorts	125 "	Colours	22 "

Carpenters

Topsail Yards	2 No.	Iron Tiller	1 No.
Lower D°	1 "	Caps	3 "
Topmasts	3 "	Pintles	4 "
Fish	1 "	Adzes	2 "
Spanker Boom	1 "	Cross Cut Saw	1 "
Topgallant Masts	2 "	Maul	1 "
" Yards	1 "	Whip Saw	1 "
Bells	2 "	Grindstone	1 "
Funnels	2 "	Pitch Pot	1 "

(Continued)

Figure 25. First page of the salvage account of HMS *Convert*. Courtesy of the Public Record Office, Kew.

Navy officers authorized the local men to continue the salvage of *Convert* and agreed to compensate them for their work; two documents sealed this arrangement.

The first was a letter from Captains Roberts and Lawford, addressed to Robert Knowles Clarke and William Bodden Sr.[33] They judged that "for the good of His Majesty's Service that the Officers & Seamen of His Majesty's Ship *Convert* lately wrecked on the east end of this Island should be removed to Jamaica as early as possible." Their opinion, however, was that in moderate weather it might be possible "to recover many Articles of her Stores Provisions &c. and you being willing to undertake so far as your abilities will allow to save whatever may be possible. We hereby authorize you, and give you the exclusive privilege of going on board for the purpose of getting out the Stores & Provisions as before mentioned for the use of His Majesty's Service, which is requested to be landed at George Town." In return for these actions, "a reasonable Salvage, and such as hath been customary in similar occasions will be allowed."

Bodden and Clarke accepted the terms of the letter and signed a document of obligation for Captains Roberts and Lawford.[34] The pledge began, "We the undersigned do hereby bind and oblige ourselves in the most solemn manner to use our utmost endeavour to save all the remaining Stores, Provisions, & Guns together with all the Materials of the Wreck of His Majesty's Ship *Convert* such as Iron work, old Copper, and Copper fastening, and to give a most faithful & just account of the same."

Bodden and Clarke owned schooners and had probably been assisting Captain Lawford with the recovery operation since *Convert* had wrecked.[35] It is not known, however, how much more salvage of the frigate the two carried out.

On 19 March 1794, while *Success* was at anchor in the bay at George Town, a schooner and a brig returning from *Convert* came to anchor alongside her. Captain Francis Roberts's log records that on 20 and 21 March a sloop and a schooner arrived with part of *Convert*'s stores, and the crew loaded them on board *Success*. Master Richard Davy's log twice notes that on 20 March a sloop arrived with stores from *Convert*, and that the crew took the goods on board.[36] Davy's log for 21 March comments, "Came alongside a Schooner with the *Convert*'s People and Luggage." The officers of *Success* were clearing them and a party was also transferring part of them to a brig. Captain Roberts's log remarks that on Saturday, 22 March, *Success* took on board part of *Convert*'s masts and yards, and by ten o'clock in the morning weighed anchor and embarked for Jamaica. Master Davy's log specifies that they received part of *Convert*'s top masts and yards. By noon *Success* was four or five leagues southeast of the east point of Grand Cayman.

On 27 March *Success* was ten or twelve leagues from Jamaica, and by 31 March the frigate was at anchor at Port Royal alongside *Europa*, *Powerful*, *Iphigenia*, and *Goelan*. Captain Roberts's log for Tuesday, 1 April 1794, comments that the ship's company was employed towing *Convert*'s masts and yards to shore, that seventeen invalids were sent to sick quarters on shore, and that at 8:00 a.m. the signal was made for a court-martial to be held on Captain Lawford, "late Commander of the *Convert*."[37]

The *Royal Gazette* reported the arrivals on 30 and 31 March of HMS *Success*, the brig *Tamerlane*, Master Gilbert, and the schooner *Union*, Master Bryan. These vessels probably carried most of the stores salvaged from *Convert*. The periodical remarked, "Arrived his Majesty's Ship *Success*, Capt. Roberts, from the Grand Caymanas. Capt. Lawford, and the other Officers of the *Convert* frigate, came in the *Success*. The stores belonging to the *Convert* frigate are on board the *Tamerlane*."[38]

On 4 April 1794, twenty-four of *Convert*'s men were discharged from *Success* into a new Royal Navy vessel, *L'Actif*.[39] The French corvette, captured by *Iphigenia*, had arrived in Port Royal on 29 March and been commissioned as a sloop of war with a complement of sixty men.[40] When *Success* sailed from Kingston Harbour on 11 April, the former master of *Convert*, Thomas Popplewell, acting as the pilot, maneuvered her out to sea from the harbor.[41]

Commodore Ford appointed the next convoy from Jamaica for 20 May, under the protection of the seventy-four-gun ship *Powerful*, commanded by Captain William Albany Otway.[42] At the end of May, the *Royal Gazette* reported that the convoy had sailed under the escort of *Powerful*, *Hound*, and *Goelan*.[43] A notice from Falmouth, included in the *Royal Gazette* of 18 June, contained news received from Cayman via the schooner *Sally and Betsey*, which informed about progress of the convoy.[44] It reported, "We are sorry to learn, by the *Sally and Betsey*, that the ship *Thomas*, belonging to Mr. Gillies, of Montego-Bay, lost her main-mast in a heavy sea, and was towed into the Caymanas by the *Hound* sloop of war." The paper continued with news that "she has since got one of the masts belonging to the *Convert* frigate, but was at the above place when the schooner sailed. The *Hound*, after towing her in, sailed to rejoin the convoy, who were lying to off the Caymanas three days." Thus, the salvage of *Convert* continued.

The Shipwrecked Merchantmen

First Lieutenant Joseph Bradby Bogue arrived in Jamaica on Thursday, 27 February 1794, with news of the wrecks of HMS *Convert* and nine of her convoy. (See appendix E for a reconstructed list of the convoy.) Two days later, on 1 March, the names of the merchantmen were published in the Marine Intelligence section of the *Royal Gazette*: *William and Elizabeth*, Goodwin; *Moorhall*, Nicholson; *Ludlow*, McLure; *Britannia*, Martin; *Richard*, Hughes; *Nancy*, Leary; *Eagle*, Ainsworth; *Sally*, Watson; and *Fortune*, Love.[45] The *Gazette*'s list of departures from Port Royal had included six of these vessels: the ship *William and Elizabeth* was bound to Bluefields; the ships *Britannia*, *Ludlow*, and *Nancy* were destined for London; the ship *Moorhall* was going to Liverpool; and the brig *Fortune* was sailing for Bristol.[46] Not mentioned in the *Gazette*'s list of departures, *Richard*, *Eagle*, and *Sally* had probably sailed from ports other than Port Royal to join the convoy.

In the late eighteenth century, *Lloyd's List*, published in London, included data on all vessels reported by Lloyd's agents or for which intelligence had been received.[47] *Lloyd's List* published the names of the nine shipwrecked merchantmen. The periodical first noted, on 18 March 1794, "The *Convert* frigate, from Jamaica to England, with the *Sally*, ——, of Kingston, and 8 others of the Convoy, were lost on the 8th of February, on the Grand Camanus, two Days after Sailing."[48] Three days later *Lloyd's List* reported that "the *Nancy*, Campbell, and the *Britannia*, Martin, of Glasgow; the *Eagle*, Ainsworth, of Kingston; the *Ludlow*, McLure, and *William and Elizabeth*, Goodwin, all for London; the *Richard*, ——, for Belfast; the *Moorhall*, ——, for Liverpool; and a Brig, were lost on the Grand Camanus; with the *Convert* frigate, and Brig *Sally* of Kingston."[49] On 28 March, *Lloyd's List* added, "The *Fortune*, Merryman, from Jamaica to Bristol, is lost on the Grand Camanus—Crew saved."[50] *Fortune* was probably the unnamed brig mentioned in the earlier report of 21 March.

In the United States, the *Maryland Journal and Baltimore Advertiser*, on 21 March 1794, printed a brief account of the wrecks of *Convert* and nine merchantmen.[51] The news had first been reported from Charleston, South Carolina, on 25 February. It recounted that Captain Manning of the brig *Eagle*, who had arrived there in eighteen days, from Kingston, Jamaica, informed that "he sailed in company with the Jamaica homeward-bound fleet, consisting of upwards of 50 sails, under convoy of the '*INCONSTANT*' of 44 guns, and that on the night of the 8th instant, the *INCONSTANT*, eight ships, and a brig, struck on the GRAND-COMMANDERS, and soon went to pieces, the cargoes were totally lost and a few men drowned." It then maintained that "a schooner belonging to Norfolk was also wrecked at the same time."

According to the *Royal Gazette*, the brig *Eagle*, Master Manning, had departed from Port Royal on 4 February. The *Gazette* does not, however, list a schooner sailing for Norfolk around this time (although the schooner *Delaware*, Master Davis, sailed for Charleston).[52] Perhaps additional research in North American archives will clarify whether ten or eleven ships actually wrecked in Grand Cayman on 8 February 1794.

The *Royal Gazette* and *Lloyd's List* agree that the following seven merchantmen of the *Convert* convoy wrecked in Grand Cayman (although *Lloyd's List* does not report the masters' names for *Moorhall*, *Richard*, or *Sally*): *William and Elizabeth*, Goodwin, *Moorhall*, Nicholson, *Ludlow*, McLure, *Britannia*, Martin, *Richard*, Hughes, *Eagle*, Ainsworth, and *Sally*, Watson, but there is some conflicting information regarding the other two vessels. Both periodicals agree that a ship called *Nancy* wrecked in Grand Cayman. The *Royal Gazette* reported that her master's name was Leary, whereas *Lloyd's List* gave the master's name as Campbell. The *Gazette* had listed both *Nancy*, under Master Campbell, and *Nancy*, under Master Leary, as having sailed from Port Royal for London.[53] And it is known that a ship called *Nancy*, with a master named Campbell, was one of nine merchantmen that rendezvoused at George Town after the shipwreck episode to take survivors on board for her voyage to Britain; Captain Lawford had given a letter to Mr. Campbell.[54] It appears, then, that *Nancy* commanded by Master Leary wrecked. Another discrepancy between the sources concerns *Fortune*. The *Royal Gazette* listed the captain's name as Love, while *Lloyd's List* gave it as Merryman—but both periodicals agree that *Fortune* was bound for Bristol.

An inconsistency also pertains to the number of shipwrecked vessels that were brigs. Captain Lawford, in his letter of 20 February to Commodore Ford, wrote that seven ships and two brigs wrecked with *Convert*. The *Royal Gazette* describes *Fortune* as a brig, and according to *Lloyd's List* the *Sally* was a brig. The bona fide ship register, *Lloyd's Register*, however, suggests that *Richard*, Master Hughes, of Belfast was also a brig.[55] If the *Royal Gazette* and *Lloyd's List* are correct in calling *Fortune* and *Sally* brigs, then the Wreck of the Ten Sail may have involved six ships and three brigs rather than seven ships and two brigs, as reported by *Convert*'s captain on viewing the wreckage, whose list of the convoy was lost in the shipwreck.

William and Elizabeth

By far the most detailed information available about the merchantmen involved in the Wreck of the Ten Sail concerns *William and Elizabeth*, Master Goodwin. Numerous issues of the *Royal Gazette* advertised for sale a wide assortment of products, shipped from Europe in *William and Elizabeth* and two other vessels. According to the ad, which was dated 6 July 1793, the goods included cotton and linen fabrics, china, saddlery, harnesses, shoes, boots, ladies' hats, telescopes, porter (a dark ale), pipes, sail canvas, copper kettles, garden hoes (among other tools), gunpowder, shot, military drums, sheet and pig lead, corn and coffee mills, iron pots and pans, scales and weights, grindstones, iron blocks with brass sheaves, oils and paints, nails and other articles of ironmongery, ship chandlery, and plantation stores.[56] The merchandise suggests that *William and Elizabeth* carried on a direct two-way trade between Britain and the West Indies, rather than in the infamous triangular trade via Africa.

A description of *William and Elizabeth* is in the 1794 volume of *Lloyd's Register of Shipping*. In the late eighteenth century, inclusion of a ship in *Lloyd's Register* did not necessarily mean that the vessel was insured at Lloyd's, but it did signify that a surveyor, retained by Lloyd's, had carried out a seaworthiness inspection of the vessel.[57] The ship-rigged *William and Elizabeth*, sheathed in metal in 1788, was 312 tons with a seventeen-foot draft when loaded and was built in the "River" in 1786. Owned by D. Shea & Company, her surveying port was London, and she was destined for Jamaica. *Lloyd's Register* rated *William and Elizabeth* A1 in 1791.[58]

Additional information about *William and Elizabeth* exists in documents regarding merchantmen registered in London. In the London Register Index the ship is registered as No. 14 on 19 January 1792, listed at 376 tons, and her master is given as Medmer Goodwin.[59] The Register of Shipping, London Foreign Trade 1790–93, contains specific details, including the names of all her owners, of which Goodwin was one, and the fact that she was British built at Deptford in Kent in 1786.[60] The register notes that the ship had three decks and a height between decks of 5 feet 6 inches.[61] There were three masts. The vessel's extreme length aloft was 114 feet 8 inches, while the extreme breadth at the broadest part, above the main wales, was 29 feet 6 1/2 inches. Her tonnage is listed as 375 tons (one ton off from the index to this register). *William and Elizabeth* was a square-sterned ship with a quarterdeck, pierced for twenty guns. The merchantman had a quarter gallery and a figurehead of Mercury. An annotation to this register entry records that *William and Elizabeth* was supposed lost.[62]

The earliest registration for *William and Elizabeth*, transcript No. 85, was dated 6 February 1787. The registers suggest that in 1787 the ship's principal dimensions and features were comparable to those recorded in 1791. The vessel had different masters, however, and several different people owned shares. The original registration shows that John Dudman in Deptford built *William and Elizabeth* and that she was launched on 7 November 1786.[63]

Moorhall

Moorhall, Master Samuel Nicholson, arrived in Port Royal from Liverpool on 18 December 1793. The commodities carried from Europe in this ship were listed in an 18 December notice that immediately appeared in the *Royal Gazette* and was also published in subsequent issues. Imports included flour, hams, cheese, potatoes, and fifty tons of coal in bulk. An advertisement describes *Moorhall* as a ship of 150 tons mounting ten double-fortified 4-pounders with small arms and men answerable. *Moorhall* was intended to sail for Liverpool on 20 January 1794 with the convoy.[64] *Lloyd's Register* also lists the ship *Moore Hall*. Despite the spelling discrepancy and the listing of a different master's name (S. Martin), archival data suggest that it is the same vessel that wrecked in Grand Cayman.[65] Built in Liverpool in 1791, the metal-sheathed ship of 149 tons had a single deck with beams, a thirteen-foot draft when loaded, and was said to be armed with eight 4-pounders. Owned by Hayhurst, the ship's surveying port was Liverpool, and the destined port was Jamaica. Lloyd's surveyors rated *Moore Hall* as A1. A register of passes, entitling *Moore Hall* to trade, shows that the vessel received pass No. 4072 on 10 September 1793.[66] At this time, she mounted ten guns. *Moore Hall*'s home port was Liverpool, her master was Samuel Nicholson, and the crew comprised twenty-four British men. On receiving the pass she was bound for Jamaica.

Ludlow

Information regarding *Ludlow* was not found in *Lloyd's Register*.[67] A 30 December 1793 advertisement in the *Royal Gazette* suggests that *Ludlow*, Master David McLure, was a new vessel on her maiden voyage—and thus, plantation built in Jamaica. The ad reveals that the ship planned to sail with the first convoy for London. *Ludlow* loaded at Port Morant on the north coast of Jamaica and sailed to Port Royal, arriving on 19 January 1794, to take on freight and passengers before departing with the *Convert* convoy.[68]

Britannia

The *Royal Gazette* noted the arrival in Port Royal, on 28 November 1793, of the ship *Britannia*, commanded by Master Daniel Martin, from Glasgow. *Britannia* had arrived with sixteen passengers on board, including "Mess. Hay, Stupart, Allardyce, Brown, Thomson, Reid; and ten steerage passengers."[69] Imports from Europe in this vessel and in *Martha*, Master Brown, are offered for sale in a 5 December 1793 notice that appeared in several issues of the *Gazette*. Merchandise on offer included madeira wine (by the pipe, hogshead, or quarter-cask), puncheons of hams, baskets of cheese, hogsheads of porter, cases of mustard, boxes of soap, puncheons of Mrs. Allan's claret, cases of pickles, boxes of perfumery, osnaburghs (heavy, course cottons in a plain weave), checks, and Irish linens. Another advertisement in the *Gazette* announced that *Britannia*, a "stout fast-sailing vessel, mounting Eight Carriage-Guns and Eight Swivels," would take on freight and passengers and would positively sail with the 20 January 1794 convoy for London.[70]

Lloyd's Register and a register of passes record details about *Britannia*.[71] Master Daniel Martin, alone among the masters of the nine shipwrecked merchantmen, died in the confusion that followed the wrecking of his ship.

Richard

The *Royal Gazette* recorded the arrival in Port Royal, on 30 November 1793, of the ship *Richard*, Master J. Hughes, from Cork. The vessel had arrived two days before the Royal Navy frigates *Success* and *Magicienne* and the remainder of the West Indian convoy from Britain. Passengers who arrived in Jamaica on board *Richard* included "Mr. Higginson, Mr. Fisher, and Mr. Elder."[72]

Although the *Royal Gazette* listed *Richard*, Hughes, as a ship, *Lloyd's List* suggests that she was a brig.[73] *Lloyd's List* agrees with the *Gazette* that the master of *Richard* was named Hughes. *Lloyd's Register* provides specific details on *Richard*.[74]

Richard is also listed in a register of foreign passes that entitled her to trade. On 7 April 1791, the British-built vessel received pass No. 1735. The register records that the brig was 176 tons and that her master was Thomas Hughes (*Lloyd's Register* identifies him as J. Hughes). *Richard*'s home port was Belfast, and the vessel's crew consisted of eleven British men. When the brig's pass was issued in 1791, she was bound for Jamaica. Presumably, *Richard* carried on trade regularly with the British West Indian colony.[75]

Nancy, *Eagle*, *Sally*, and *Fortune*

The same eighteenth-century sources were consulted for *Nancy*, Master Leary, *Eagle*, Master Ainsworth, *Sally*, Master Watson, and *Fortune*, Master Love or Master Merryman. The names *Nancy* and *Sally*, and to a slightly lesser extent *Eagle* and *Fortune*, were so commonly bestowed on merchantmen, none of which aligned with the correct master's name, that it is impossible to conclusively identify any of these as the ships or brigs that wrecked in Grand Cayman, barring discovery of additional information.

Lloyd's List remarks that the brig *Sally*, with no master's name given, and *Eagle*, Master Ainsworth, were of Kingston. While these merchantmen may have been British-built or plantation-built vessels, current research suggests that both were registered in Jamaica.[76] The *Royal Gazette* and *Lloyd's List* both note that the brig *Fortune* was bound to Bristol, although they disagree on the master's name. The *Royal Gazette* remarks that *Nancy*, Master Leary, was bound for London. Perhaps knowledge of the ports with which these ships and brigs were associated will eventually enable them to be positively identified.

Salvage Efforts

Reports from the Cayman Islands received in Jamaica in 1794 suggest that the nine luckless merchantmen of the Wreck of the Ten Sail were partially salvaged but also quickly destroyed by natural forces. The *Royal Gazette* reported the arrival in Port Royal from the Cayman Islands of the sloop *Lark*, Master Freeman, on 23 March and the brig *Surprise*, Master Wylie, on 28 March. The *Gazette* also remarked, "If we may credit the last accounts from the Caymanas, the prospect of saving much from the vessels wrecked there is very indifferent. The continued high winds and the peculiar situation on which the ships struck, render the approach extremely dangerous."[77]

A week later, the *Royal Gazette* listed the arrival in Port Royal, on 29 March, of the sloop *Marlborough*, Master Ball, from Grand Caymans. In the same issue, a notice dated 29 March from Montego Bay reported, "Wednesday evening the sloop *Mercury*, Babb, returned from the Grand Caymanas, which he left at noon the 21st inst. Capt. Babb informs, that the vessels unfortunately lost at that island, are almost all beat to pieces; the produce saved amounts to only about 50 hogsheads of sugar, 150 puncheons of rum, 600 bags of piemento, 100 bags of cotton, much damaged, and some tons of wood."[78]

Although additional reports about the shipwrecks did not appear in the *Royal Gazette*, in the following months sea traffic continued between Grand Cayman and Jamaica. Some of this traffic can probably be attributed to continued salvage activities associated with the Wreck of the Ten Sail. On 6 April 1794, the sloops *Sea-Flower*, Master Russell, and *Alert*, Master Hay, arrived in Port Royal from the Cayman Islands, followed by the schooner *Little Ann*, Master Smith, on 10 April.[79] The *Sea-Flower* sailed again from Port Royal for Cayman on 21 April, and the next day the sloop *Industry*, Master Wright, arrived in Port Royal from Grand Cayman.[80] On 2 May 1794, the schooner *Friendship*, Master Delisser, arrived in Port Royal from Grand Cayman.[81] The sloop *Fly*, Master Dixon, departed Jamaica for the Cayman Islands on 11 May, followed by *Industry* on 14 May.[82] On 27 May, *Sea-Flower* arrived back in Port Royal from Cayman; she departed again for Grand Cayman on 4 June.[83] News reported on 18 June from the Jamaican port of Falmouth included the arrival there of the schooner *Sally and Betsey* from Cayman.[84] On 24 June 1794, the sloop *Fly* arrived at Port Royal from Grand Cayman.[85] It appears that salvage activities continued on the shipwrecked merchantmen for months after the *Royal Gazette* reported that little of the cargoes could be saved. Meanwhile, Caymanians salvaged what they could from *Convert*.

The Remainder of the Convoy

On 9 February 1794, the day following the shipwreck, Captain Lawford sent a message, via a canoe, to the few merchantmen that waited in the offing at the east end of Grand Cayman, asking the masters of these vessels to assemble at the Hogsties on the west end of the island. The ships *Louisa*, Harrison, *Alfred*, Bryan, *Llandovery*, Adams, *Nancy*, Campbell, *Barbados*, Moore, and *Jane*, Gammell, and the brigs *Betsey and Susan*, Harvey, *Countess of Galloway*, Elgin, and *Mars*, King, responded to his request.[86] Captain Lawford then distributed a circular to each master asking him to take on board his ship as many survivors as could possibly be accommodated.

Lloyd's Register identifies several of these merchantmen and their respective masters. *Alfred* was a 400-ton ship, built in Philadelphia in 1776. The vessel's draft was sixteen feet. In 1791 *Alfred* underwent a "good repair" in London and was sheathed with metal. *Louisa*, a 329-ton ship with a sixteen-foot draft, was built in 1784 and sheathed in 1792. *Llandovery* was built on the Thames River in 1777. She was 287 tons with a draft of fifteen feet. *Llandovery* underwent a good repair in 1787 and was sheathed in 1792. London was the surveying port for the ships *Alfred*, *Louisa*, and *Llandovery*. *Jane* was a 201-ton ship, built in Newfoundland in 1783. The vessel received repairs in 1791, was copper sheathed, and had a draft of fourteen feet. Liverpool was *Jane*'s surveying port.[87]

Documents regarding *Llandovery*'s registry in London on 25 June 1793 indicate that her master was William Adams and that she was a 289-ton square-sterned ship with three masts, two decks, a quarterdeck, and quarter gallery.[88] Pierced for ten guns, *Llandovery* was 100 feet long.[89]

In the register of passes entitling ships to trade, three of the rescuing merchantmen are listed. A pass granted to *Louisa* in February 1793 describes the vessel as a British-built ship of 323 tons. Her captain was Thomas Harrison, and her home port was London. *Louisa* carried two guns, employed fifteen British men and five foreign men, and was bound for Jamaica. *Nancy* is identified by a pass issued in April 1793, before a voyage to Jamaica. The home port of this British-built ship was Greenock, and her master was Robert Campbell. The vessel was 103 tons and carried eight guns. *Nancy*'s crew comprised eleven British and three foreign men. The brig *Countess of Galloway* is also listed in the register of passes, but the pass was granted in June 1794, after her return to Britain. At the time of issue, the brig was bound to North America. This 103-ton, British-built vessel was of Wigton in Scotland. Her master was William Elgin, and her crew consisted of two British and five foreign men.[90]

According to the *Royal Gazette*, the small convoy departed Grand Cayman on 13 February with "Bryan, in the *Alfred*, to act as Commodore."[91] Although the nine merchantmen intended to put into Havana for supplies and were carrying letters from Captain Lawford requesting assistance from the governor there, it appears that one, and perhaps three, of the vessels did not do so. The Marine Intelligence section of the *Royal Gazette* reported in late March that "an American vessel is arrived at St. Ann's, which fell in with, and supplied with some articles of provisions, in the Gulph Stream, the ship *Llandovery*, Adams, one of the ships under the convoy of the *Convert*, and of the ten that sailed from the Caymanas for the Havannah, but which were afterwards separated by a violent gale of wind."[92]

In its next issue, the *Gazette* clarified the earlier report with a 29 March statement from Montego Bay: "The sloop *Sally*, Miner, from North-Carolina, which arrived at Port Antonio, last Tuesday fe'nnight, in lat. 28-1/2 spoke the ship *Llandovery*, Adams, one of the January fleet, short of provisions; Capt. Miner supplied Capt. Adams with what provisions he could spare."[93] Apparently, a winter storm had dispersed the nine-ship convoy and caused *Llandovery* to bypass Havana; it is also possible that two brigs were separated from the others and missed the Spanish port. It is unclear whether these merchantmen rejoined one another, but all three vessels safely reached Britain. *Lloyd's List* records the arrival in Dover on 10 April 1794 of the ship *Llandovery*, Master Adams, and the brig *Mars*, Master King. By 13 April the brig *Betsey and Susan*, Master Harvey, also reached Dover. *Mars* sailed on to the Thames River port of Gravesend, arriving on 13 April, as did *Betsey and Susan*, which arrived three days later.[94]

The remaining six merchantmen did reach Havana, as did the ship *Lion*, Master King. *Lloyd's List* notes, "Captain Souter, of the *Royal Charlotte*, arrived at the Cowes from Jamaica, parted the *Lion* off the Havannah, which Place he intended to put into."[95] It is possible that survivors were taken on board the *Lion* on the day of the shipwrecks in Grand Cayman, or else that the vessel received shipwreck victims that earlier had been put on board the other rescue vessels. As the advertisement in the *Royal Gazette* had boasted, the *Lion* was "a fast-sailing copper-sheathed ship, mounting 18 double-fortified Four Pounders."[96] The *Gazette*'s Marine Intelligence section of 12 April 1794 remarks, "Several ships of the late unfortunate fleet from this island had reached the Havannah, but there being no opportunity of a Spanish convoy at the time, they proceeded on their voyage. It is said that the Governor handsomely offered them the protection of a ship of the line, if they would wait ten days, which they declined."[97] No doubt the Spanish governor of Havana also gave the British merchantmen provisions.

Lloyd's List reported on 11 April 1794 that "the *Alice*, Smith, arrived at Liverpool, from Jamaica; sailed from the Havannah on the 26th of February, in Company with the *Alfred*, Bryan; *Louisa*, Harrison; *Barbadoes*, Moore; *Lion*, King; *Countess of Galloway*, Elgin; and *Nancy*, Campbell; for London. *Jane*, Gannuel, for Bristol; and *Hero*, Galbreath, for Liverpool; and parted with them in Lat.30.25. Long.70.52."[98] *Alice*, Master Smith, also called at Havana and may have carried shipwreck survivors, but this vessel did not sail in convoy with the others. *Alice* was a 220-ton ship, advertised to be a fast sailer mounting six carriage guns.[99] It is unclear whether *Hero*, Master Galbreath, was one of the *Convert* convoy. This vessel was not listed among the late January and early February departures from Jamaica printed in the *Royal Gazette* and was not among the arrivals in Britain recorded in *Lloyd's List* through 30 May 1794.

The remaining seven merchantmen reached Great Britain unharmed. *Jane* arrived in Bristol and *Louisa* appeared in Plymouth on 19 April 1794. These two ships had sailed in convoy with the others after leaving Havana, but they probably sprang out ahead of the small fleet on nearing home. *Alfred*, *Nancy*, *Barbados*, *Countess of Galloway*, and *Lion* sailed together into Penzance, on the southwest coast of Britain, on 23 April; all continued on to the London port of Gravesend, arriving on 27 April.[100] *Louisa* eventually sailed into the Thames River and reached Gravesend on 13 May.[101] The reconstructed list of the *Convert* convoy (appendix E) documents the arrival in Britain, according to *Lloyd's List*, of each of the merchantmen that departed Jamaica with the fleet.

Several members of the *Convert* convoy did not reach Britain. *Lloyd's List* reported on 29 April 1794 that "the *Susannah*, McIsaac, from Jamaica to London, was left at the Havannah leaky."[102] The *Royal Gazette*'s departure list called *Susannah* a snow, but it is certainly possible that she was the leaky vessel—described by Captain Lawford as a schooner—that delayed the fleet at the outset. Regardless, this merchantman's luck did not improve. The *Royal Gazette*'s Marine Intelligence section of 21 June noted: "On the 28th of April arrived at Charleston, the brig *Susannah* of this port, taken by the *Sans Pareille* French Privateer. The *Susannah* was last from the Havanna."[103] *Lloyd's List* reported that "the *Susannah*, McIsaac, from Jamaica and Havannah to London, is taken and carried into Charleston."[104] On the other side of the Atlantic, France took another prize: "The *Peggy*, Robertson, from Jamaica to London, is taken by a French Frigate, and carried into Brest."[105] *Peggy* was an American-built, ship-rigged vessel from Greenock, armed with six guns and with a crew of eleven. When the 171-ton ship received a pass to trade in May 1793, she was bound to Barbados.[106]

The *Royal Gazette* also remarked the arrival in Britain of ships from the *Convert* convoy. A few dates differ slightly from those reported in *Lloyd's List*, but not significantly. The mid-May issue of the *Royal Gazette* reported on the arrival in the Downs of ships from the dispersed West India fleet, including "the *Martha*, Brown; the *Arethusa*, Dodds; and the *Atalanta*, Forbes." In addition, "the *Royal Charlotte*, Souter" arrived at Cowes. Intelligence revealed that "the *Arethusa* parted with the *Amelia* in lat.47.30. long.13.20.west, and presently afterwards fell in with four large French ships of war, one of which chased her, but she escaped by steering a different course, in very hazy weather. The next day, she fell in with the *Betsey* of Providence, an American ship, that had been chased by one of the above men of war, two of which are 44 gun frigates. They had with them two Dutch prizes."[107]

The *Gazette*'s 31 May Marine Intelligence section listed the following arrivals in Britain from Jamaica: "The *Jane*, Gammell; *St. Thomas*, Drew; *Betsey*, Kent; *Amelia*, Aires; *Thomas Henry*, Kirkpatrick; *Catherine*, Singleton; *Cowley*, George; *Prince*, Gordon; *Norfolk*, Jessup; *Sarah*, Potter; *New Lioness*, Ritchie. The *Prince*, Gordon, from this island, is arrived at Ramsgate, and on shore there."[108] On 14 June, it noted, "The *Leviathan*, Warden, from this island, arrived at London the 18th of April, and the *Betsey and Susan*, Harvey, on the 15th."[109] On 28 June, the *Gazette* reported, "The *Leviathan*, Warden, from this island, arrived at Gravesend the 21st of April. The *Lyon*, King; *Alfred*, Bryan; *Barbadoes*, Moyre; *Nancy*, Campbell; and *Countess of Galway*, Elgin; from this island, are arrived at Penzance."[110]

Captain Lawford's Court-Martial

In his letter of 3 April 1794 to Secretary of the Admiralty Philip Stephens, John Ford penned that HMS *Success* had arrived at Port Royal from "the Caymaynas on the 30th of March with Captain Lawford, the Officers, & part of the Company of the *Convert*, I immediately gave Directions for a Court Martial to be assembled in order to try them for the Loss of that Ship, and enclose herewith a Copy of the Sentence of the Court upon that occasion, and of the Orders Captain Lawford was under."[111]

A court-martial was standard for the loss of any naval ship. All officers and crew were tried. The commander in chief on the station would convene the court-martial but could not serve on the court. The case would be tried by no fewer than five or no more than thirteen captains or admirals, the second in command on the station usually presiding. The person on trial was allowed counsel, while the court was advised on legal matters by the judge advocate. Ultimately, the court's judgment was arrived at by vote.[112]

The Trial

On 30 March 1794, John Ford, commodore and commander in chief of His Majesty's ships and vessels at Jamaica, ordered a court-martial to inquire into the conduct of Captain John Lawford, the officers and company of His Majesty's late ship *Convert* at the time the frigate and nine ships of her convoy wrecked, on 8 February 1794, on the reefs of Grand Cayman while proceeding to Great Britain "agreeably to the Order of the said Commander in Chief, and to Try them for the same Accordingly."[113]

The court-martial was held on board HMS *Success* on 1 April (figure 26). The transcript of the trial comprises a summary of the court's orders and its conclusions; a copy of Lawford's letter of 20 February to Commodore Ford; a copy of the Commodore's original orders for the convoy on 5 January; detailed questioning of Lawford, his officers, and Richard Davy, the Sailing Master of *Success*, together with cross-examination by Lawford; and a closing statement of the court's findings.

Captain Francis Roberts of *Success*, the senior captain on the Jamaica station, presided. Other members of the court included the captains of the four vessels found at anchor in the harbor at Port Royal when *Success* arrived from Grand Cayman: Patrick Sinclair of *Iphigenia*, William Albany Otway of *Powerful*, George Gregory of *Europa*, and George H. Stephens of *Goelan*. Judge Advocate R. Holmes was present.

Captain Lawford and the officers and company of *Convert* who were present in Jamaica were brought into court, and Commodore Ford's order that the court-martial be held was read. Before the trial, the members of the court and the judge advocate took oaths as required by an act of Parliament titled "an Act for amending, explaining, and reducing into one Act of Parliament, the Laws relating to the Government of His Majestys Ships, Vessels, and forces by Sea."

John Lawford's letter from Grand Cayman of 20 February 1794, describing the shipwreck episode to John Ford, and Commodore Ford's 5 January orders to Captain Lawford to escort the convoy to Britain were read to the court. After the documents were admitted as evidence, the court asked Captain Lawford if he had charges to make against any of *Convert*'s officers or crew regarding the loss of the frigate or their later conduct. He had none. Subsequently, five of *Convert*'s officers were brought before the court for questioning; Third Lieutenant John Allen, however, was unable to offer any firsthand evidence.

First to be admitted and sworn was First Lieutenant Bogue. The court

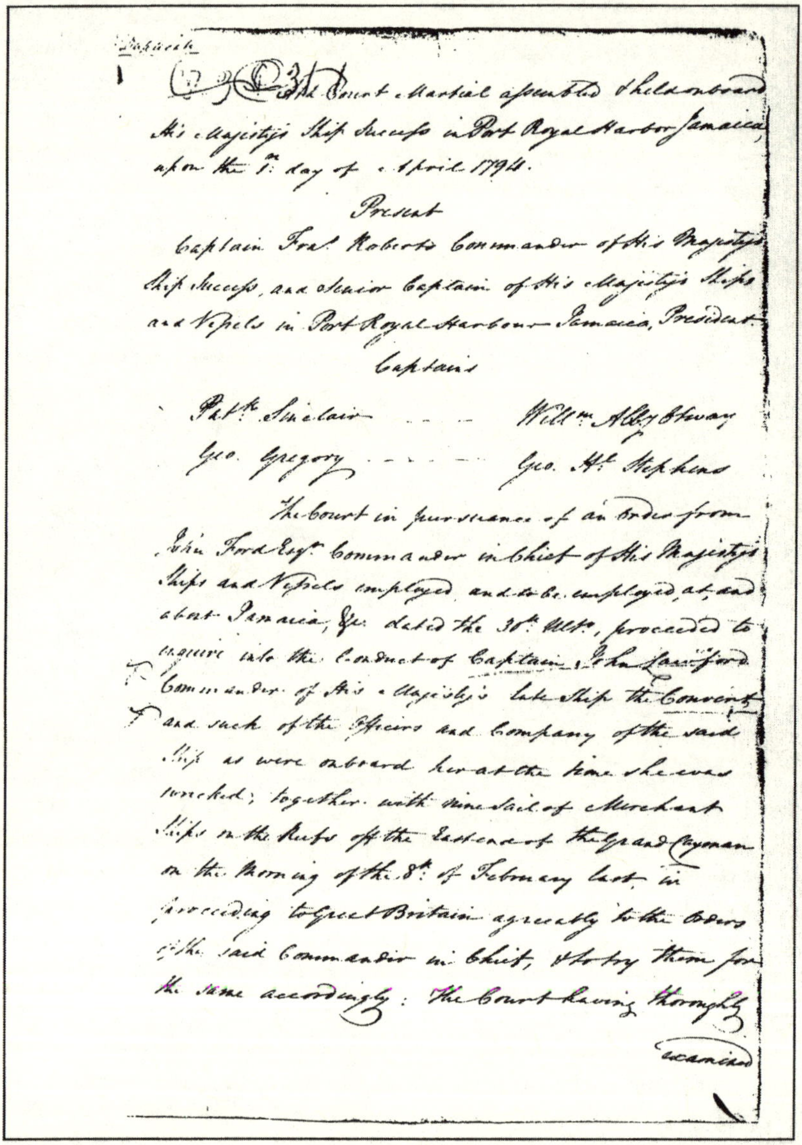
The Court Martial assembled & held on board His Majesty's Ship Success in Port Royal Harbor Jamaica, upon the 1st day of April 1794.

Present

Captain Fras. Roberts Commander of His Majesty's Ship Success, and Senior Captain of His Majesty's Ships and Vessels in Port Royal Harbour Jamaica, President.

Captains

Patk. Sinclair — Willm. Albany Otway

Geo. Gregory — Geo. Hy. Stephens

The Court in pursuance of an Order from John Ford Esqr. Commander in Chief of His Majesty's Ships and Vessels employed and to be employed, at, and about Jamaica, &c. dated the 30th Ulto., proceeded to enquire into the Conduct of Captain John Lawford Commander of His Majesty's late Ship the Convert and such of the Officers and Company of the said Ship as were on board her at the time she was wrecked; together with nine sail of Merchant Ships on the Reefs off the East end of the Grand Cayman on the Morning of the 8th of February last, in proceeding to Great Britain agreeably to the Orders of the said Commander in Chief, & to try them for the same accordingly: The Court having thoroughly examined

Figure 26. Excerpt from the court-martial of Captain John Lawford. Courtesy of the Public Record Office, Kew.

asked him to describe the circumstances regarding *Convert* from the time that the convoy departed Jamaica to the time the frigate went ashore in Grand Cayman. He explained that on 6 February 1794, the convoy had sailed from the west end of Jamaica. They steered west-northwest until evening and then furled *Convert*'s sails so as not to outsail the "bad sailing vessels." When his watch began at 8:00 a.m. on 7 February, the frigate was assisting a leaky schooner that had fired a distress signal, and the convoy was standing by. The convoy sailed again at noon, and at 1:00 p.m. *Convert* sailed ahead of the fleet to sight the land (Grand Cayman). At two thirty, two guns were fired from behind, and Lawford ordered that the crew be summoned and that the frigate stand back into the fleet. The distress signal had been fired by the same leaky schooner, which feared that *Convert* would leave it. *Convert* led the fleet, steering west-northwest until 5:45 p.m. At that time her sails were furled and her course was altered to the west, to show the convoy the intended course and the sail to carry for the night, and a signal was made to that effect. In the next few hours, *Convert* fired swivels at a few merchantmen that were disobediently running ahead of her; otherwise, little of note happened before Lieutenant Bogue was relieved at 8:00 p.m. At 2:30 a.m. on 8 February, he was awakened and told there was firing ahead. He arrived on deck and saw the sails being hoisted. The helm was ordered "to be put a port, in order to haul to the Northward," when the master called out from forward "a ship ahead almost close to us." The merchant ship on the other tack "drove athwart hawse and carried away our Jibb Boom." It took ten minutes to get clear of the other vessel. As *Convert* was maneuvering to stand to the northward, the merchantman again fell on board the starboard bow and "paid the Ship off before the Wind." Before they could extricate themselves, *Convert* struck while the master was forward, clearing anchors and sounding. The sails were furled and the crew was taking down the topgallant yards and masts when the carpenter reported a leak. In ten minutes the water was up to the orlop deck. The ship had bilged and could not be saved. The boats were hoisted out, and, with great difficulty, all but five people were saved.

Captain Lawford then took up the questioning. Lieutenant Bogue testified that the master had taken a good observation with a sextant at noon on 7 February. The master had informed him, as officer of the watch, when the sun had come up.

During the voyage, *Convert* had frequently signaled the sternmost ships to make more sail and the headmost vessels to shorten sail and keep to their stations, but their crews had paid little attention. A 6-pounder had been moved from the quarterdeck to the forecastle to facilitate the firing of shots to make them comply. Bogue believed that all possible efforts had been made to save *Convert*. He did not know if there was any error in the compasses used on board. When they had shortened sail the second time, Jamaica was out of sight, and by the master's reckoning they believed that they were within eighteen leagues of Cayman. On 7 February, during Bogue's watch, between six and eight in the evening, *Convert* was steered west, and after that time he did not know her course. At 8:00 p.m., when Bogue was relieved by Second Lieutenant Earnshaw, all but one or two vessels were astern, and those were falling back because they had been fired at. The convoy was generally well collected, and signal guns and signal lights were always kept in readiness in case they were needed in the night. The only order Bogue had had to deliver to Lieutenant Earnshaw was to steer west.

Second Lieutenant William Earnshaw was then admitted and sworn. He testified that he had not been on deck when the convoy left Jamaica between noon and one o'clock in the afternoon on 6 February. They had steered W by N 1/2 N until between eleven o'clock and noon on 7 February, at which time *Convert* was brought to, to wait for the convoy.

At six o'clock they bore up and steered west. Earnshaw's first watch began at 8:00 p.m. Captain Lawford, with great anxiety, had delivered orders to the second lieutenant at ten, telling him to keep ahead of the convoy, to keep the merchantmen in their stations, to keep a commanding view of the fleet, and to be particular about the course that was steered. Earnshaw had obeyed all these orders. Lawford also had told Earnshaw that when he was relieved by the master he should ask him to "prick off the run of the Ship upon the Chart" from the departure in Jamaica, to be certain that it was correct, and to work the back bearings and distance from Jamaica. Earnshaw passed these orders on to the master. A quarter of an hour before he was relieved, the second lieutenant went around the ship and observed that the convoy was well collected. At midnight, when he was relieved, *Convert*'s course was west. During the middle watch, Earnshaw was awakened and told that a ship ahead had fired guns and that the crew had been summoned. He went up on deck, to the forecastle, to find the frigate's topsails set and one of the merchantmen almost on board her, and he informed the officers on the quarterdeck. They unsuccessfully tried to "weather the ship." The merchantman, on the other tack, luffed up, and not seeing *Convert*, as it was very dark, ran on board the starboard bow. A man on the foreyard called out, "Land and Breakers ahead, close on Board us." As *Convert* cleared the merchant ship and maneuvered to haul to the northward, she struck.

Captain Lawford then questioned Lieutenant Earnshaw, who also apparently believed that all efforts had been made to save *Convert*. In general, he said, the convoy had disregarded *Convert*'s signals. After leaving Jamaica, the convoy had had moderate breezes until the following day at noon, when the wind died. Later in the afternoon, the winds picked up again and blew fresh breezes until the ship struck; that evening there were also squalls. According to Earnshaw, it had been a hazy, cloudy night, and they could not see very far. During his watch (eight to midnight) on 7 February, the topsails were furled and the fore topmast staysail was set occasionally to keep the ship in her station. The second lieutenant thought that *Convert* might have cleared the reefs in hauling to the northward if the merchantman had not fallen on board her. He had heard the master of the merchantman that fired the distress signal say that there were three vessels on shore before his ship struck, and that another brig and ship had passed close to him while standing out to clear the reefs. One of these vessels, the ship, had also struck twice before clearing them.

Third Lieutenant John Allen was admitted and sworn, but then dismissed. He had been unable to do his duty that evening because of a wounded arm.

Master Thomas Popplewell was subsequently called into the court and sworn. The *Convert*'s logbook was produced, and he testified that it contained a true account of "the Transactions of the Ship." Like the others, he was asked to relate the circumstances of the loss of *Convert*. He noted that at noon on 6 February, South Negril bore east a distance of about twelve leagues, the observed latitude being 18° 09′ north. They steered W by N 1/2 N until eight the next morning when they brought to, to wait for the convoy to collect. At noon on 7 February they bore away west-northwest, the observed latitude being 18° 47′ north. He reckoned that Grand Cayman bore NW 1/2 N about eighteen leagues. An hour later, at one o'clock, *Convert* had sailed ahead of the convoy, steering the same course until three in the afternoon, to make land. When they heard a gun fired from astern, they sailed back to the fleet and found that the signal had been made by a schooner that had sprung a leak. They tacked and steered west-northwest until five forty-five and then altered the course to the west. They maintained that course until twelve thirty in the morning of 8 February. The master then changed the course to west-northwest until two thirty, when a gun was heard. A second gun was heard, and its flash bore southwest from them. Popplewell notified Captain Lawford, who immediately came up on deck. Lawford gave orders to steer for the flash. All hands were rallied and the topsails were set when people on the foreyard called out "Land ahead and Breakers." *Convert* was hauled to the northward. A merchant ship on the other tack was near her. The people forward called out "hard a Starboard," but before anything could be done the merchantman fell on board

Convert. Eventually they were able to extricate themselves, the frigate being before the wind and the other vessel's head to the southeast. The ships collided again, and before they could disengage themselves they were very near the reef. As the merchantman cleared the frigate, *Convert* struck the reef.

Popplewell's answers to questions put by the court reveal that he believed the compasses on board *Convert* were good, but he had never taken an amplitude or azimuth to prove them. He said he had been through the Gulf of Florida several times and usually steered west-northwest from the west end of Jamaica to the Cayman Islands. He had always found that course to carry him to the southward of the Caymans, sometimes so far south that he didn't see them. He considered the Caymans to be fifty-two leagues from the west end of Jamaica. In light winds he had sometimes found a current to set him to the westward when sailing from Jamaica to the Caymans, but in fresh breezes he did not have any reason to think there was any current. He believed that his observations between Jamaica and the Caymans were good and could be depended on. He had the direction of the course *Convert* was to steer, with the approval of the captain, from the time the frigate left Jamaica until it wrecked.

The court pointed out that, by the log, there was no distance recorded for the ship on 7 February between noon and 4:00 p.m. They questioned this omission. *Convert*'s master said that the winds were light, and the ship made so little progress that the heaving of the log (not the logbook), a device for measuring the vessel's speed through the water, or the distance that she had sailed, was omitted as inconsequential. In working the ship's way, he had not allowed for any distance to be run for those four hours on the course set in the logbook, W by N 1/2 N. When he worked the bearings to Grand Cayman (NW 1/2 N, eighteen leagues), at noon on 7 February, he had not allowed anything for a current because he wasn't aware of one. He found his reckoning by observation to agree with the record. He had the watch when *Convert* went ashore. The weather on that night, during his watch, had been "dark, Cloudy, and blowing Fresh." *Convert*'s course had been changed from west to west-northwest at midnight because Popplewell considered that they were far enough to the south and west, and also clear of the Cayman Islands. Northerly winds were prevailing, and he deemed it advisable to haul to the northward in order to make Cape Corrientes on the western tip of Cuba. In Captain Lawford's presence, at midnight, Popplewell pricked off on the chart the run of the ship and the bearings and distance of the Cayman Islands, before advising that the course be altered to the northward, but he had not worked the distance back to Jamaica. When he advised altering the course, he believed that Cayman bore north-northeast twelve leagues. At noon on 7 February,

Master's Mate Hutchins and Midshipmen Campbell and Sherwin had observed with him. He allowed a variation of half a point to the east in correcting his courses. Popplewell attributed his being so far off course, and out of his reckoning, to a strong northerly current, pointing to these factors as the cause of the shipwrecks. The masters of vessels that sailed to Cayman from Jamaica to salvage the cargoes pointed out that they too had been set considerably to the northward of their reckoning by currents. When the convoy sailed from Jamaica, however, he had no suspicion that there was any current. When he first saw the breakers, they were on *Convert*'s starboard bow, and the ship's head was to the southwest. At noon on 7 February, the master had taken his observation with a sextant that he had used for three or four years. Finally, Popplewell told the court that he had gone through the Gulf of Florida several times in the merchants' service, not the king's service. He had been master of a brig of about two hundred tons and had made the voyage about twelve times.

Convert's master was further questioned by Captain Lawford. Popplewell indicated that they had spoken with the crews of various merchantmen that sailed to Cayman from Jamaica after the wreck occurred, and all were driven to the north of their reckoning. One had even made Little Cayman (some ninety miles northeast of Grand Cayman) instead of Grand Cayman. HMS *Success* had also been to the north of her reckoning. Popplewell believed that if the ships of the convoy had kept to their stations, with nothing between *Convert* and the breakers, they would have had enough time to warn the merchantmen to haul off. No ships went ashore after *Convert* signaled for the convoy to disperse and provide for their own safety, except one that had previously been struck by another ship. That ship ran aground after daylight to save the lives of the people on board. He also believed that *Convert* would have cleared the reefs if she had not been struck, and that all possible efforts had been made to save the frigate and warn the convoy to save themselves. He had observed the latitude almost every day while they were on shore in Grand Cayman and reckoned the latitude where *Convert* went ashore to be 19° 26′ N.

Master's Mate James Hutchins was then sworn. Other than testifying to the logbook's authenticity and his own observation, with a reliable instrument, of the latitude at noon on 7 February (18° 47′ N), Hutchins was unable to offer much information. He had been berthing the crew and numbering hammocks, so did not know why no distance had been allowed in the ship's log between noon and four o'clock in the afternoon on 7 February. He had stood watch with Second Lieutenant Earnshaw between 8:00 p.m. and midnight.

The court subsequently examined Lieutenant Bogue about the ship's log.

He said that he came up on deck as officer of the watch at noon on 6 February, when the convoy departed Jamaica. When asked about the fact that no distance was allowed the ship from noon to 4:00 p.m. on 7 February, he said that he believed it had been marked on the log board by Midshipman Campbell, the mate of the watch, and must have been left out in copying; he did not know what figures were marked, or if the instrument for measuring the distance had been used during the four-hour period. Under questioning by Captain Lawford, Bogue said that he believed *Convert* would have cleared the breakers if the merchant ship had not run on board her a second time.

Bogue said he believed that every effort had been made to save *Convert* and to ensure the safety of the merchantmen. He also believed that if the ships of the convoy had kept to their stations, with nothing between *Convert* and the breakers, that they might have been warned in time to haul off. Lawford asked Bogue if he remembered seeing him on deck on 8 February after the alarm was sounded. Bogue replied that Captain Lawford was on deck before him.

Midshipman Colin Campbell was admitted and sworn. He remembered the departure from Jamaica on 6 February, and was the mate of the watch on 7 February from noon until four o'clock in the afternoon. He was confident that the log board had been marked during the watch but did not know what distance was recorded during those four hours. He did not know why no distance was allowed the ship in the logbook during the watch, and could not say if the instrument for measuring the distance had been used.

Richard Davy, master of *Success*, stated that the latitude where *Convert* went ashore was 19° 25′ or 19° 26′ N. When questioned by Captain Lawford, he said that in his passage from Jamaica to the Caymans in *Success*, he had found there to be a considerable northerly current, which had set *Success* nine to ten leagues north of his reckoning.

After the examinations concluded, Captains Roberts, Sinclair, Otway, Gregory, and Stephens deliberated. The court's opinion was that "the Misfortune was occasioned by a strong Current setting the Ships very considerably to the Northward of their Reckoning, and doth therefore adjudge that the said Captain John Lawford Commander of His Majesty's late Ship the *Convert*, the Officers and Company of the said Ship, be acquitted, and they are hereby acquitted accordingly."[114]

Oceanographic Data and the Court's Findings

Modern oceanographic research on the currents and oceanography of the Caribbean supports the conclusions drawn in the court-martial. The Equa-

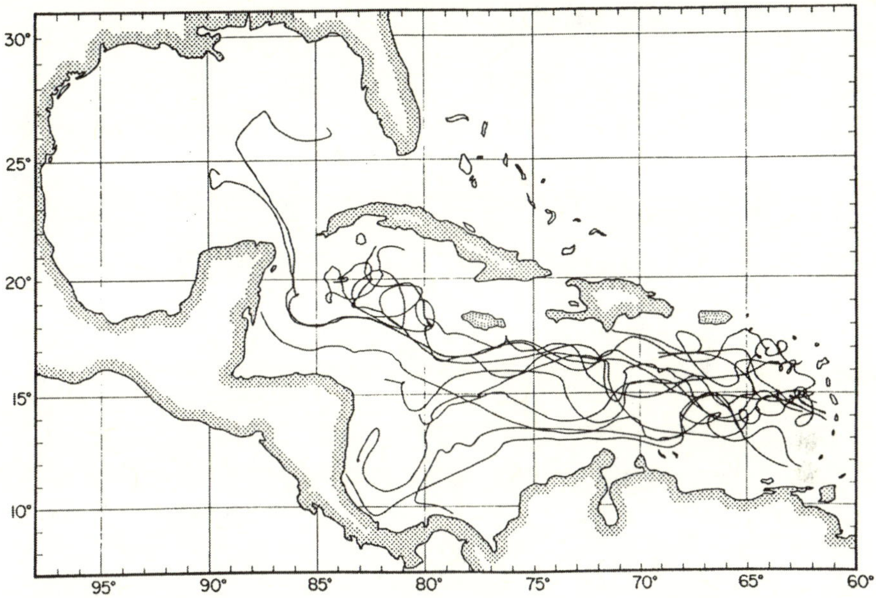

Map 13. Satellite-tracked drifting buoy data. West of Jamaica the current has a distinct northward component with active eddying in the Cayman Islands area. Figure 2 from Robert L. Molinari et al., "Surface Currents in the Caribbean Sea as Deduced from Lagrangian Observations," *Journal of Geophysical Research* 86, no. C7 (1981): 6537–42, copyright by the American Geophysical Union.

torial Current is the region's prime influence. Entering the Caribbean Sea from the south, through the Lesser Antilles, it flows predominantly westward, and then exits through the Yucatán Channel where it joins the Gulf Stream (see map 4). Oceanographic investigations, including studies based on satellite-tracked drifting buoy data, suggest that west of Jamaica the Equatorial Current has a distinct northward component with very active eddying in the Cayman Islands area (map 13).[115] The accompanying illustration is a "Composite plot of buoy trajectories collected in the Caribbean Sea and Gulf of Mexico from October 1975 through June 1976." As such the research scientifically documents the presence of irregular currents and eddies that surely could have contributed to the *Convert*'s being out of her reckoning when the frigate was lost on the East End reefs of Grand Cayman, in the 8 February 1794 Wreck of the Ten Sail.

8

What Remains

Links to the Past

From the sixteenth century to modern times, the reefs of the low-lying Cayman Islands have claimed hundreds of ships of more than fifteen nationalities, among them the Dutch West Indiaman *Dolphijn* (1630); the British sloop HMS *Jamaica* (1715); the Spanish brigantine *San Miguel* (1730); the pirate ship *Morning Star* (1722); merchantmen of British, Spanish, Norwegian, North, South, and Central American, and Canadian origin; Caymanian schooners; a twentieth-century Liberty ship; and other vessels. But the most famous shipwreck disaster in Cayman's history remains the Wreck of the Ten Sail.

Earlier chapters provided a historical and geographical context for HMS *Convert* and nine of her merchant convoy and described in detail the events surrounding the wrecking. Folklore has linked the 225-year-old episode with the present. And yet there is more. The seas hold vestiges of the ten British ships that, on 8 February 1794, ventured too near the windward reefs of Grand Cayman.

The captains and crews of the Wreck of the Ten Sail heavily salvaged their ships, and later Caymanians continued the efforts. The remaining features and artifacts, affected by exposure to the sea, eventually reached a state of equilibrium, occasionally disturbed by violent weather. During recent times, however, the shipwrecks have suffered the impact of modern human intervention.

Over the past half century, snorkelers and scuba divers have recovered many items from the shipwrecks of the Cayman Islands, including those located on the eastern reefs of Grand Cayman. Many of these collectors are curiosity seekers, fascinated by an object or desirous of a cannon or an anchor for display in front of a home, hotel, or business. Most of them have been unaware that they are contributing to the destruction of rare and nonrenewable historical information and material culture. When people unscientifically remove artifacts from their archaeological contexts, those artifacts lose their ability to tell the story of Cayman's past. Without proper treatment, the usual fate of marine artifacts, particularly iron objects, is rapid deterioration and eventual loss.

In the past twenty-five years, international attention has contributed to developing formal instruments to protect underwater cultural heritage, including the ICOMOS International Charter on the Protection and Management of Underwater Cultural Heritage (1996), which prescribes best practice, and the UNESCO Convention on the Protection of the Underwater Cultural Heritage (2001), a legal document; both can be accessed online. Additionally, the author has contributed to publications related to the status of protection of underwater cultural heritage in the Cayman Islands and the Caribbean region, which are available.[1]

In an attempt to regulate the recovery of objects from the islands' historical shipwrecks, the Cayman Islands government enacted the Abandoned Wreck Law (5 of 1966) (1997 Revision). This law claims all historical shipwrecks located on the seabed of the islands' territorial waters (twelve nautical miles) for more than fifty years, with ownership of artifacts "vested in Her Majesty in right of Her Government of the Islands." While this clause provides blanket protection for historical shipwrecks, the law has fundamental deficiencies. First, it does not recognize shipwrecks as cultural property. Second, it ensures that the government receives a percentage of the value of artifacts from shipwrecks, and once the government enters into an agreement, it is obliged to return to the prospector at least one-half of the value of the wreck. If the government retains salvaged artifacts, it must pay the prospector a percentage of their appraised value. Essentially, the government gives up rights to more than 50 percent of a shipwreck and then pays the prospector to buy it back. Violators of the Abandoned Wreck Law may be fined up to CI$2,000 and/or imprisoned for up to two years; unlawfully held artifacts from abandoned wrecks may be seized.[2]

In the 1990s the Ministry of Culture established a Marine Archaeology Committee with a view to achieving new legislation. Since this legislation has yet to be enacted, the committee can study and benefit from the exemplary standards set in the 1996 ICOMOS International Charter on the Protection and Management of Underwater Cultural Heritage and the 2001 UNESCO Convention on the Protection of the Underwater Cultural Heritage.

The Cayman Islands government established the Abandoned Wreck Law largely in response to its receipt of applications from treasure hunters to prospect for and salvage wrecks in Caymanian waters. Fortunately, the government has not granted licenses to these salvage groups, so the law has succeeded in preventing large-scale, indiscriminate excavation of historical shipwreck sites. But the small-scale removal of objects, one at a time, went unchecked for many years. In 1991, however, when the Wreck of the

Ten Sail Project's underwater archaeological work began, marine enforcement officers (in charge of environmental concerns) began to assist the archaeologists in informing people that it is unlawful to collect artifacts from shipwreck sites. Since that date, the Cayman Islands National Museum has consistently worked to educate the public by demonstrating that underwater archaeology and conservation of marine artifacts from shipwrecks is vital if Caymanians are to preserve the tangible remains of their maritime heritage for future generations to study and enjoy. And of course, intact wrecks on the seabed are a major attraction for visiting divers.

Over the past three decades, the National Museum, Department of Environment, National Archive, and National Trust, assisted at times by the Legal Department, have worked together on a variety of issues related to historical shipwrecks and land-based maritime heritage sites. They have advised ministries on protection of sites and on the need to develop appropriate legislation. Site inventories have grown. These agencies formed a Maritime Heritage Partnership that advocates a three-tiered approach—to protect, manage, and interpret the Islands' maritime heritage sites. They have worked toward the creation of a dedicated Cayman Islands Maritime Archaeology Program (CIMAP, pronounced "Sea Map") to develop and implement the initiatives of the partnership, which they would serve as advisors and facilitators. In 2003, they launched their first initiative, a land-based Maritime Heritage Trail, accessible to all, that widely promotes the Islands' maritime legacy. Encompassing thirty-six sites located throughout the three Cayman Islands, the interactive trail, interpreted through a colorful poster/brochure and signs marking the trail stops, combines heritage, education, and recreational tourism. A second initiative is to create a series of shipwreck preserves, the first being at the site of the *Glamis*, built in Dundee, Scotland, in 1876 and wrecked under Norwegian flag in 1913. Certain robust shipwreck sites, such as *Glamis*, are suitable for interpretation for snorkelers and divers. At these sites people can visit shipwrecks that are not fragile and that have legal protection and a management plan in place. A third initiative involves earlier sites that are sensitive and fragile—for example, HMS *Convert* and the Wreck of the Ten Sail, and HMS *Jamaica*, lost after chasing pirates. These sites, deserving of special protection, study, and management, have even greater potential to reveal unique histories available nowhere else in the world. Publications, museum exhibitions, and filmed documentaries can result to share knowledge with the public. CIMAP could bring together and develop all aspects of maritime archaeology undertaken in the Cayman Islands during the past four decades, for the benefit of the public, through education, culture, environment, and tourism.

Archaeology before 1990

At the request of the Cayman Islands government, the Institute of Nautical Archaeology (INA), a nonprofit scientific and educational organization based at and affiliated with Texas A&M University, conducted a professional underwater archaeological survey of Little Cayman, Cayman Brac, and Grand Cayman during the summers of 1979 and 1980.[3] In the mid-1980s, with permission from the government, the Indiana University Department of Physical Education, Scuba Research and Development Group (SRD) conducted noninvasive fieldwork on shipwreck sites that were possibly associated with the Wreck of the Ten Sail.[4]

The 1979 and 1980 Institute of Nautical Archaeology Surveys

In 1978 the Cayman Islands government initiated inquiries aimed at having a scientific archaeological survey conducted to locate and evaluate the shipwreck resources of the Cayman Islands. Their representatives approached the Institute of Nautical Archaeology. Although INA had not previously sponsored fieldwork in the Caribbean, it agreed to assist the Cayman Islands. Roger C. Smith, a research associate with INA, led a team of experienced archaeologists in two phases of underwater fieldwork in 1979–80. According to Smith, INA initiated the Cayman Islands Project for two reasons: a survey was obviously needed, and the work might demonstrate to other West Indian nations that "scientific scrutiny, rather than the hunt for treasure, can bring aspects of national heritage to light."[5] The resulting field investigations were the first scientific surveys for historical shipwrecks ever conducted in the Cayman Islands.

To locate sites, the INA team used remote sensing devices including a magnetometer, visual survey methods, and information offered by local informants. They targeted likely shipwreck areas, particularly Cayman's fringing reefs, for the search. In 1979 they used remote sensing procedures, accompanied by visual methods, for the survey of Little Cayman. In 1980, during the surveys around Grand Cayman and Cayman Brac, the team, including this author, placed more emphasis on visual search techniques. Visual survey proved to be extremely effective in the clear waters of Cayman, especially in shallow reef zones that are inaccessible to boats. Smith describes the methods used: "After a site was located, its precise position was surveyed from existing benchmarks and plotted on a master chart of the areas covered by the investigation. Features such as anchors, cannons, ship's structure, and fittings were carefully measured and recorded. Limited testing by selective excavation or surface sampling was undertaken to obtain diagnostic artifacts useful in determining a general date or cultural affiliation for each site. These artifacts often included pottery sherds, clay smoking-pipe fragments, bits and pieces of ship's equipment, or crew's possessions."[6] After the artifacts were examined, measured, typed, and photographed, most were returned to the sites from which they had been recovered. Researchers, however, kept certain items for further analysis or public display because of their historical significance.[7]

During 1979 and 1980, INA archaeologists recorded fifty-five archaeological sites on Grand Cayman, seventeen sites on Little Cayman, and five sites on Cayman Brac.[8] Most of these sites were associated with shipwrecks, but several were terrestrial sites. Maps and documentary files detailing site locations, features, and tentative interpretations about these seventy-seven sites form the core of the National Shipwreck Inventory, which has grown to over 140 sites in 2019.[9] Most of the artifacts that were recovered during the Cayman Islands Project were later buried in labeled bags at their sites of origin. Although a law had been passed in 1979 mandating the establishment of the Cayman Islands National Museum, there was not yet a public repository to curate the artifacts; a museum officer was appointed in the mid-1980s, and the National Museum officially opened to the public in 1990. Nonetheless, artifacts that were not returned to the sea after the conclusion of the INA survey were stored as part of the future National Museum's collections. Roger Smith held the Cayman Islands Project photographs and the drawings of artifacts recovered during the fieldwork until he published the *Maritime Heritage of the Cayman Islands*, after which time he deposited data with the Cayman Islands National Museum.[10]

During the Cayman Islands Project, the INA team was to locate and record shipwrecks situated around all three of the Cayman Islands; they spent a month surveying exclusively the reefs of Grand Cayman's East End (map 14). Smith pointed out that twenty-four shipwreck-related sites were located on this six-mile stretch of windward reef, and he called the area "a virtual graveyard of unfortunate vessels."[11] Artifacts observed on these sites varied from ceramics and glass to cannons and anchors and suggested that the sites ranged in date from the late eighteenth century until the mid-1960s. While in-depth study of the shipwrecks was not among the goals of the Cayman Islands Project, the INA crew concluded that several sites were likely to represent remains of HMS *Convert* and the wrecked merchantmen of her convoy.

One site, designated GC 017, held buried cannons thought to be from the frigate *Convert*.[12] At least two guns had been removed earlier from this general area for display on land, but the project identified and plotted the locations of five others; one had been taken from the site and dropped half a mile away, across the East End Sound toward shore. The transported cannon, recognized by its dimensions and inscriptions as a piece of French

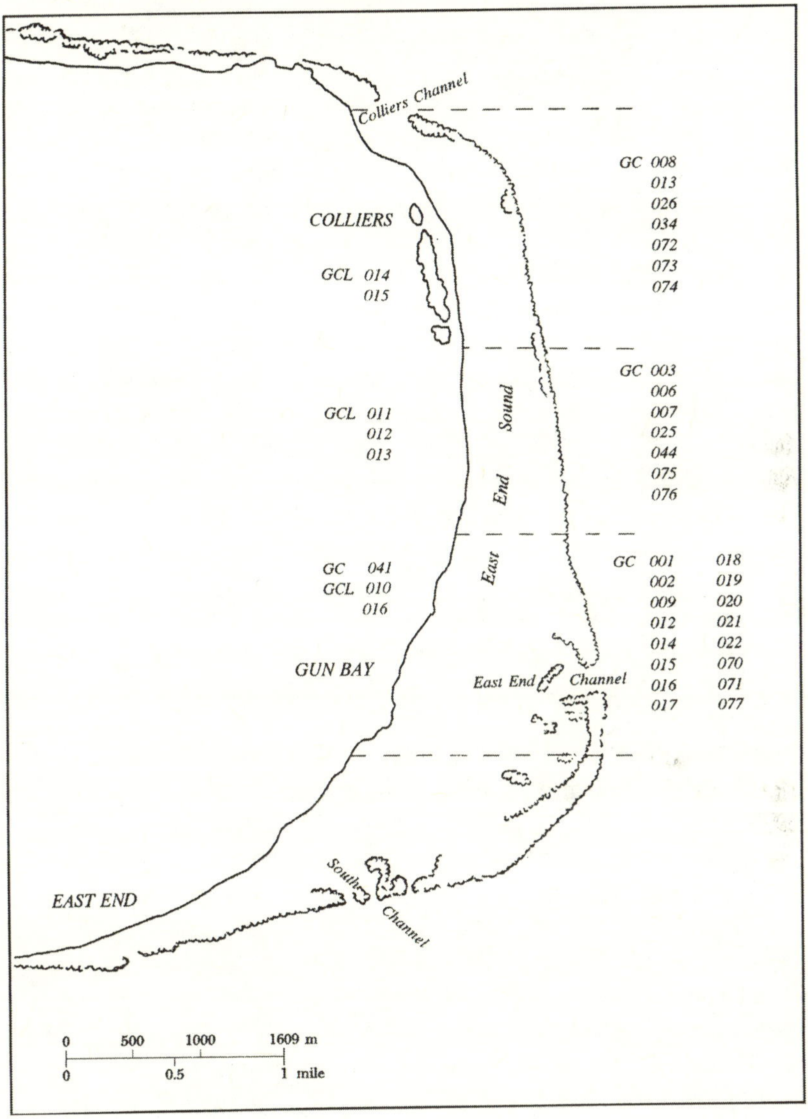

Map 14. East End reefs of Grand Cayman with general shipwreck zones containing archaeological sites investigated in 1980 and/or 1991. Drawn by R. L. Craig.

ordnance, bore markings on the base ring and trunnions that would eventually be used to identify it precisely: on the end of the left trunnion were the letters "BA" (the right trunnion remained concreted); on the base ring was inscribed "A ◦ 1781" and "N°45 ◦ P3347."[13] This site and other possible Wreck of the Ten Sail sites were further investigated in 1991 and are discussed in detail later in this chapter.

The Indiana University Scuba Research and Development Group Surveys

Indiana University's Department of Physical Education, Scuba Research and Development Group (SRD), headed by Charles Beeker, approached the Cayman Islands government in the mid-1980s and secured permission to investigate possible Wreck of the Ten Sail sites. The SRD group had permission to locate and document sites through remote sensing, mapping, photography, and video recording, but not to excavate or collect artifacts. SRD received small grants for the survey from the Cayman Islands government, the Professional Association of Diving Instructors (PADI), and Indiana University. The SRD surveys were field-school projects and took place in three sessions, each lasting a few weeks. Fifteen to twenty sport divers from the university, who were learning the fundamentals of underwater archaeology from an experienced nautical archaeologist retained by SRD, documented the sites.[14] While the 1980 INA survey located and professionally recorded more sites at East End than SRD, Beeker's group found several new sites. Most of their documentation, however, involved three shipwreck-related sites located in the vicinity of East End Channel, one shipwreck site in East End Sound, and a beach site, all previously recorded by the INA team.[15] Sites GC 001, GC 002, and GC 021 are post-eighteenth-century sites, clearly not related to *Convert* and her convoy; GC 017 and GC 041 have late eighteenth-century components and are almost certainly associated with the Wreck of the Ten Sail.[16]

Fieldwork organizer Charles Beeker wrote to individuals and archival repositories in Britain and France seeking information about *Convert* and about artifacts found on the eighteenth- and nineteenth-century sites. In a letter written on 7 April 1986, French naval scholar Jean Boudriot identified a specific cannon described by Beeker. It had recently been salvaged from site GC 017.[17] Boudriot explained that from Beeker's description, *Convert*, ex-*Inconstante*, was armed with 12-pounder cannons (long-pattern guns) that conformed to the official French Regulations of 1779. He suggested that Beeker's cited weight for the gun, 2,200 kg, was not accurate, pointing out that 1,650 kg was more likely (he speculated that concretions on the cannon might account for the difference).[18] Boudriot interpreted the inscriptions that Beeker had observed on the gun: "BA" indicated the name of the master of the forge, Baynaud; "FN" identified the forge where the gun was cast, Forge-Neuve, an ironworks near Angoulême in Charente, France (see map 6); "1781" was the year the gun was cast; and "N°25" indicated the cast number (chronological, starting anew at N°1 each year). Boudriot told Beeker that the inscription "P33" indicated the weight of the gun in *livres* but suggested that the last two numbers were missing; according to the manufacturing standards the weight theoretically should have been "P3350." Boudriot said that two fleurs-de-lis were the trademark of Forge-Neuve. He wrote that Baynaud owned another forge, located in Ruelle, with a trademark featuring three fleurs-de-lis, always printed on the base ring.[19] Boudriot's identification of the cannon from site GC 017 suggests that it is a piece of the original French ordnance placed on board *L'Inconstante* and lost when the frigate wrecked.

A Quest for Cannons

Before undertaking the underwater archaeology phase of the Wreck of the Ten Sail Project the investigative team, including the author, decided to carry out some background research. We knew that numerous cannons had been salvaged from shipwreck sites located in the waters of Grand Cayman, particularly from East End. Therefore, beginning in December 1990, we conducted a search for cannons displayed on land. The plan was to discover the locale from which each cannon had been recovered and to determine whether any might be associated with the Wreck of the Ten Sail. By late 1991 the author, assisted by volunteers Jeanne Masters and Arthur and Helene Schindler, had photographed and measured about thirty cannons and obtained their salvage history. We found that nine guns were almost identical in their measurements and overall appearance. Among them were Baynaud's Forge-Neuve 1781 long-pattern 12-pounder, cast "N°45" (recorded by INA in 1980), and cast "N°25" (described and precisely identified by the SRD project in 1986). All came from site GC 017, located in the sound at East End.[20]

These French 12-pounders were cast according to the Regulations of 1778–79. They were long-pattern guns, specified in the Regulations to be 2.413 m in length from the face of the muzzle to the back of the base ring; in reality, due to casting variances in guns cast before about 1786, lengths often varied up to 2 or 3 cm from the standard. The bore diameter was to be 120.7 mm (see figure 7 and figure 9).[21]

One person raised three of the cannons, designated OR 18, OR 26, and OR 27, in the 1970s. He told us that he had cured the iron guns in fresh water for a year, after which he had scrubbed them with a wire brush. In the 1980s they were displayed in front of a business called the Sea Aquarium, but today they are located in the front yards of private residences. Although the original inscriptions have exfoliated with layers of rust corrosion, the salvager did record some details. He reported that OR 18, which is currently displayed in his front yard, bore the inscription "A 1781 N°R1333"; he did not record trunnion marks (figure 27). It is apparent that 1781, the

Figure 27. Cannon OR 18. Photograph by M. E. Leshikar-Denton.

date of casting, is correct, but the "N°R1333" is probably a misreading of the cannon's combined cast number and weight. We do not know what the "A" signifies, but "A" was also recorded on the cast "N°45" cannon (it may relate to the year and cast number or refer to Angoulême, the location of Forge-Neuve). When we recorded OR 18 in December 1990, the gun was in fair condition. It was freshly painted silver, with black bands; a black cannonball sealed the bore.

A second gun, designated OR 26, was marked "A 1781 N°6 P3308"; this suggests that the cannon was the sixth long-pattern 12-pounder cannon that was cast at an unidentified French forge in 1781. The weight, 3308 *livres*, may be slightly in error, or the gun may be lighter than the standard 3350 *livres*. In January 1991, OR 26 was in fair condition. Although it had been painted black, little paint remained. The cannon was spalling chunks of iron corrosion products.

According to the salvager, some of the markings on OR 27 came off when he was chipping the encrustation from the gun. Nonetheless, in November 1991, when the team recorded the cannon, we could discern traces of numbers and letters. The number 17 on the base ring probably represents part of the date; the letters "FN," which were legible on the right trunnion, suggest that the cannon was cast at Forge-Neuve. In November 1991, OR 27 was unpainted, but the surface was in fair condition. It is assumed that a rust inhibitor, such as a product containing phosphoric acid, must have been repeatedly applied to the surface in the past. This cannon, which is said to have been recovered in the 1970s, is mounted on a concrete carriage with the date 2-11-82 carved into it. The carriage is the same one that the cannon was mounted on at the Sea Aquarium, so the date may be associated with that venture.

At least four of the remaining six guns were lifted in the 1980s. Earl Smith removed OR 05 from the sea (figure 28). He had received approval from the Cayman Islands government, in a letter of 28 June 1979, to salvage two cannons from East End, although it is not known if a license for the work was prepared. The letter stipulated that the guns would remain the property of the government and "that the restoration of the cannons be carried out with acceptable conservation techniques."[22] Smith built a concrete vat around OR 05 and filled it with rainwater. He constructed a windmill-type device to keep the water circulating and left the gun in the fresh water from 1982 to 1985. Subsequently, he mounted the cannon in his front yard and painted it with a thick black automobile lacquer. OR 05 is the cannon that the 1980 INA crew had found transported halfway across the sound at East End. The INA team had noted its markings: "BA" on the left trunnion; "A ° 1781" and "N°45 ° P3347" on the base ring. By December 1990, when the artifact was recorded, the lettering had disappeared with rust corrosion, but Earl and Pat Smith noted that the letters "FN" had been apparent on the right trunnion at the time of salvage. They had kept two pieces of encrustation, one from a trunnion and the other from the base ring, which revealed the imprints "BA" and "81 [graphic fleurs-de-lis] N." These imprinted encrustations are now part of the National Museum Collection.

I noted three fleurs-de-lis when I examined the base-ring encrustation, but this is not consistent with the marking for a Forge-Neuve cannon that Jean Boudriot described to Charles Beeker in 1986 (two fleurs-de-lis). Thus, I assumed that the encrustation impression was misinterpreted. Nonetheless, I asked Jean Boudriot and David H. Roberts about this inconsistency. In a 19 April 1992 letter on behalf of Jean Boudriot, David Roberts reaffirmed that the Ruelle guns had three fleurs-de-lis, and he further noted that they were distinguished from the Forge-Neuve guns ("FN") by the mark "RV"; both carried the "BA." In a subsequent letter of 9 May 1992, however, Boudriot and Roberts wrote, "According to the registers for receiving guns at Rochefort Archives, there would be three fleurs-de-lys on the base ring."[23]

The Smiths' information filled in gaps regarding OR 05, and thus we know that the French cannon was cast in 1781, that its cast number was 45, that it weighed 3347 *livres*, and that it was forged at Baynaud's Forge-

A

B

Figure 28. *A*, cannon OR 05 as displayed in 1990. Photograph by M. E. Leshikar-Denton. *B*, trunnion detail showing "BA" in 1980. Photograph by K. C. Smith. *C*, base ring detail showing "No 45 ° P33." in 1980. Photograph by K. C. Smith. *D*, base ring detail showing "A ° 1781 (three graphic fleur de lys) N" in 1986. Photograph by Indiana University.

C

D

Figure 28. (*continued*)

Neuve, near Angoulême in Charente. The three fleurs-de-lis on the encrustation mold confirm that OR 05 was intended for Rochefort. This fact supports the theory that OR 05 was part of the original ordnance used aboard the Rochefort-built frigate *L'Inconstante*. In 1990 the team noted that OR 05 was in fair, bordering on poor, condition.

In November 1991, we documented OR 28 in the yard of a private residence. It had recently been moved there, but its salvage history and details of how it came to be in that location were not clear. The current keeper of the cannon thought that it was one of three guns previously displayed at the Sea Aquarium. Since three other cannons have been reported by the original salvager to be the Sea Aquarium cannons, the numbers do not add up. No inscriptions were discernible on the trunnions or base ring. Although the cannon had not been painted, it was in fair, bordering on poor, condition.

Three guns, OR 09, OR 10, and OR 11, are currently in public possession. The Cayman Islands National Trust displays OR 09 and OR 10 at Guard House Park at the entrance to Bodden Town. People raised the cannons in the early 1980s for display in Bodden Town during an annual festival called Pirates Week. Pat Smith of Gun Bay, who made written notes at the time the guns were salvaged, pointed out that at least one of these cannons had the letters "BA" and "FN" on the trunnions. She also noted that it bore the inscription "1781 N13 P3." Although the information is not complete, it suggests that the gun was cast in 1781 at Baynaud's Forge-Neuve and that the cast number was 13. In December 1990, when we recorded the cannons, none of the previously mentioned markings were evident. OR 09 and OR 10 were sparsely coated with a tar-like substance, and both were in poor condition.

A local resident donated OR 11 to the Cayman Islands National Trust prior to our survey. Most of the cannon's markings had disappeared with rust corrosion, but a faint "N—3" was discernible. When we recorded OR 11 in December 1990, it was in fair condition. The National Trust attempted to conserve this gun in the 1990s, but in 2001 turned its custody over to the National Museum. Subsequently, the museum set it up in electrolytic treatment, which was interrupted by Hurricane Ivan in 2004. At that point the gun was stored in a rust-inhibiting electrolyte, and completion of its conservation is pending.

Another cannon, OR 22, was retrieved from the sea in 1982, subsequently returned to the sea, and then recovered again.[24] When it was recorded in January 1991, it was stored in a concrete vat and was partially immersed in fresh water. Although the iron surface was cracking, the numbers and letters "1781 N°25 ° P3" were evident on the base ring; parts of the

Figure 29. Cannon OR 22 showing "N°25" on the base ring. Photograph by M. E. Leshikar-Denton.

gun were still encrusted (figure 29). OR 22 is the cannon that Jean Boudriot identified in 1986 for Charles Beeker of SRD. In 1991 the gun was in good, bordering on fair, condition. Subsequently, it was painted blue and mounted in the front yard of a private residence.

In 1993 OR 30, a cannon identical to the previously recorded nine guns, was discovered in a vat of water at a local marina. It was said to have been raised in the 1980s but was immersed again in the sea adjacent to the marina until its removal to the vat. The cannon retained its coralline encrustation and seemed to be in good condition. The National Museum made initial efforts to acquire custody of this cannon to conserve it through electrolytic treatment, but this never reached fruition. The gun has been moved, but its present location is not known.

Today, the Department of Environment monitors and protects site GC 017, from which these ten French cannons came. I discuss the Wreck of the Ten Sail Project's documentary work there under "Current Underwater Archaeology."

Other guns that we found during our survey of cannons located on land differed in style from the ten French guns. Salvors recovered Cannon OR 06 from the sea adjacent to the beach at Gun Bay, East End. The dimensions of this iron gun, including an overall measurement of 2.56 m (about 8 ft. 5 in.) from the face of the muzzle to the rear of the base ring, suggest that it is an eighteenth-century 9-pounder of British manufacture.[25] Unfortunately, it is in poor condition. Two other cannons remain buried in the sand adjacent to the area where OR 06 once lay.

Other guns located on land were vaguely reported to have come from East End. None of these pieces of ordnance are similar to the French guns from GC 017, but several had similar dimensions to OR 06. These also may be eighteenth-century British cannons, but because they are mostly in poor condition, and because their exact provenience is not known, they will not be discussed here.

The survey team recorded OR 21, a late eighteenth- or early nineteenth-century carronade with trunnions, at an East End residence in January 1991. On examination, it exhibited corrosion indicative of sea exposure. Efforts to research its origin have been unsuccessful.[26]

A Quest for Shipwrecks

Between July and November 1991, the author, assisted by a crew of avocational archaeology volunteers, conducted an underwater search for the wrecks of HMS *Convert* and her convoy. I obtained permission from the Cayman Islands government to carry out the fieldwork, under the auspices of the Cayman Islands National Museum. All of the volunteers were island residents who met each day to survey or catalog; thus, the usual housing and provisioning logistics associated with similar projects were eliminated. The Wreck of the Ten Sail Project was also supported in part by a Texas A&M University grant, and with the help of other generous individuals and organizations.

Background Information

Archaeological recording of shipwreck sites that were possibly associated with the Wreck of the Ten Sail began in the 1980s. The Institute of Nautical Archaeology's Cayman Islands Project and Indiana University's Scuba Research and Development group surveys did not center exclusively on locating and studying shipwrecks from this one eighteenth-century episode. Nonetheless, initial documentation of East End's shipwreck sites, particularly assessments carried out by the 1980 INA team, provided an excellent foundation and starting point for the Wreck of the Ten Sail Project.

At the outset of the underwater archaeological fieldwork in July 1991, we considered it practical to review the data related to the wrecks of *Convert* and her convoy. Oral history had traditionally placed the shipwrecks on Grand Cayman's East End, and previous archival research had confirmed the location. New information discovered in Britain's Public Record Office in February 1991 had further defined the search area. The *Royal Gazette* (22 February–1 March 1794) stated that HMS *Convert*, *William and Elizabeth*, *Britannia*, *Ludlow*, *Nancy*, *Moorhall*, *Richard*, *Fortune*, *Eagle*, and *Sally* wrecked together on the northeast end of Grand Cayman.[27] Significantly, during the 1980 Cayman Islands Project our crew had located eighteenth-century materials largely in this geographical zone.

The vessels were salvaged by their owners or their owners' representatives soon after wrecking and almost certainly were further salvaged by the Caymanians of the time. Since the ships had been lost on the windward reefs of Grand Cayman, they were vulnerable to nature's periodic tempests, including hurricanes, over the course of two hundred years. And especially during the previous thirty years, snorkelers and scuba divers had removed numerous artifacts, ranging from ceramic jars and copper nails to cannons, from the eastern reefs of Grand Cayman.

It is particularly useful that, on capture of *L'Inconstante* from the French, the British made an inventory of items belonging to the frigate; the Admiralty kept this record (see appendix A). The Admiralty acquired the sails, rigging, ordnance, and stores, along with the hull, for His Majesty's Service. Included were the frigate's twenty-six 12-pounder cannons and six 6-pounders and the carpenter's stores of 80 tons of pig iron ballast in 1,600 pigs. Since *Convert* sailed for Europe two months after her capture, it is logical to assume that the frigate's ordnance and stores changed little before her journey. The vessel would have undergone a major refit in Great Britain rather than in Jamaica. Thus, we were able to compare the postcapture inventory of *L'Inconstante* with the salvage account of *Convert* prepared by Royal Navy officers after the frigate wrecked and develop hypotheses about artifacts that might remain on the archaeological site—always keeping in mind that Caymanians carried out substantial further salvage.

The salvage account of *Convert* (see appendix F) reveals that some of the gunner's stores, including four swivels and eighteen gun carriages, were recovered by the Royal Navy, but apparently the 12- and 6-pounder cannons, along with much of the round and double-headed shot, were not immediately saved. They also recovered the stream anchor and kedge, but not the bower or sheet anchors. The salvage account did not mention the pig iron ballast. It appears, then, that when Captains Francis Roberts and John Lawford left Grand Cayman in HMS *Success*, the primary and secondary ordnance, sundry ordnance stores, the largest anchors, and substantial quantities of pig iron ballast, among many other items, were still aboard *Convert*.

The officers believed, however, that in moderate weather further salvage would be possible. Today, I can attest to the fact that there are days each year when the foaming East End reef settles into a mill-pond state, so the assessment was absolutely correct. Therefore, they gave William Bodden Sr. and Robert Knowles Clarke, two prominent Caymanians who owned some of the island's schooners, the exclusive right to "undertake so far as your abilities will allow to save whatever may be possible." They were to land the recovered goods at George Town, with compensation for their work. Bodden and Clarke agreed "to save all the remaining Stores, Provisions, & Guns together with all the Materials of the Wreck of His Majesty's Ship *Convert* such as Iron work, old Copper, and Copper fastening, and to give a most faithful & Just account of the same."[28] As mentioned earlier, Bodden and Clarke had probably been involved in helping Captain Lawford salvage *Convert* before the officer left Grand Cayman. They undoubtedly continued the recovery efforts, and the archaeology suggests that they were successful. Nonetheless, substantial material believed to belong to *Convert* remains on the seabed of East End Sound. And surprisingly, the Cayman Islands National Museum recently discovered fragments of possible *Convert* ceramics during emergency excavation of a historical stepwell in George Town that had been filled in with surrounding material during the late 1800s (see figure 1).

The Survey

The 1991 underwater archaeological fieldwork on the Wreck of the Ten Sail was designed to locate or relocate late eighteenth-century shipwreck sites that might be associated with *Convert* and the merchantmen; to document major features such as cannons, anchors, ships' fittings, and ballast, while determining the physical extent of the sites; to assess the remains and make recommendations regarding further investigation and future management of the resources; and to recover, conserve, and analyze samples of artifacts encountered during the survey. In 2019, with this book, I intend to bring the fascinating archival and archaeological discoveries together for a wide audience and excite the next generation of researchers to take it further.

We knew at the outset of the 1991 project that the sites previously recorded by the 1980 INA team might have been changed by storm activity over the centuries. Both Hurricane Allen in 1980 and Hurricane Gilbert in 1988 had undoubtedly affected the reefs and seabed; twentieth-century shipwrecks had collapsed in situ, with parts of them being carried over the reef into the lagoon.[29] And since that time Hurricane Ivan in 2004 seriously affected Grand Cayman.

In addition to considering recent changes, we attempted to determine whether any human modifications had affected the seabed, reefs, or channels of East End over the previous two hundred years. No specific information was available from various Cayman Islands government departments at the time, so we took a different approach. We examined the first printed British Admiralty chart of Grand Cayman, dated 1790, and based on a survey conducted by George Gauld in 1773 (see map 5). Gauld documented that a "Large Reef of Rocks" surrounded the eastern end of the island. He denoted present-day South Channel on his map as "Channel of 7 f." but did not indicate a cut in the region of East End Channel, which today is the largest channel.[30] While the information does not prove the absence of a channel, it suggests that if such a cut existed, it was not of great size or was infrequently used. A century later, an 1882 Admiralty chart of Grand Cayman showed Colliers Channel, East Channel, and South Channel, with the water depth in East Channel varying from 1 to 1.75 fathoms.[31] The *Caymanian* newspaper in its first issue, dated 2 March 1908, published a notice regarding the reef in the vicinity of East End Channel—highlighting major changes underway: "Mr. White of Cayman Brac is engaged in blowing a passage through the reef here. This, when completed will enable the vessels of large size to enter and leave the harbour and thus enhance the shipping possibility of this outport of Grand Cayman."[32] In 1990, Phoebe Watler Spence remarked that in the 1950s both East End Channel and South Channel were dredged or widened. She also recalled that the lagoon was deeper in earlier times, suggesting that sediments have built up in the East End Sound.[33]

Modern studies provide additional information about the physical nature of the offshore zone at East End. Grand Cayman experiences minimal tidal fluctuations, with a maximum range of 60 cm and an average range of 30 cm. But geologist Brian Jones points out that "at the mouths of small bays, sounds or channels through the reefs, strong tidal currents can result due to funneling."[34] This is certainly the case for the three East End channels. The water entering the sound over and through the reef, especially at high tide or during rough weather, must subsequently leave the sound. When large amounts of seawater are forced into the sound, exiting channel currents become strong.

During underwater archaeological surveys in calm weather, we observed common East End Sound currents. While working inside the lagoon between East End Channel and Colliers Channel, the survey team detected opposite flow patterns toward the two cuts in the reef. About midway between Colliers Channel and East End Channel the sea seems to flow toward shore. But from the mid-reef area toward the north, there is a gentle northward flow toward Colliers Channel; to the south, there is a southward current that carries much of the water leaving the sound through East End Channel. Current velocity increases in the channels. The winds that affect

East End are typically the eastern trade winds. During the summer months they blow from the southeast or east, and in the winter months generally from the northeast. Winter cold fronts can bring strong northeast or northwest winds. The Cayman Islands are also subject to occasional hurricanes between June and November.

At East End the fringing reef, made up of living corals, dead reefs, and coarse coral-boulder ramparts, stretches from headland to headland to create the lagoon locally called East Sound or East End Sound. The boulder ramparts have accumulated primarily through hurricane-associated wind and wave action, which severely affects the eastern shore of Grand Cayman.[35] Parts of the reef are generally above sea level, and other areas are periodically exposed during low tides, but much of the reef remains submerged. Brian Jones writes that behind the reef crest, formed of coral fragments broken from the fore-reef, is a relatively barren lagoon floor zone of "poorly sorted sheet gravels and sands that are composed of fragments of corals, sea-urchins, conch shells, sponges etc." He notes that toward land the grain size of the sediment decreases and there are scattered corals, followed by patch reefs surrounded by sand deposits and turtle grass (*Thalassia*).[36] Seaward, beyond the reef, "the seafloor slopes gradually to about 30 m and then plunges to the ocean depths."[37] Shipwreck debris exists in clusters along the reef and seabed in all of these zones.

We conducted the 1991 survey for ships of the Wreck of the Ten Sail intermittently between July and November (continuously between August and October), because the sea conditions at East End are generally calmest during summer and fall. The region of intensive reconnaissance began on the south side of East End Channel and extended northward for three miles to Colliers Channel, because archival documents and previous archaeological surveys suggested that the wrecks were located on the northeastern reefs (see map 14).[38] We were aware that the remains of *Convert* and nine merchantmen might be scattered on the fore-reef, strewn up on or buried within the reef proper, or located inside the East End Sound.

Many ships have wrecked over the centuries at East End, and in some cases the remains of different vessels overlap one another, creating complex site formation patterns. Consequently, the team carefully assessed shipwrecks to determine their formation processes and in what period they occurred. The 1991 investigation, focusing chiefly on late eighteenth-century sites, relied heavily on visual search techniques, assisted by the use of underwater metal detectors for site location and to further define site features and boundaries. Future research in the deep sandy zones of East End Sound, as well as in deeper offshore areas beyond the reef, could benefit from the addition of remote sensing techniques using a magnetometer and other innovations.

We began with a visual survey of the entire inside of the reef in parallel lines, with crew members spaced about 20 m apart, to a distance of approximately 140 m from the reef. We worked our way from East End Channel northward to Colliers Channel. In this zone, water depths ranged from 0 m to seldom more than 4 m. Once we anchored the survey boat, a person using a metal detector swam parallel to and almost on top of the reef; here the swimmer might find heavy iron objects, sometimes well disguised, on or near the coral boulder ramparts. Other team members swam in parallel lines about 20 m shoreward of each other. Another sweep, inshore of the first, was made to return to our anchored boat. In practice, when the crew found a site or a group of sites they would closely investigate the remains, and then would proceed with the general survey. We assessed many sites within a few hours, others took days, and one site, GC 012, involved almost a month of documentation.

All surveyors looked for vestiges of shipwrecks such as anchors, ballast, ordnance, ships' fittings, copper sheathing, ceramics, and glass. When a team member discovered such artifacts, the crew gathered and determined and recorded a visual shore range. The geographical coordinates of most of the sites—those that were originally discovered during the 1980 INA survey and sighted from benchmarks on land—are recorded in the National Shipwreck Inventory files of the Cayman Islands National Museum.[39] Next, the team conducted a careful reconnaissance of the area, from on top of the barrier reef toward shore.

The highest concentrations of artifacts often followed the East End Sound currents, suggesting common breakup patterns and site-formation processes for shipwrecks. From the mid-reef southward toward East End Channel, distributed remains frequently followed in a southwesterly direction along the bottom of the lagoon. From the mid-reef northward toward Colliers Channel, shipwreck materials usually extended northwestward along the seabed. At times, we observed shipwreck-related artifacts more than 300 m shoreward of the reef. If we determined that a particular site comprised post-eighteenth-century materials, we made notations but did not continue recording. We more thoroughly investigated possible eighteenth-century sites. The team collected samples of artifacts from most sites and subsequently treated them to remove calcareous deposits and salts; team members stabilized, cataloged, drew, and photographed these materials. Today the National Museum houses and curates these artifacts.

The clues to individual sites varied. We first detected several far shoreward of the reef, while others were more conspicuous near the natural barrier or right up on top of it. We discovered few shipwreck sites later on the outside of the reef that did not also have components within the East End Sound.

Once we had inspected the inner reef, the fore-reef was also visually surveyed, in parallel lines, by swimmers and by divers being towed behind a boat on special diving "tow boards." We worked from the shallow reef zone out toward the deep ocean drop-off. In depths to about 15 m our methods were practical, but in deeper water visual survey by snorkelers was less effective. We considered it likely, however, that most vessels that ran aground at East End broke up in shallow water and were scattered across the reef into the lagoon. Prevailing wind and ocean currents would have contributed to this phenomenon and process of site formation. Nonetheless, future magnetometer work in the fore-reef zone should be conducted before considering that the area has been completely surveyed, since storms may have redeposited shipwreck remains in deeper water. It is also possible that other ships, not targeted for the 1991 investigation, might have struck the reef and later foundered in deeper water.

Another excellent method for archaeologically locating shipwreck features on the outer reef is to follow trails of artifacts from inside the lagoon right over the coral boulder ridge to the outside. Although coarse coral rubble sometimes conceals artifacts on the reef crest, and close inspection can be impossible in submerged areas where swimmers must navigate in waves breaking over fire coral, we frequently found related shipwreck features on both sides of the reef. Sea conditions, however, were often too dangerous to allow the survey team to traverse the coral barrier. Thus, when occasional calm days occurred, the crew walked, swam, or belly-surfed back and forth over the reef adjacent to sites where shipwreck remains had earlier been detected on the lagoon side.

In addition to crossing the reef whenever possible to search for related shipwreck components, the crew worked on the seaward side from an anchored boat when a particular site, or particular sections of the fore-reef, required careful investigation using scuba. Given the usual rough sea conditions on the fore-reef of East End, even in the calm months, it is important to remember that during a handful of days each year the sea becomes as calm as a millpond. In 1991 during those few tranquil October days, the crew could clearly see archaeological features on the fore-reef, from the boat, before getting into the water.

During the 1991 field-survey phase of the Wreck of the Ten Sail Project, the team relocated and reassessed all sites previously recorded by the INA crew and the SRD group, from about one-quarter of a mile south of East End Channel to Colliers Channel. The field crew also explored and documented previously undiscovered features of known sites as well as several new sites.[40]

During the 1991 investigation, the team examined over thirty shipwreck-related sites. We believe that near-contiguous GC 012 and GC 017 comprise remnants of *Convert*. Other eighteenth-century sites are likely to be vestiges of the merchantmen. And many sites are clearly nineteenth- and twentieth-century shipwrecks. Remains that may be associated with HMS *Convert*, *William and Elizabeth*, *Britannia*, *Ludlow*, *Nancy*, *Moorhall*, *Richard*, *Fortune*, *Eagle*, and *Sally* are described in the following pages. I mention post-eighteenth-century sites to provide an overview of all types of shipwrecks in the survey area. In the course of our research, we ruled out these later sites as candidates for the Wreck of the Ten Sail.

The French Cannon Site, GC 017

It is no secret that cannons lay buried within a shallow sand bank, sometimes called Sand Cay, on the inside of the eastern reef of Grand Cayman. After recounting R. Tulloh Coe's story of the Wreck of the Ten Sail, Commissioner George Hirst, in his 1910 *Notes on the History of the Cayman Islands* mentioned the presence of cannons on the Gun Bay reef. He discounted rumors that a fort once stood there, emphasizing that Coe's story clearly showed that "it was exactly on this spot the 'wreck of the ten sail' took place."[41] The ten cannons salvaged from the area, now located on land, attest to the fact that the French Cannon Site is still well known today. Although stories persist about a fort on the reef, archaeological research favors Hirst's hypothesis.

In 1980, Marshall Watler of Gun Bay told the members of the 1980 Cayman Islands Project that there were cannons located northwest of the East End Channel. The INA crew noted that the guns were within a turtle grass–covered sand flat in about eight feet of water. They designated the site GC 017, searched the area visually and with metal detectors, and documented their findings. There was a disturbed area from which one cannon (OR 05) had recently been salvaged. The team later discovered the gun buoyed at a new location halfway across the East End Sound. They noted that there were at least four more buried cannons spread in a southeasterly to northwesterly direction. The cascabel of one of the four pieces of ordnance was visible in the excavation trench of the one that had been salvaged. The INA crew reasoned that magnetic anomalies near two of the guns, unlikely to be cannons, might be ammunition. The remaining four cannons located adjacent to the recent salvage pit were probably among those subsequently retrieved in the 1980s.

The INA crew identified the transported cannon as an eighteenth-century French gun, which suggested it might be from *Convert*, ex-*Inconstante*. An encrusted lead cover, a device commonly used on loaded ordnance at sea to keep the powder dry, covered its touch hole.

The Cayman Islands Project suggested that no permits be issued for salvage of the remaining guns, pointing out the probable relationship of GC 017 to the Wreck of the Ten Sail. It also recommended that the site not be further disturbed, except by professional archaeologists and until conservation facilities and personnel were available on the island.[42]

In the mid-1980s Indiana University's SRD group investigated GC 017. The field-school crew explored the area visually and with metal detectors. They plotted the positions of at least six guns, mapped general magnetic areas, and noted the probable former positions of salvaged cannons, marked by disturbed sand patches in the field of turtle grass. The SRD group, assuming that the cannons had been salvaged from the Royal Navy frigate and then deposited on the sandbar, identified GC 017 as the "cannon transport site for the wreck *Convert.*" They suggested that the area contained no additional artifacts but recommended that further salvage of cannons not be allowed.[43]

When we initiated the archaeology phase of the 1991 Wreck of the Ten Sail Project, we knew that East End's Sand Cay had previously been mined for cannons; they had been found ornamentally displayed around the island. In fact, by late 1991 the survey team had discovered nine of the ten salvaged 12-pounders from site GC 017 on land. In 1794, however, the Royal Navy had not recovered *Convert*'s twenty-six such guns, or the six 6-pounders. Thus, we hoped that cannons and additional parts of the shipwreck might remain in situ.

On 15 April 1991, before the summer field season began, two of us had the opportunity to photograph the French Cannon Site and the surrounding area from a helicopter. We conducted a metal-detector survey of GC 017 several days later. This preliminary reconnaissance revealed at least eight large magnetic targets on the site. We thought seven were possible cannons, and one was a large L-shaped feature. Most of these artifacts were buried in turtle grass, sand, and coral rubble, but two cannons were exposed. Fortunately, both guns retained protective coralline encrustations. Hand-fanning around the base of one of these cannons, I observed poorly preserved bits of wood. It was unclear whether these fragments could be remnants of a gun carriage or even part of a ship's deck. Nonetheless, the presence of wood beneath a cannon and features other than cannons on the site suggested to me that Sand Cay might be where part of *Convert* came to rest after being cast over the reef. Even in the twentieth and twenty-first centuries, large portions of ships that previously wrecked on the fore-reef were tossed over the reef and into the lagoon by severe storms. We considered the French Cannon Site a prime site for test excavations.

Also in April 1991, the Cayman Islands National Museum sought permission from the Cayman Islands government for the project team to conduct test excavations during the proposed underwater archaeology phase of the Wreck of the Ten Sail Project. The government granted permission for a survey and for collection of surface artifacts, but conditional consent to carry out excavations came after the 1991 field season was over. Thus, even today the site is still intact for testing when resources become available.

Although the project plans had included placing several trenches across GC 017 to determine whether parts of the hull or deck of a ship survived within Sand Cay, the work was limited to a detailed visual and metal-detector survey of the site, which took place in October 1991. Using incised-numbered PVC stakes and nylon line, the crew established a 20 × 30 m grid, in water depths of about 0.5 to 3 m, over the concentration of magnetic features located within the turtle grass–covered sandbar (figure 30).

A visual survey revealed little artifactual material on the surface other than a few miscellaneous nineteenth-century floor tiles and ceramic sherds from known East End Channel wrecks, thought to have been deposited in the area by storm activity. The team also noted a few pieces of slag ballast and bits of shingle or pebble ballast, both of which also occur on nearby sites. Cannons nos. 10 and 11 remained uncovered, as they had been in April 1991, while an unknown person had recently exposed the top of cannon no. 2.

Following the visual inspection, we carried out a controlled metal-detector survey, grid by grid, until the entire area had been surveyed for magnetic features. Subsequently, we recorded the dimensions and orientations of major anomalies, thought to be cannons, which we defined as precisely as possible and plotted on the map. The team carried out minimal ground-truthing on shallow targets, but deep targets could not be defined without excavation. Thus, we recognized seven features (nos. 2, 3, 4, 6, 9, 10, and 11) as probable 12-pounder cannons and one L-shaped iron encrustation (no. 14) as a possible ship's member. Six targets (nos. 1, 5, 7, 8, 12, and 13) remained unidentified, but their magnetic signatures and positions within the group suggest that most are probably cannons. Although five features (nos. 1, 7, 8, 12, and 13) seem to be shorter than the others, we do not know whether their magnetic readings indicate smaller cannons such as 6-pounders, 12-pounders buried off the horizontal plane, or other iron objects. The survey crew also detected at least nine small magnetic anomalies on the site.

After recording the magnetic targets of GC 017, we removed the nylon line delineating the grids. We drove the numbered PVC stakes at the corners of the grids into the seabed, with about 10 cm remaining exposed, leaving them in place for future work at the site. We reburied cannon no. 2, which the team had found partially exposed.[44]

Discussions with Charles Beeker of SRD, in the context of our map,

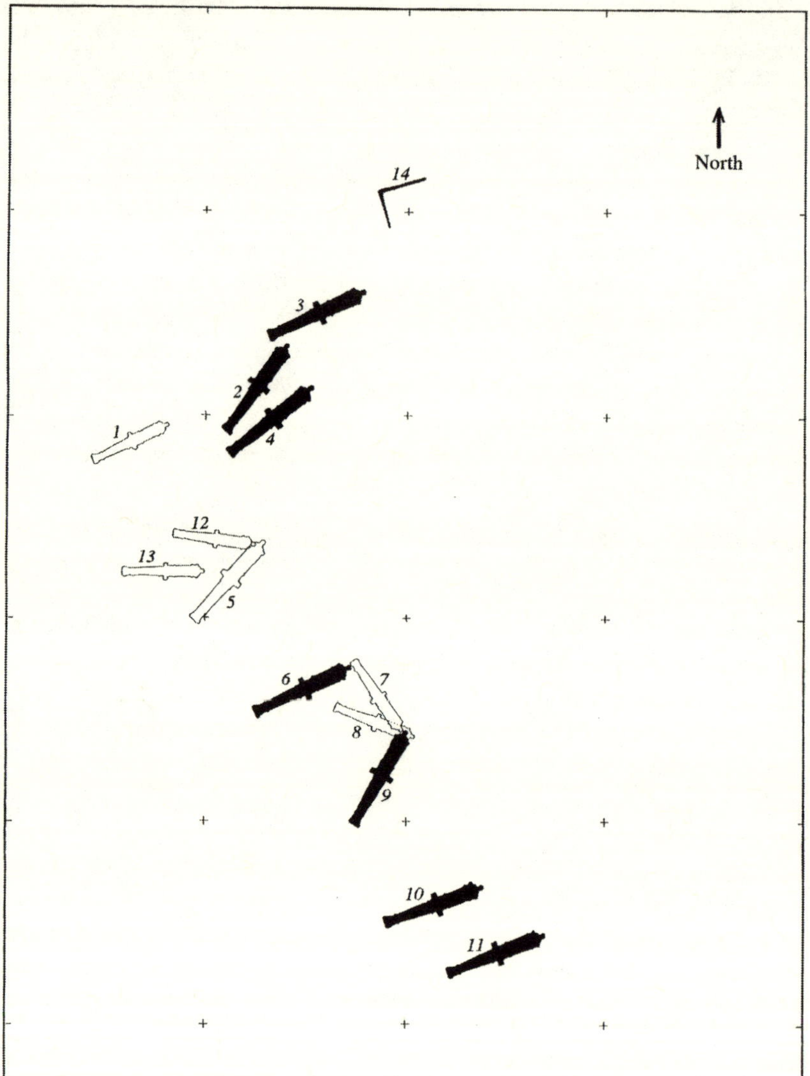

Figure 30. French Cannon Site, GC 017. Drawn by M. E. Leshikar-Denton.

suggest that nine previously salvaged cannons were removed as follows: four from southeast of cannon no. 11, three from between nos. 10 and 11, and two from the vicinity of nos. 5 and 6. The provenience of the tenth salvaged cannon now on land is unknown.

Beeker once observed, in situ, the cannons that were located between nos. 10 and 11, after the surrounding sediment had been excavated, and they were stacked on old wooden boards or planks. He believes that they were positioned this way when they were salvaged from *Convert* in the 1790s.[45] His hypothesis may be correct, as the French Cannon Site is adjacent to East End Channel, which today is relatively deep and wide. But I question whether East End Channel was sufficiently deep and wide in the eighteenth century to accommodate vessels capable of transporting numerous cannons, most weighing over 3,000 pounds, from offshore into the lagoon. And since Captains Lawford and Roberts requested that William Bodden Sr. and Robert Knowles Clarke bring salvaged guns and stores to George Town, it is unlikely that so many guns would have ended up on a submerged sandbar in East End Sound instead. In fact, if the guns were recovered from the wreck by island schooners, it would probably have been far easier and more practical to carry them to the west side of Grand Cayman. If, on the other hand, the Caymanians salvaged the cannons from *Convert* for use on Grand Cayman, there would have been no reason to leave them in the sea. Finally, if *Convert*'s gundeck and associated ordnance was carried over the reef into the shallow sound, this may actually explain why the heavy cannons were not recovered and transported to George Town in the eighteenth century; this is the theory that seems most plausible to me. In 2019, the research question of whether GC 017 is a salvage site deposition or the location where part of *Convert* came to rest still remains to be answered through test excavations. It is envisioned that CIMAP archaeologists can take up this issue.

The French Cannon Site is one of the Cayman Islands' most important underwater heritage sites. Continued efforts should be made to protect it from vandalism, and scientific archaeological investigations should be appropriately planned and carried out to further define its historical significance. Principally, the site should be evaluated in its entirety, but we must also recognize that the large collection of contemporaneous French cannons, lost in a single episode, are in themselves a unique and important resource. The site holds local, regional, and international significance.

The Probable Frigate Spillage Site, GC 012

In 1980 the Cayman Islands Project assessed GC 012 as a possible Wreck of the Ten Sail site. The INA team called it the "Pebble Ballast Wreck."

They noted that the site was located parallel to the reef immediately north of East End Channel and extended northward over a distance of about one-third of a mile.[46] During the 1991 Wreck of the Ten Sail Project, the area was surveyed in more detail, and it was determined that this zone encompasses the wreckage signatures of several shipwreck sites, two of which are characterized by pebble ballast. The pebble ballast on the two sites, however, is distinctly different. The area also includes another site with slag ballast. The 1991 project redefined GC 012 as the northernmost shipwreck, clearly a late eighteenth-century site.

GC 012, as defined in 1991, is located several hundred meters to the northeast of the French Cannon Site and may represent a spillage trail toward it.[47] Crushed and buckled pieces of copper sheathing in the reef and across the site suggest that parts of the hull of a copper-clad ship ground across the reef in this area. The Probable Frigate Spillage Site includes surface artifacts ranging from ships' fittings, ballast, and ammunition to ceramics and glass. It extends from the reef toward the west-southwest, over an area exceeding 100 × 160 m. Directly between the southwest extremity of GC 012 and GC 017 there are deep sand deposits covered by thick beds of turtle grass that may conceal artifacts, but none were observed on the surface between the sites.

Swimmers and scuba divers conducted visual and metal-detector surveys of the fore-reef adjacent to GC 012 to depths of about 15 m. The team hoped to find anchors and tons of pig iron ballast but discovered none on the seaward side of the reef. In fact, there is a surprising absence of shipwreck features on the fore-reef. Since the reef is a high-energy zone made up of dead coral rubble that builds and shifts, it is possible that parts of the wreckage are buried within the reef. It is also possible that much of the ship was carried into the East End Sound where it was subsequently scattered, salvaged, or buried.

Somewhat barren mixed sand and coral rubble areas adjacent to the coral boulder reef characterize the seabed that encompasses GC 012. Moving shoreward, there are isolated coral heads and patch reefs surrounded by finer sand and coral rubble. In spite of the presence of large quantities of artifacts on the surface of the site, the materials are somewhat difficult to detect by the untrained eye. Encrusted iron objects, lying on the surface or protruding from the sand and rubble, appear very similar to chunks of eroded and broken coral. Living coral frequently encrusts ceramics, glass, bricks, and pebble ballast. The natural disguise protects the site, to some degree, from vandalism.

In 1991 we determined that although the surface artifacts of the Probable Frigate Spillage Site are widely dispersed and large shipwreck features such as anchors appear to be absent, the site is nonetheless very important. In fact, the range of surface artifacts we discovered at GC 012 exceeds the variety found on all the other East End sites that we surveyed. Many of these late eighteenth-century artifacts support the hypothesis that GC 012 represents part of the Royal Navy frigate *Convert*. The team devoted over a month to documenting the site and processing the artifact collection.

We based the size of the study area on the surface distribution of related artifacts—essentially, the shipwreck signature. At first we defined an 80 × 100 m zone. During the survey, however, we extended the boundaries to encompass over 100 × 160 m of seafloor; here we carried out documentation and a controlled surface collection (figure 31). After we established primary and secondary datums, we divided the site into units, delineated by incised-numbered PVC stakes and nylon line and arbitrarily gave them alphabetical designations.[48] Most of the units were 20 × 20 m, two were 20 × 30 m (CC and DD), and those that encompassed part of the reef were 20 × 45 m (JJ, V, X, Z, BB, and EE). The team designated units II and LL so that we could include a few artifacts found beyond the primary grid.

The team also surveyed the zones surrounding the established grid: to the north, no artifacts were observed; to the east and northeast, no significant material was observed on the reef crest or seaward, except a copper drift bolt embedded in the fore-reef; to the west, turtle grass beds may conceal a buried, shoreward scatter of artifacts; to the south, shipwreck debris from nineteenth- and twentieth-century wrecks obscures the diminishing scatter of eighteenth-century GC 012 artifacts; to the southwest, across more than 200 m of turtle grass, lies GC 017, which may or may not be directly related to GC 012. We systematically surveyed each unit within the established GC 012 grid in parallel lines, both visually and with metal detectors. During low tide, water depths in this zone ranged from almost 0 m on the reef to 1.4 m on the western boundary. We documented surface artifacts by two methods. First, since the site is much affected by storm activity and light artifacts such as glass and ceramic sherds and small pebble ballast are widely dispersed, the provenience of these items is recorded simply by unit. During the 1991 survey, the team collected all observed surface ceramics, all diagnostic glass sherds, and samples of pebble ballast. (These archaeological materials are curated at the Cayman Islands National Museum.) We documented the exact provenience of copper, lead, and iron artifacts, and bricks, as well as some broken molds of iron artifacts (with a few exceptions) on the master map of GC 012 surface artifacts (figure 32). We consecutively numbered these master map artifacts, totaling almost 550 objects for the whole site. (The original GC 012 master map includes the numerical designation of each artifact, but due to the scale these numbers

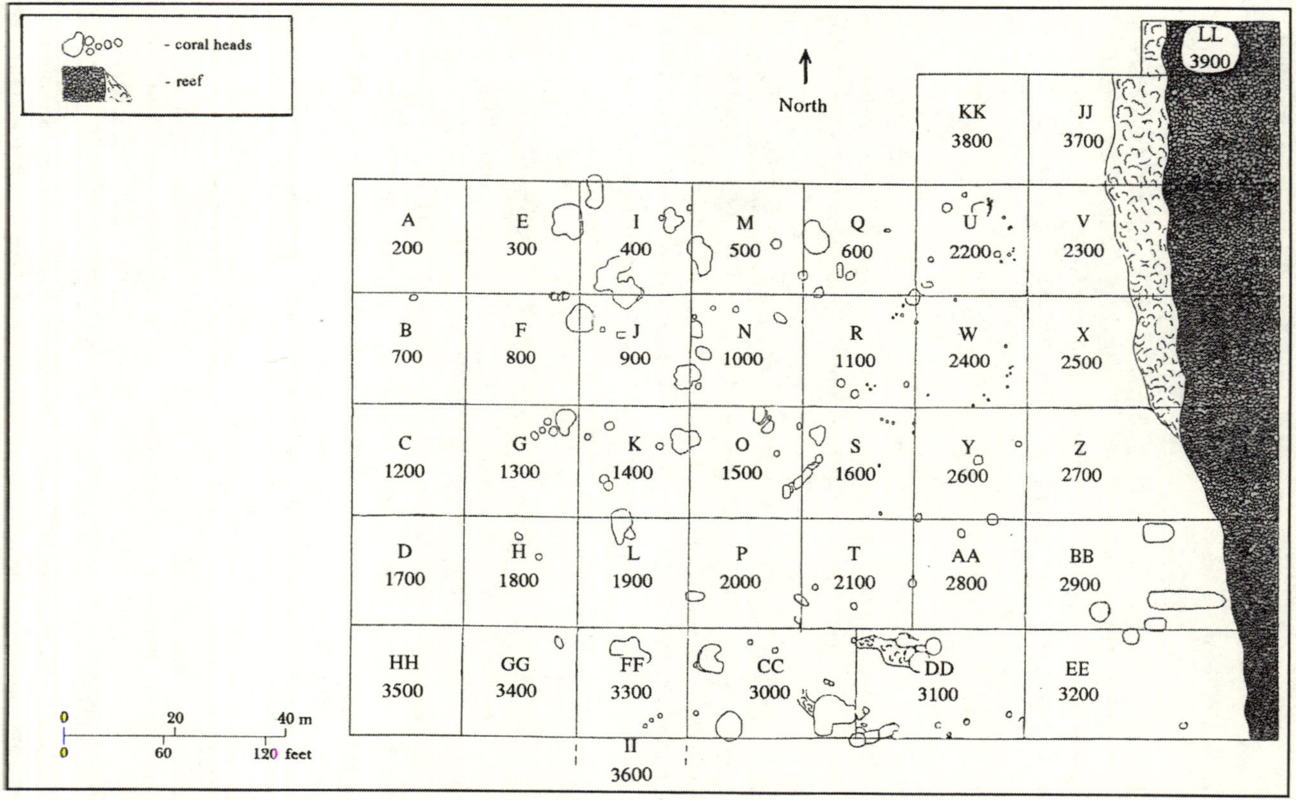

Figure 31. Key to the grids for the Probable Frigate Spillage Site, GC 012. Drawn and compiled by M. E. Leshikar-Denton and R. L. Craig.

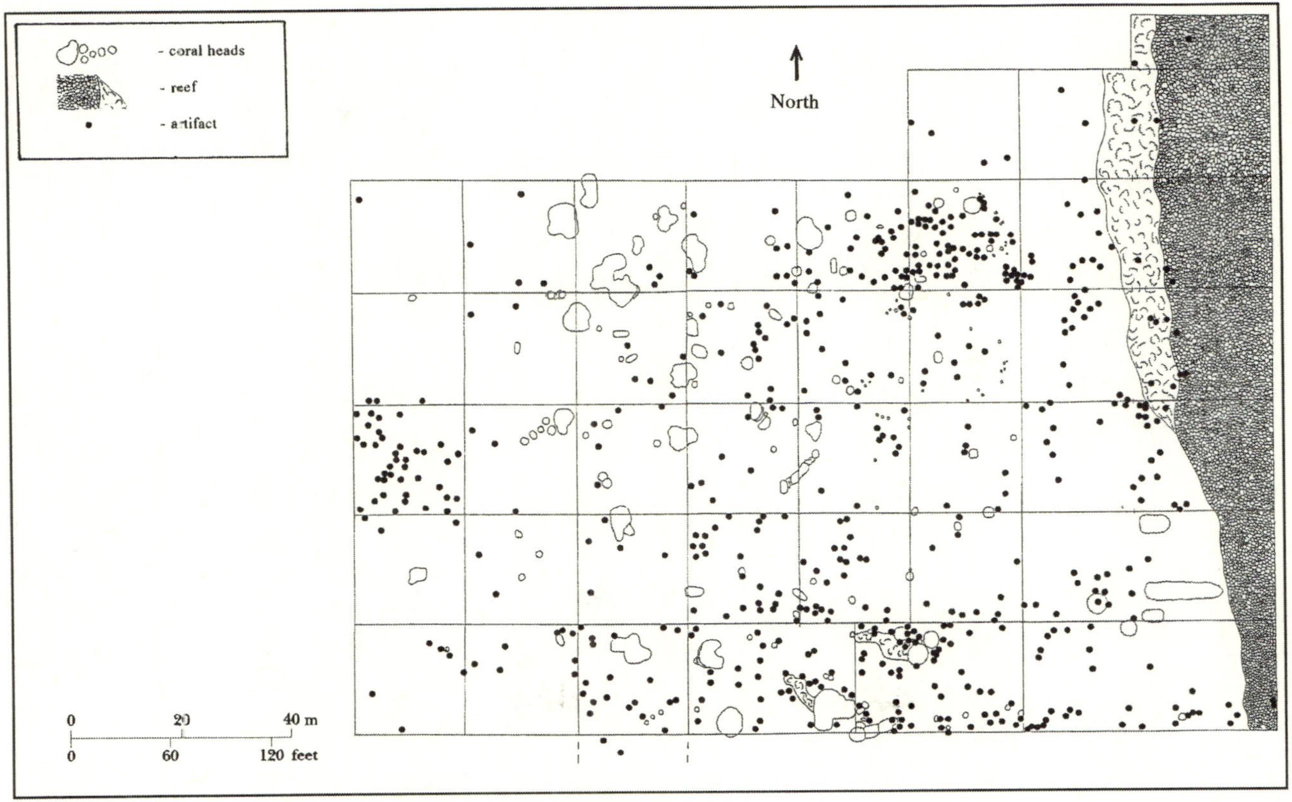

Figure 32. Distribution of artifacts plotted on the master map of the Probable Frigate Spillage Site, GC 012. Drawn and compiled by M. E. Leshikar-Denton, Jeanne Masters, and R. L. Craig.

are omitted in figure 32). Our team collected all copper items and bricks, as well as most lead artifacts. We did not collect iron artifacts, which are often heavily encrusted and much less stable than copper and lead objects, with the exception of a few samples of recognizable items such as cannonballs and bar shot. But since the provenience of iron artifacts is recorded, archaeologists will have the option to recover them when adequate conservation facilities are in place on Grand Cayman.

The project team cataloged all collected objects from site GC 012. We identified the artifacts from each unit by lot number and gave them consecutive inventory numbers within that lot (although the system of decimal numbering of classes of artifacts varies). Artifacts with master map numbers also have the unique artifact inventory numbers.

In addition to cataloging artifacts collected from GC 012, we treated them to remove calcareous deposits and salts, stabilized them for storage, and sketched them. Inventory numbers were either tagged to the artifact, written on a ziplock bag containing the object, or applied to the surface of the item. We photographed many artifacts with black-and-white film on a scaled background.

Analysis of the artifacts from the Probable Frigate Spillage Site suggests that they date to the late eighteenth century and contribute to our understanding of the Wreck of the Ten Sail. Among ship-related artifacts observed on the site are ships' fittings, copper and lead sheathing, copper and iron fasteners, and items associated with the standing and running rigging (figure 33A). There are several iron chain plates, eyebolts, hooks, and rope thimbles. There is a remnant of a lignum vitae sheave with a brass coak, part of a ship's block that perhaps would have been used for the ship's rigging or for handling the guns (figure 33B).[49] The sheave coak is similar to a style commonly used in the Royal Navy in the late eighteenth century.[50] There are whole and broken bricks, perhaps from brick ovens, and tiles. The team discovered three identifiable pieces of pig iron ballast in the northeastern grids that conform to a size commonly used on French warships; we collected one whole and one broken piece.[51] Abundant shingle ballast is spread across the whole site, helping define its boundaries and clarify the wreck formation process.

The collection includes artifacts that contribute to the story of shipboard life, including possible tools and objects associated with victualing, like ceramics and glass. Although we did not discover whole bottles, dark-green glass bottle fragments conform to late eighteenth-century British styles (figure 34A).[52] The team collected sherds of various types of ceramics, from a few bits of Chinese porcelain to fragments of British creamware,

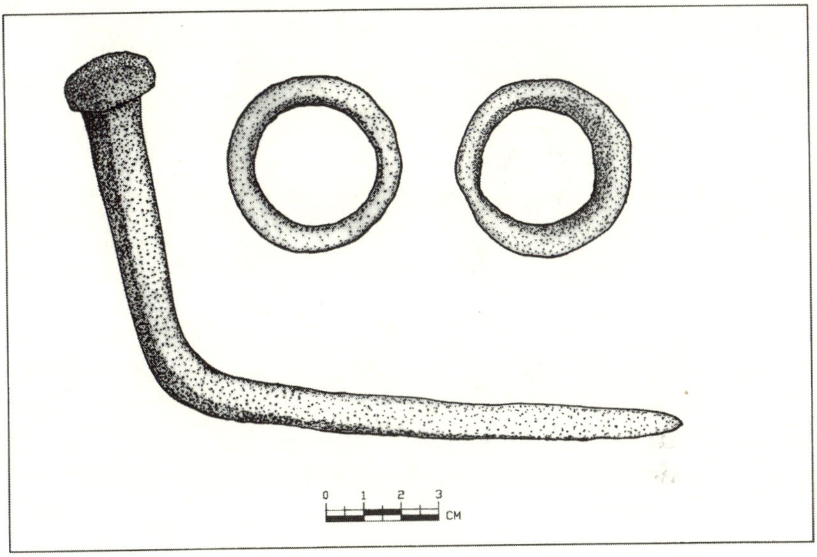

A

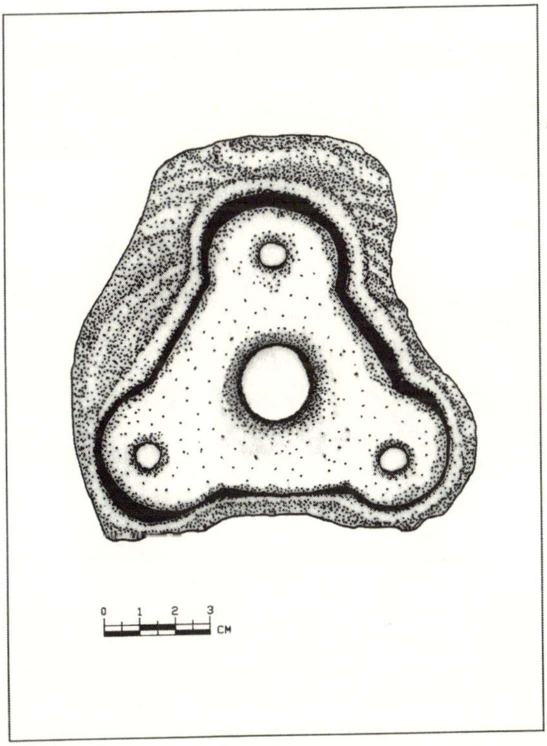

B

Figure 33. *A*, copper nail (1900.7.1) and copper rings (*left*, 3100.5.1; *right*, 3100.12.1) from site GC 012. Drawn by M. E. Leshikar-Denton. *B*, remnant of lignum vitae sheave with brass coak (2100.4.1) from site GC 012. Drawn by Helene Schindler.

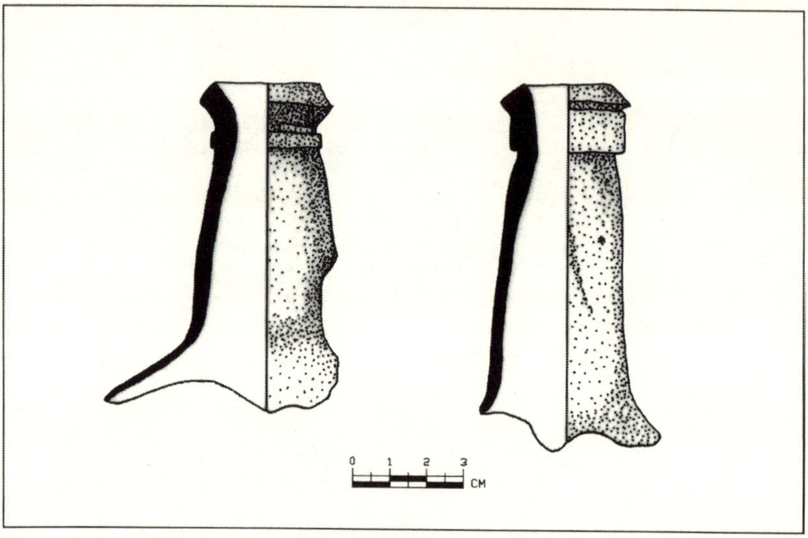

A

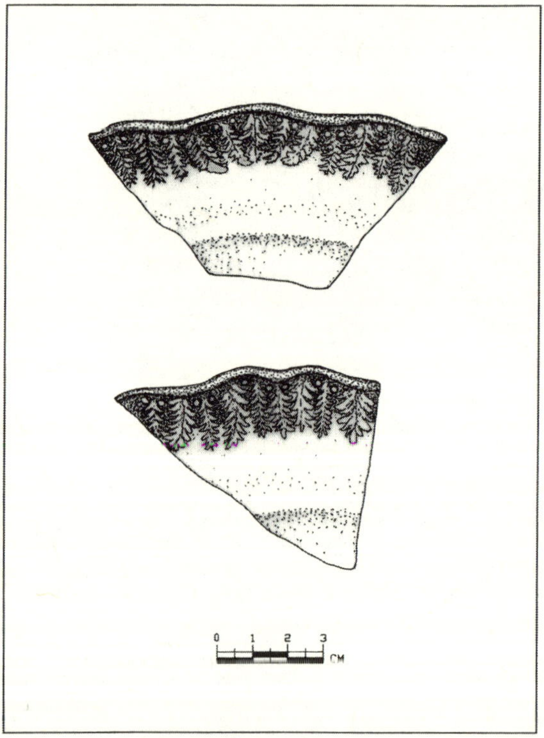

B

Figure 34. *A*, dark-green glass bottle necks with lip and string rim finishes typical of the late eighteenth century (*left*, 800.7.1; *right*, 1700.9.1). *B*, pearlware rim sherds with blue molded-plume borders (*top*, 800.1.1; *bottom*, 1300.5.2). *C*, unidentified metal-alloy spoon, lightly encrusted with coralline growth (3500.1.1). All from site GC 012 and drawn by M. E. Leshikar-Denton.

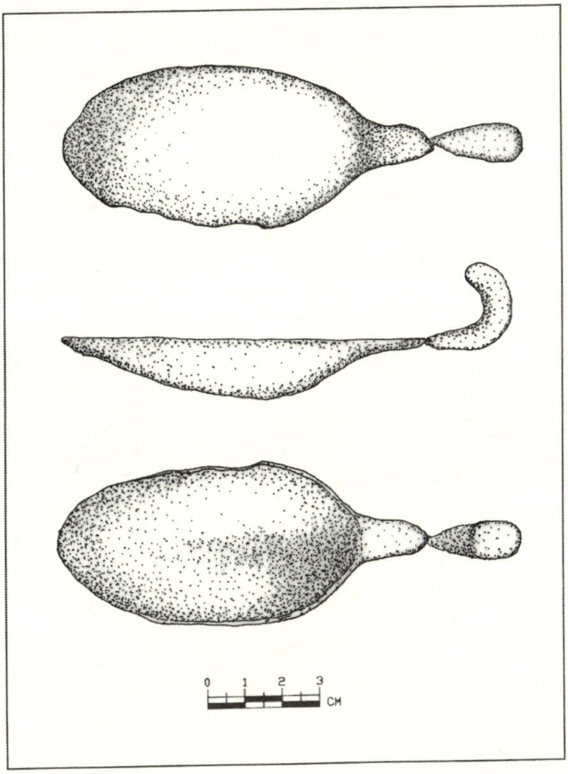

C

Figure 34. (*continued*)

pearlware, basaltes, stoneware, and glazed and unglazed earthenware (figure 34B), and two unidentified metal-alloy spoons (figure 34C).

A swivel gun yoke and gunner's stores, including about thirty-eight whole or partial pieces of bar shot, at least thirty-five identifiable cannonballs, and lead shot provide evidence of an armed ship. Although many remain encrusted in the sea, most of the cannonballs on the Probable Frigate Spillage Site appear to be the right caliber to be fired from the 12-pounder cannons located nearby on the French Cannon Site. Jean Boudriot and David Roberts reported the following average shot diameters: 11.7 cm for a 12-pounder, 10.2 cm for an 8-pounder, and 9.3 cm for a 6-pounder.[53] Artifact no. 2400.4.1 is an iron cannonball measuring 11.4 cm in diameter, from GC 012 (figure 35).

GC 012 is an unusual shipwreck site, and a fragile one. While many artifacts have been disguised and protected by coralline growth, the site has

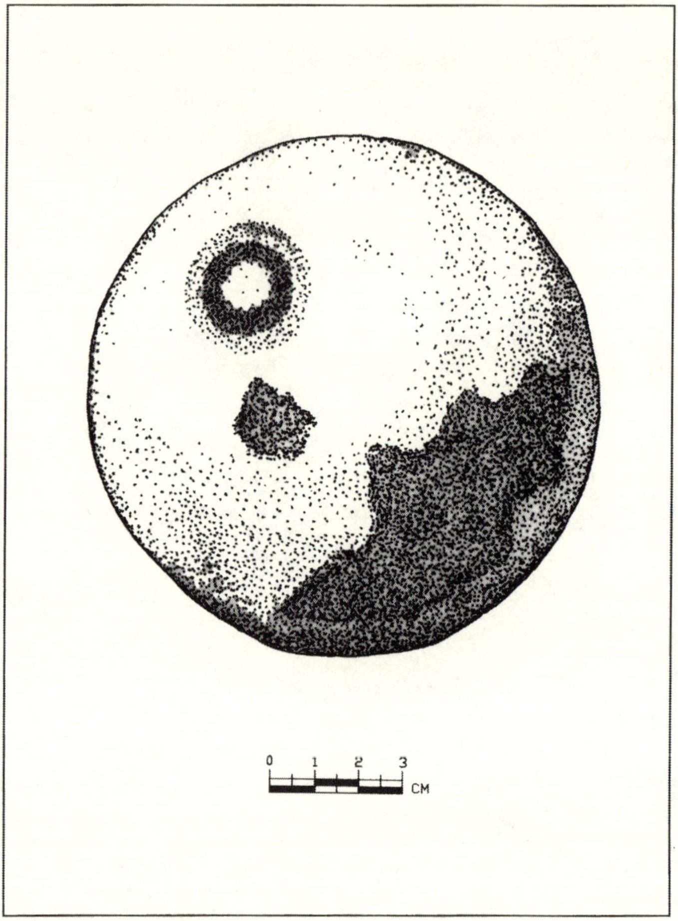

Figure 35. Twelve-pounder iron cannonball (2400.4.1) from site GC 012. Drawn by M. E. Leshikar-Denton.

also been repeatedly "excavated" by nature. In this location, it is probable that sediment shifts, periodically burying or uncovering artifacts on the seabed. The site's exposure enables a wide variety of artifacts to be easily identified. At the same time, their presence on the surface leaves them endangered during stormy weather and makes them accessible to curiosity seekers.

The Probable Frigate Spillage Site, like the French Cannon Site, probably includes remains of HMS *Convert*. It is, however, a more exposed and vulnerable site that requires stringent protection from vandalism. In the early 1990s the Cayman Islands National Museum aspired to create a wet-site conservation laboratory to treat objects from the sea; in 2019 it is unfortunate that no such dedicated facility exists. While further collection and conservation of selected iron objects that are exposed on the surface of GC 012 is appropriate, adequate conservation facilities first need to be in place. Further archaeological investigations, including excavations in selected areas to address special research questions, could be carried out, but only after the issue of adequate conservation is addressed.[54]

The Probable Salvage Campsite, GC 041, and Other Terrestrial Sites

Site GC 041, first recorded in 1980, is a terrestrial site located on the beach opposite GC 012 and GC 017. After Hurricane Allen the INA team noticed large quantities of ceramic sherds and some ships' fittings eroding from the beach in this area. The ceramics were similar to those found at GC 012, and the INA team thought the site related to the Wreck of the Ten Sail. During the summer of 1991, agreeing with the earlier assessment, we secured permission from two landowners to conduct a controlled surface collection of ceramics and glass. The team carried out the collection in 10 m corridors between the road and the sea, over about 90 m of beachfront. Few metal objects were seen, but these heavy objects often remain buried while ceramic and glass sherds are thrown to the surface by crabs. Late eighteenth-century British wine bottle and ceramic fragments, including abundant creamwares and pearlwares in edge-decorated, transfer-printed, hand-painted, and annular ware designs were abundant on the site. Since East End was relatively unpopulated in the late eighteenth century, there can be little doubt that Captain Lawford and his men, and possibly the crews of the merchantmen, used this area as a campsite while they were salvaging the ships of the Wreck of the Ten Sail. It is also likely that these people discarded damaged goods in the area. In addition to eighteenth-century artifacts, however, we found a considerable variety of material dating throughout the nineteenth century and into the twentieth century.

In the sea adjacent to GC 041 is a freshwater spring, which surely contributed to the site's popularity as a salvage campsite, not only for ships of the Wreck of the Ten Sail but also for numerous other ships that have wrecked on the East End reef over the centuries. The owner of the north parcel of land containing GC 041 told us that his grandfather had a wattle-and-daub home landward of the beach area.[55]

To the south of GC 041, near the base of Gun Bluff, is a smaller concentration of ceramic material that dates between the eighteenth and the twentieth century. The site has been designated GCL 016.[56] In this location a piece of pig iron ballast is set vertically into the ground as a boundary marker. The landowner said that the iron pig was found in the vicinity. Charles Beeker also told me that several buried cannons are located nearby and, with the help of a metal detector, the team determined that these guns remain buried in the sea adjacent to the beach. GCL 016 is probably related to the Wreck of the Ten Sail and is likely to have been associated with other shipwreck salvage activities that have occurred over the centuries.

The team noted additional terrestrial sites along the beach at East End in 1991 and 1993, designating them as GCL 010, GCL 011, GCL 012, GCL 013, GCL 014, and GCL 015.[57] Sites GCL 013 and GCL 014 are characterized by dark-green glass fragments and pieces of slate; they may relate to shipwreck site GC 003, located on the reef nearby, which is discussed below. All of the other sites include glass and ceramic fragments dating to the late eighteenth century or nineteenth century but also include minimal twentieth-century material. All of these sites may relate to salvage of the Wreck of the Ten Sail and later shipwrecks, but GCL 015 also appears to have been a homestead.[58]

Northern Survey Zone: GC 026, GC 072, GC 073, and GC 074

The merchantmen of the Wreck of the Ten Sail ranged in tonnage from about 150 to 376 tons. They carried perishable cargoes, and their crews probably largely salvaged their guns and hardware. Therefore, it is not surprising that the sites of the merchant wrecks are not extensive. Ballast, iron and copper fasteners, minimal amounts of glass and ceramics, and occasionally an anchor characterize most. Sparse remains can make it difficult to date a site.

The 1980 INA team recorded GC 026. They wrote that the site was located within the East End Sound and that its features included lightly scattered iron objects and late eighteenth- or early nineteenth-century ceramic sherds, such as shell-edged pearlware and annular ware, but no ballast. Tilefish burrows using the ceramics were observed on the site. When GC 026 was assessed in 1991 in the northern zone of our survey area, late eighteenth-century shell-edged pearlware and annular ware were observed up to 80 m west of the reef in depths of about 1.5 m. The team also noted small quantities of dark-green glass, a copper fastener, and a few iron fasteners. In addition, we discovered homogeneous ballast, 10 to 25 cm in diameter, now identified as high-copper-content slag.[59] The presence of this slag on the shipwreck suggests a probable Industrial Revolution solution to ballasting the vessel and fits nicely into the Wreck of the Ten Sail time frame. In fact, research points to a possible point of origin for the ballast, in the rich copper mines of Amlwch, Wales; owing to its density, copper slag, a by-product of copper smelting, was exported from Amlwch to Liverpool and other major British ports for ballasting large ocean-going sailing vessels.[60] The slag ballast extends in a 20 m wide corridor from the sandy lagoon floor across the top of the dry reef (40 m wide), and small amounts are concreted to the seabed of the fore-reef. We also observed a few encrusted iron ships' fittings farther seaward. It is possible that other features are buried in the sand and rubble of the lagoon. GC 026 probably holds remains of a Wreck of the Ten Sail merchantman.

The 1991 survey team recorded site GC 073 about 70 m south of GC 026. It includes a sparse scatter of small round and flat pebble ballast and dark-green glass fragments, including a push-up bottle base. Since the ballast is distinctly different from that found at the former site, it must be the remains of another vessel. It is located directly inside the reef from a late nineteenth- or early twentieth-century riveted iron-hull ship, GC 008, but may not be related to it. The artifacts observed at GC 073 in 1991 were too sparse to provide positive identification of the site.

Identified during the 1991 survey, GC 072 and GC 074 are located in the northern survey zone. GC 072 is an ephemeral site consisting of a few copper and iron fasteners and fragments of dark-green glass, all within about 70 m of the reef. We did not find artifacts on the fore-reef adjacent to this site. The lack of ballast on the site suggests that a small part of a vessel came to rest there.

About 200 m south of GC 072, and possibly associated with it, lies site GC 074. Sparse dark-green glass found up to 150 m from the reef, and small quantities of ballast on the reef and scattered shoreward characterize the site. We observed a single poorly fired red brick or thick tile on the site and found two large stoneware jar sherds that may relate to it more than halfway to shore. We did not observe features seaward of the reef. The presence of ballast stones strewn across the reef suggests the location of a shipwreck, but the small quantity of widely scattered material is not sufficient to identify the site as the primary remains of a wrecked merchantman. Interestingly, the stone ballast on GC 74 appears to be identical to that found on GC 075 (discussed below) which is located about 400 m to the south, suggesting a possible common port.[61]

Central Survey Zone: GC 003, GC 006, GC 025, GC 044, GC 75, and GC 076

The INA survey team documented GC 003 as a site on the lagoon side of the reef characterized by late eighteenth- or early nineteenth-century green glass fragments, large quantities of slate ballast, and ship's hardware, including a chain plate and iron fasteners. The 1980 team did not observe shipwreck debris on the adjacent fore-reef. Located in the central survey zone, we surveyed GC 003 again in 1991. Inside the reef our team noted large chunks (30 cm diameter) of angular slate as well as smaller slabs and fragments. This ballast was extensive on the reef and parallel to it and trailed to a sparse scatter up to 300 m west. The team encountered small amounts of dark-green glass and iron fasteners with the spillage of slate and recorded additional shipwreck materials on the fore-reef and up to 50 m seaward. There were large quantities of shattered slate as well as iron ship's fittings, copper fasteners, and remnants of wood embedded in the seafloor. Although we did not find diagnostic glass and ceramics, the site is a good candidate for the Wreck of the Ten Sail.

About 100 to 130 m south of GC 003 is GC 006, another site recorded during the 1980 Cayman Islands Project. One can detect it from a boat in fair weather because it includes a windlass assembly on the reef that protrudes above sea level, even at high tide. The survey team noted a 60 to 70 m scatter of ballast parallel to the inner reef that spread westward over 100 m of seafloor. They documented numerous fasteners and an iron cannon in the lagoon. Features on the fore-reef included two wooden-stocked anchors, two iron-stocked anchors (without their stocks), a pile of anchor chain, a larger iron windlass assembly, hawse pipes, and chain plates. Also observed were copper sheathing and tacks, and the neck of an earthenware olive jar. The team assessed the site to be an armed wooden sailing ship, probably dating to the first half of the nineteenth century. But the INA team noted that it might relate to the Wreck of the Ten Sail.

The 1991 team noted the same principal features at GC 006 as the earlier group. We also documented that within the reef there are numerous magnetic targets, including a couple of concentrations of cannonballs and expanding shot. The encrusted cannon appears to be an eighteenth-century British 9-pounder. It is located about 40 m northwest of the exposed windlass. Although Charles Beeker reported that the gun had once been moved a short distance from its original location, his group found and returned it to the correct area, and there are cannonballs nearby. There seems to be at least two principal types of stone ballast on the site (10–30 cm diameter), one angular and the other more round. There are ship's fittings, copper sheathing and fasteners, lead, and green glass. The current project suggests that the anchors and some of the ships' fittings on GC 006 date to the first half of the nineteenth century, while the cannon is earlier. Thus, it appears that the site may actually encompass the remains of at least two shipwrecks, and one may be a Wreck of the Ten Sail merchantman.

About halfway between GC 003 and GC 006, on the seaward side of the reef and embedded in it, there is a wooden-stocked long-shank anchor, which could belong to a third and earlier site. We discovered it in 1991 and designated it as GC 076. The 3.5 m (ca. 11.5 ft.) long anchor has one fluke embedded in the seafloor and the other is broken. The shank faces northwest toward the reef. One person reported to me more recently that years ago, he had removed a wrought-iron swivel gun from a location nearby, which he showed me. The site is complicated, including several shipwreck signatures. The swivel gun is similar (or perhaps the same gun) as OR 24, which, though in poor condition, is now in the custody of the National Museum. If the cannon and anchor truly are associated, the area could hold remains of one of the earliest shipwrecks found in the waters of Grand Cayman, disguised by later shipwrecks.

The 1991 team located and recorded GC 075, almost 200 m north of GC 003. The site is characterized by large concentrations of stone ballast (10–30 cm diameter) that are concreted on the reef and scattered shoreward. The team observed piles of ballast and scattered ballast on the fore-reef along with fragments of copper sheathing, tacks, and fasteners. We noted a few ships' fittings and fragments of glass. Although we found no diagnostic ceramics and glass, we concluded that GC 075 could be a Wreck of the Ten Sail merchantman.

When GC 044 was recorded in 1980 on the fore-reef, it was said to include an isolated wooden-stocked anchor, at least one iron object on the reef, and sparse, scattered "river rock" ballast. The INA team did not observe artifacts on the inside of the adjacent reef. They assessed the anchor to be a common style used on medium-draft merchantmen of the late eighteenth and early nineteenth centuries. One fluke was embedded in the seafloor, and the shank pointed shoreward as though it had been cast to hold a vessel off the reef. Since few features were recorded on the site, the INA team theorized that the ship that lost the anchor might have been extensively salvaged, pulled off the reef, or dispersed by storms.

When we explored GC 044 in 1991, we found it to be more extensive than previously thought. It includes substantial quantities of fist-sized slag ballast, identical in composition to that found at GC 026, pointing to a similar loading point or port of origin.[62] Along the top of the reef, our team discovered a near solid pile of this ballast that extends north and south for 45 m. It trails in short westerly fingers toward shore for about 30 m and then thins out considerably, but we observed sparse ships' fittings, copper sheathing, and fasteners up to 150 m from the reef. We collected a few green glass and earthenware olive-jar sherds and examined the 3.2 m (10.5 ft.) long anchor; its shank points to the southwest, in the breaking waves on the fore-reef. About 33 m northeast of the anchor, we discovered a pile of encrusted pig iron ballast (about 15 × 15 × 48 cm). It consists of between twenty and thirty pigs scattered in a northerly direction. Approximately 6.5 m east of the pig iron is what appears to be a 50 m long scour pit containing additional fist-sized slag ballast as well as copper drift-bolt fragments and nails. The team identified iron features, including ship's fittings, dispersed throughout the site.

At first, our team thought site GC 044 might be a possibility for the frigate *Convert* because of the presence of pig iron ballast. The pigs, however, we found not to be of dimensions standard for ballast used on eighteenth-century French warships, and the size of the anchor was more appropriate for a merchantman. Furthermore, little ceramic and glass material and no ordnance were apparent on the site. GC 044 is likely to be the site of a Wreck of the Ten Sail merchantman.

Site GC 025, located in East End Sound, was recorded by the INA team in 1980 as an isolated deposit of shipwreck material from an unknown source. The group described a light concentration of ballast over 30 m^2 of seafloor, which did not extend toward the reef and also observed iron fasteners and late eighteenth- or early nineteenth-century green glass sherds. They suggested that the site might be a portion of a larger wreck site located elsewhere. In 1991, our team observed small cobbles of flint pebble ballast, small amounts of dark-green glass (including diagnostic bottle lips), and ceramic sherds (including a green transfer-print pearlware mug sherd) on GC 025. We noted small clusters of pebbles on the reef, inside the reef, and dispersed lightly toward shore, along with small fragments of copper sheathing. The largest concentration of material was located about 150 to 175 m from the reef in a 50 m wide zone. On the fore-reef, we observed a few pieces of iron embedded in the seafloor. The glass and ceramic fragments located on this shipwreck site suggest that it dates to the early nineteenth century.[63] It is therefore unlikely that GC 025 is associated with the Wreck of the Ten Sail.[64]

Southern Survey Zone: GC 009, GC 022, GC 070, GC 071, and GC 077

Site GC 009 is located around two large coral formations in the middle of the inside passage through East End Channel, where there is generally a strong outflowing current. In 1980 the INA team observed an intact late-style Spanish olive jar, numerous olive-jar fragments, a brick, and small quantities of green glass on the site. These materials probably date to the late eighteenth century. Informant Marshall Watler told the survey team that at least six or eight intact olive jars had previously been recovered from the site. The INA team noted that the ceramics appeared to have no associated provenience. In 1991 we did not see much of the olive-jar material around the coral formations, but a significant amount may be buried in the sandy seabed.

Site GC 022, recorded in 1980 as "East End Channel Debris," encompasses GC 009 and includes most of East End Channel. The INA team suggested that it contained assorted material from several shipwrecks, which had probably been thrown into the lagoon during storms and carried out again through the channel. Among artifacts observed on the site were green glass fragments, ceramic sherds, copper sheathing, copper and iron fasteners, olive-jar sherds, tiles, bricks, and several iron ships' structural components. Significant amounts of ballast were not apparent on the site but may be buried. The team assessed most of the shipwreck debris as corresponding to the late eighteenth century. In 1991 we observed similar materials in East End Channel, and the survey team discovered one of the bags of artifacts that the INA team had buried at the conclusion of the 1980 field season. Although the plastic bag had deteriorated, the artifacts, duct tape, and labeled tag had survived two hurricanes in a protected pocket of the seabed. Considering that a passage was blown through the reef here in 1908 and that the channel has been modified in more recent times, it would not be surprising that a merchantman from the Wreck of the Ten Sail had actually wrecked in this area.

There is a long-shank anchor, typical of the late eighteenth century, located in the fore-reef area of East End Channel in 9 meters of water. We recorded it in 1991 as GC 077, but Charles Beeker had previously shown it to me. The anchor might be associated with GC 009, GC 022, or an undiscovered shipwreck in the vicinity, and it is likely to be associated with the Wreck of the Ten Sail. The encrusted anchor is about 3.73 m long (12 ft. 3 in.). In considering whether this anchor might relate to HMS *Convert*, it was determined that it may be too small to be the frigate's best bower (4.19 m long [13 ft. 9 in.]) or sheet (4.11 m long [13 ft. 6 in.]) anchor; it could be the small bower anchor (slightly smaller than the best bower and sheet anchors).[65] The stream and kedge anchors, as mentioned earlier, were salvaged in 1794.

Site GC 070 is the designation given in 1991 to the southern pebble ballast concentration in the INA team's former GC 012, located about 150 m west of the reef in East End Sound. The distinctive large flint pebble ballast is associated with creamwares and pearlwares in edge-decorated, hand-painted, transfer-printed, and annular ware designs, stonewares, and dark-green and brown bottle glass (diagnostic sherds of glass were not found in 1991). These may be late eighteenth-century artifacts, but the style of application of the blue band on shell-edged pearlware sherds and a red transfer-print fragment suggest that an early nineteenth-century date is more likely. Mid to late nineteenth- and twentieth-century ships have wrecked on the fore-reef and scattered across the reef in this vicinity too; thus, it is difficult to determine whether earlier shipwreck material extends toward the reef. Nonetheless, it is possible that a Wreck of the Ten Sail merchant ship was lost here and that GC 070 represents her remains.

Site GC 071, recorded in 1991, is also located within the former INA team's GC 012, slightly southeast of GC 070. It is characterized by angular chunks of slag ballast (10–30 cm diameter) that extend parallel to the reef for about 50 m and scatter toward the west-southwest. Although some slag is visible on the reef, it is not apparent on the fore-reef, which is heavily concreted in this area. Within the southern zone of the slag ballast spillage is a pocket of small pebble ballast, similar to that observed on site GC 012; it is associated with green glass fragments and pearlwares in shell-edged, hand-painted and annular ware patterns. The pebble ballast concentration appears to be from another site, overlapped by the slag ballast, but we did not give it a separate designation. We noted copper sheathing on the site. GC 071 is located just north of the remains of the wreck of a late nineteenth- or early twentieth-century riveted iron-hulled ship (GC 018). It is located southwest of the wreckage of a late nineteenth-century composite-built sailing vessel, GC 016, and may relate to it. It may, however, represent yet another shipwreck in the area. No clearly diagnostic materials were apparent on the site.[66]

Post-Eighteenth-Century Sites

All of the sites included in this section were recorded during the 1980 phase of the Cayman Islands Project. Gun Bay resident Marshall Watler originally reported most of them to project director Roger Smith. Data included in the site files prepared by the INA team are mentioned first, followed by assessments made in 1991.[67]

Site GC 001, located in the mid-lagoon at East End, includes the gunwale of a relatively large sailing vessel. It is partially buried, but wooden strakes and top-timbers, iron members, and chain plates with remnants of wooden deadeyes protrude above the turtle grass–covered seabed over a distance of 25 m. The 1980 INA project suggested that the site might relate to GC 012, located near the reef. As mentioned earlier, however, the INA team's GC 012 extends about 530 m and encompasses several shipwreck sites. GC 001 is not associated with the present, more closely defined, GC 012. In 1991 we concluded that GC 001 probably contains the remains of a nineteenth-century sailing vessel. While the site is not from the Wreck of the Ten Sail, the survival of the articulated gunwale of a ship in the soft sediments of East End Sound suggests that large parts of other vessels may also exist in buried contexts.

Both the 1980 INA investigation and the 1991 survey suggest that GC 002 includes the remains of a late nineteenth-century composite-built wooden sailing ship. Barrels of cement; numerous red tiles from Marseille, France; a windlass assembly; iron ship's members and fittings; and copper sheathing lie scattered across the seabed on the south side of East End Channel, with most artifacts concreted in place. We noted minimal ballast and no anchors on the site. Recently discovered documents and a photo of the brig *August* lead me to believe that this site is the remains of the Norwegian ship *August* that was built in Sweden in 1872 and wrecked under Norwegian flag in March 1897, en route from Marseille, France, to Progreso, Mexico.[68] I have seen identical red tiles, dating to this period, used in Mexican hacienda construction near Campeche, Mexico. It is also fascinating that in 2003 we discovered remnants of the red Marseille tiles during excavation of the old stepwell located adjacent to the waterfront in George Town, attesting to the salvage of shipwreck materials from East End that were transported and landed on the west side of Grand Cayman (see figure 1). Apparently this was common practice over several centuries, at least as early as the 1794 Wreck of the Ten Sail.

Assessments by INA and the 1991 project agree that GC 007 represents the remnants of a late nineteenth-century composite-built wooden sailing ship, scattered from the fore-reef into East End Sound. A Trotman anchor, two other iron-stocked anchors, anchor chain, a windlass assembly, iron ship's members and fittings, and copper sheathing characterize the site. The 1991 team also observed chunks of fist-sized slag ballast.

The 1980 project concluded that GC 008, located near Colliers, probably wrecked in the twentieth century. The site consists of sections of a metal-hulled ship made up of plates of iron or steel riveted together, but appears to lack hardware associated with either sailing rigging or engine apparatus. The 1991 project concluded that the vessel might date to either the end of the nineteenth century or the twentieth century.

In 1980, the INA team recorded several sites in the survey zone that date to the twentieth century. Site GC 013, also near Colliers, comprises substantial remains of a large iron-hulled sailing ship, including anchors. Fragments of the ship have been carried up onto the reef. Marshall Watler of Gun Bay told the INA crew that the site was that of the *Glynnis*, which wrecked at the turn of the century, while other people mentioned the names *Marabelle* and *Metusala*. The crews of both the 1980 and 1991 surveys did not find associated artifacts on the inside of the reef. However, in 1991 the team noted buried magnetic anomalies in a shallow shoal in that vicinity. In 2003–4 this site was mapped, including two anchors, numerous hull fragments, iron chain plates with wooden deadeyes, a windlass, a capstan, a rudder stock with tiller, a rudder frame, the jib boom, multiple bollards, and the wheel. A year after Hurricane Ivan, in September 2005, on a calm day, two more anchors were discovered almost up on the reef. This shipwreck is *Glamis*, built in Dundee, Scotland, in 1876 and lost under Norwegian flag in 1913.[69] We now have a wealth of information about *Glamis*, from her sailing, wrecking, and salvage history to photographs, and even a connection with the living descendants of the ship's Norwegian owners. The Cayman Islands Maritime Heritage Trail Partnership (National Museum, Department of Environment, National Trust, and National Archive) is seeking to interpret *Glamis* as the first shipwreck preserve in the Cayman Islands.

Information obtained by the Cayman Islands Project suggests that *Rimandi Mibaju*, site GC 014, was an ore freighter, carrying a cargo of bauxite, that wrecked north of East End Channel in 1964. Parts of the superstructure of this modern steel ship were above water in 1980, before Hurricane Allen passed near Grand Cayman. During that storm high seas pounded the ship, causing her to collapse below sea level. Much of the vessel is strewn on the seabed of the fore-reef, but some parts of the ship span the reef into the sound. In 1991 a local resident was allowed, after the fact, to salvage the ship's brass propeller. A fortuitous twist of fate resulted in a change of plan; the propeller is now on public display in a park dedicated to the Wreck of the Ten Sail, at East End.

Ridgefield, site GC 015, wrecked on the south side of East End Channel in about 1962. The large steel Liberty ship is said to have been built in 1943–44 with the original name of *James A. Butts* and to have seen action during World War II. During Hurricane Allen (1980) the forward deck of the wreck collapsed, and in Hurricane Gilbert (1988) parts of the ship were carried over the reef into East End Sound. *Ridgefield* rests on an earlier wreck, GC 020. In 1991, we observed its brass propeller embedded halfway into the ballast pile of the older vessel. Around this time, the government prevented a salvage attempt on the propeller. In 1991 three segments of the ship were still visible above sea level: the bow and bits of the superstructure outside the reef, and a large part of the midsection within the lagoon. In 2019, small parts of these features still protrude above the water.

According to the 1980 survey, site GC 016 appears to be the wreck of a post-1850s composite-built wooden sailing ship. It is located on the fore-reef, adjacent to and partially beneath *Rimandi Mibaju*. Principal features include four large anchors, the windlass assembly, a section of an iron mast, and numerous iron ships' members and fittings. The 1991 crew agreed that GC 016 dates to the nineteenth century.

In 1980 Marshall Watler identified GC 018 as *Lilly*. The site comprises the bow of a late nineteenth- or early twentieth-century sailing vessel with a riveted iron hull and wooden decks. Marshall Watler told the INA crew that the wreckage had washed over the reef. *Lilly*, still visible above sea level, is embedded in a turtle grass–covered sandbar within the lagoon on the north side of East End Channel. The 1980 team suggested that GC 018 might be related to GC 019 and/or GC 021, sites situated on the fore-reef on opposite sides of East End Channel. The 1991 crew concluded that the site is associated with GC 019. They discovered pieces of riveted iron hull, matching those observed on GC 018, to the northeast of GC 018 on the reef and within the sound, opposite GC 019. The bow feature still protrudes above the water's surface in 2019.

Site GC 019 was originally recorded to consist of a single iron-stocked anchor, which is located northeast of *Lilly*, in 2 m of water, on the seaward side of the barrier reef. The anchor is embedded in and concreted to the coral boulder ramparts. As discussed, the two sites appear related.

Site GC 020 extends from beneath the stern of *Ridgefield* on the fore-reef, over the reef, and into East End Sound. It consists of the remains of a post-1850s composite-built wooden sailing vessel with at least three iron-stocked anchors (two of them being Trotman anchors). In 1980 the survey team noted copper sheathing, a windlass assembly, iron ships' fittings, and quarried ballast stones on the site. By 1991 *Ridgefield*'s brass propeller, about 5 m in diameter, was embedded halfway into the earlier ship's ballast, now identified as fist-sized chunks of slag, as related.

In 1980 the INA crew documented GC 021, an iron-hulled sailing vessel of the late nineteenth or early twentieth century, located on the outer reef south of East End Channel. The site contains three iron-stocked anchors, sections of the iron hull and masts, hawse pipes, mooring bits, a capstan, a windlass assembly, and other wreckage. By 1991 the site remained relatively unchanged.

The INA team recorded site GC 034, the solid lead keel of a modern sailing yacht, in 1980 near Colliers Channel. It was said to have belonged to a vessel named *Wander IX* that ran aground but was pulled off again in 1963. The keel was salvaged in 1991 for its metal value, by the same local resident who lifted the *Rimandi Mibaju* propeller; in a similar twist of fate, this lead keel is now displayed along with that propeller in the Wreck of the Ten Sail Park.

Summary

The professional archaeological fieldwork carried out by INA during the 1980s phase of the Cayman Islands Project laid the foundation for the more detailed study conducted from 1990 through 1993. Thirty underwater sites and eight terrestrial sites have been located within a defined survey zone at East End. The French Cannon Site, GC 017, and the Probable Frigate Spillage Site, GC 012, appear to represent the remains of the Royal Navy frigate *Convert*. Salvage activity and the forces of nature have disturbed both sites, but they still hold a tangible record about *Convert*, ex-*Inconstante*, and the people who sailed her, information that is available through no other source. The Probable Salvage Campsite, GC 041, contained large amounts of eighteenth-century material that suggests it was the principal salvage campsite used by Captain Lawford and his men, and possibly the crews of the merchantmen. Site GCL 016 and perhaps additional terrestrial sites also feature components that suggest they were salvage campsites related to the *Convert* convoy.

The merchantmen of the Wreck of the Ten Sail are difficult to identify precisely, but hypotheses can be made. GC 026 is believed to represent the remains of one of the merchant vessels, while GC 072 and GC 073 are too sparse to classify. GC 074 may be the partial remains of a merchantman and might be affiliated with GC 075, a probable Wreck of the Ten Sail merchantman. Sites GC 003 and GC 044 are excellent candidates for two of the merchant vessels. It is possible that GC 006 contains two or three wreck sites, and that one may be a Wreck of the Ten Sail merchantman. The long-shank anchor designated GC 076 is likely to be affiliated with an earlier shipwreck. Sites GC 009, GC 022 and GC 077, all located in the vicinity of East End Channel, could be the dispersed remains of one of the merchantmen, with perhaps the long-shank anchor designated as GC 077 being more probably associated with HMS *Convert* as her small bower anchor. Site GC 070 is a remote possibility for a Wreck of the Ten Sail merchantman, but may instead date to the early nineteenth century. Site GC 071 overlaps a deposit of eighteenth-century artifacts from an unknown source, but diagnostic materials were not clearly associated with the slag ballast that represents the site. While GC 071 might be affiliated with a late nineteenth-century wreck, it could be earlier; slag ballast has been found on both eighteenth- and nineteenth-century sites. GC 025 is probably an early nineteenth-century wreck. Sites GC 001, GC 002, GC 007, GC 008, GC 013, GC 014, GC 015, GC 016, GC 018, GC 019, GC 020, and GC 021 are undoubtedly nineteenth- and twentieth-century sites. GC 034, a twentieth-century lead keel, was recovered from the seabed.

Conclusion

Archival research on Cayman's 1794 Wreck of the Ten Sail has focused on the construction, service life, and wrecking of a frigate between 1789 and 1794. This brief span of time was an extraordinary period in the history of the Caribbean, Europe, and the world. In the archives of Great Britain, France, and Jamaica I discovered eighteenth-century documents that tell the story of this warship and provide a window into the social history of the era from both French and British perspectives. It is rare to have such a rich record.

In March 1789, King Louis XVI of France gave instructions to name a new 12-pounder frigate *L'Inconstante*; two months later the ship was under construction in the Royal Dockyard of Rochefort. The shipwright St. Pennevert built *L'Inconstante* according to a draft by Jean Denis Chevillard, who created his plan in the era when eighteenth-century French naval design had reached its pinnacle. Although France built more than one hundred 12-pounder frigates between 1748 and 1798, only eight had the same design as *L'Inconstante.*

The French Revolution erupted in Paris in July 1789 while *L'Inconstante* was under construction at Rochefort. After minor delays, the dockyard launched the frigate on 9 September 1790 and was sheathing the vessel in copper by December. The vessel was fitted out for service the following year. The French Navy gave *L'Inconstante*'s command to Alexandre Joseph Riouffe, Capitaine de Vaisseau, whose orders were to serve in the troubled French Caribbean colony of Saint-Domingue.

After an aborted attempt to sail to the West Indies in January 1792, *L'Inconstante* again embarked on 12 April 1792. Eight days later France declared war on Austria, beginning the French revolutionary wars. France abolished the French monarchy, established the first French Republic, and executed King Louis XVI by guillotine, during Captain Riouffe's tour of duty in the Caribbean. Social, political, and military upheavals also gripped the French colony of Saint-Domingue.

When news reached Jamaica on 29 March 1793 that France had declared war on Britain on 1 February, Commodore John Ford's forces immediately captured all French vessels in Port Royal and Kingston Harbours and dispatched the Jamaica squadron on patrol missions around Saint-Domingue. The following September, British forces landed on Saint-Domingue and took possession of Jérémie and the harbor and fortress at Le Môle St. Nicolas. On 25 November 1793, while *L'Inconstante* was returning to Port-au-Prince from a convoy mission to Petit Trou, His Majesty's ships *Penelope*, Captain B. S. Rowley, and *Iphigenia*, Captain Patrick Sinclair, captured the French frigate. Captain Riouffe was among the French officers and seamen who died of wounds received in the brief engagement.

British men sailed the French prize to Jamaica, where the Royal Navy acquired the hull, sails, rigging, ordnance, and stores. The High Court of Vice Admiralty adjudicated the case and distributed the net proceeds of the prize money among *L'Inconstante*'s captors. As there was already an *Inconstant* in His Majesty's Service, Commodore Ford renamed the frigate *Convert*. He gave her command to Captain John Lawford, with *Convert*'s first mission assigned to escort a homeward-bound merchant fleet to Britain.

After acquiring a crew of officers and seamen by assignment, recruitment, and impressment, *Convert* collected her merchant convoy. The fleet sailed from Jamaica on 6 February 1794, but a leaky merchantman delayed its progress, so *Convert*'s officers did not sight Grand Cayman before sunset on 7 February. At midnight, when Master Thomas Popplewell reckoned that the fleet was clear of Grand Cayman, he obtained Captain Lawford's permission to shift the convoy's course more to the northward. The voyage ended in the early morning hours of 8 February 1794 when a disastrous chain of events resulted in the loss of *Convert* and nine ships of her merchant convoy on the windward reefs of Grand Cayman.

Captain Lawford endeavored to save *Convert*'s passengers and crew, and with the help of the island's inhabitants few lives were lost. Captain Daniel Martin of the wrecked merchant ship *Britannia* was one of eight people who drowned. The Caymanians were suffering hardships from a recent hurricane and could not support the shipwreck victims on Grand Cayman. Thus, Lawford sent most of the people off to Europe in other ships of the convoy. He sent a report of the wrecking to the Admiralty and dispatched First Lieutenant Bradby Bogue to Jamaica to inform Commodore Ford. *Convert*'s officers and thirty seamen camped on the East End beach and salvaged goods from *Convert*.

Commodore Ford was patrolling the waters near Saint-Domingue when he received news of the shipwreck disaster. He immediately dispatched HMS *Success*, Captain Francis Roberts, to Grand Cayman. Before *Success* departed Grand Cayman at the end of March with *Convert*'s officers, remaining crew, and salvaged stores, Captains Roberts and Lawford signed agreements with Caymanians William Bodden Sr. and Robert Knowles Clarke to continue the salvage of *Convert*.

The crews of the shipwrecked merchantmen also salvaged their vessels, but they lost a large percentage of the perishable cargoes. Most of the remainder of the dispersed *Convert* convoy safely reached Britain, with the exception of *Susannah*, McIsaac, captured by a French privateer and *Peggy*, Robertson, taken prize by a French Navy frigate.

A court-martial held aboard HMS *Success* on 1 April 1794, tried Captain Lawford, the officers, and crew of *Convert* for the loss of His Majesty's ship. The court honorably acquitted all, attributing the misfortune to a strong current taking the convoy to the north of their reckoning.

The narrative of *L'Inconstante*'s career and loss of HMS *Convert*, as revealed through archival sources, has laid a solid foundation for understanding the ships and people of Cayman's 1794 Wreck of the Ten Sail. There are additional records, however, in the archives of Britain, France, and Jamaica that will enable future researchers to further investigate particular ships, individuals, and events.

Caymanian oral history and folklore on the Wreck of the Ten Sail adds a dimension to this investigation often overlooked in historical studies and archaeological projects. This book has provided a background to remembrances and surviving tales of the shipwrecks in the Cayman Islands. Connecting the past with the present, the colorful folklore reveals the Wreck of the Ten Sail to be a significant event in the history of the Cayman Islands, which attained local value in Caymanian society and lives on as the most well-remembered and told story of Cayman's many shipwreck tales. It matters little that the stories are inconsistent with the historical and archaeological record. The current study has identified the potential for a thorough analysis of Caymanian shipwreck and wrecking folklore—including, of course, the Wreck of the Ten Sail.

Archaeological investigations have shown that in addition to a rich archival record and delightful folklore, archaeological remains of the Wreck of the Ten Sail exist. Within a 5 km survey zone, archaeologists identified thirty underwater sites and eight terrestrial sites dating between the late eighteenth century and the twentieth century. The French Cannon Site, GC 017, and the Probable Frigate Spillage Site, GC 012, appear to represent the remains of His Majesty's ship *Convert*, while the Probable Salvage Campsite, GC 041, contains related artifacts. All of these sites, although altered by salvage activities and violent storms, still contain tangible evidence of *Convert*, ex-*Inconstante*, and thereby can convey information about late eighteenth-century shipboard life and the naval warships of France and Britain. While historical studies of the French revolutionary and Napoleonic wars are abundant, few vessels from this time period have been archaeologically studied.

Many identified sites hold remains of the merchant ships and brigs of the Wreck of the Ten Sail. These have the potential of providing a physical record of Britain's merchant navy in the late eighteenth century.

The East End reefs of Grand Cayman are a significant historical shipwreck zone, where Wreck of the Ten Sail sites have been located, documented, and assessed. All of these archaeological sites are worthy of protection by the Cayman Islands government, and this is still being accomplished through creative use of the Abandoned Wreck Law.

The Cayman Islands featured this Wreck of the Ten Sail research in the Cayman Islands during the bicentenary of the disaster in 1994. The National Museum presented an exhibit that brought archaeology into the public eye, and government officials and museum staff, including the author, enjoyed escorting Britain's reigning monarch, Queen Elizabeth II, and Prince Philip through it (figure 36). The Cayman Islands Postal Service created a special stamp issue, the Currency Board minted a commemorative coin, the National Archive published a book with Cayman Free Press, and the Visual Arts Society held an art competition. The museum facilitated public lectures and radio and television appearances to increase awareness. The Cayman Islands government also acknowledged the importance of historical wrecks when it created the land-based Wreck of the Ten Sail Park at East End, also dedicated by the queen in 1994, and providing a view of the reefs where HMS *Convert* and part of her convoy wrecked.

In the Cayman Islands, four decades of successive projects, from INA and Roger Smith's Cayman Islands Project in 1979–80 up to the present National Museum and Maritime Heritage Trail and Shipwreck Preserve Partnerships, have laid foundations of research, awareness, protection, management, and interpretation of shipwreck sites. As present National Museum director and archaeologist, I am advocating for the Cayman Islands government to further support steps undertaken to establish CIMAP, the proposed Cayman Islands Maritime Archaeology Program, and to coordinate with the United Kingdom on protection of HMS *Convert*, since as a British warship, the frigate's remains technically belong to the United Kingdom. At long last, plans for further scientific investigation into the Wreck of the Ten Sail, among other sites, can go forward at a quicker pace. Site investigation and recovery, conservation, and analysis of artifacts, now

Figure 36. Her Majesty Queen Elizabeth II and Prince Philip tour the *Wreck of the Ten Sail* exhibit at the Cayman Islands National Museum. Photograph by Lennon Christian, courtesy of Cayman Islands Government Information Services.

and in the future, will result in a collection of artifacts and a body of information that can be used in interpretive displays in the Cayman Islands for the education and enjoyment of the public. They tell a story of Cayman, the Caribbean, Europe, and the world—a story that took place 225 years ago.

I began this research ten years after experiencing the summer of 1980 as an INA team member on the Cayman Islands Project. At the time I had no idea that by 1986 the Cayman Islands would become my home and that I would spend the next three decades and more researching, protecting, and interpreting historical sites, shipwrecks, and artifacts in these Caribbean islands, with the support of dedicated and aware people and institutions. Many opportunities and challenges have come my way, and progress is evident. While time can seem long and trying, in perspective it is short and fleeting. Contributions each of us has made illuminate elements of the past that speak to our awareness in the present and contribute to the formation of the future. I have benefited and built on work started by others, and now look to the future with the knowledge that others will pick up the torch and make their own contributions. I wish them fair winds and calm seas.

Appendix A

Inventory of *L'Inconstante*

Inventory and Appraisement of the Sails, Rigging, Ordnance and Stores from *L'Inconstante* That Were Acquired for His Majesty's Service

> Pursuant to an Order from John Ford Esqr Commodore and Commander in Chief & & & date the 30th November 1793, and to us directed ~

We whose Names are hereunto Subscribed have been on board the Frigate *L'Inconstant* and there have taken a strict and Careful Survey of such of her Sails, Rigging and Stores, as are fit for His Majesty's Service and find them to be as herein set forth with our Appraisement Annexed (Viz^{t})

Boatswain Stores

Canvas	N°	3 .... 200 Yards		New
"	"	5 50 Yards		"
Cables of	17^{ins}	..........2 N°	(90 f^{ms} Each)	⅓ Worn
" "	17	.... 20 fath^{ms}	....	Bridles
Messenger	9	1 N°	(45 f^{ms})	New
Cablet of	7	.... 21 f^{ms}	.....	"
	4½	.... 30 "	.....	"
Hawser "	5	........................209 "	.....	"
"	4½	........................101 "	.....	"
"	4	213 "		"
Rope of	3½^{ins}	...... 6 Coils	(108 f^{ms} Each)	New
" "	3½	.....20 f^{ms}........................		"
" "	3	...... 6 Coils	(108 f^{ms} Each)	"
" "	3	.....80 fath^{ms}......................		"
" "	2½	...... 4 Coils	(108 f^{ms} Each	"
" "	2	...... 8 "	(108 " .. " ..	"
" "	1½	...... 4 "	(108 " .. " ..	"
" "	1	...... 6 "	(108 " .. " ..	"

White Rope 4½	70 fath^ms^		"
" " 3½	25 fath^ms^		"
" " 1½	200 "		"
" " 1	100 "		"

	C : q^ts^ : l^b^		
Anchors of	30 : 3 : 1	Four	Serviceable
" "	9 : 2 : 16	One	
" "	6 : 1 : 10	One	
Iron Hanks		48	
Grapnel Boat	40 l^b^	1	
" "	25	1	
" "	20	1	
" Fire & Chain		2	
" Hand & Chain		2	
Hooks Tackle		24	
Traveller Jibb		1	
Thimbles of Sorts		31	
Leads Deepsea		1	
" Hand		1	

Sails

Boom Driver	1 N^o^	New
Flying Jibb	1 "	"
D^o^	1 "	⅓ Worn
D^o^	1 "	½ d^o^
Fore Course	1 "	New
" Topsails	3 "	"
" " Gall^t^ Royal	1 "	½ Worn
Main Course	1 "	New
" D^o^	1 "	¾ Worn
" Topsail	1 "	"
" " Gall^t^ Sail	1 "	New
" " " Royal	1 "	½ Worn
Mizen Course	1 "	New
" Topsail	1 "	"
" " Gall^t^ Sail	1 "	¾ Worn
Stay Sail Main	1 "	New
" " Mizen	1 "	½ Worn
" " Main Top	1 "	D^o^
" " Fore Top	1 "	New
" " Fore Top	1 "	⅔ ^ds^ Worn
" " Main Top Gall^t^	1 "	D^o^
" " Middle	1 "	¾ Worn
Studdingsail Main	2 "	New
" " " Top	1 "	"
" " Fore Top	1 "	⅔ ^ds^ Worn
" " Fore Top	1 "	½ Worn
" " Mizen Top	1 "	New
" " Fore	1 "	⅔ ^ds^ Worn

Boat Sails	2 "		½ Worn
Standing Rigging Complete			½ Worn

Carpenters Stores

Handscrew	1 N°	Serviceable
Iron Ballast 1600 Pigs	80 Tons	
Goose Neck with Bolts}	1 N°	
Hinges Scuttle	2½ p^r	
Chain Pump Wheel	2 N°	

All which Sails, Rigging and Stores, We find to be as against Each Article express't, and we think the Boatswain's Stores to be worth the sum of One Thousand Seven Hundred and Seventy three Pounds Five Shillings and Seven Pence, and the Carpenters Five Hundred, and Thirty Eight Pounds, Seven Shillings and Six Pence Sterling. Total Two Thousand, three Hundred, and Eleven Pounds Thirteen Shillings and One Penny Sterling Exchange at £ 40. . p^rCent Equal to Three Thousand, two Hundred and Thirty Six Pounds Six Shillings and Three Pence Currency ~

And we do declare that we have made and taken this Survey and Appraisement with such Care and Equity that (if required) We are ready to make Oath to the Impartiality of our Proceedings

In Witness whereof We have hereunto set our Hands at His Majesty's Yard at Port Royal this 20th day of December 1793 ~

Willm Smith	Naval Storekeeper
Saml Sherwin	Master of the *Alligator*
Robt Farris	Master of the *Musquito*

(A Copy)
Jn° Ford

Inventory and Estimation of Sundry Ordnance and Ordnance Stores taken on board the French Frigate *L'Inconstant*

				T : C : Q	£	S	D
Iron Ordnance	12 p^{drs}	26 N°		42 . 18 . 0			
	6 d°	6 "		5 . 2 . 0			
	at £16 p^{r} Ton			48 . 0 . 0	768	0	0
			S	£ S . D			
Ship Carriages with Beds and Coins	12 p^{drs}	26 N°	@70/	91 . 0 . 0			
	6 "	6	@50	15 . 0 . 0	106	0	0
Round Shot	12 p^{drs} 1460 N°		T C Q l^{bs}	£			
	6 " 170 "		8 . 5 . 2 . 4	@12p^{r} ton	99	6	3
		No	£ S D				
Grape Shot	12 p^{drs}	250@3/6 ea	43 . 15 . 0				
	6 "	58 1/9	5 . 1 . 6		48	16	6
Langrage Shot	12 "	210@4/ ea	42 . 0 . 0				
	6 "	55@2/	5 . 10 . 0		47	10	0
Dbleheaded Shot	12 "	150@4/ea	30 . 0 . 0				
	6 "	20@2/	2 . 0 . 0		32	0	0
Parchment Cartridges	12 p^{drs}		800 N° @/4		13	6	0
			£ S D				
Cases of Wood	12 p^{drs}	23N° @4/	4 . 12 . 0				
	6 "	6 @2"	12 . 0		5	4	0
Ladles & Wadhooks	12 p^{drs}	4 "	1 . 10 . 0				
	6 "	1 "	4 . 6		1	14	6
Spunges	12 p^{drs}	28 N° @3/			4	4	0
				Carried Over	1126	1	3

Item	No.		Rate	£	S	D	£	s	d
Brought Over						£	1126	1	3
				£	S	D			
Corned Powder {whole Barrels 29 @ £7				203	0	0			
Corned Powder {half do 9				31	10	0			
							234	10	3
Parchment Cartridges filled with Powder } 12pdrs 356No; 6 " 25 } Weight 1474 lbs @ 1/							73	14	0
Cartridges wth do							4	15	0
Match 84 lbs @ 1/							4	4	0
Powderhorns 25 No @ 1/							1	5	0
Priming Irons 35 "								3	0
Aprons of Lead, large	21	No	@ 1/6				1	11	6
Wood handspikes	25	"	@ 1/				1	5	0
Crows of Iron 4½ ft	31		@ 7/6				10	17	0
Tackles Complete wth Blocks & Hooks } 2½ins.	32	No	@ 5/				8	0	0
Hand Grenades	60	No	@ 1/6				4	10	0
Bright Muskets	85	No	@ 15/	63	15				
Bayonets	15		@ 2/6	1	17	6			
							65	12	6
Pole Axes	38		@ 2/	3	16	0			
Strong Pikes	29		@ 2/6	3	12	6			
							7	8	6
						Sterling £	1543	16	9
						Equal in Jamaica Currency to	2161	7	6

Office of Ordnance
Jamaica 21 Dec. 1793

Nichl Lechmere
H: A: Genet

(Copy)
Jno Ford

Source: Public Record Office, Kew, England (PRO), Admiralty Records (ADM) 1/245, Admiralty and Secretariat Papers, "Jamaica 1793 & 94 Admiral John Ford Esqr." Enclosure in Commodore John Ford to Philip Stephens, Secretary of the Admiralty aboard the *Europa*, off Jérémie, 5 February 1794.

Appendix B

Condemnation of *L'Inconstante*

The following has been transcribed from Jamaica Archives, High Court of Vice Admiralty, Ships' Papers, "*L'Inconstante* to HMS *Penelope*, Taken 25th November 1793, Condemned."

Monition:

JAMAICA, Is. GEORGE the Third, by the Grace of God, of GREAT-BRITAIN, FRANCE, and IRELAND King, and of JAMAICA Lord, Defender of the Faith, &c. To HUGH HOLSON, Esquire, Marshal of our Court of Vice-Admiralty of our said Island of Jamaica, or to any of his lawful Deputies, Greetings. Whereas our trusty and well-beloved the Honourable SAMUEL WHITEHORNE, Esquire, Judge Surrogate and Commissary of our said Court, doth order and decree to call and cite before him, on a certain day and time, and after the form and manner herein after prescribed, all manner of persons whatsoever, (except the subjects and vassals of France, or others inhabiting within the countries, territories, or dominions of France) That have, or pretend to have, any just claim, right, title or interest of, in, or to a certain Armed Ship or vessel of War called—*La Inconstant*—whereof one Jean Riouffe—late was or pretended to be master, her tackle, apparel, and furniture, and the goods, wares, merchandize, Slaves, Specie and effects on board her, taken and seized by Bartholomew Samuel Rowley Esquire Commander of our Ship of War *Penelope* and Patrick Sinclair Esquire Commander of our Ship of War *Iphigenia* their Several and respective Officers, Marines and Mariners—which said Armed Ship or vessel is now riding at anchor in the harbour of Kingston in the Island aforesaid, and within the jurisdiction of this Court.

We Therefore will, require, and strictly command You, or any of Ye, that by affixing of this Monition at some public place, at our towns of St. Jago de la Vega, Kingston, and Port-Royal, at the time of public concourse of merchants, You warn and monite all and every person and persons whatsoever, (except such person or persons who are excepted and precluded as aforesaid) that have, or pretend to have, any just claim, right, title, or interest of, in, or to the said Armed Ship or vessel, called—*La Inconstant*—whereof the said Jean Riouffe—late was or pretended to be master, her tackle, apparel, and furniture, and the goods, wares, merchandize, Slaves, Specie and effects on board her, taken and seized as aforesaid, That they be and appear before our said Judge, within our town of St. Jago de la Vega, on Tuesday next, being the tenth—day of December inst. between the hours of Eight and Twelve in the forenoon of the same day, then and there to shew some just, reasonable, and lawful cause (if any they can) why the said Armed Ship or vessel, her apparel, and furniture, and the Goods, Wares, Merchandize, Slaves, Specie and Effects taken and seized as aforesaid, should not be forfeited and confiscated to the use of the said Bartholomew Samuel Rowley and Patrick Sinclair Commanders as aforesaid their Several and respective officers, seamen, marines, and Mariners for and by reason that the said Armed Ship or vessel, her tackle, apparel, and furniture, and the goods, wares, merchandize, Slaves, Specie and effects aforesaid, did, at the time of the capture and seizure aforesaid, belong to and were the property of some or one of the subjects of France, or persons inhabiting the territories or countries of France, between whom and us, it is public and notorious, that there was and still is hostility and war.

AND We further require and command You, that You intimate, or cause to be intimated, as We do intimate by these presents to all persons in general (except such persons who are excepted and precluded as aforesaid) That if they do not appear at the time and place aforesaid, and, when there, shew some just, reasonable, and lawful cause to the contrary, the said Judge of our said Court will proceed and pronounce the said Armed Ship or vessel, her tackle, apparel, and furniture, and the goods, wares, merchandize, Slaves, Specie and effects aforesaid, taken and seized as aforesaid, to be rightfully and lawfully seized, and to be a just and lawful prize to the use of the said Bartholomew Samuel Rowley and Patrick Sinclair Commanders as aforesaid their Several and respective—officers, seamen, marines, and Mariners as goods forfeited and confiscated to them for the reasons aforesaid. And if the persons hereby monited do not appear at the time and place aforesaid, their absence will be deemed and accounted as consumacy. And what you have done in the premises you shall certify to us or to our said Judge of our said Court, with these presents. Dated at St. Jago de la Vega, in our said Court, and under the seal of the same, this fifth day of December in the year of our Lord one thousand seven hundred and ninety three and of our reign the thirty fourth.

W[m] Walker Dep Reg Cur Vi Adm

Libel:

Jamaica Is.
In the Court of Vice Admiralty}

The Advocate General at the Relation of Bartholomew Samuel Rowley Esquire Commander of His Majesty's Ship of War *Penelope* Patrick Sinclair Esquire Commander of His Majesty's Ship of War *Iphigenia* their Several and Respective Officers, Marines and Mariners—

against—

A Certain Armed Ship or Vessel called *La Inconstant* her Guns Tackle furniture Ammunition and Apparel and all and Singular the Goods Wares Merchandize Slaves Specie and effects on board her—

Be it Remembered that on the fifth—day of December in the Year of our Lord One Thousand Seven Hundred and Ninety three Came George Crawford Ricketts Esquire His Majesty's Advocate General for the said Island who for and on behalf of our Sovereign Lord the King in this behalf prosecuted against a certain Armed Ship or Vessel called *La Inconstant* whereof one Jean Riouffe late was or pretended to be Master her Guns Tackle furniture Ammunition and Apparel and all and Singular the Goods Wares Merchandize Slaves Specie and effects on board her taken and Seized as French Property and goods and lawful Prize on the High Seas and within the Jurisdiction of this Court by the said Bartholomew Samuel Rowley Esquire Commander of His Majesty's Ship of War *Penelope*, Patrick Sinclair Esquire Commander of His Majesty's Ship of War *Iphigenia* their Several and Respective Officers, Marines and Mariners. In pursuance of His Majesty's Royal Proclamation bearing Date on or about the Eleventh day of February One Thousand Seven Hundred and Ninety three which recites That Whereas diverse injurious proceedings have lately been had in France in derogation of the Honor of His Majesty's Crown and of the Just Rights of His Subjects, and also That Whereas Several unjust seizures have been there made of the Ships and Goods of His Majesty's Subjects contrary to the law of Nations and to the faith of Treaties and also That Whereas the said acts of Unprovoked Hostility have been followed by an open declaration of War against His Majesty and His Ally the Republic of the United Provinces his said Majesty being therefore determined to take such Measures as were Necessary for Vindicating the Honor of his Crown and for procuring Reparation and Satisfaction for his injured Subjects was pleased by and with the advice of his Privy Council to order and it was thereby ordered that general reprisals should be granted against the Ships Goods and Subjects of France so that as well his Majesty's Fleet and Ships as also all other Ships and Vessels that should be Commissioned by Letters of Marque or general reprisals or otherwise by his Majesty's Commissioners for Executing the Office of Lord High Admiral of Great Britain should and might lawfully Seize all Ships Vessels and goods belonging to France or to any Persons being Subjects of France or inhabiting within any of the Territories of France and bring the same to Judgment in any of the Courts of Admiralty within any of His Majesty's Dominions And the said George Crawford Ricketts Advocate General as aforesaid for and on behalf of our Sovereign Lord the King doth Article Allege Aver Propound and Say that the said Ship or Vessel called *La Inconstant* her Guns Tackle furniture Ammunition and Apparel and all and Singular the Goods Wares Merchandize Slaves Specie and effects on board her on or about the Twenty fifth day of November in the said year of our Lord One Thousand Seven Hundred and Ninety three were taken and Seized as French Property and good and lawful Prize on the High Seas and within the Jurisdiction of this Court by the said Bartholomew Samuel Rowley, Patrick Sinclair their Several and Respective Officers, Marines and Mariners. And the said George Crawford Ricketts Advocate General as aforesaid on the behalf aforesaid doth further Article Allege Aver Propound and Say that the said Ship or Vessel called *La Inconstant*, her Guns Tackle furniture Ammunition and Apparel and all and Singular the Goods Wares Merchandize Slaves Specie and effects on board her did at the time of such taking as aforesaid belong unto the State or Government of France between whom and our said Sovereign Lord the King it is Public and Notorious there then was and now is Hostility and War Subsisting—

Whereupon and upon all and Singular the premises the said George Crawford Ricketts Advocate General as aforesaid humbly prays that the said Ship or Vessel called—*La Inconstant* her Guns Tackle furniture Ammunition and Apparel and all and Singular the Goods Wares Merchandize Slaves Specie and effects on board her taken and Seized as aforesaid may be adjudged to be lawful Prize and may be confiscated and Condemned to the use of our said Sovereign Lord the King and that the same may be sold and the price and prices of all and every part and part thereof may be applied and distributed to and among the Captors According to His Majesty's Royal Proclamation And that this Libel may be received—

G^{eo} C. Ricketts
C^{ha} William Alder, Proctor

Appendix C

Biographical Sketch of John Lawford

During this investigation of the Wreck of the Ten Sail, biographical information about Captain John Lawford of HMS *Convert* came to light that deals almost exclusively with the Royal Navy officer's career; clues to his personal life emerge from his family tree and will and that of his wife. John Lawford was born in 1756/57 and baptized on 3 July 1757 in Portsea St. Marys Hants. He married Anna Maria Holden in 1803 when he was about forty-seven years old and she was forty-five; a review of their wills suggests that while they did not have their own children, they maintained other close family ties and enjoyed friendship with a variety of people from different walks of life. John Lawford died on 22 December 1842 at the age of eighty-six. His wife died eleven years later at the age of ninety-five.[1]

Details about Lawford's advancement in the Royal Navy are available in sources located at the Public Record Office and the National Maritime Museum in England. He became a lieutenant in the Royal Navy at the age of twenty-one, on 23 December 1777. Ten years later, on 1 December 1787, he achieved the rank of commander. John Lawford was promoted to post captain on 1 December 1793. He became Rear Admiral of the Blue on 1 August 1811, Rear Admiral of the White on 4 December 1813, and Rear Admiral of the Red on 4 June 1814. He attained the status of Vice Admiral of the Blue on 12 August 1819 and Vice Admiral of the White on 19 July 1821. He achieved the rank of Admiral of the Blue on 22 July 1830 and progressed to Admiral of the White on 10 January 1837 and Admiral of the Red on 23 November 1841. He was awarded the title of Knight Commander of the Bath in 1838.[2]

According to Pitcairn-Jones, John Lawford was commissioned into twelve Royal Navy ships and vessels over the course of his naval career.[3] In 1778, he became second lieutenant on *Active* and in 1780 held the same post on *Namur* (90 guns). He served as first lieutenant on *Crown* (64) in 1784 and on *Leander* (50) in 1787. In 1790 he was commander of the sloop *Hound*

(16) and in 1794 became captain of the frigate *Convert* (36).[4] Lawford was captain of *Agincourt* (64) in 1797 and of *Romney* (50) in 1798. He became captain of *Polyphemus* (64) in 1800, of *Invincible* in about 1801, and of *Audacious* (74) in 1805. In 1806 he took his last command as captain of *Impetueux*.[5] He served aboard this 74-gun ship until 1 August 1811 when, at about age fifty-five, he was promoted to the rank of rear admiral.

When John Marshall published his *Royal Naval Biography* in 1823 he included a biography for John Lawford, Vice Admiral of the White. At the time the book was published Lawford was about sixty-seven years old and resided at Shoarne, near Rochester, Kent. Marshall wrote:

> At the period of the Spanish armament, in 1790, this officer commanded the *Hound* sloop, stationed in the Channel. During the two succeeding years we find him in the same vessel at Jamaica. He was made post, Dec. 1st, 1793, into the *Convert* of 36 guns, which vessel was lost on the Grand Caymanes, in the West Indies, on the 8th March, in the following year.[6]
>
> Captain Lawford's next appointment was to the *Agincourt*, 64; from her he removed, about the spring of 1798, to the *Romney* of 50 guns. In the summer of the same year, being entrusted with the command of a small squadron, he fell in with a Swedish frigate having under her convoy a number of vessels, bound to different ports in the Mediterranean, laden with naval stores. Upon doubts which Captain Lawford entertained respecting the line of conduct he should pursue on so delicate an occasion, he immediately sent an express to the Admiralty, whilst with his squadron, he kept the convoy in view. On the return of his messenger with instructions for the detention of the merchant vessels, our officer desired Sir Charles Lindsay and Captain Raper to communicate them in the civilest terms to the Swedish Commodore; who shewed his instructions to repel force by force, if any attempt were made to board the vessels under his charge, and declared that he would protect them to the last. The crew of the Swedish frigate were immediately at quarters, matches lighted, and every preparation made for an obstinate resistance. In the night, possession was taken of most of the vessels; the commander of the convoy making many movements, which were narrowly watched by the *Romney*, keeping close under his lee, lower-deck guns run out, and every man at his station. In the morning an armed boat sent by the Swedish frigate, took out by force the British officer who had been left on board one of the vessels; at the same time the Commodore sent an officer of his own to Captain Lawford, to complain that he had taken ad-

vantage of the night to get possession of his charge, which was unobserved by him, or he would assuredly have defended them to the last. Upon further conference, and representation of the impracticability of resistance to such a superior force, he at length agreed to go into Margate Roads, and returned the British officer who had been detained on board his frigate.

Some months after, judgment was passed in the High Court of Admiralty, that all the merchantmen, with their several cargoes, should be condemned (being laden with naval and military stores, bound to France); but that the private adventures of the masters should be restored. The prizes were calculated to be worth 600,000*l.* The judge, Sir W. Scott, now Lord Stowell, asserted upon this occasion:

> 1st, That the right of visiting and searching merchantmen upon the high seas, whatever be the ships, cargoes, or destination, is an incontestable right of the lawfully commissioned cruizers of a belligerent nation.
>
> 2nd, That the authority of the sovereign of the neutral country being interposed in any manner of mere force, cannot legally vary the rights of a lawfully commissioned belligerent cruizer; and
>
> 3rd, That the penalty for the contravention of this right is the confiscation of the property so with-held from visitation and search.

In the autumn of 1799, the *Romney* formed part of the expedition sent against the Helder, and was with Vice-Admiral Mitchell, at the surrender of the Dutch squadron commanded by Rear-Admiral Storey. Captain Lawford subsequently removed into the *Polyphemus* of 64 guns, which ship was attached to Lord Nelson's division at the attack upon the Danish line of defence before Copenhagen, April 2, 1801, and sustained a loss of 5 men killed, and 24 wounded.

On the 7th Dec. 1804, our officer being on a cruize off Cape St. Mary, fell in with and captured the *Santa Gertruyda*, a Spanish frigate of 36 guns, from Peru and Mexico, bound to Corunna, with a cargo consisting of cocoa, coffee, hides, platina, drugs, cochineal, cotton, and several rich private ventures, together with 1,215,000 dollars in specie (The *Lively* frigate, Captain G.E. Hamond, was in sight at the time of the above capture). This valuable prize parted company in a violent gale of wind on the 16th, and on Christmas day carried away her mainmast, and had her rudder choked. Fortunately she was fallen in with by the *Harriet* armed ship, which took her in tow, and after beating about the Channel for several days, brought her safe to Plymouth on the 10th Jan. 1805.

In the ensuing summer, Captain Lawford was appointed to the *Audacious* of 74 guns; and from her removed, towards the close of the year, into the *Impetueux*, another third rate, in which ship he continued on Channel service until the 1st Aug. 1811. He was then advanced to the rank of Rear-Admiral.

Our officer has never, we believe, hoisted his flag. His commission as Vice-Admiral bears date Aug. 12, 1819.

Residence.—Shoarne, near Rochester, Kent.[7]

Biographical details about John Lawford also appear in an obituary notice that was published in the April 1843 issue of the *Gentleman's Magazine.* Omitting a lengthy paraphrase, which is clearly based on the Marshall biography, the article is presented because it includes additional information:

ADM. SIR JOHN LAWFORD, K.C.B.

Dec. 22. At his residence, Grove-road, St. John's-wood, aged 86, Admiral Sir John Lawford, K.C.B.

This much respected old officer had been a commissioned officer in the navy for sixty-five years, and served as First Lieutenant of the *Nimrod*, 98 guns, in the battle of the 12th April, 1782, that ship being Lord Rodney's second astern on that day. . . . He became a Vice-Admiral in 1819, and Admiral in 1837. He was nominated a Knight Commander of the Bath in 1838.

Sir John Lawford married, in 1803, a daughter of the Rev. Mr. Holder, Rector of Barsom, Suffolk.[8]

The obituary states that he served as first lieutenant of the *Nimrod*, the ship that was Lord Rodney's second astern in the battle of 12 April 1782 (Battle of the Saints). Yet Pitcairn-Jones lists Lawford as second lieutenant of the *Namur* from 1780, with his next commission as first lieutenant of the *Crown* in 1784.[9] The discrepancy is probably the result of confusion about the ship's name: the *Namur*, Fenshaw, a 90-gun ship with a crew of 750 men, along with the *Duke* (90), Gardner, and *Canada* (74), Cornwallis, flanked Admiral Sir George Rodney's *Formidable* (90) as the four ships broke through the enemy's line in the Battle of the Saints.[10] There were no ships of the line named *Nimrod* with Admiral Rodney on that day. Most likely, then, John Lawford was aboard the *Namur* for the Battle of the Saints.

Genealogical data about John Lawford also proved elusive in the 1990s. I wrote to the Kent Archives in Maidstone, to the Kent Family History Society, and to about fourteen Lawford families whose names appeared in telephone directories in the Medway and North West Kent area. Although various people kindly attempted to find information, little of substance emerged. Living descendants of John Lawford were not identified, although a reply from L. S. Lawford suggested that Admiral Sir John Lawford, KCB, had been granted armorial bearings.

Correspondence with P. L. Dickinson at the College of Arms in London revealed that armorial bearings were indeed granted to Captain John Lawford in 1803, who at the time was residing at Portsmouth, Hampshire:

ARMS	Quarterly Gules and Erminois on a bend cotised wavy Argent an anchor erect Sable between two estoiles Azure
CREST	On a wreath of the colours A demi lion Ermine holding between his paws a naval coronet Gold in the mouth a branch of olive proper
MOTTO	IN UTRUMQUE PARATUS

The College of Arms did not have a pedigree of John Lawford's family entered in its records, and therefore no official biographical information about the Royal Navy officer is registered there. P. L. Dickinson noted, however, that John Lawford impaled the Arms of a Holden family with those of his own. This is the usual way of representing a marriage heraldically: the shield is divided vertically down the center and the Arms of the husband are placed on the left-hand side and those of the wife's family on the right.[11]

In more recent times, I did a search on the internet and, to my surprise, came upon Lawford's family tree and the wills of Admiral Sir John Lawford, KCB (1757–1842), and Lady Anna Maria Lawford, née Holden (ca. 1758–1853), transcribed by Clive Lawford on his family website. He is not a direct descendent of John Lawford, and I have not been able to firmly establish their connection.[12]

John Lawford lived a long and apparently interesting life. His active naval career spanned the American War of Independence, the French revolutionary wars, and most of the Napoleonic Wars. In his lifetime, he witnessed sweeping social, political, and economic changes in the world and the remarkable technological advances of the Industrial Revolution. He also had a long and successful marriage and accumulated considerable wealth. On their respective deaths, John and Anna Maria Lawford judiciously distributed their possessions among their extended families as well as among friends, associates, employees, and personal servants. After providing for his wife during her lifetime and tending to personal matters, his will takes on the form of a detailed share-out plan reminiscent of naval practice; hers is very personal and includes a sum for the care of her dog. Undoubtedly additional information exists about this fascinating man, and a study of his life is a worthwhile subject for future research.

Appendix D

Data from the Muster Table of HMS *Convert*

The following table includes information extracted from the muster table of HMS *Convert*. The original document contains the following columns:

Bounty Paid
N°
Entry
Year
Appearance
Whence and whether Prest or not
Place and Country where Born
Age at Time of Entry in this Ship
N° and Letter of Tickets
MENS NAMES
Qualities
D. D.D. or R. [Discharged, Discharged Dead, or Run]
Time of Discharge
Whither or for What Reason

Also present are additional columns concerning clothes and beds supplied by the navy, wages, and so forth. Most of the information that appears in the original muster table is included in the selection below; however, some data has been omitted (e.g., location of discharge and the costs for clothing and beds), and a few columns have been combined. Several columns were blank in the original. Many of the abbreviations that appear in the original have been spelled in full for the reader; abbreviations that remain are generally as they appear in the original. The transcription of names reflects the author's best attempt to decipher the original handwriting. Dates are in the American style (month/day/year).

Bounty Paid	N°	Entry Year Appearance	Whence and whether Prest or not	MENS NAMES	Qualities	D. D.D. R.	Time of Discharge Year
Convert's Complement 220 Men began Wages and Sea Victualling p/Order from Commodore Ford Dated 1 December 1793							
	1	12/1/93	*Hound* p/Commission 12/1/93	John Lawford	Captain		
	2	"	Pt. Royal	Wm Buttler	his Servant		
	3	"	"	William Forder	"	DD	1/7/94
	4	"	"	John Mawby	"		
	5	"	"	John Silver Sword	"	DD	12/21/93
	6	"	"	Robert Panton	"		
	7	"	"	John Lewellin	"		
	8	"	"	John Baptisma	"		
	9	"	"	David Rieussett	"		
	10	"	"	Alex^r^ Innes	"		
	11	"	p/Admiralty Order	Widows' Men (1)	Able Seaman		
	12	"	"	" " (2)	Able Seaman		
	13	"	p/Warrant	Joseph Blease	Cook		
	14	"	"	John Austin	his Servant		
	15	"	p/Commission 12/1/93	William Earnshaw	2nd Lieutenant		
	16	"	Pt. Royal	Rick Walker	his Servant		
	17	"	p/Warrant 12/1/93	John Doran	Surgeon's 1st Mate		
£5	18	"	Pt. Royal Vol^r^	Thomas Flinn	Able Seaman		
				" "	Carpenter's Crew 12/22/93		
£5	19	"	"	Samuel Leek	Able Seaman		
				" "	Yeoman/Sheets 12/22/93		

£5	20	"	"	Ab^{m} Hutchings	Able Seaman		
£5	21	12/2/93	"	Ariek Linman	Able Seaman		
	22	"	"	Henry Bligh	Able Seaman	R	1/4/94
	23	"	"	Jacob Corason	Able Seaman	R	1/10/94
	24	"	"	Joseph Losanto	Able Seaman	R	1/22/94
£5	25	"	"	George Henesey	Able Seaman		
	26	"	"	Benjamin Jones	Able Seaman	DD	12/21/93
	27	"	"	Lewis Lewis	Able Seaman	DD	12/18/93
£5	28	"	"	Fran^{s} Francisco	Able Seaman		
£5	29	"	"	William Parry	Able Seaman		
				" "	Quartermaster's Mate 12/5/93		
£5	30	"	"	Edward Norman	Able Seaman		
£5	31	"	"	Aaron Crauford	Able Seaman		
£5	32	"	"	Michael Dorgan	Able Seaman		
	33	"	"	Daniel Green	Able Seaman	DD	12/16/93
£5	34	"	"	James Sands	Able Seaman		
	35	"	"	Danl Butterworth	Able Seaman	R	1/11/94
£5	36	12/2/93	Pt. Royal Vol^{r}	Peter Wilson	Able Seaman		
				" "	Clerk 12/6/93		
£5	37	"	"	James Barron	Able Seaman		
	38	12/4/93	p/Warrant 12/1/93	John Scott	Purser		
	39	"	*Hound*	Thomas Cowap	his Servant	D	12/30/93 request
	40	"	"	Saml Luffingam	Purser's Steward		
	41	"	p/Warrant 12/3/93	Thomas Popplewell	Master		
	42	"	Pt. Royal	Thomas Garnett	his Servant	DD	12/30/93
	43	"	p/Warrant 12/3/93	Roger Kirby	Boatswain		

Continued on the next page

Bounty Paid	N°	Entry Year Appearance	Whence and whether Prest or not	MENS NAMES	Qualities	D. D.D. R.	Time of Discharge Year
	44	"	Pt. Royal	James Heighney	his Servant		
	45	"	"	John Hancock	"		
	46	"	*Marie Antoinette* p/Warrant 12/1/93	George Innes	Gunner	DD	12/23/93
	47	"	Pt. Royal	Joseph Stow	his Servant	D	"
	48	"	"	John Stow	"	D	"
	49	12/5/93	*Hound* p/List	John Pering	Midshipman		
	50	"	"	James Hutcheon	Clerk		
				" "	Master's Mate 12/6/93		
	51	"	"	Robert Forbes	Midshipman		
	52	"	"	Samuel Brown	Gunner's Mate		
	53	"	"	Richard Dyer	Able Seaman		
				" "	Yeoman/Powder Room 12/6/93		
	54	"	"	Samuel Childs	Able Seaman		
				" "	Quartergunner 12/6/93		
	55	"	"	Thomas Dougal	Able Seaman		
				" "	Coxswain 12/6/93		
	56	"	"	William Gray	Able Seaman	DD	12/30/93
	57	"	"	Wm Marshall	Able Seaman		
				" "	Quartermaster 12/6/93		
	58	"	"	Fran^{s} Stevens	Able Seaman		
				" "	Quartermaster 12/6/93		
	59	"	"	John Gray	Able Seaman	DD	12/9/93
	60	"	"	Henry Croker	Able Seaman		

				" "	Corporal 12/6/93		
	61	"	"	Rick Finlay	Able Seaman	DD	12/20/93
	62	"	"	W^{m} McDaniel	Able Seaman		
	63	"	"	And^{w} McDaniel	Able Seaman		
£5	64	"	D^{o} Volunteer	James Middleton	Able Seaman		
				" "	Corporal 12/6/93		
	65	12/6/93	p/Warrant 12/3/93	William Cruise	Carpenter	DD	
	66	"	Pt. Royal	Geo F Cruise	his Servant	DD	12/13/93
	67	"	"	Wm Augt Cruise	"	D	
	68	"	"	Wm Truscott	Midshipman	D	1/20/94 into *Success*
£5	69	"	Volunteer	James Furnace	Able Seaman		
	70	"	"	George Pinder	Able Seaman	R	1/22/94
£5	71	"	"	John Lister	Able Seaman	R	2/5/94 Bluefields
£5	72	"	"	John Hoderaft	Able Seaman		
£5	73	"	"	John Bonker	Able Seaman		
£5	74	"	"	John Webster	Able Seaman		
£5	75	12/5/93	Volunteer	Laur^{ce} Brailey	Able Seaman		
£5	76	"	"	Vill^{rs}Wilkinson	Able Seaman		
£5	77	"	"	Thos Williams	Able Seaman		
£5	78	"	"	Wm Stanburry	Able Seaman		
£5	79	"	"	James Smith	Able Seaman		
£5	80	"	"	George Wood	Able Seaman		
				" "	Boatswain's Mate 12/7/93		
	81	"	Pt. Royal Vol^{r}	Peter Dryden	Able Seaman	DD	1/12/94
	82	12/14/93	Pt. Royal	John Batters	Carp^{rs} Servant	D	
	83	12/17/93	p/Commission 12/10/93	John Allen	3rd Lieutenant		
	84	"	Pt. Royal	Penelope	his Servant		

Continued on the next page

Bounty Paid	N°	Entry Year Appearance	Whence and whether Prest or not	MENS NAMES	Qualities	D. D.D. R.	Time of Discharge Year
	85	12/18/93	P/Commission 12/1/93	Joseph Bradby Bogue	1st Lieutenant		
	86	"	Pt. Royal	Richard Bogue	his Servant		
	87	"	Volunteer	William Ashton	Able Seaman	DD	1/13/94
£5	88	"	"	Wm Williams	Able Seaman		
	89	"	"	John McNutt	Able Seaman	R	1/28/94
£5	90	"	"	Richard Smith	Able Seaman		
	91	"	*Penelope*	Joseph Potts	Able Seaman	DD	1/7/94
£5	92	12/21/93	*Alligator*	Th^os C Sherwin	Midshipman		
	93	"	Pt. Royal Vol^r	James McGraw	Able Seaman	R	1/10/94
£5	94	"	"	Pat^k Gallagher	Able Seaman		
£5	95	"	Volunteer	Peter Ryan	Able Seaman		
£5	96	"	"	John Foy	Able Seaman		
£5	97	"	"	Charles Groby	Able Seaman		
£5	98	"	"	Colin Campbell	Able Seaman		
£5	99	"	"	Ab^m Finnemore	Able Seaman		
£5	100	"	"	Peter Thomas	Able Seaman		
	101	"	Prest	Robert Wingate	Able Seaman	R	1/14/94
	102	"	Prest	Edward Mullin	Able Seaman		
£5	103	"	Volunteer	James Mitchell	Able Seaman		
£5	104	"	"	William Pearcy	Able Seaman		
	105	"	"	John Whitaker	Able Seaman	DD	1/7/94
£5	106	"	"	Thomas Briggs	Able Seaman		
£5	107	"	"	John Morton	Able Seaman		
£5	108	"	"	James Cole	Able Seaman		
£5	109	"	"	John Hunter	Able Seaman		

	110	"	"	Samuel Daniel	Able Seaman	D	1/17/94
£5	111	"	"	William Hughes	Able Seaman		
£5	112	"	"	Andrew Wilson	Able Seaman		
				" "	Carpenter's Crew 1/1/94		
£5	113	"	"	Robert Martin	Able Seaman		
				" "	Carpenter's Mate 1/1/94		
£5	114	"	"	John Battey	Able Seaman		
£5	115	"	"	John Iveson	Able Seaman		
£5	116	"	"	John Sundell	Able Seaman		
	117	"	"	Thomas Taylor	Able Seaman	R	1/22/94
	118	"	"	Peter Swad	Able Seaman	R	1/10/94
	119	"	Prest	George Hayes	Able Seaman	R	1/12/94
£5	120	"	Volunteer	Dennis Larey	Able Seaman		
£5	121	"	Pt. Royal Vol[r]	Thomas Young	Able Seaman		
£5	122	"	"	Richard Sammons	Able Seaman		
£5	123	"	"	Henry Lobb	Able Seaman		
				" "	Quartermaster's Mate 1/1/94		
£5	124	"	"	Thomas Loyd	Able Seaman		
	125	"	Prest	James Walker	Able Seaman	R	1/18/94
	126	"	"	Talent Boeson	Able Seaman	R	1/8/94
	127	"	"	Tucker Hall	Able Seaman	R	1/27/94
	128	"	"	Joseph Highim	Able Seaman	D	1/17/94 p/order
	129	"	"	Solomon	Able Seaman	R	1/28/94
£5	130	"	Volunteer	Alex[r] Dower	Able Seaman		
£5	131	"	"	Joseph Tonkinson	Able Seaman		
£5	132	12/21/93	Volunteer	Thomas Gurdin	Able Seaman		

Continued on the next page

Bounty Paid	Nº	Entry Year Appearance	Whence and whether Prest or not	MENS NAMES	Qualities	D. D.D. R.	Time of Discharge Year
	133	12/22/93	"	Richard Miller	Able Seaman	DD	1/3/94
	134	"	"	Wm Connely	Able Seaman	DD	1/8/94
£5	135	"	"	Step^{n} Dunglinson	Able Seaman		
£5	136	"	"	John Byram	Able Seaman		
£5	137	"	"	Edward Finigin	Able Seaman		
£5	138	"	"	Owen Roberts	Able Seaman		
£5	139	"	"	James Corcoran	Able Seaman		
				" "	Quartermaster 1/1/94		
	140	"	"	Henry Williams	Able Seaman	DD	1/1/94
	141	"	Pt. Royal	Edwd Crodsdaile	Capt Servant		
£5	142	"	Volunteer	John Quilliam	Able Seaman		
£5	143	"	"	John Curlett	Able Seaman		
	144	12/24/94	*Penelope*	Nick^{s} Pascoe	Able Seaman	D	1/27/94 Supern^{s} list being invalided
	145	"	"	James Mayon	Able Seaman		
	146	"	"	Owen Sulliven	Able Seaman	DD	1/26/94
	147	"	"	Robert Pierce	Able Seaman		
	148	"	"	Robert Cummins	Able Seaman		
£5	149	"	"	Charles Bayley	Able Seaman		
£5	150	"	Pt. Royal Vol^{r}	Henry Mills	Able Seaman		
£5	151	"	"	Pat^{k} Wickman	Able Seaman		
	152	"	"	W^{m} McKenny	Able Seaman	DD	1/4/94
	153	"	"	James Tennent	Able Seaman	DD	1/8/94
	154	"	"	Charles Smith	Able Seaman	DD	1/10/94
£5	155	"	"	William Belt	Able Seaman		

£5	156	"	"	John Goster	Able Seaman		
£5	157	"	"	John Seaman	Able Seaman		
	158	"	"	John Myers	Able Seaman	DD	1/1/94
£5	159	"	"	George Read	Able Seaman		
£5	160	"	"	John Thomas	Able Seaman		
£5	161	"	"	John Hurt	Able Seaman		
	162	"	"	James Langdon	Able Seaman	R	1/11/94
£5	163	"	"	John Witherman	Able Seaman		
£5	164	"	"	Alex Stewart	Able Seaman		
£5	165	"	"	Hugh Johnson	Able Seaman		
	166	"	"	William Croy	Able Seaman	DD	1/14/94
	167	"	Prest	Matthew Murch	Able Seaman	R	1/18/94
	168	"	Prest	William Wilson	Able Seaman	R	1/28/94
£5	169	"	Volunteer	Jn° Goldsberry	Able Seaman		
				" "	Quartergunner 1/1/94		
£5	170	"	"	Thomas Moore	Able Seaman		
£5	171	"	"	Wm Williams	Able Seaman		
£5	172	"	"	Thomas Dorlin	Able Seaman	DD	2/10/94 Grand Cayman
£5	173	"	"	Luke Dixon	Able Seaman		
	174	"	"	William Harley	Able Seaman	R	1/28/94
	175	"	Prest	Corn^{s} Swim	Able Seaman	R	1/22/94
	176	"	Prest	R Bransfield	Able Seaman	D	1/17/94 p/order
£5	177	"	Volunteer	Thomas Beck	Able Seaman		
£5	178	"	"	Ch^{r} Mason	Able Seaman		
	179	"	"	Charles Foster	Able Seaman	R	1/14/94
£5	180	"	"	John Blanden	Able Seaman		

Continued on the next page

Bounty Paid	Nº	Entry Year Appearance	Whence and whether Prest or not	MENS NAMES	Qualities	D. D.D. R.	Time of Discharge Year
	181	"	Prest	Thomas Rowe	Able Seaman	R	1/27/94
£5	182	"	Volunteer	John Campbell	Able Seaman		
				" "	Yeoman/Sheets 1/1/94		
£5	183	"	"	Thomas Peters	Able Seaman		
£5	184	"	"	John Clarke	Able Seaman		
				" "	Quartermaster's Mate 1/1/94		
£5	185	"	"	Wm Scurfield	Able Seaman		
£5	186	"	"	Ja^s Sanderson	Able Seaman		
£5	187	12/24/93	Volunteer	James Fitt	Able Seaman		
£5	188	"	"	Wm Masters	Able Seaman		
£5	189	"	"	Robt McMillan	Able Seaman		
£5	190	"	"	Evan Harper	Able Seaman		
	191	"	"	Robert Manning	Able Seaman	DD	1/17/94
£5	192	"	"	John Smith	Able Seaman		
£5	193	"	"	Michael Cain	Able Seaman		
	194	"	Prest	Ezekiel Banks	Able Seaman	R	1/14/94
£5	195	"	Volunteer	Samuel Hather	Able Seaman	DD	2/4/94
	196	"	"	William Hart	Able Seaman	DD	1/20/94
£5	197	"	"	Henry F Hardacre	Able Seaman	DD	1/27/94
	198	12/31/94	Pt. Royal	John James	Master's Servant		
£5	199	"	Volunteer	John Pouncet	Able Seaman		
	200	"	Pt. Royal	Tim^y Coakley	Purser's Servant		
£5	201	"	Pt. Royal Vol^r	Joakin Hesse	Able Seaman	D	1/27/94 *Mosquito* in lieu

£5	202	"	"	Henry Crookman	Able Seaman		
£5	203	"	"	Peter Rooney	Able Seaman		
£5	204	"	"	Joseph Evans	Able Seaman		
£5	205	"	"	Joseph Robertson	Able Seaman		
£5	206	"	"	John Gooff	Able Seaman		
£5	207	"	"	Tho[s] Williams	Able Seaman		
£5	208	"	"	Isaac Fudge	Able Seaman		
£5	209	"	"	Robert Davis	Able Seaman		
£5	210	"	"	John Robinson	Able Seaman		
£5	211	"	"	David James	Able Seaman		
£5	212	"	"	John Boyne	Able Seaman		
£5	213	"	"	Math[w] Charleton	Able Seaman		
£5	214	"	"	John Saunders	Able Seaman		
	215	"	"	Peter Cronyen	Able Seaman	R	1/27/94
£5	216	"	"	Richard Nein	Able Seaman		
	217	"	"	James Barrow	Able Seaman	D	1/27/94 Civil Law by habeas corpus
£5	218	"	"	James Ellis	Able Seaman		
	219	1/5/94	*Penelope*	Colin Campbell	Able Seaman		
				" "	Master's Mate 1/6/94		
	220	1/6/94	p/Warrant 1/2/94	William Dixon	Gunner		
	221	"	Pt. Royal	W[m] Dixon (2)	Gunner's Servant		
	222	"	"	Joseph Stow	"		
	223	"	p/Warrant 12/2/93	William Porter	Surgeon		
	224	"	Pt. Royal	James Anderson	his Servant		
£5	225	"	Volunteer	Rich[d] Golding	Able Seaman		
£5	226	"	"	Martin Bayne	Able Seaman		

Continued on the next page

Bounty Paid	Nº	Entry Year Appearance	Whence and whether Prest or not	MENS NAMES	Qualities	D. D.D. R.	Time of Discharge Year
£5	227	"	"	Roger Mathews	Able Seaman		
£5	228	"	"	Samuel Clarke	Able Seaman		
£5	229	"	"	Peter Johnson	Able Seaman		
£5	230	"	"	Isaac Smith	Able Seaman		
	231	1/8/94	Pt. Royal	Isaac Smith	Capt^s Servant		
£5	232	"	Volunteer	John Gillespie	Able Seaman		
£5	233	"	"	John Agnew	Able Seaman		
£5	234	"	"	Colin Graham	Able Seaman		
£5	235	"	"	John Drummond	Able Seaman		
£5	236	"	"	Harry Beck	Able Seaman		
£5	237	"	"	John Stewart	Able Seaman		
£5	238	"	"	Walter Buchan	Able Seaman		
				" "	Armorer's Mate 1/12/94		
£5	239	"	"	Joseph Mallony	Able Seaman		
				" "	Quartergunner 1/12/94		
£5	240	1/8/94	Volunteer	George Lavender	Able Seaman		
£5	241	"	Pt. Royal Vol^r	James Wright	Able Seaman		
£5	242	"	"	William Gowens	Able Seaman		
£5	243	"	"	Joseph Foster	Able Seaman		
				" "	Quartergunner 1/12/94		
£5	244	"	"	Richard King	Able Seaman		
	245	"	"	Thomas Quaile	Able Seaman	R	1/28/94
	246	"	"	Saml Carpenter	Able Seaman	R	1/20/94
£5	247	"	"	David Kelly	Able Seaman		
	248	"	Prest	James Robertson	Able Seaman	R	1/28/94

£5	249	"	Volunteer	Henry Edwards	Able Seaman		
£5	250	"	"	Peter Crawford	Able Seaman		
£5	251	"	"	Joseph Cambrick	Able Seaman		
£5	252	"	"	James Jenkins	Able Seaman		
£5	253	"	"	Thos Richardson	Able Seaman		
£5	254	"	"	John Thomas	Able Seaman		
£5	255	"	"	William Passley	Able Seaman		
£5	256	"	"	John Gammel	Able Seaman		
£5	257	"	"	John McDonald	Able Seaman		
£5	258	"	"	David Davis	Able Seaman		
£5	259	"	"	John Conner	Able Seaman		
£5	260	"	"	John Ruslin	Able Seaman		
	261	"	"	Michael Dowling	Able Seaman	R	1/28/94
£5	262	"	"	Thomas Reece	Able Seaman		
£5	263	"	"	John Singleton	Able Seaman		
£5	264	"	"	Samuel Pepper	Able Seaman		
£5	265	"	"	David Ellis	Able Seaman	DD	1/28/94
£5	266	"	"	Rick Abbot	Able Seaman		
£5	267	"	"	John Jennings	Able Seaman		
£5	268	"	"	John Martin	Able Seaman		
£5	269	"	"	Samuel Pearson	Able Seaman		
£5	270	"	"	William Tick	Able Seaman		
£5	271	"	"	William Powell	Able Seaman		
£5	272	"	"	John Mathews	Able Seaman		
	273	"	"	Roger West	Able Seaman	R	1/27/94
£5	274	"	"	Thomas Allen	Able Seaman		
£5	275	"	"	Wm Jeffreys	Able Seaman		

Continued on the next page

Bounty Paid	N°	Entry Year Appearance	Whence and whether Prest or not	MENS NAMES	Qualities	D. D.D. R.	Time of Discharge Year
£5	276	"	"	George Moore	Able Seaman		
£5	277	"	"	Pedro Vidal	Able Seaman		
£5	278	"	"	Thos Blackston	Able Seaman		
	279	"	Prest	Bryan McGee	Able Seaman	R	1/26/94
	280	"	Volunteer	John Bryan	Able Seaman	DD	1/27/94
£5	281	"	"	Thomas Boden	Able Seaman		
£5	282	1/26/94	"	John Buchanan	Able Seaman		
£3:10s	283	1/27/94	"	Hugh Marr	Ord^{y} Seaman		
£5	284	1/28/94	*Mosquito*	James Duffie	Able Seaman		
			Vol^{r} in lieu		Carpenter's Crew 2/2/94		
	285	2/6/94	Volunteer	William Henesey	Able Seaman		
	286	"	"	John Forbes	Able Seaman		
	287	"	"	David Davis	Able Seaman		
	288	"	"	James Williams	Able Seaman		
	289	"	"	R^{d} Swanston	Able Seaman		
	290	"	"	Johan Schoburg	Able Seaman		
	291	"	"	Alex^{r} Carter	Able Seaman		

List of Supernumeraries Borne for Victuals only

Bounty Paid	N°	Entry Year Appearance	Whence and whether Prest or not	MENS NAMES	Qualities	D. D.D. R.	Time of Discharge Year
	1	12/1/93	Pt. Royal	Jean Legros	Pilot	D	1/20/94
	2	1/14/94	Pt. Royal Hospital	Joseph Gibbs	Able Seaman		
	3	1/18/94	"	Giles Ross	M^{r} at Arms		
	4	1/21/94	*Success*	James Gathers		DD	2/4/94
	5	"	"	John Farewell		DD	2/4/94

	6	"	"	John Buckley
	7	1/26/94	*Hermione* Invalided	Lieu^{t} Brice
	8	1/28/94	*Europa* Hospital Invalided	John Randle
	9	"	"	William Horell
	10	"	"	George Brown
	11	"	"	William Welch
	12	"	"	Thomas Bowman
	13	"	"	Walter Ross
	14	"	"	Richard Burn
	15	"	*Penelope* D^{o}	George Burt
	16	"	"	Jer^{h} Dailey
	17	"	"	John Hutchinson
	18	"	*Ipheginia* D^{o}	John Provin
	19	"	"	William Clarke
	20	"	"	Edward Jones
	21	"	*Success* Invalided	John Robinson
	22	"	"	Andrew Hogg
	23	"	"	John Ford
	24	"	*Alligator* D^{o}	John Ray
	25	"	"	John Burgen
	26	"	*Convert* D^{o}	Nicholas Pascoe
	27	"	*Mosquito* D^{o}	James Perkins
£5	28	1/27/94	"	John Dalley
£5	29	"	"	John Potter
	30	1/28/94	*Spitfire* D^{o}	Wm Lawrence
	31	"	*Flying Fish* D^{o}	Wm Williams

Continued on the next page

Bounty Paid	N^{o}	Entry Year Appearance	Whence and whether Prest or not	MENS NAMES	Qualities	D. D.D. R.	Time of Discharge Year
		List of Non Commissioned Officers & Privates borne for whole allowance of all species p/order of Captain Lawford					
	1	1/25/94	Pt. Royal	Thomas Hill	Sergeant		
	2	"	"	Jer^{h} Martin	"		
	3	"	"	Thomas Long	"		
	4	"	"	Robert Manson	"		
	5	"	"	John Sprowle	"		
	6	"	"	Edward Forster	"		
	7	"	"	Robert Morrison	"		
	8	"	"	George Hindman	"		
	9	"	"	John Witheral	Corporal		
	10	"	"	John Knowlton	"		
	11	"	"	Samuel Thomas	"		
	12	"	"	Henry Hawkins	"		
	13	"	"	Robert Gray	"		
	14	"	"	Thomas Lewis	"		
	15	"	"	John Younger	"		
	16	"	"	Ja^{s} Abercrombie	"		
	17	"	"	Arrindale Carbey	"		
	18	"	"	George Law	"		
	19	"	"	George Ried	Drummajor		
	20	"	"	Samuel Monday	Drummer		
	21	"	"	James Kershaw	"		
	22	"	"	Thomas Kershaw	"		
	23	"	"	William Askins	Private		

24	"	"	Joseph Watson	"
25	"	"	Alex^{r} Smith	"
26	"	"	Thos Henderson	"
27	"	"	Jonath^{n} Chauner	"
28	"	"	Twig Roberts	"
29	"	"	John Plunket	"

List of a Prisoner and Eight Invalids belonging to the 1st Regiment of Royals & 62nd Regiment of Foot & Royal Artillery victualled at 2/3^{ds} allowance of all species of provisions p/order of Captain Lawford

1	1/26/94	from Packet sent by S^{r}J Jervis from Barbados for England	Jean Jeung	
2	1/28/94	Pt. Royal 1st Reg^{t} Royals Invalided	James Campbell	Private
3	"	"	Michael D	
4	"	"	John Hall	
5	"	"	John Rae	
6	"	"	Peter Kearns	
7	"	"	John Long	
8	"	62nd Regiment	William Hussey	Sergeant
9	"	Royal Artillery	James Webburn	Private

Source: Original muster table signed by Captain John Lawford, Purser John Scott, Master Thomas Popplewell and Boatswain Roger Kirby, Public Record Office, Kew, England (PRO), Admiralty Records (ADM) 36/11476, Ships' Muster Books, Muster Table of HMS *Convert*, 1793–94.

Appendix E

Ships in the *Convert* Convoy, 1794

The following table is a reconstructed list of the *Convert* convoy based on the author's interpretation of available data compiled from the 1793 and 1794 volumes of the *Royal Gazette* (National Library of Jamaica, Institute of Jamaica, Kingston, and Public Record Office, Kew, England, respectively) and the 1794 volumes of *Lloyd's Register* and *Lloyd's List*. While the list has been thoughtfully compiled, it should not be taken as definitive. Several vessels not mentioned here also arrived in Britain from Jamaica in late April and May 1794. There are some discrepancies: for example, occasionally the captain's name for a specific ship recorded at departure differs from that recorded at arrival. There are numerous possible reasons for such discrepancies: (1) if the master of a vessel died during the voyage, the ship would arrive with a different master; (2) a mistake in names or other information may have occurred on either side of the Atlantic; or (3) perhaps there were, in fact, two ships of the same name, and these were distinguished by the different masters' names (a common practice). Superscript letters *a*, *b*, and *c* have been assigned to the sources of the conflicting data (see notes at the end of the table). All of the arrival information (except that for the *Atalanta*) is from *Lloyd's List*. A dash occupies cells for which data is currently unavailable. An asterisk marks cases in which two recorded individuals may in fact be the same person. (S) = ship. (Bg) = brig. (Snow) = snow. (Sch) = schooner.

	Ship	Captain	Bound to	Arrived at	Date
		The Wreck of the Ten Sail			
1	HMS *Convert*	John Lawford	Bluefields, Great Britain	Wrecked/Grand Cayman	8 Feb
2	*William and Elizabeth* (S)	Medmer Goodwin	Bluefields	Wrecked/Grand Cayman	8 Feb
3	*Britannia* (S)	Daniel Martin	London	Wrecked/Grand Cayman	8 Feb
4	*Ludlow* (S)	David McLure	London	Wrecked/Grand Cayman	8 Feb
5	*Nancy* (S)	Leary[a]/Campbell[b]	London	Wrecked/Grand Cayman	8 Feb
6	*Moorhall* (S)	Samuel Nicholson	Liverpool	Wrecked/Grand Cayman	8 Feb
7	*Richard* (Bg)[c]	J. or Thomas Hughes	Belfast	Wrecked/Grand Cayman	8 Feb
8	*Fortune* (Bg)[a]	Love[a]/Merryman[b]	Bristol	Wrecked/Grand Cayman	8 Feb
9	*Eagle* (S) (of Kingston)	Ainsworth	—	Wrecked/Grand Cayman	8 Feb
10	*Sally* (Bg)[b] (of Kingston)	Watson	—	Wrecked/Grand Cayman	8 Feb
		Ships that waited several days in Grand Cayman to carry survivors			
11	*Llandovery* (S)	W. Adams	—	Dover	10 Apr
12	*Mars* (Bg)	King	—	Dover	10 Apr
				Gravesend	13 Apr
13	*Betsey and Susan* (Bg)	Harvey	London	Dover	13 Apr
				Gravesend	16 Apr
14	*Jane* (S)	Gammell	Bristol	Havana[d]	—
				Bristol	19 Apr
15	*Louisa* (S)	Thomas Harrison	London	Havana[d]	—
				Plymouth	19 Apr
				Gravesend	13 May

16	*Alfred* (S)	B. Bryan	London	Havana[d]	—
				Penzance	23 Apr
				Gravesend	27 Apr
17	*Nancy* (S)	Robert Campbell	London	Havana[d]	—
				Penzance	23 Apr
				Gravesend	27 Apr
18	*Barbados* (S)	Moore	Bluefields, London	Havana[d]	—
				Penzance	23 Apr
				Gravesend	27 Apr
19	*Countess of Galloway* (Bg)	William Elgin	London	Havana[d]	—
				Penzance	23 Apr
				Gravesend	27 Apr
			Other ships in the convoy		
20	*Alice* (S)	Bryan Smith	Liverpool	Havana[d]	—
				Liverpool	10 Apr
21	*Lion* (S)	Finnan[a]	Bluefields	—	—
		Thomas King[a,b]	London	Havana[d]	—
				Penzance	23 Apr
				Gravesend	27 Apr
22	*Susannah*[e] (Snow)	McIsaac	Bluefields, London	Left at Havana[b]	—
				Captured, taken into Charleston[a,b]	28 April
23	*Diana* (Snow)	Thompson	—	Deal	15 Mar
				Gravesend	18 Mar

Continued on the next page

	Ship	Captain	Bound to	Arrived at	Date
24	*Arethusa* (S)	Smith[a]	Bluefields	—	—
		Dodds[a,b]	—	Deal	19 Mar
25	*Grange*	Hutchison	—	Dover	20 Mar
				Gravesend	23 Mar
26	*Thomas Henry* (S)	Kirkpatrick*[a,b]	Bluefields	Cork	20 Mar
		Fitzpatrick*[b]	—	Plymouth	29 Mar
		Fitzpatrick*[b]	—	Gravesend	8 Apr
		Kirkpatrick*[a,b]	Bluefields	Gravesend	25 May
27	*Royal Charlotte* (S)	Souter	Bluefields	Cowes	20 Mar
				Portsmouth	27 Mar
				Gravesend	2 Apr
28	*Catherine* (S)	Singleton*[a,b]	London	Dartmouth	20 Mar
		Sinclair*[b]	—	Gravesend	6 Apr
29	*St. Thomas*	Drew	—	Bristol	20 Mar
30	*Gascoigne* (S)	Bibbye	Bluefields	Liverpool	20 Mar
31	*Betsey* (Bg)	Richard Kent	Bluefields, Liverpool	Liverpool	20 Mar
32	*Cyclops* (S)	Patrick Fairweather	Liverpool	Liverpool	20 Mar
33	*Amelia*	Aires	—	Portsmouth	21 Mar
				Gravesend	2 Apr
34	*Sally*	Potter*[b]	—	Falmouth	21 Mar
	Sarah (Snow)	Potter*[a,b]	—	Gravesend	3 Apr
35	*Martha* (S)	Robert Brown	London	Gravesend	23 Mar
				Gravesend	23 May
				Deal	24 May
36	*Leviathan*	Warden	—	Cork	24 Mar
				Portsmouth	16 Apr

37	*Nereus* (S)	McIver	—	Scilly	26 Mar
				Gravesend	2 Apr
38	*Margaret*	McConochy	—	Dover	26 Mar
				Gravesend	2 Apr
39	*Eliza-Ann* (S)	Hughes[a]	Dublin	—	—
		Marshall[b]	—	Liverpool	31 Mar
40	*Hawke*	Hill	—	Liverpool	31 Mar
41	*Prince*	Gordon	—	Ramsgate (on shore)	1 Apr
				Gravesend	13 Apr
42	*Cowley* (S)	Richard George	London	Dover	1 Apr
43	*Lord Charlemont* (S)	Richard Pindar	Bluefields, Liverpool	Liverpool	1 Apr
44	*Lord Rodney*	Johnson	—	Liverpool	1 Apr
45	*William*	—	—	Liverpool	1 Apr
46	*Norfolk*	Jessup	—	Gravesend	3 Apr
47	*New Lioness*	Ritchie	—	Deal	4 Apr
48	*Nile* (Bg)	Bowden	London	Gravesend	6 Apr
49	*Fanny* (S)	Withall	—	Gravesend	8 Apr
50	*St. Mary's Planter*	Dixon	—	Dover	9 Apr
				Gravesend	16 Apr
51	*Friends* (Bg)	McDonald	Belfast	Belfast	10? Apr
52	*Flora* (Bg)	Davidson	London	Gravesend	2 May
53	*Elizabeth*	Burton	—	Bantry Bay	? Apr
				Gravesend	12 May
54	*Atalanta* (Bg)	Forbes	—	The Downs[a]	—
55	*Peggy*[f] (S)	Robertson	Bluefields, London	Captured, taken into Brest[b]	—

Continued on the next page

	Ship	Captain	Bound to	Arrived at	Date
56	*Dispatch*[g] (Bg)	Pattison[a]	London	—	—
		Walker[b]	Lancaster	near Isle of Tory, in distress[b]	—
57	*Constant* (Bg)	Miles	North Carolina	—	—
58	*Molly* (Bg)	Willey	Baltimore	—	—
59	*Delaware* (Sch)	Davis	Charleston	—	—

[a] *Royal Gazette*
[b] *Lloyd's List*
[c] *Lloyd's Register*
[d] Departed 26 February 1794.
[e] The *Susannah* was reported by *Lloyd's List* on 29 April 1794 to have been left at Havana in a leaky condition. Less than two months later, on 13 June 1794, the same source reported that she had been captured and taken into Charleston. The *Royal Gazette* (21 June 1794) reported that she was captured by a French privateer and taken into Charleston on 28 April 1794, noting that she was last from Havana.
[f] According to *Lloyd's List* (20 May 1794), the *Peggy* was captured by a French frigate and taken into Brest.
[g] Although doubtful, it is possible that the *Dispatch*, for which no arrival was recorded, was the same as the unnamed brig that arrived near the Isle of Tory in distress, as reported by *Lloyd's List* on 8 April 1794.

Appendix F

Salvage Account of HMS *Convert*

An Account of Stores saved from the Wreck of His Majesty's Ship *Convert*

Boatswains					
Sails	22	N°	Boats Grapnels	2	N°
Pieces of Canvas	3	"	Fire and Chain	1	"
Hammocks Covers	4	"	Tackle Hooks	8	"
Compasses	3	"	Travellers	2	"
Stream Cable	1	"	Marline Spikes	2	"
Hawsers	2	"	Anchor Stream	1	"
Messengers	2	"	" Kedge	1	"
Topsail Sheets	3	"	Time Glasses	6	"
Buoy	1	"	Lengths of Junk	37	"
Leather Buckets	8	"	Boats	4	"
Cat Blocks	2	"	" Oars	18	"
Coils of Rope	8½	"	" Masts	6	"
Spare Tackles	8	"	" Sails	6	"
Blocks of Sorts	125	"	Colours	22	"

Carpenters					
Topsail Yards	2	N°	Iron Tiller	1	N°
Lower d°	1	"	Caps	3	"
Topmasts	3	"	Pintles	4	"
Fish	1	"	Adzes	2	"
Spanker Boom	1	"	Cross Cut Saw	1	"
Topgallant Masts	2	"	Maul	1	"
" Yards	1	"	Whip Saw	1	"
Bells	2	"	Grindstone	1	"
Funnels	2	"	Pitch Pot	1	"
Hoops for Mast	2	"	Copper Brace	1	"
Bolts	5	"	" Bolts	2	"
Links & Plates	1	"	" Boiler	1	"
Nuts for the Winch	2	"	also sundry Iron Work & loose Copper		

Gunners Stores

a remnant of 5½ inch rope for Breechings			Tackles wth Blocks & Hooks	10	N°
Round Shot	228	N°	Blocks dble & Sgle	46	"
Grape	304	"	Hooks-pairs	24	"
Tincase	200	"	Melting Ladle	1	"
Ladles with Staves	6	"	Muskets	89	"
Spunges with Staves & rammer heads	9	"	Bayonets	10	"
Rope Spunges and rammer heads	11	"	Cartouch Boxes	8	"
Wadhooks with d°	5	"	Swords	39	"
Budge Barrel	1	"	Scabboards for d°	39	"
Copper hoops	3	"	Belts for d°	20	"
Lanthorn dark	1	"	Pistols	41	"
Priming Irons	20	"	Pole Axes	7	"
Aprons of Lead	9	"	Strong Pikes	27	"
Powder horns	8	"	Vice Standing	1	"
Crows of Iron	8	"	Cases of Wood	8	"
Linch Pairs	16	"	Handspikes	18	"
Forelocks	22	"	Gun Carriages	18	"
			Swivels	4	"

Purser's Stores

Casks of Beef	16	N°
Ullage Cask of Rum	1	"
Bags of Bread	3	"

John Lawford
(Copy)
Jn° Ford

Source: Public Record Office, Kew, England (PRO), Admiralty Records (ADM) 1/245, Admiralty and Secretariat Papers, "Jamaica 1793 & 94, Admiral John Ford Esqr.," Enclosure in: Commodore John Ford to Philip Stephens, Secretary of the Admiralty, aboard the *Europa*, Port Royal, Jamaica, 3 April 1794.

Notes

The following abbreviations are used throughout the notes:

AN	Archives Nationales, Paris, France	
AR	Archives du Port de Rochefort, Rochefort, France	
CINA	Cayman Islands National Archive	
CINM	Cayman Islands National Museum	
JA	Jamaica Archives, Spanish Town	
MDHD	Ministry of Defense, Hydrography Department, Somerset, England	
NLJ	National Library of Jamaica, Institute of Jamaica, Kingston	
NMM	National Maritime Museum, London, England	
PRO	Public Record Office, Kew, England	
	ADM	Admiralty Records
	BT	Board of Trade Records
	CO	Colonial Office Records
SHM	Ministère de la Défense, Service Historique de la Marine, Château de Vincennes, France.	

Preface

1. Narrative description of the Wreck of the Ten Sail taken from Margaret Leshikar-Denton, "Tracing the Wreck of the Ten Sail," in *Beneath the Seven Seas*, ed. George F. Bass (London: Thames and Hudson, 2005), 206 (with minor edits).

2. It is common today to hear the incident described in this book referred to as "the Wreck of the Ten Sails." The traditional nautical expression, however, is "Ten Sail," and that is how the incident was first referred to in print, in George Hirst's *Notes on the History of the Cayman Islands* (1910). Many of the documents cited in the bibliography use the term "sail" to mean "one or more sailing ships." I have chosen to honor the traditional usage, which evidence indicates was standard at the time these events occurred.

3. Saint-Domingue was the name of the western part of Hispaniola, which was under French control throughout most of the eighteenth century. Today this region is the Republic of Haiti.

4. George S. S. Hirst, *Notes on the History of the Cayman Islands* (Kingston,

Jamaica: P. A. Benjamin, 1910), 115–16. Neville Williams, *A History of the Cayman Islands* (Grand Cayman: Government of the Cayman Islands, 1970), 28.

5. Roger C. Smith, *The Maritime Heritage of the Cayman Islands* (Gainesville: University Press of Florida, 2000), 152–61.

6. Much of the information from the 1979–80 survey is included in files that were created for each archaeological site recorded. These unpublished files are part of the National Shipwreck Inventory held by the Cayman Islands National Museum (hereafter CINM).

Chapter 1

1. Hirst, *Notes on the History*, 115–16.

2. Williams, *History of the Cayman Islands*, 28.

3. More recent publications on the wreck and on Cayman Islands history in general, whose authors carried out in-depth research in several countries, include Margaret E. Leshikar-Denton and Philip Pedley, eds., *Our Islands' Past*, vol. 2, *The Wreck of the Ten Sails* (George Town, Grand Cayman: Cayman Islands National Archive and Cayman Free Press, 1994); Smith, *Maritime Heritage*; Michael Craton and the New History Committee, *Founded upon the Seas: A History of the Cayman Islands and Their People* (Kingston, Jamaica: Ian Randle Publishers, 2003); and Leshikar-Denton, "Tracing the Wreck of the Ten Sail."

4. The original tapes of the interviews were deposited in the Cayman Islands National Archive (hereafter CINA), which administers the Memory Bank, now called the Oral History Program.

5. Phoebe Watler-Spence, interview by Margaret E. Leshikar, 14 November 1990, CINA, Memory Bank.

6. Marshall Watler, interview by Margaret E. Leshikar, 4 January 1991, CINA, Memory Bank.

7. Edison Jackson, interview by Margaret E. Leshikar, 4 January 1991, CINA, Memory Bank.

8. Mary Antoinette Wood Levy, interview by Margaret E. Leshikar, 24 January 1991, CINA, Memory Bank.

9. Barrett Welcome, Ethellen Jackson, William Allen McLaughlin, William Warren Conolly, Phoebe Watler Spence, Nina Watler Conolly, [Katy Rochelle?] Wood, Mary Antoinette Wood Levy, and Doris Wood, interviewed by Anita Ebanks, 1982–83, CINA, Memory Bank, Wreck of the Ten Sail. These interviews are cited collectively because they are archived together in the Memory Bank.

10. The name of this narrator is derived from the name spoken on a poor-quality tape, as best I could understand it. The interviewer could not precisely recall the narrator's name. Phoebe Watler Spence suggests that the person may have been Lydia Rachel Rankine, for she does not recall anyone by the name of Katy Rochelle Wood from East End; she noted that Lydia Rachel Rankine's daughter said that her mother would play tricks on people by giving them different names.

Chapter 2

1. Placement of ocean currents in map 4 is based on Paul Pinet, Acetates to Accompany *Oceanography: An Introduction to the Planet's Oceans* (New York: West Publishing, 1992), acetate 8.

2. Roger C. Smith, "Treasure Ships of the Spanish Main: The Iberian-American Maritime Empires," in *Ships and Shipwrecks of the Americas*, ed. George F. Bass (London: Thames and Hudson, 1988), 85.

3. Brian Jones, E. B. Lockhart, and C. Squair, "Phreatic and Vadose Cements in the Tertiary Bluff Formation of Grand Cayman Island, British West Indies," *Bulletin of Canadian Petroleum Geology* 32 (1984): 382–83.

4. Brian Jones, "A Field Guide to the Geology of the Cayman Islands" (manuscript, University of Alberta, 1988), 1; "Geology of the Cayman Islands," in *The Cayman Islands: Natural History and Biogeography*, ed. M. A. Brunt and J. E. Davies (Boston: Kluwer Academic, 1994), 13–49.

5. Craton and the New History Committee, *Founded upon the Seas*; Smith, *Maritime Heritage*.

6. Hirst, *Notes on the History*; Williams, *History of the Cayman Islands*; Edwin B. Doran, "A Physical and Cultural Geography of the Cayman Islands" (PhD diss., University of California at Berkeley, 1953).

7. Samuel Eliot Morison, *Admiral of the Ocean Sea: A Life of Christopher Columbus* (London, Little, Brown, 1970), 636–37.

8. Smith, *Maritime Heritage*, 25–28; Craton and the New History Committee, *Founded upon the Seas*, 1–19.

9. Smith, *Maritime Heritage*, 58–66; Craton and the New History Committee, *Founded upon the Seas*, 2, 21.

10. Mary Frear Keeler, ed., *Sir Francis Drake's West Indian Voyage, 1585–1586* (London: Hakluyt Society, 1981), 38, 68, 113, 203–4; Craton and the New History Committee, *Founded upon the Seas*, 16.

11. Smith, *Maritime Heritage*, 151; Craton and the New History Committee, *Founded upon the Seas*, 17.

12. Ministry of Defense, Hydrography Department, Somerset (hereafter MDHD), q43 Ag 1, Admiralty Chart of Grand Cayman with Notations by George Gauld, 1773.

13. National Library of Jamaica, Institute of Jamaica, Kingston (hereafter NLJ), MS. 72, Nugent Papers, Report on the Cayman Islands by Edward Corbet, 21 June 1802, fol. 10.

14. Williams, *History of the Cayman Islands*, 6–7; Craton and the New History Committee, *Founded upon the Seas*, 35.

15. Hirst, *Notes on the History*, 17–18; Smith, *Maritime Heritage*, 63. Smith includes an excerpt from Public Record Office, Kew, England (hereafter PRO), Colonial Office Records (hereafter CO) 308/1, Instructions for Thomas Windsor, Lord Windsor, Governor of our Island of Jamaica, in the West Indies, 21 March 1662.

16. Smith, *Maritime Heritage*, 60–61.

17. Williams, *History of the Cayman Islands*, 8–10; Smith, *Maritime Heritage*, 8, 23–26, 91–95.

18. Williams, *History of the Cayman Islands*, 10–11, Craton and the New History Committee, *Founded upon the Seas*, 26–27.

19. Hirst, *Notes on the History*, 20, 24; Craton and the New History Committee, *Founded upon the Seas*, 27. Hirst cites the Minutes of the Council of Jamaica dated 12 August 1671, which contains the proclamation of amnesty.

20. Hirst, *Notes on the History*, 250.

21. Hirst, *Notes on the History*, 28.

22. Williams, *History of the Cayman Islands*, 21; Smith, *Maritime Heritage*, 66–67. Smith cites an excerpt from PRO, CO 137/48, Memorial of John Sharpe on behalf of the inhabitants of Jamaica and the merchants trading there, to the Duke of Newcastle, 13 November 1738.

23. Hirst, *Notes on the History*, 33; Williams, *History of the Cayman Islands*, 12–16; Smith, *Maritime Heritage*, 103–11; Craton and the New History Committee, *Founded upon the Seas*, 28–30.

24. Smith, *Maritime Heritage*, 37–38.

25. Smith, *Maritime Heritage*, 151–52.

26. Hirst, *Notes on the History*, 32, 67.

27. Hirst, *Notes on the History*, 37–65; Williams, *History of the Cayman Islands*, 17–19. More information has been discovered about these land grants in recent years; they are described in detail in Craton and the New History Committee, *Founded upon the Seas*, 36–42.

28. Hirst, *Notes on the History*, 67–108.

29. MDHD, q43 Ag 1.

30. The growth of the slave population is described in Craton and the New History Committee, *Founded upon the Seas*, 63.

31. MDHD, q43 Ag 1; MDHD, Ag 1 196 fol. 2; MDHD, U 10 AG1.

32. PRO, CO 700/West Indies 23, Maps and Plans in PRO II: America and the West Indies, Catalog No. 2972, West Indies (1773–75) 1790.

33. Williams, *History of the Cayman Islands*, 21.

34. MDHD, q43 Ag 1.

35. PRO, CO 142/22, Jamaica Miscellaneous, Shipping Returns, 1784–1807; PRO, CO 142/23, Jamaica Miscellaneous, Shipping Returns, 1795–98.

36. PRO, CO 142/23, fol. 66.

37. Hirst, *Notes on the History*, 140.

38. Williams, *History of the Cayman Islands*, 26–27.

39. Williams, *History of the Cayman Islands*, 26.

40. NLJ, MS.72, Nugent Papers, Corbet's Report, fol. 3–4. Corbet's Report can also be found in Smith, *Maritime Heritage*, App. 3, and in Philip Pedley, ed., *Our Islands' Past*, vol. 1, *Edward Corbet's Report and Census of 1802 on the Cayman Islands* (George Town, Grand Cayman: Cayman Islands National Archive and Cayman Free Press, 1992).

41. NLJ, MS.72, Nugent Papers, Corbet's Report, fol. 1–20.

42. Williams, *History of the Cayman Islands*, 31; Craton and the New History Committee, *Founded upon the Seas*, 90–91, 93.

43. Jamaica Archives, Spanish Town, Jamaica (hereafter JA), 1B/5/3/18, fol. 128, 131, Council of Jamaica Minutes 1771–84, 25 February 1777. In the minutes, reference is made to a request by William Bodden Senior for a renewal of his commission as captain in the militia of the Cayman Islands. Mr. Bodden was still acting in this capacity in 1802 when Edward Corbet visited the island.

Chapter 3

1. William Doyle, *The Oxford History of the French Revolution* (Oxford: Oxford University Press, 1990), 32.

2. For further information about timber used by the French Navy from the

seventeenth century into the Napoleonic era, see Jean Boudriot, "Propos sur les bois de marine sous l'Ancien Régime," *Neptunia* 182 (1991): 12–18; Paul W. Bamford, *Forests and French Sea Power, 1660–1789* (Toronto: University of Toronto Press, 1956); P. E. Herbin de Halle, *Des bois propres au service des arsenaux de la marine et de la guerre, ou développement et rapprochement des lois, règlemens et instructions concernant la recherche, le martelage et l'exploitation des arbres propres aux constructions navales, de l'artillerie, etc.* (Paris: S. C. L'Huillier, 1813).

3. Jean Boudriot, *The Seventy-Four Gun Ship*, vol. 1, *Hull Construction*, trans. David H. Roberts (Annapolis: Naval Institute Press, 1986), 6.

4. Archives du Port de Rochefort (hereafter AR) 1 E 256, Correspondance de la Cour avec l'Intendant de la Marine à Rochefort, Direction générale Port R pour l'Intendance, no. 18, 14 March 1789.

5. Lavery, *Nelson's Navy*, 11.

6. Michael Lewis, *The History of the British Navy* (Baltimore: Penguin Books, 1962), 172–74.

7. Brian Lavery, *Nelson's Navy: The Ships, Men, and Organization, 1793–1815* (London: Conway Maritime Press, 1989), 40. The degree to which the British and French shared common seafaring practices and shipbuilding technologies in the late eighteenth century becomes apparent when one consults contemporary marine dictionaries; the French gave British equivalents and the British gave French equivalents for most entries. For examples, see Daniel Lescallier, *Vocabulaire des termes de marine, anglois et françois* (Paris: L'Imprimerie Royale, 1777); William Falconer, *An Universal Dictionary of the Marine; or, A Copious Explanation of the Technical Terms and Phrases Employed in the Construction, Equipment, Furniture, Machinery, Movements, and Military Operations of a Ship* (London: T. Cadell, 1769).

8. Lavery, *Nelson's Navy*, 278.

9. For details about the progress of students training to be shipwrights, see Boudriot, *Hull Construction*, 12–14. For examples of French treatises on building and rigging ships, see Pierre Alexandre Laurent Forfait, *Traité élémentaire de la mâture des vaisseaux: À l'usage des élèves de la marine* (Paris: Clousier, 1788); Daniel Lescallier, *Traité pratique du gréement des vaisseaux et autres batimens de mer: Ouvrage publié par ordre du Roi, pour l'instruction des élèves de la marine, sous le Ministère de M. de Fleurieu* (Paris: Clousier, 1791); Honore Sebastien Vial de Clairbois, *Traité élémentaire de la construction des vaisseaux, à l'usage des élèves de la marine, composé and publié, d'après les ordres de M. le Marechal de Castries, Ministre and Secrétaire d'Etat au Département de la Marine* (Paris: Clousier, 1787).

10. Many works on naval architecture published in Britain included drafts of ships from other countries—for example, John Charnock, *An History of Marine Architecture, Including an Enlarged and Progressive View of the Nautical Regulations and Naval History, both Civil and Military, of All Nations, Especially of Great Britain; Derived Chiefly from Original Manuscripts, as Well in Private Collections as in the Great Public Repositories, and Deduced from the Earliest Period to the Present Time*, 3 vols. (London: R. Faulder and 28 other publishers, 1800–1802); *European Magazine: A Collection of Papers on Naval Architecture, Originally Communicated through the Channel of the European Magazine* (London: European Magazine, 1791–93).

11. Lavery, *Nelson's Navy*, 20, 40, 278. Examples of contemporary British works on naval architecture and the rigging of ships include David Steel, *The Elements and Practice of Rigging and Seamanship*, 2 vols. (1794; reprint, London: Sim Com-

fort Associates, 1978); David Steel, *The Elements and Practice of Naval Architecture*, 2 vols. (1805; reprint, London: Sim Comfort Associates, 1977); Marmaduke Stalkartt, *Naval Architecture or the Rudiments and Rules of Ship Building*, 2 vols. (London: J. Boydell, J. Dodsley, and J. Sewell, 1781–87); William Sutherland, *The Ship Builder's Assistant* (London: Mount and Davidson, 1794).

12. Lavery, *Nelson's Navy*, 40.

13. Lavery, *Nelson's Navy*, 279; Jean Boudriot, *The Seventy-Four Gun Ship*, vol. 3, *Masts, Sails, Rigging*, trans. David H. Roberts (Annapolis: Naval Institute Press, 1987), 250–55.

14. Jean Boudriot, *The Seventy-Four Gun Ship*, vol. 2, *Fitting Out the Hull*, trans. David H. Roberts (Annapolis: Naval Institute Press, 1986), 156.

15. Boudriot, *Hull Construction*, 6.

16. Boudriot, *Masts, Sails, Rigging*, 251, 254–55.

17. Boudriot, *Masts, Sails, Rigging*, 251, 256–57; Lavery, *Nelson's Navy*, 19, 279. For a detailed discussion of the development and history of the French frigate, see Jean Boudriot and Hubert Berti, *The History of the French Frigate, 1650–1850*, trans. David H. Roberts (East Sussex, England: Jean Boudriot Publications, 1993).

18. Boudriot, *Masts, Sails, Rigging*, 250–59. Simplified drafts of the various types of ships in the French Navy are also included in this source.

19. Lavery, *Nelson's Navy*, 279.

20. Lavery, *Nelson's Navy*, 20.

21. Lavery, *Nelson's Navy*, 40.

22. For a breakdown of the rating scale, accompanied by a listing of the number and caliber of guns carried by each type of ship, see J. J. Colledge, *Ships of the Royal Navy* (Annapolis: Naval Institute Press, 1987), 12–13.

23. The forty-four-gun two-deckers would make a comeback in the late eighteenth and nineteenth centuries in US Navy Constitution-class frigates, which were responsible for US victories in the War of 1812.

24. Lavery, *Nelson's Navy*, 49.

25. Colledge, *Ships of the Royal Navy*, 12–13; Lavery, *Nelson's Navy*, 40–57. Lavery gives numerous examples of drafts of the various types of ships in the Royal Navy.

26. The *rôle de bord* of *L'Inconstante* suggests that the frigate carried forty guns, although an inventory taken after her capture records only thirty-six. Jean Boudriot and Hubert Berti, *Frégate la Belle-Poule 1765 de l'ingénieur Guignace, historique des frégates de 12 et monographie* (Paris: A.N.C.R.E., 1985), 12, lists thirty-six guns. Boudriot and Berti, *The History of the French Frigate*, p. 157, lists *L'Inconstante*'s armament as twenty-six 12-pounders and eight 6-pounders; pp. 121–72 are dedicated specifically to 12-pounder frigates.

27. Boudriot, *Hull Construction*, 10.

28. Lavery, *Nelson's Navy*, 280; Bernard Cros, "Les ingénieurs de la marine aux XVII et XVIII siècles," *Neptunia* 170 (1988): 7–18.

29. For details about the evolution of the *frégate légère*, see Jean Boudriot, "La frégate dans la marine royage, 1660–1750, la frégate légère," *Neptunia* 181 (1991): 27–31.

30. Boudriot and Berti, *Frégate la Belle-Poule*, 6.

31. Boudriot and Berti, *Frégate La Belle-Poule*, 11–13; Boudriot and Berti, *History of the French Frigate*, 156–57, provides similar but slightly different tabulations.

32. Boudriot and Berti, *Frégate La Belle-Poule*, 6–13.

33. Boudriot and Berti, *Frégate La Belle-Poule*, 11–13. The names of 21 shipwrights who collectively designed 89 of the 104 12-pounder frigates built between 1748 and 1798, and the numbers of vessels constructed according to the plans of each, follow: Guignace (14), J. M. B. Coulomb (12), Chevillard the Younger (9), Haran (8), Ginoux (7), Sané (6), Forfait (5), Secondat (5), Chevillard the Elder (4), Raffeau (3), Lamothe Père (3), J. L. Coulomb (2), Pénetreau (2), Groignard (2), Morineau (1), Duhamel (1), Chapelle fils (1), Poumet (1), Estienne (1), Bombelle (1), and Vial du Clairbois (1). Boudriot and Berti, *History of the French Frigate*, 156–57, provides similar but slightly different tabulations.

34. Boudriot and Berti, *Frégate La Belle-Poule*, 11–13; Boudriot and Berti, *History of the French Frigate*, 156–57. These two publications include copies of the plans of several 12-pounder frigates, drawn by various shipwrights in the half century between 1748 and 1798. Special attention is given to *La Belle-Poule*, for which drafts and detailed drawings are provided, including deck arrangements and sail plans.

35. Boudriot and Berti, *Frégate La Belle-Poule*, 10, 30, 32; Jean Boudriot and David H. Roberts, personal communication (letters to the author), 19 April and 9 May 1992. (Roberts is a colleague of Boudriot; he translates many of Boudriot's works from French to English.) Figure 2 is one of six engravings by Pierre Ozanne provided to Margaret Leshikar-Denton from Boudriot's personal collection.

36. Boudriot and Roberts, letter, 9 May 1992.

37. Boudriot and Berti, *Frégate La Belle-Poule*, 11–13; Boudriot, *Hull Construction*, 23. One French foot or *pied* is equivalent to 32.5 cm, whereas an English foot is equivalent to 30.5 cm.

38. Boudriot and Berti, *Frégate La Belle-Poule*, 11–13; Boudriot and Roberts, letters, 19 April and 9 May 1992; Boudriot, *Masts, Sails, Rigging*, 260; Norman Hampson, *La marine de l'an II, mobilisation de la flotte de l'océan, 1793–1794* (Paris, 1959). For further information about *La Charmante* and *La Junon*, including plans of these frigates, see Patrick Villiers, *La marine de Louis XVI de Choiseul à Sartine*, vol. 1 (Paris: J. P. Debbane, 1985), 400–401, 415–18.

39. Boudriot and Roberts, letter, 9 May 1992.

40. Boudriot and Roberts, letter, 9 May 1992; David Lyon, G. Slatter, and David Topliss, National Maritime Museum, personal communications with author, 1991–93. The drafts are preserved in the National Maritime Museum as: *L'Unité*, Reg. no. 6247 (digital reproduction ID J6091), Stern and Profile, As Taken; Reg. no. 6250 (digital reproduction ID J6088), Decks, As Taken; Reg. no. 6248, Profile, As Fitted; Reg. no. 6249, Decks, As Fitted.

41. AR, 2 G2 25, 2 G2 34, Devis d'armement et de campagne, la frégate *la Gracieuse*, devis de retour de campagne; Boudriot and Berti, *Frégate La Belle-Poule*, 28.

42. Boudriot and Berti, *Frégate La Belle-Poule*, 11–13.

43. Villiers, *La marine de Louis XVI*, 1: 400–401, 414–18.

44. Boudriot and Berti, *Frégate La Belle-Poule*, 11–13. Current research has not revealed the ultimate fate of the latter four frigates.

45. Boudriot and Berti, *Frégate La Belle-Poule*, 11–13.

46. For detailed information about the administration of the ports and dockyards, see Boudriot, *Hull Construction*, 10–15.

47. AR, 1 E 256, Direction générale Port R pour l'Intendance, no. 18, copy of a letter of 14 March 1789. Here the title of Monsieur le Comte, or Count, is in-

cluded with the names of the men exchanging official letters. By early 1790, when Navy administration correspondence began to come from Paris rather than from Versailles, the titles were dropped and the individuals are addressed simply as Monsieur. Hereafter in the text, names cited in correspondence will be given by surname.

48. AR, 1 E 256, Direction générale Port R pour l'Intendance, no. 18, copy of a letter of 14 March 1789, Pour modèle, comparaison du résumé de l'etat de situation des vaisseaux du 1 Mai 1789 avec l'inventaire du magasin général.

49. AR, 1 E 256, Direction générale Port R, no. 34, letter of 16 May 1789. The estimated labor cost was 5,900 livres, assuming the currency abbreviation refers to the French livre [pound].

50. AR, 1 E 261, Correspondance de la Cour avec l'Intendant de la Marine à Rochefort, Direction des constructions, Rochefort, 26 June 1789.

51. AR, 1 E 256, Direction générale Port R pour l'Intendance, no. 69, copy of a letter of 21 November 1789.

52. AR, 1 E 261, Intendance général, no. 75, letter of 25 September 1789.

53. AR, 1 E 262, Correspondance de la Cour avec l'Intendant de la Marine à Rochefort, Direction du port, no. 1, Rochefort, 10 January 1790.

54. AR, 1 E 262, Intendance générale pour l'Intendance, no. 20, copy of a letter of 26 March 1790.

55. AR, 1 E 262, Intendance générale, no. 27, letter of 23 April 1790.

56. AR, 1 E 262, Intendance générale, no. 31, letter dated 30 April 1790.

57. Boudriot, *Masts, Sails, Rigging*, 260.

58. AR, 1 A 122, Correspondance du Commandant de la Marine à Rochefort avec la Cour, 1790.

59. AR, 1 E 262, Intendance générale, no. 165, letter of 28 December 1790.

60. AR, 1 E 262, Direction du port, no. 2, Rochefort, 10 January 1791.

61. AR, 3 E2 35, Rôle d'équipage, la frégate *L'Inconstante*, commandée par M. Riouffe Major de Vaisseau, rôle de bord, 21 November 1791 to 25 November 1793; PRO, Admiralty Records (hereafter ADM) 1/245, Admiralty and Secretariat Papers, "Jamaica 1793 & 94 Admiral John Ford Esqr.": John Ford, Commodore and Commander in Chief of His Majesty's Ships and Vessels at Jamaica, to Philip Stephens, Secretary of the Admiralty, aboard the Europa, off Jérémie, 5 February 1794, and Enclosure: Inventory and appraisement of *L'Inconstante*.

62. Jean Boudriot, personal collection.

63. Boudriot and Roberts, letters, 19 April and 9 May 1992.

64. AR, 1 E 256, Direction générale Port R pour l'Intendance, no. 43, copy of a letter of 13 June 1789.

Chapter 4

1. Sir James Barskett, *History of the Island of St. Domingo: From Its First Discovery by Columbus to the Present Period* (1818; reprint, London: Frank Cass, 1972), 114–53.

2. Ministère de la Défense, Service Historique de la Marine, Château de Vincennes (hereafter SHM), CC7 ALPHA 2151, Dossier individuel de Alexandre Joseph Riouffe. Numerous documents in this class detail Riouffe's career in the French Navy and the ships on which he served.

3. AR, 1 E 268, Correspondance de la Cour avec l'Intendant de la Marine à

Rochefort, Officier militaire pour l'Intendance, no. 293, copy of a letter of 17 November 1791.

4. SHM, CC7 ALPHA 2151, Rochefort, services du citoyen Riouffe Capitaine de Vaisseau, extrait des rôles d'équipages déposés au bureau général des armemens de ce port, 22 Nivôse et 28 Pluviôse l'an 3 de la Republique francaise (11 January and 16 February 1795). The dates in this reference are according to the French Revolutionary Calendar, which was the official calendar of France from 24 November 1793 to 31 December 1805; the first day of the calendar began on 22 September 1792, immediately after the establishment of the first French Republic. The calendar was divided into twelve months of thirty days each, and the remaining five days were feast days; in leap year the last day of the year was Revolution Day.

5. AR, 1 E 271, Correspondance de la Cour avec l'Intendant de la Marine à Rochefort, Extrait de l'equipage de deux frégates armées en flûte, et celui d'une flûte, 17 November 1791.

6. AR, 1 E 271, Port R et arsenaux pour l'Intendance, no. 294, copy of a letter of 17 November 1791.

7. AR, 1 E 268, Commis aux revues aux approvisionnement, no. 316, letter of 27 November 1791.

8. AR, 1 E 271, Port R & arsenaux pour l'Intendance, no. 322, copy of a letter of 3 December 1791; Riouffe's instructions are included in Archives Nationales, Paris (hereafter AN), C/7 276, Dossier personnel de Alexandre Joseph Riouffe.

9. AR, [1 E 271], Artillerie et colonies, no. 330, letter from the Minister of the Navy in Paris to Charlot in Rochefort, 8 December 1791.

10. AR, [1 E 271], Colonies, no. 353, letter from the Minister of the Navy to Charlot, 17 December 1791.

11. AR, 1 A 122, Correspondance du Commandant de la Marine à Rochefort avec la Cour, 1791.

12. Jean Favier, director, Archives Nationales, Paris, personal letter to Charles Beeker, Indiana University, 21 May 1986.

13. AR, 3 E2 35, Rôle d'équipage, la frégate *L'Inconstante*, commandée par M. Riouffe Major de Vaisseau, rôle de bord, 21 November 1791 to 25 November 1793.

14. AR, 3 E2 35, Rôle d'équipage, la frégate *L'Inconstante*, commandée par M. Riouffe Major de Vaisseau, rôle de bord, 21 November 1791 to 25 November 1793.

15. Barskett, *History of the Island of St. Domingo*, 154–57.

16. William Doyle, *The Oxford History of the French Revolution* (Oxford: Oxford University Press, 1990).

17. Lewis, *History of the British Navy*, 174; Lavery, *Nelson's Navy*, 281.

18. AR, 3 E2 35, *L'Inconstante*, rôle de bord.

19. Lavery, *Nelson's Navy*, 282.

20. C. L. R. James, *The Black Jacobins, Toussaint L'Ouverture, and the San Domingo Revolution* (London: W. H. Allen, 1989), 31.

21. Captain Thomas Southey, *A Chronological History of the West Indies*, vol. 3 (1827; reprint, London: Frank Cass, 1968), 37.

22. James, *Black Jacobins*, 31.

23. James, *Black Jacobins*, 122.

24. James, *Black Jacobins*, 118–19.

25. Barskett, *History of the Island of St. Domingo*, 154–57.

26. Barskett, *History of the Island of St. Domingo*, 157–59; James, *Black Jacobins*, 118–23; Southey, *Chronological History*, 53–54.

27. Barskett, *History of the Island of St. Domingo*, 154–59; Southey, *Chronological History*, 54.

28. NLJ, "French Navy, Account Given in to the National Convention of the State of the French Navy, Sept. 23," *Royal Gazette* 15, no. 1 (1793). This periodical, published weekly on Saturdays, often published intelligence gathered about France.

29. SHM, CC7 ALPHA 2151, La municipalité du Môle, Séance du 29 janvier 1793 L'an premier de La République Francaise.

30. PRO, ADM 1/245, Admiralty and Secretariat Papers, "Jamaica 1793 & 94 Admiral John Ford Esqr.": John Ford, Commodore and Commander in Chief of His Majesty's Ships and Vessels at Jamaica, to Philip Stephens, Secretary of the Admiralty, aboard the *Providence*, Port Royal, Jamaica, 14 April 1793 and Enclosure: A List of French Vessels seized in the Port of Kingston on 29 March 1793. In the Public Record Office, the dispatches and enclosures in ADM 1/245 are bound together and titled "Jamaica 1793 & 94 Admiral John Ford Esqr." John Ford was, however, commodore and commander in chief of His Majesty's ships and vessels at Jamaica until 12 April 1794, when he was promoted to rear admiral.

31. PRO, ADM 1/245, John Ford to Philip Stephens, aboard the *Providence*, Port Royal, Jamaica, 12 May 1793 and Enclosure: A List of French Prizes taken by the Squadron under the Command of John Ford between 14 April and 12 May 1793. British documents refer to the captured French corvette as *le Goelan*; the French called her *le Goéland* (seagull).

32. Southey, *Chronological History*, 37.

33. British documents consistently refer to a place called Aux Cayes, but attempts to find such a place on both modern and historical maps have so far been unsuccessful. There is, however, a place called Les Cayes on the south coast of Saint-Domingue, and it is possible that the two names refer to the same location.

34. PRO, ADM 1/245, Extract of a letter from Captain Rowley of His Majesty's Ship *Penelope* dated at Sea 3 June 1793, enclosure in John Ford to Philip Stephens, 9 June 1793.

35. PRO, ADM 1/245, A List of the Squadron under the Command of John Ford . . . and the Services they are employed on 12 May 1793, enclosure in John Ford to Philip Stephens, 12 May 1793; Southey, *Chronological History*, 74.

36. Barskett, *History of the Island of St. Domingo*, 159–65; James, *Black Jacobins*, 126–28; Southey, *Chronological History*, 67–69.

37. PRO, ADM 1/245, Disposition of the Squadron under the Command of John Ford . . . on 8 September 1793, enclosure in John Ford to Philip Stephens, 8 September 1793.

38. Southey, *Chronological History*, 74.

39. Barskett, *History of the Island of St. Domingo*, 163–75; James, *Black Jacobins*, 135; Southey, *Chronological History*, 69–70.

40. AN, Marine BB/4/28, fol. 86–95, Dossier *L'Inconstante*.

41. James, *Black Jacobins*, 31.

42. AR, 3 E2 35, *L'Inconstante*, rôle de bord.

43. JA, High Court of Vice Admiralty, Ship's Papers, "*L'Inconstante* to HMS *Penelope*, Taken 25th November 1793, Condemned."

Chapter 5

1. F. R. Augier, S. C. Gordon, D. G. Hall, and M. Reckord, *The Making of the West Indies* (Trinidad and Jamaica: Longmans Caribbean, 1990), 98–99.

2. The explanation of prize money is based on largely parallel descriptions related by naval historians Michael Lewis and Brian Lavery: Lewis, *A Social History of the Navy, 1793–1815* (London: George Allen and Unwin, 1960), 315–33; Lavery, *Nelson's Navy*, 116.

3. Lavery, *Nelson's Navy*, 116.

4. PRO, ADM 1/245, Admiralty and Secretariat Papers, "Jamaica 1793 & 94 Admiral John Ford Esqr.": John Ford, Commodore and Commander in Chief of His Majesty's Ships and Vessels at Jamaica, to Philip Stephens, Secretary of the Admiralty, aboard the *Europa*, Port Royal, Jamaica, 13 January 1793.

5. "Admiral Sir John Lawford, K.C.B." (obituary), *Gentleman's Magazine*, April 1843, 426.

6. PRO, CO 137/92, Jamaica Original Correspondence, 18 November 1793 to 7 February 1794, John Lawford to the Governor of Baccalar, aboard the *Hound*, St. George's Kay, 5 March 1793, enclosure in Adam Williamson, Lieutenant Governor and Commander in Chief in and over His Majesty's Island of Jamaica and the Territories thereon depending in America, Chancellor and Vice Admiral of the same, to Henry Dundas, Secretary of State for War, Kings House, Jamaica, 13 December 1793.

7. Southey, *Chronological History*, 70. William Bligh of the *Providence* was the famous Bligh who, several years before, had suffered the mutiny of his crew on the *Bounty*.

8. PRO, ADM 1/245, Captain William Hargood to John Ford, aboard the *Hyæna*, Port Antonio, Jamaica, 27 January 1793, enclosure in John Ford to Philip Stephens, 3 February 1793.

9. The British spelling of Cap Français was Cape Francois.

10. The *Triton, Falcon*, and *Helena* were no longer with the squadron in Jamaica.

11. PRO, ADM 1/245, John Ford to Philip Stephens, aboard the *Providence*, Port Royal, 14 April 1793, and Enclosure 9: A List of the Squadron under the Command of John Ford . . . and the Services they are employed on 14 April 1793, Enclosure 10: A List of French Vessels seized in the Port of Kingston on 29 March 1793, and Enclosure 11: A List of French Prizes taken by the Squadron between 1 and 14 April 1793.

12. PRO, ADM 1/245, John Ford to Philip Stephens, aboard the *Providence*, Port Royal, Jamaica, 12 May 1793, and Enclosure: John Lawford to John Ford aboard the *Hound*, off Belize, Honduras, 14 April 1793.

13. Although the British spelled the French frigate's name with an "A," this vessel was the frigate *L'Embuscade*, which was under construction at Rochefort at the same time as *L'Inconstante*.

14. PRO, ADM 1/245, Extract of a Letter from Mr. Miller to Lord Dunmore, Charlestown, 18 April 1793, Enclosure in John Ford to Philip Stephens, 9 June 1793.

15. PRO, ADM 1/245, A List of the Squadron under the Command of John Ford . . . and the Services they are employed on 12 May 1793, . . . on 9 June 1793, . . . on 14 July 1793, Enclosures in dispatches from John Ford to Philip Stephens

between 12 May and 14 July 1793; PRO, ADM 7/782, Registers of Convoys 1793–97, Ships from Jamaica under Convoy of the *Proserpine* Frigate, Captain Alms, arrived 3 September 1793. It is supposed that the *Fly* joined the home-bound fleet because she escorted vessels from Port Antonio to Bluefields where the convoy assembled, and she is absent from subsequent lists of Ford's squadron in Jamaica.

16. PRO, ADM 1/245, A List of French Vessels seized in the Port of Kingston on 29 March 1793, A List of the French Prizes taken by the Squadron under the Command of John Ford between 1 and 14 April 1793, . . . between 14 April and 12 May 1793, . . . between 14 May and 9 June 1793, . . . between 10 June and 11 July 1793, Enclosures in dispatches from John Ford to Philip Stephens between 14 April and 11 July 1793.

17. PRO, ADM 1/245, John Ford to Philip Stephens, aboard the *Providence*, Port Royal, Jamaica, 12 May 1793.

18. Southey, *Chronological History*, 74.

19. Captain Rowley of the *Penelope* did not sail with the Europe-bound convoy on 12 June, but it seems that Lawford believed he would do so.

20. PRO, ADM 1/245, John Ford to Philip Stephens, aboard the *Providence*, Port Royal, Jamaica, 12 May 1793, and Enclosure: A List of the Squadron . . . on 12 May 1793; PRO, ADM 1/245, John Ford to Philip Stephens, aboard the *Providence*, Port Royal, Jamaica, 17 May 1793; PRO, ADM 1/245, John Ford to Philip Stephens, aboard the *Goelan*, Port Royal, Jamaica, 11 August 1793, and Enclosure: John Lawford to John Ford, aboard the *Hound*, off Belize River, 26 June 1793.

21. PRO, ADM 7/782, A List of Ships and Vessels brought under Convoy of HMS *Hector*, George Montague Comdr., from Jamaica to England between 22 July and 4 October 1793; PRO, ADM 7/782, Ships from Jamaica under Convoy of the *Hannibal*, Captain Colpoys, arrived 1 October 1793; PRO, ADM 1/245, John Ford to Philip Stephens, aboard the *Goelan*, Port Royal, Jamaica, 11 August 1793, and Enclosure: Disposition of the Squadron under the Command of John Ford . . . on 11 August 1793.

22. NLJ, *Royal Gazette* 15, no. 44 (26 October–2 November 1793), 22–23.

23. PRO, ADM 1/245, John Ford to Philip Stephens, aboard HMS *Goelan*, Port Royal, Jamaica, 11 August 1793, and Enclosure: Disposition of the Squadron . . . on 11 August 1793. The *Serpent* sloop was no longer with the squadron by this time.

24. PRO, ADM 1/245, John Ford to Philip Stephens, 8 September 1793, and Enclosure: Disposition of the Squadron under the Command of John Ford . . . on 8 September 1793.

25. Southey, *Chronological History*, 74.

26. PRO, ADM 1/245, John Ford to Philip Stephens, aboard the *Europa*, Port Royal, Jamaica, 24 November 1793, and Enclosure: Disposition of the Squadron under the Command of John Ford . . . on 24 November 1793.

27. NLJ, *Royal Gazette* 15, no. 48 (23–30 November 1793), 22–23.

28. PRO, CO 137/92, Adam Williamson to Henry Dundas, Kings House, Jamaica, 13 December 1793, and Enclosures. As British Commissary in the Bay of Honduras, John Lawford was involved in settling disputes, chiefly regarding infractions committed by British settlers who persisted in cutting mahogany outside of the limits prescribed by the Treaty of 1783 and Convention of 1786 between Spain and Britain. The British had fewer complaints about Spanish infractions. Lawford's

role was difficult, and at times misunderstandings arose between the British magistrates of the district, who tried to suppress complaints about unauthorized cutting of wood on the Spanish side of the boundary, and himself.

29. PRO, CO 137/92, Adam Williamson to Henry Dundas, Kings House, 16 January 1794, and Enclosure: John Lawford to Adam Williamson, HMS *Convert*, Port Royal, 20 December 1793.

30. PRO, CO 137/92, Henry Dundas to Adam Williamson, Whitehall, 6 March 1794.

31. Lavery, *Nelson's Navy*, 51.

32. NLJ, *Royal Gazette* 15, no. 48 (23–30 November 1793), 23.

33. AR, 3 E2 35, Rôle d'équipage, la frégate *L'Inconstante*, commandée par M. Riouffe Major de Vaisseau, rôle de bord, 21 November 1791 to 25 November 1793.

34. PRO, ADM 1/245, B. S. Rowley to John Ford, aboard the *Penelope*, Port Royal, Jamaica, 30 November 1793, Enclosure in John Ford to Philip Stephens, aboard the *Europa*, Port Royal, Jamaica, 7 December 1793.

35. Use map 9 and figure 12 together for a more detailed understanding of the courses sailed by HMS *Penelope* and *Iphigenia* between 20 and 26 November 1793. Please note that data were recorded in ships' logs from midday to midday.

36. Presumably, these vessels had people aboard who were unsympathetic to the new French Republic and its civil commissioners in Saint-Domingue, as it is known that the parish of Saint-Marc gave itself up to the British in December.

37. PRO, ADM 52/3276, Master's Logs, A Log of the Proceedings of the *Penelope*, B. S. Rowley, Commander, by John Douglas, Master, from 31 August 1793 to 10 June 1794.

38. PRO, ADM 1/3992, Lloyds 1793–1804, Extract of a personal letter from Jérémie dated 27 November 1793 and received in London on 27 January 1794, forwarded by Thomas Taylor of Lloyd's Coffee House to Philip Stephens, 27 January 1794.

39. PRO, ADM 1/2059, Captain's Letters, 1793–94, "L," John Lawford's Commission into the *Convert*, 1 December 1793. John Lawford was promoted to post captain, a term used to describe a full captain who commanded a ship of the sixth rate or higher.

40. PRO, ADM 1/245, John Ford to Philip Stephens, aboard the *Europa*, Port Royal, Jamaica, 7 December 1793, and Enclosure: A List of the Squadron under the Command of John Ford . . . on 7 December 1793.

41. PRO, ADM 1/245, John Ford to Philip Stephens . . . 7 December 1793, and Enclosure . . . 7 December 1793.

42. NLJ, *Royal Gazette*, 15, no. 48 (23–30 November 1793), 23, no. 49 (30 November–7 December 1793), 22–23. French documents recorded that Captain Riouffe's left arm received the wound and was subsequently amputated.

43. JA, High Court of Vice Admiralty, Ship's Papers, "*L'Inconstante* to HMS *Penelope*, Taken 25th November 1793 Condemned."

44. AN, Marine BB/4/28, fol. 86–95, Dossier *L'Inconstante*, copie de la déclaration du citoyen Leissegues Lieutenant de Vaisseau sur le sort de la frégate *L'Inconstante* commandée par le deu Riouffe Capitaine de Vaisseau, 27 June 1794, and Extrait de la journée du combat de la frégate l'Inconstante . . . as described by Officier de Marine Ouinet (see note 49).

45. SHM, CC7 ALPHA 2151, Dossier individuel de Alexandre Joseph Riouffe.

46. Official French documents give this officer's full name as Alexandre Joseph Riouffe and commonly refer to him as Joseph Riouffe. Apparently, he was also known as Jean Riouffe.

47. JA, High Court of Vice Admiralty, *L'Inconstante* to HMS *Penelope*.

48. The name of the commander of *Le Goelan* is spelled three ways in two documents. A previously cited British account spells the name *Leisseguese*, while in this French letter the name is spelled both as *Leissegues* and *Lesseigues*.

49. It is probable that the officer whose name is spelled Boisguere in the cited French document is the same man as Second Lieutenant Augustin de Boyery, who appeared in the previously cited British document. It is difficult to decipher the exact spelling of the name of the other officer in the cited French document (Ouinet), which also occurs in the accompanying *Extrait de la journée du combat* . . . ; it is possible that it is Ouimet or Omnes.

50. AN, *Marine* BB/4/28, fol. 86–95, Dossier *L'Inconstante*, déclaration du citoyen Leissegues.

51. The testimony given by Naval Officer Ouinet is not dated but was given after Lieutenant de Vaisseau Leissegues's 27 June 1794 statement; the events that Ouinet describes begin with the capture of *L'Inconstante*, cover the period of his imprisonment in Jamaica, and end with his arrival in Brest on 13 July 1794.

52. Although the word *bateaux* is plural, the document refers to *un bateaux*, in the singular.

53. The small number of men on board the British frigates can be attributed to difficulties in completing the complements of the Royal Navy vessels stationed in Jamaica in the first year of war with France; the squadron had been sent to the West Indies on a peacetime mission.

54. Although Ouinet referred to forty-four guns, *L'Inconstante*'s official documents suggest that she was designed to carry forty.

55. Ouinet seems to be stating that the gun captain wanted to continue firing after *L'Inconstante* lowered her flag, but it is not clear whether the gun captain knew that the flag had been lowered.

56. Ouinet mixed up his dates here, as 2 December was a Monday.

57. I did not encounter any documentary corroboration of these serious allegations.

58. In this source the name of the corvette is spelled *Goillant*, but it is almost certainly the same vessel referred to in British accounts as *Le Goelan*. There is no clear identification given for Doctor Renal.

59. Captain Riouffe's dying words, as related by Ouinet, are a bit confusing. The English paraphrase relates the statements as accurately as possible.

60. Hypolite Valliet Riouffe's name is spelled in numerous ways in this class of documents; the most common spelling is reflected in the text.

61. SHM, CC7 ALPHA 2151, Dossier individuel de Alexandre Joseph Riouffe. Many of the documents included within this class exhibit Revolutionary Calendar dates. If only Revolutionary dates occur on referenced documents, standard calendar dates will still be given.

62. PRO, ADM 52/3276, Master's Log of HMS *Penelope*; PRO, ADM 1/2059, John Lawford's Commission.

63. PRO, ADM 1/245, Inventory and appraisement of the sails, rigging, ordnance, and stores from *L'Inconstante*, ordered on 30 November 1793 and completed

on 20 and 21 December 1793, Enclosure in John Ford to Philip Stephens, aboard the *Europa*, off Jérémie, 5 February 1794.

64. PRO, ADM 1/245, John Ford to Philip Stephens, aboard the *Europa*, Port Royal, Jamaica, 7 December 1793, and Enclosure: A List of the Squadron under the Command of John Ford . . . on 7 December 1793.

65. Lavery, *Nelson's Navy*, 116; Lewis, *Social History of the Navy*, 318.

66. JA, High Court of Vice Admiralty, *L'Inconstante* to HMS *Penelope*.

67. JA, High Court of Vice Admiralty, *L'Inconstante* to HMS *Penelope*. Naval storekeeper William Smith purchased the hull, etc., as per valuation for £19,844.10s.3d, and Nicholas Lechmere of the Office of Ordnance acquired the ordnance, stores, etc., for the Admiralty for £2,161.7s.6d. Various merchants bought the water casks, thirteen hogsheads of wine, thirteen barrels of beef, fourteen barrels of pork, seventy-five barrels of flour, one hogshead of taffia (inferior rum), three hogsheads of salt, five hogsheads of calavances (chick peas), ten bags of calavances, two hogsheads of vinegar, thirty-five casks of bread, thirteen sails, two awnings, and 4,242 pounds of cordage for a total of £828.18s.9d. The complete sale of the frigate and her stores resulted in proceeds of £22,834.16s.6d. The entire sum was subsequently allocated to various parties. Expenses associated with pilotage into Port Royal were £15.10s.5d; court fees amounted to £119; and the cost of hiring a vessel to transport stores from Port Royal was £208.17s.6d. Appraisal costs totaled £73.10s for the hull, rigging, and stores and £11.5s for the water casks. Wharfage and weighing sundries incurred a fee of £98.15s; cooperage cost £40.5s; charges for advertisements and a crier at the sales of the stores came to £6; the fee for lodging a copy of the sales in the Register's Office was £5.10s; and 5 percent commission on the complete sale totaled £1,141.14s.9d, presumably paid to the relators' agent, Benjamin Waterhouse. The remaining sum of £21,114.8s.10d was disbursed to His Majesty's ships *Penelope* and *Iphigenia*.

68. Lewis, *Social History of the Navy*, 318–19, 330–33; Lavery, *Nelson's Navy*, 116. The standard share-out in force at the time was three-eighths to the captain or captains; one-eighth divided equally among the captains of marines and army, sea lieutenants, master, and physician; one-eighth divided among the lieutenants of marines and army, secretary of admiral, principal warrant officers, master's mates, and chaplain; one-eighth divided between the midshipmen, inferior warrant officers, principal warrant officer's mates, and marine sergeants; and two-eighths, or one-fourth, divided among the rest of the crew. Flag officers such as an admiral—in this case, Commodore Ford—and his junior flag officers received one of the captain's eighths.

Chapter 6

1. Lavery, *Nelson's Navy*, 269.

2. Lavery, *Nelson's Navy*, 273.

3. PRO, ADM 1/245, Admiralty and Secretariat Papers, "Jamaica 1793 & 94, Admiral John Ford Esqr.": John Ford, Commodore and Commander in Chief of His Majesty's Ships and Vessels at Jamaica, to Philip Stephens, Secretary of the Admiralty, 9 June 1793, and Enclosure: A List of the Squadron under the Command of John Ford . . . on 9 June 1793; PRO, ADM 7/782, Registers of Convoys 1793–97, Ships from Jamaica under Convoy of the *Proserpine* Frigate, Captain

Alms, arrived 3 September 1793. The *Fly* may also have sailed with the homebound June convoy (see chapter 6, note 15).

4. PRO, ADM 1/245, John Ford to Philip Stephens, aboard the *Goelan*, Port Royal, Jamaica, 11 August 1793; PRO, ADM 7/782, A List of Ships and Vessels brought under Convoy of HMS *Hector*, George Montague Comdr., from Jamaica to England between 22 July and 4 October 1793; PRO, ADM 7/782, Ships from Jamaica under Convoy of the *Hannibal*, Captain Colpoys, arrived 1 October 1793.

5. JA, 1B/5/3/20, Council of Jamaica Minutes, May 1792 to May 1799, 7 August and 12 November 1793. As a result of pleas from merchants, the Assembly of Jamaica asked that Jamaican ports be opened to neutral vessels. Many British ships had been captured by French ships of war and privateers in American seas, and such action was deemed necessary because Commodore Ford could not provide protection for British ships that might be sent from Jamaica to North America for supplies. Lieutenant Governor Adam Williamson permitted the ports to be opened to neutral vessels for a limited period.

6. Lavery, *Nelson's Navy*, 130.

7. Lavery, *Nelson's Navy*, 113.

8. PRO, ADM 36/11476, Ships' Muster Books, Muster-Table of HMS *Convert*, 1793–94. The ship's crew did include one carpenter's mate and three carpenter's crew.

9. Lavery, *Nelson's Navy*, 88, 99.

10. The purser's servant also came from the *Hound*, but he was counted earlier in the group of ten warrant officers' servants. The eleven men ranked as petty officers from the *Hound* comprised two midshipmen, a master's mate, a gunner's mate, a yeoman of the powder room, a quartergunner, a coxswain, two quartermasters, and two corporals. From the remaining thirty-seven able seamen volunteers, five petty officer assignments were made: a carpenter's crew, a yeoman of the sheets, a quartermaster's mate, a clerk, and a boatswain's mate.

11. PRO, ADM 1/245, John Ford to Philip Stephens, aboard the *Providence*, Port Royal, Jamaica, 14 April 1793.

12. Lavery, *Nelson's Navy*, 117–23.

13. JA, 1B/5/3/20, Council Minutes, 3 December 1793.

14. JA, 1B/5/3/20, Council Minutes, 3 December 1793.

15. Lavery, *Nelson's Navy*, 120.

16. NLJ, *Royal Gazette* 15, no. 49 (30 November–7 December 1793), 23.

17. *Royal Gazette* 15, no. 52 (21–28 December 1793), 22.

18. PRO, ADM 36/11476, Muster-Table of HMS *Convert*. From the ranks of the eighty-four volunteers, seven petty officer assignments were made: a carpenter's crew, a carpenter's mate, two quartermaster's mates, a quartermaster, a quartergunner, and a yeoman of the sheets.

19. Lavery, *Nelson's Navy*, 120.

20. PRO, ADM 36/11476, Muster-Table of HMS *Convert*. The additional eighty-four men included a gunner, two gunner's servants, a surgeon and his servant, a master's servant, a purser's servant, a master's mate from the *Penelope*, a captain's servant, two able seamen who had been impressed, and seventy-three volunteer able seamen. Three petty officer appointments were made from among the volunteer seamen (one armorer's mate and two quartergunners).

21. JA, 1B/5/3/20, Council Minutes, 17 July 1794.

22. PRO, ADM 36/11476, Muster-Table of HMS *Convert.*

23. PRO, ADM 1/245, John Ford to Philip Stephens, aboard the *Europa*, Le Môle St. Nicholas, 22 January 1794.

24. PRO, ADM 1/5331, Courts-Martial, February to December 1794, April 1—Captain John Lawford, the Officers and Company of the *Convert*, for the loss of her, John Ford to John Lawford, Captain of HMS *Convert*, aboard the *Europa*, off Port au Prince, 5 January 1794. A copy of Ford's 5 January 1794 instructions to John Lawford are also included as an Enclosure in: PRO, ADM 1/245, John Ford to Philip Stephens, aboard the *Europa*, Port Royal Harbour, Jamaica, 3 April 1794. Ford's instructions in the latter copy are, however, misdated 5 February 1794.

25. PRO, CO 141/1, Government Gazettes, *Royal Gazette* 16, no. 2 (4–11 January 1794), 23.

26. JA, 1B/5/3/20, Council Minutes, 20 January 1794.

27. JA, 1B/5/3/20, Council Minutes, 20 January 1794.

28. PRO, ADM 36/11476, Muster-Table of HMS *Convert.*

29. PRO, CO 141/1, *Royal Gazette* 16, no. 3 (11–18 January 1794), 19.

30. PRO, ADM 1/245, John Ford to Philip Stephens, aboard the *Europa*, off Jérémie, 5 February 1794, and Enclosures.

31. PRO, ADM 1/245, John Ford to Philip Stephens, aboard the *Europa*, off Jérémie, 5 February 1794, and Enclosures.

32. PRO, CO 141/1, *Royal Gazette* 16, no. 4 (18–25 January 1794), 17.

33. PRO, ADM 36/11476, Muster-Table of HMS *Convert.*

34. Lavery, *Nelson's Navy*, 150.

35. Lavery, *Nelson's Navy*, 113.

36. PRO, ADM 36/11476, Muster-Table of HMS *Convert.*

37. PRO, CO 141/1, *Royal Gazette* 16, no. 5 (25 January–1 February 1794), 22.

38. PRO, CO 141/1, *Royal Gazette* 16, no. 10 (1–8 March 1794), 23.

39. Lavery, *Nelson's Navy*, 269–71.

40. Lavery, *Nelson's Navy.*

41. David MacGregor, *Fast Sailing Ships, Their Design and Construction, 1775–1875* (Annapolis, Naval Institute Press, 1988), 13. In another excellent work, *Merchant Sailing Ships, 1775–1815* (London: Conway Maritime Press, 1985), MacGregor discusses numerous types of merchant ship hulls that could be rigged as ship, snow, brigantine, schooner, or sloop, among other rigs. The reader is referred to this volume for a description of the range of merchant vessels that might have composed the *Convert* convoy.

42. Lavery, *Nelson's Navy*, 271.

43. PRO, CO 141/1, *Royal Gazette* 16, no. 5 (25 January–1 February 1794), 22–23; no. 6 (1–8 February), 22–23.

44. MacGregor, *Merchant Sailing Ships*, 109–14.

45. William Falconer, *Falconer's Marine Dictionary* (New York: Augustus M. Kelley, 1970; reprint of *An Universal Dictionary of the Marine*, 1780, first published in 1769), 50.

46. MacGregor, *Merchant Sailing Ships*, 139–46.

47. MacGregor, *Merchant Sailing Ships*, 81.

48. MacGregor, *Merchant Sailing Ships*, 92–98.

49. NLJ, *Royal Gazette* 15 (1793); PRO, CO 141/1, *Royal Gazette* 16 (1794). There were also advertisements for several vessels that intended to sail with the "first convoy" but that actually sailed later. Among these vessels were the *Betsey*, Master Gibson; *Belisarius*, Master Cleland; and *Gipsey*, Master Tobin.

50. MacGregor, *Fast Sailing Ships*, 14.

51. NLJ, *Royal Gazette* 15, no. 50 (7–14 December 1793), 1.

52. PRO, CO 141/1, *Royal Gazette* 16, no. 1 (28 December 1793–4 January 1794), 1, 17.

53. PRO, CO 141/1, *Royal Gazette* 16, no. 5, 22; PRO, CO 141/1, *Royal Gazette* 16, no. 6, 22. In the lists of vessels that arrived at or sailed from Port Royal, the name of each merchantman occurs first, followed by the surname of the vessel's master. While the ships *Lion*, Finnan, and *Arethusa*, Smith, which occur in the Jamaica departure list, are not accounted for as arrivals in Britain in either *Lloyd's List* (in March and April 1794) or the *Royal Gazette*, *Lion* (or *Lyon*), King, and *Arethusa*, Dods (or Dodds), are recorded in both publications as arriving in Britain from Jamaica. It is likely that there was only one *Lion* and one *Arethusa* in the fleet. It is possible that the masters died and that the ships arrived with different masters. However, there are ads in several issues of the 1793 *Royal Gazette* that refer to the ship *Lion*, King, suggesting that this ship intended to sail with the winter convoy, so it may be that the name Finnan was simply a mistake in the departure list.

54. PRO, CO 141/1, *Royal Gazette* 16, no. 4, 22.

55. PRO, CO 141/1, *Royal Gazette* 16, no. 6, 22.

56. PRO, ADM 1/5331, John Lawford's Court-Martial, John Lawford to John Ford, Island of Grand Cayman, 20 February 1794. A copy of Lawford's 20 February 1794 letter to John Ford is also included as an Enclosure in: PRO, ADM 1/245, John Ford to Philip Stephens, aboard the *Europa*, Port Royal Harbour, Jamaica, 3 April 1794. The two transcriptions vary slightly in punctuation, spelling, and an occasional word, but their overall content is the same.

57. Lavery, *Nelson's Navy*, 307.

58. PRO, CO 141/1, *Royal Gazette* 16, no. 7 (8–15 February 1794), 19.

59. PRO, CO 141/1, *Royal Gazette* 16, no. 5, 23; PRO, CO 141/1, *Royal Gazette* 16, no. 6, 23.

60. NLJ, *Royal Gazette* 15, no. 50 (1793), 1.

61. PRO, ADM 1/245, John Ford to Philip Stephens, aboard the *Europa*, off Jérémie, 5 February 1794, and Enclosures.

62. PRO, ADM 36/11476, Muster-Table of HMS *Convert*.

63. PRO, CO 141/1, *Royal Gazette* 16, no. 5 (1794), 22.

64. PRO, ADM 1/5331, John Lawford's Court-Martial, John Lawford to John Ford, 20 February 1794. In Captain Lawford's 20 February 1794 letter to Commodore Ford, in which he describes the circumstances of the convoy as well as the wrecking of ten ships, he recalls that three vessels of the convoy, which were bound to America, were schooners. It is possible, however, that one was a schooner and two were brigs, as suggested previously in the text, based on information in the *Royal Gazette*. The *Convert*'s list of the convoy did not survive, and approximately nineteen names of vessels that left Jamaica with the convoy were not found in the departure documents that were consulted. Information about vessels arriving in Britain, however, combined with the departure data, provides details that enable a

reasonably accurate reconstruction of the convoy. This list is presented in chart form in appendix E.

Chapter 7

1. Richard Pares, *War and Trade in the West Indies 1739–1763* (London: Frank Cass, 1963), 303–4.

2. PRO, ADM 7/782, Registers of Convoys 1793–97, A List of Ships and Vessels brought under Convoy of HMS *Hector*, George Montague Comdr., from Jamaica to England between 22 July and 4 October 1793.

3. Lavery, *Nelson's Navy*, 309–10.

4. PRO, ADM 1/5331, Courts-Martial, February to December 1794, April 1—Captain John Lawford, the Officers and Company of the *Convert*, for the loss of her, John Ford, Commodore and Commander in Chief of His Majesty's Ships and Vessels at Jamaica, to John Lawford, Captain of HMS *Convert*, aboard the *Europa*, off Port au Prince, 5 January 1794. A copy of Ford's 5 January 1794 instructions to John Lawford are also included as an Enclosure in: PRO, ADM 1/245, Admiralty and Secretariat Papers, "Jamaica 1793 & 94, Admiral John Ford Esqr.": John Ford to Philip Stephens, Secretary of the Admiralty, aboard the *Europa*, Port Royal Harbour, Jamaica, 3 April 1794. The latter copy of Ford's instructions is, however, misdated 5 February 1794.

5. PRO, ADM 1/5331, John Lawford's Court-Martial, John Lawford to John Ford, Island of Grand Cayman, 20 February 1794. This letter is extensively paraphrased and quoted in the following pages. It does not include modern standard punctuation, and sentences are often separated by semicolons or colons rather than periods. When a quotation is used from this letter, the original punctuation is retained, except at the end of the quoted material, where a period is used if it is structurally the end of a sentence. A copy of Lawford's 20 February 1794 letter to John Ford is also included as an Enclosure in PRO, ADM 1/245, John Ford to Philip Stephens, 3 April 1794. The two transcriptions vary slightly in punctuation, spelling, and an occasional word, but their overall content is the same.

6. PRO, ADM 1/5331, John Lawford's Court-Martial.

7. PRO, ADM 1/5331, John Lawford's Court-Martial.

8. PRO, ADM 1/5331, John Lawford's Court-Martial.

9. PRO, ADM 1/5331, John Lawford's Court-Martial.

10. PRO, ADM 1/5331, John Lawford's Court-Martial.

11. PRO, CO 700/West Indies 23, Maps and Plans in PRO II: America and the West Indies, Catalog no. 2972, West Indies (1773–75) 1790. The cited map, which appears as map 5, is the first printed version of George Gauld's map of Grand Cayman. There are three hand-drawn versions of the map, dated 1773, that are located in the Ministry of Defense, Hydrography Department, Somerset: q43 Ag 1, Admiralty Chart of Grand Cayman with Notations by George Gauld, 1773; Ag 1 196 fol. 2; and U 10 AG1.

12. PRO, ADM 1/2059, Captain's Letters, 1793–94, "L," John Lawford to the Commanders of the Merchant Ships and Vessels off the Island of Grand Cayman, East End of the Island of Grand Cayman, 9 February 1794.

13. PRO, ADM 1/2059, The Inhabitants of Grand Cayman to John Lawford,

George Town, Grand Cayman, 12 February 1794. Signatures on the petition include George Turnbull, George Turnbull for William Bodden, Joseph Dalby, Robert Knowles Clarke, Thomas Thomson, William Gerat Prescott, Hugh Mitchell, and James Hoy.

14. NLJ, *Royal Gazette* 15, no. 51 (14–21 December 1793), 23. The dates vary by a couple of days in the two accounts of the Grand Cayman hurricane, but it was surely the same storm.

15. NLJ, *Royal Gazette* 15 (1793); PRO, CO 141/1, Government Gazettes, *Royal Gazette* 16 (1794). The *Royal Gazette* was checked for the dates 26 October 1793 through 1 March 1794, inclusive.

16. PRO, ADM 1/2059, John Lawford to the Masters of the Merchantmen, George Town, Grand Cayman, 13 February 1794.

17. PRO, ADM 1/5331, John Lawford's Court-Martial. Havana is spelled several ways in various documents; when these sources are quoted, the spelling is as it appears in the original.

18. PRO, ADM 1/2059, John Lawford to the Governor of Havannah, George Town, Grand Cayman, 13 February 1794. There are two copies of this letter in the referenced class of documents, which vary slightly. The more complete version is quoted.

19. John Lawford's 13 February 1794 letter to the Admiralty is among the Public Record Office documents in the class ADM 1/2059. This letter contains much of the same information that Lawford includes in his 20 February 1794 letter to Commodore Ford. In regard to the convoy, however, Lawford informed the Admiralty that there were fifty-eight square-rigged ships for Europe and three schooners for America. In his letter to Ford he wrote that there were fifty-five square-rigged vessels for Europe and three schooners for America.

20. PRO, ADM 1/5331, John Lawford's Court-Martial.

21. PRO, ADM 1/5331, John Lawford's Court-Martial.

22. PRO, CO 141/1, *Royal Gazette* 16, no. 9 (22 February–1 March 1794), 22–23.

23. PRO, CO 141/1, *Royal Gazette* 16, no. 10 (1–8 March 1794), 22.

24. PRO, CO 141/1, *Royal Gazette* 16, no. 11 (8–15 March 1794), 22.

25. PRO, CO 141/1, *Royal Gazette* 16, no. 5 (25 January–1 February 1794), 22.

26. PRO, ADM 1/2059, John Lawford to Philip Stephens, George Town, Grand Cayman, 13 February 1794.

27. PRO, CO 141/1, 16 (1794), no. 10, 23.

28. PRO, ADM 1/245, John Ford to Philip Stephens, 3 April 1794.

29. PRO, ADM 51/1158, Captain's Log of HMS *Success*, Francis Roberts, 13 February 1794 to 31 August 1794; PRO, ADM 52/3427, Master's Log of HMS *Success*, Richard Davy, 19 February 1794 to 20 July 1794.

30. The days recorded in the referenced logs run from noon to noon, so 14 March began shortly after the *Success* made sail for the *Europa*.

31. PRO, ADM 51/1158, Captain's Log of HMS *Success*; PRO ADM 52/3427, Master's Log of HMS *Success*.

32. PRO, ADM 1/245, An Account of the Stores saved from the Wreck of His Majesty's Ship *Convert*, Enclosure in John Ford to Philip Stephens, 3 April 1794.

33. PRO, ADM 1/245, Francis Roberts, Captain of HMS *Success*, and John

Lawford to Robert Clarke and William Bodden Senior, 19 March 1794, Enclosure in John Ford to Philip Stephens, 3 April 1794.

34. PRO, ADM 1/245, Obligation signed by William Bodden Senior and Robert Knowles Clarke to save the stores of the *Convert*, 19 March 1794, Enclosure in John Ford to Philip Stephens, 3 April 1794.

35. NLJ, *Royal Gazette* 15, no. 51 (1793), 23.

36. There may have been only one sloop, which Davy mentioned twice in his log.

37. PRO, ADM 51/1158, Captain's Log of HMS *Success*; PRO ADM 52/3427, Master's Log of HMS *Success*.

38. PRO, CO 141/1, *Royal Gazette* 16, no. 14 (29 March–5 April 1794), 22–23.

39. PRO, ADM 51/1158, Captain's Log of HMS *Success*; PRO ADM 52/3427, Master's Log of HMS *Success*.

40. PRO, ADM 1/245, John Ford to Philip Stephens, 3 April 1794.

41. PRO, ADM 51/1158, Captain's Log of HMS *Success*; PRO ADM 52/3427, Master's Log of HMS *Success*.

42. PRO, ADM 1/245, John Ford to Philip Stephens, 3 April 1794.

43. PRO, CO 141/1, *Royal Gazette* 16, no. 23 (31 May–7 June 1794), 22.

44. PRO, CO 141/1, *Royal Gazette* 16, no. 25 (14–21 June 1794), 23.

45. PRO, CO 141/1, *Royal Gazette* 16, no. 9, 22–23.

46. PRO, CO 141/1, *Royal Gazette* 16, no. 5, 22; PRO, CO 141/1, *Royal Gazette* 16, no. 6, 22.

47. Barbara Jones, information officer at Lloyd's Register of Shipping, London, letter to the author, 11 March 1992.

48. *Lloyd's List*, 1793–94 (Farnborough, Hants: Gregg International Publishers, 1969; reprint), no. 2595, 18 March 1794.

49. *Lloyd's List*, no. 2596, 21 March 1794.

50. *Lloyd's List*, no. 2598, 28 March 1794.

51. Hornbake Library, University of Maryland, Microfilm AN41.16.M3—Reel 5, *Maryland Journal and Baltimore Advertiser*, 21 March 1794.

52. PRO, CO 141/1, *Royal Gazette* 16, no. 5 (1794), 22; no. 6 (1794), 22.

53. PRO, CO 141/1, *Royal Gazette* 16, no. 6 (1794), 22.

54. PRO, ADM 1/2059, John Lawford to the Masters of the Merchantmen, 13 February 1794.

55. *Lloyd's Register* 1794 (reprint, London: Gregg Press, 1969), *Richard*, Hughes.

56. NLJ, *Royal Gazette* 15, no. 44 (26 October–2 November 1793), 7.

57. Barbara Jones, Lloyd's Register, letters to the author, 27 December 1991, 11 March 1992.

58. *Lloyd's Register*, 1794, *William and Elizabeth*, Goodwin.

59. PRO, Board of Trade Records (hereafter BT) 111/1, Indexes to Transcripts, Ships Registered in London 1786–1854, Index 1786–1802, A–Z, London. Despite the discrepancy between the London Register and *Lloyd's List* with regard to tonnage, it is apparent that the data are for the same ship.

60. PRO, BT 107/9, Transcripts and Transactions: Series I, Register of Shipping, London Foreign Trade 1790–93, 1792, no. 14, *William and Elizabeth*.

61. The *William and Elizabeth* had two earlier registrations that had been canceled before the 1792 registration. On 16 February 1791 the ship had been registered as no. 52 in the transcripts. At this time the *William and Elizabeth* had the

same owners and master as in 1792, but the vessel may have had some physical differences. The register for 1791 notes that the *William and Elizabeth* had two decks, rather than the three decks described in 1792. But the 5-foot, 6-inch space between decks listed in 1791 is identical to that in the later registration. It is unclear whether an error was made in transcribing information from one transcript to the next, or whether an actual modification was made in the structure of the ship. The other primary features were the same as those listed in 1792. In the 1791 registration the *William and Elizabeth* is described as a frigate-built ship with quarterdeck and forecastle; PRO, BT 107/9, 1791, no. 52, *William and Elizabeth.*

62. PRO, BT 107/9, 1792, no. 14, *William and Elizabeth.*

63. PRO, BT 107/8, Transcripts and Transactions: Series I, Register of Shipping, London Foreign Trade 1787–89, 1787, no. 85, *William and Elizabeth.*

64. NLJ, *Royal Gazette* 15, no. 51 (1793), 22–23. The name of the ship is spelled in two ways in the *Gazette*: *Moorehall* and *Moorhall.*

65. *Lloyd's Register*, 1794, *Moore Hall*, S. Martin.

66. PRO, ADM 7/112, Register of Passes 1792–95; PRO, ADM 7/113, Register of Passes 1792–95, Index, no. 4072, *Moore Hall*, Nicholson. Such a pass was held on board as evidence to British cruisers that the vessel was engaged in legitimate trade.

67. The name of the *Ludlow*'s master is spelled in several different ways in the *Royal Gazette* and *Lloyd's List*: McLewer, McClure, and McLure.

68. PRO, CO 141/1, *Royal Gazette* 16, no. 4 (18–25 January 1794), 1, 22.

69. NLJ, *Royal Gazette* 15, no. 48 (23–30 November 1793), 22–23.

70. NLJ, *Royal Gazette* 15, no. 49 (30 November–7 December 1793), 17–19.

71. *Lloyd's Register*, 1794, *Britannia*, Martin; PRO, ADM 7/112 and 113, no. 3198, *Britannia*, Martin. *Lloyd's Register* records that the *Britannia* was a 206-ton ship-rigged vessel, sheathed with metal, with a draft of fourteen feet when loaded. The *Britannia* was built in Scotland in 1788 and owned by McNeil and Company, and her master was D. Martin. The vessel's surveying port was Greenock, Scotland, and her destined port was recorded as New York. The *Britannia*'s rating by *Lloyd's* was A1. A register of passes, entitling her to trade, notes that the *Britannia*, Daniel Martin, was a British-built ship of 205 tons, of Greenock. Ten British men and three foreign men were employed on board the vessel. On 28 January 1793, when the *Britannia's* pass (no. 3198) was issued, she was bound for New York.

72. NLJ, *Royal Gazette* 15, no. 49 (1793), 22–23.

73. None of the other merchant vessels with the name *Richard* that appear in *Lloyd's Register* are recorded as voyaging between Belfast and Jamaica. Only one *Richard* was listed with a captain by the name of Hughes, and that is the brig discussed in the text. Also, the brig *Richard*, Hughes, disappears from the annual volumes of *Lloyd's Register* after 1794.

74. *Lloyd's Register*, 1794, *Richard*, Hughes. The 176-ton vessel had a single deck with beams, was last sheathed with metal in 1792, and had a draft of thirteen feet when loaded. The *Richard* was built in Hull in 1776 and had received thorough repairs in both 1782 and 1792. She was owned by Scott and Company. The brig's surveying port was Belfast, and the destined port was Jamaica. The *Richard*, which received an E1 rating from Lloyd's, was noted as a "Constant Trader."

75. PRO, ADM 7/141, Register of Foreign Passes 1784–94; PRO, ADM 7/142, Register of Foreign Passes 1784–94, Index, no. 1735, *Richard*, Hughes.

76. The Public Record Office in England has some miscellaneous shipping return documents for Jamaica (Kingston, Saint Lucea, Montego Bay, Savannah-la-Mar) as follows: CO 142/21,22,23, Jamaica Miscellaneous, Shipping Returns, 1783–1807. None of them includes information around the date of the Wreck of the Ten Sail. Neither British nor Jamaican archives turned up any documentary evidence of ships registered in Kingston during this time.

77. PRO, CO 141/1, *Royal Gazette* 16, no. 13 (22–29 March 1794), 22.

78. PRO, CO 141/1, *Royal Gazette* 16, no. 14 (29 March–5 April 1794), 23.

79. PRO, CO 141/1, *Royal Gazette* 16, no. 15 (5–12 April 1794), 22. In the *Royal Gazette* the sloop *Sea-Flower* is sometimes listed as *Seaflower*, and the master, Russell, is sometimes listed as Russel.

80. PRO, CO 141/1, *Royal Gazette* 16, no. 17 (19–26 April 1794), 22.

81. PRO, CO 141/1, *Royal Gazette* 16, no. 19 (3–10 May 1794), 22.

82. PRO, CO 141/1, *Royal Gazette* 16, no. 20 (10–17 May 1794), 22.

83. PRO, CO 141/1, *Royal Gazette* 16, no. 22 (24–31 May 1794), 22; no. 23 (31 May–7 June 1794), 22.

84. PRO, CO 141/1, *Royal Gazette* 16, no. 25 (14–21 June 1794), 23.

85. PRO, CO 141/1, *Royal Gazette* 16, no. 26 (21–28 June 1794), 22.

86. The spelling of the names of the merchantmen (and their masters) is inconsistent in the various documents examined. The most frequent spelling is presented in the text, while direct quotes retain the spelling as it appears in the individual document.

87. *Lloyd's Register*, 1794, *Alfred*, Bryan; *Louisa*, Harrison; *Llandovery*, Adams; *Jane*, Gammel.

88. The tonnage differs slightly from that given in *Lloyd's Register*, a common occurrence.

89. PRO, BT 111/1 and BT 107/9, 1793, no. 129, *Llandovery*, Adams.

90. PRO, ADM 7/112 and 113, no. 3542, *Louisa*, Harrison; no. 3460, *Nancy*, Campbell; no. 5443, *Countess of Galloway*, Elgin.

91. PRO, CO 141/1, *Royal Gazette* 16, no. 10 (1794), 23.

92. PRO, CO 141/1, *Royal Gazette* 16, no. 13, 22. Captain Lawford gave directions to nine merchantmen, but a tenth ship may have joined the small convoy after their departure from Grand Cayman.

93. PRO, CO 141/1, *Royal Gazette* 16, no. 14, 23.

94. *Lloyd's List*, no. 2602, 11 April 1794; no. 2603, 15 April 1794; no. 2604, 18 April 1794.

95. *Lloyd's List*, no. 2597, 25 March 1794.

96. NLJ, *Royal Gazette* 15, no. 50 (1793), 1.

97. PRO, CO 141/1, *Royal Gazette* 16, no. 15 (1794), 23.

98. *Lloyd's List*, no. 2602, 11 April 1794.

99. NLJ, *Royal Gazette* 15, no. 50 (1793), 1.

100. *Lloyd's List*, no. 2605, 22 April 1794; no. 2606, 25 April 1794; no. 2607, 29 April 1794.

101. *Lloyd's List*, no. 2612, 16 May 1794.

102. *Lloyd's List*, no. 2607, 29 April 1794.

103. PRO, CO 141/1, *Royal Gazette* 16, no. 25 (1794), 22.

104. *Lloyd's List*, no. 2620, 13 June 1794.

105. *Lloyd's List*, no. 2613, 20 May 1794.

106. PRO, ADM 7/112 and 113, no. 3686, *Peggy*, Robertson.

107. PRO, CO 141/1, *Royal Gazette* 16, no. 20 (1794), 22. *Lloyd's List* does not report the arrival in Britain of the *Atalanta*, Forbes, within the time frame of the other *Convert* convoy arrivals.

108. PRO, CO 141/1, *Royal Gazette* 16, no. 22, 23.

109. PRO, CO 141/1, *Royal Gazette* 16, no. 24 (7–14 June 1794), 22.

110. PRO, CO 141/1, *Royal Gazette* 16, no. 26, 22.

111. PRO, ADM 1/245, John Ford to Philip Stephens, 3 April 1794.

112. Lavery, *Nelson's Navy*, 217.

113. PRO, ADM 1/5331, John Lawford's Court-Martial.

114. PRO, ADM 1/5331, John Lawford's Court-Martial.

115. Robert L. Molinari and others, "Surface Currents in the Caribbean Sea as Deduced from Lagrangian Observations," *Journal of Geophysical Research* 86, no. C7 (1981): 6537–42; Arnold L. Gordon, "Circulation of the Caribbean Sea," *Journal of Geophysical Research* 72, no. 24 (1967): 6207–23; John M. Morrison and Worth D. Nowlin Jr., "General Distribution of Water Masses within the Eastern Caribbean Sea during the Winter of 1972 and Fall of 1973," *Journal of Geophysical Research* 87, no. C6 (1982): 4207–29.

Chapter 8

1. Margaret E. Leshikar-Denton, "Caribbean Maritime Archaeology," in *Encyclopedia of Global Archaeology*, ed. Claire Smith (New York: Springer, 2014), 1160–68; "Caribbean Maritime Archaeology," in *The Oxford Handbook of Maritime Archaeology*, ed. A. Catsambis, B. Ford, and D. L. Hamilton (New York: Oxford University, 2011), 629–59; "Foundations in Management of Maritime Cultural Heritage in the Cayman Islands," in *Underwater Cultural Heritage at Risk*, ed. R. Grenier, D. Nutley and I. Cochran, (Paris: International Council on Monuments and Sites) 23–25; "The Situation in the Caribbean," in *Patrimonio cultural subacuático / Underwater Cultural Heritage*, ed. V. Marín, (Havana: UNESCO, 2004), 85; "Tracing the Wreck of the Ten Sail," in *Beneath the Seven Seas*, ed. G. F. Bass (London: Thames and Hudson, 2005), 206–9; "Problems and Progress in the Caribbean," in *International Handbook of Underwater Archaeology*, ed. C. Ruppé and J. Barstad (New York: Kluwer Academic / Plenum Press, 2002), 283–85; Margaret E. Leshikar-Denton and Pilar Luna Erreguerena, eds., *Underwater and Maritime Archaeology in Latin America and the Caribbean* (Walnut Creek, CA: Left Coast Press, 2008); Margaret Leshikar-Denton and Bert Ho, *The Probable* Glamis *Site: Archaeological Mapping and Potential for a Shipwreck Preserve, Grand Cayman, Cayman Islands* (Cayman Islands: CINM, 2004); Margaret E. Leshikar-Denton and Philip Pedley, eds., *Our Islands' Past*, vol. 2, *The Wreck of the Ten Sails* (George Town, Grand Cayman: Cayman Islands National Archive and Cayman Free Press, 1994); Margaret E. Leshikar-Denton, Matthew A. Russell, and Amanda M. Evans, eds., "Special Issue: Navigating Contentious Waters: International Responses to the 2001 UNESCO Convention on the Protection of the Underwater Cultural Heritage," *Journal of Maritime Archaeology* 5, no. 2 (2010); Margaret E. Leshikar-Denton and Della A. Scott-Ireton. "Underwater Archaeology," in *Encyclopedia of Caribbean Archaeology*, ed. Basil A. Reid and Grant Gilmore III (Gainesville: University Press of Florida, 2014), 341–48; "Creativity in Maritime Heritage Management in the Cay-

man Islands," in *Caribbean Heritage*, ed. Basil A. Reid (Kingston: University of the West Indies, 2012), 345–55; "The Cayman Islands Experience: Yesterday, Today, and Tomorrow," in *Underwater and Maritime Archaeology in Latin America and the Caribbean*, ed. Margaret E. Leshikar-Denton and Pilar Luna Erreguerena (Walnut Creek, CA: Left Coast Press, 2008); "A Maritime Heritage Trail and Shipwreck Preserves for the Cayman Islands," in *Out of the Blue: Public Interpretation of Maritime Cultural Resources*, ed. J. H. Jameson and D. A. Scott-Ireton (New York: Springer, 2007), 64–84.

2. *Abandoned Wreck Law* (5 of 1966–1997 Revision) Cayman Islands Government; Prosecutions for violations in 2002 are on record and have resulted in cases of imprisonment and fines. The value of the Cayman dollar is fixed to the US dollar; a CI dollar is worth about US$1.20.

3. Smith, *Maritime Heritage*, xvii; CINM, Institute of Nautical Archaeology (INA) communications and reports.

4. CINM, Indiana University Scuba Research and Development Group communications and reports; Personal communication with Charles Beeker, formerly head of the SRD group, and subsequently director of the Office of Underwater Science and Educational Resources in the School of Health, Physical Education and Recreation at Indiana University.

5. Roger C. Smith, "The Maritime Heritage of the Cayman Islands: Contributions in Nautical Archaeology" (master's thesis, Texas A&M University, 1981), v–xiv.

6. Smith, *Maritime Heritage*, 7–8.

7. Smith, "Maritime Heritage," ix.

8. Smith, *Maritime Heritage*, xvii.

9. Smith, *Maritime Heritage*, 17; CINM, National Shipwreck Inventory files. Specific shipwreck site locations are confidentially held by the government.

10. Roger Smith subsequently served as the Florida State underwater archaeologist, until his recent retirement.

11. Smith, "Maritime Heritage," xiii.

12. Sites recorded during the Cayman Islands Project were given certain designations. Each archaeological site had a prefix: LC for Little Cayman, CB for Cayman Brac, and GC for Grand Cayman. Following the prefix, sites were numbered consecutively in the order in which they were recorded. This classification and numbering system has been retained for the National Shipwreck Inventory.

13. CINM, National Shipwreck Inventory, GC 017 site file. In 1990 the transported cannon, now located on land, was given the designation OR 05; the significance of this identification number is explained in the section "A Quest for Cannons."

14. CINM, SRD communications and reports; Charles Beeker, personal communication with author, 1991.

15. CINM, SRD communications and reports.

16. CINM, National Shipwreck Inventory files. The SRD group identified the five sites by different designations, but the CINM National Shipwreck Inventory numbers (retained from INA numbers) are used to avoid confusion.

17. In 1990 this cannon from GC 017 was designated OR 22; the significance of this identification number is explained in the section "A Quest for Cannons."

18. I do not know whether Charles Beeker was told by someone else how much

the cannon weighed, whether he weighed it himself, or whether he estimated its weight.

19. Jean Boudriot, letter to Charles Beeker, 7 April 1986 (copy given to Margaret Leshikar-Denton by Charles Beeker). On 9 May 1992, Jean Boudriot and David H. Roberts wrote to me, "The *Regulations of 1767* ordered that the base ring should be engraved with the year of casting, the weight, and the cast number (starting anew each year). With the adoption in 1786 of a new system of guns, put into production in the second half of 1788, new casting marks were adopted in 1789."

20. CINM, Grand Cayman Cannon Survey files. These research files, deposited by Margaret Leshikar-Denton in the National Museum, contain the photographs, measurements, history-of-salvage details, present locations, and current guardianship data of these cannons. Each gun was identified by the prefix OR, for ordnance, and then it was numbered according to the chronology in which it was recorded. Unless otherwise footnoted, all the data in this section of chapter 8 are included in the referenced files.

21. Jean Boudriot and David H. Roberts, letters to author, 19 April and 9 May 1992.

22. CINM, Grand Cayman Cannon Survey files, letter of 28 June 1979 from the Cayman Islands Government to Stephen E. Smith (copy provided to Margaret Leshikar-Denton by Pat Smith).

23. Boudriot and Roberts, letters to author, 19 April and 9 May 1992. In the 9 May letter Boudriot and Roberts provided further information about the two forges owned by Baynaud. They wrote: "In 1762 Louis Baynaud took over the forge at Ruelle which had been set up in 1751 with letters patent in the name of the Marquis de Montalembert; his poor management forced him to hand over to Baynaud, and when the latter died in October 1774 the forge closed down. It started up again in the second half of 1777, under the management of Baynaud's son Mathieu, assisted by a relative Loulaigue who was an experienced forgemaster. In 1783 a major contract was signed with Ruelle and Forge-Neuve, for six years' supply of guns. Baynaud was responsible for Ruelle and Loulaigue for Forge-Neuve. Guns cast at Ruelle should have the letters RV on the face of the right trunnion, and BA on the left. Those cast at Forge-Neuve [after 1783] would have FN on the right trunnion and DL on the left."

24. After its presumed unauthorized salvage in 1982 for a private individual, Charles Beeker and Roger Smith discovered the gun and returned it to the sea, but to no avail, as it was retrieved again. Fortunately, since the Wreck of the Ten Sail Project commenced in the early 1990s, no additional unauthorized cannon salvage is known to have been carried out.

25. H. L. Blackmore, *The Armouries of the Tower of London*, vol. 1, *Ordnance* (London: Her Majesty's Stationery Office, 1976), 401–2.

26. CINM, Grand Cayman Cannon Survey files.

27. PRO, CO 141/1, *Royal Gazette* 16 (1794), 22 February to 1 March, no. 9, 23.

28. PRO, ADM 1/245, Admiralty and Secretariat Papers, "Jamaica 1793 & 94 Admiral John Ford Esqr.": John Ford, Commodore and Commander in Chief of His Majesty's Ships and Vessels at Jamaica, to Philip Stephens, Secretary of the Admiralty, 3 April 1794, and Enclosures: Francis Roberts, Captain of HMS *Success*, and John Lawford to Robert Clarke and William Bodden Senior, 19 March 1794;

Obligation signed by William Bodden Senior and Robert Knowles Clarke to save the stores of the *Convert*, 19 March 1794.

29. Hours before the winds of Hurricane Allen reached Grand Cayman, the INA team had seen the waters of the East End lagoon turn to mud and, near Gun Bluff, move southward like a river. We had watched the decks of the Liberty ship *Ridgefield* (aground since 1962) buckle under violent seas on the East End reefs. From shore, we had also witnessed the visible remains of the bauxite ore freighter *Rimandi Mibaju* (aground since 1964) disappear beneath the surf.

30. PRO, CO 700/West Indies 23, Maps and Plans in PRO II: America and the West Indies, Catalog no. 2972, West Indies (1773–75) 1790.

31. CINA, Admiralty Chart of Grand Cayman (London, published under the Superintendence of Captain Sir Frederick J. Evans, 30 December 1882).

32. CINA, *The Caymanian* 1, no. 1, 2 March 1908.

33. CINA, Memory Bank tape, Narrator Phoebe Watler Spence, interviewed by Margaret E. Leshikar, 14 November 1990.

34. Brian Jones, "A Field Guide to the Geology of the Cayman Islands" (Manuscript, University of Alberta, 1988), 2.

35. Jones, "Field Guide to the Geology," 8, 14, 60.

36. Jones, "Field Guide to the Geology," 60, 63–64.

37. Jones, "Field Guide to the Geology," 5.

38. In 1991 the southeast reefs were not investigated.

39. Geographical coordinates for all new sites discovered are to be updated with GPS.

40. Site data were deposited by Margaret Leshikar-Denton into the National Shipwreck Inventory files housed at the CINM. Wreck of the Ten Sail Project field notes, maps, and artifact collections were also deposited by Margaret Leshikar-Denton into the National Museum.

41. Hirst, *Notes on the History*, 115–16.

42. CINM, National Shipwreck Inventory, GC 017 site file.

43. CINM, SRD communications and reports; Charles Beeker, personal communication, 1991.

44. CINM, National Shipwreck Inventory files, and Wreck of the Ten Sail Project field notes and maps.

45. CINM, SRD communications and reports; Charles Becker, personal communication, 1991.

46. CINM, National Shipwreck Inventory, GC 012 site file.

47. Henceforth the designation GC 012 is used to describe the site as redefined in 1991.

48. The grids were established with the use of a compass and fiberglass tapes. They exhibit a small margin of error, which is considered acceptable due to the dispersed nature of the site.

49. J. Philip Dering of the Texas A&M University Palynology Laboratory identified a sample of wood from this sheave [2100.4.1] as lignum vitae.

50. David Steele, *The Elements and Practice of Rigging and Seamanship*, vols. 1 and 2 (London: Sim Comfort Associates, 1978; reprint of the original edition: London, 1794); Fred W. Hopkins and Donald G. Shomette, "The *DeBraak* Legacy: An Analysis of Eighteenth-Century Rigging," *American Neptune* 51, no. 3 (1991): 156–63. Steele uses the word "coak," while Hopkins and Shomette prefer "bushing."

51. Boudriot and Roberts, letters to author, 19 April and 9 May 1992. They suggest that in the eighteenth century, iron ballast pigs weighing about 50 or 100 pounds were commonly used. These pigs would be about 4 inches square in section, 1 foot long for the 50-pound pig and 2 feet long for the 100-pound pig. On site GC 012 the ballast pigs seem to be of the 100-pound variety.

52. Olive R. Jones, *Cylindrical English Wine and Beer Bottles, 1735–1850* (Ottawa, Ontario: Parks Canada, 1986); Olive R. Jones and E. Ann Smith, *Glass of the British Military, 1755–1820* (Ottawa, Ontario: Parks Canada, 1985).

53. Boudriot and Roberts, letters to author, 19 April and 9 May 1992.

54. CINM, National Shipwreck Inventory files and Wreck of the Ten Sail Project field notes and maps.

55. CINM, National Shipwreck Inventory files and Wreck of the Ten Sail Project field notes and maps.

56. Terrestrial sites located on Grand Cayman now receive designations beginning with the prefix GCL. Shipwreck sites continue with the GC prefix, which was originated by the 1979–80 Institute of Nautical Archaeology project.

57. All of the referenced East End terrestrial sites except GC 041, GCL 014, and GCL 016 were recorded in March 1993. George Sparling, Duncan McCleod, Arthur and Helene Schindler, and Margaret Leshikar-Denton combined survey efforts with William Keegan, Anne Stokes, and Reed Toomey of the Florida Museum of Natural History during their survey for prehistoric sites. The corridor of land between the road and the sea was intensively searched from Gun Bluff to Colliers. Although no prehistoric sites were identified, Keegan, Stokes, and Toomey are acknowledged for their assistance in locating historic sites.

58. CINM, Terrestrial Site Inventory files.

59. Margaret Leshikar-Denton wishes to acknowledge Michael Savarese, Charles Vitaliano, Clifford Ambers, and Rebecca Robinson, the Department of Geological Sciences, and the Underwater Science and Educational Resources Office for their analysis (using transmitted light microscopy, scanning electron microscopy, X-ray diffraction, and electron microprobe analysis) of the ballast from sites GC 026, GC 044, and GC 017. Also acknowledged are two research grants funded by the National Science Foundation that purchased and maintain the SEM facility at Indiana University: (1) NSF grant #PCM8212660 awarded to Indiana University's Biology Department for the purchase of the SEM; and (2) NSF grant #EAR8617504 awarded to Dr. Robert Wintsch from the Department of Geological Sciences for the purchase of the back scatter electron detector. The electron microprobe facility in the Department of Geological Sciences at Indiana University was purchased with funds provided by NSF grant #EAR9103509 and from the Keck Foundation.

60. Amlwch History, Amlwch Port Heritage Trail, http://www.amlwchhistory.co.uk.

61. CINM, National Shipwreck Inventory files and Wreck of the Ten Sail Project field notes and maps.

62. The slag from sites GC 026, GC 044, and GC 017 was identified by Michael Savarese, Charles Vitaliano, Clifford Ambers, and Rebecca Robinson of the Department of Geological Sciences at Indiana University.

63. Jones, *English Wine and Beer Bottles.*

64. CINM, National Shipwreck Inventory files and Wreck of the Ten Sail Project field notes and maps.

65. Boudriot and Roberts, letters to Margaret Leshikar-Denton, 19 April and 9 May 1992. These anchor measurements conform to standard sizes used on French 12-pounder frigates, but unknown factors could have resulted in variations from the norm.

66. CINM, National Shipwreck Inventory files and Wreck of the Ten Sail Project field notes and maps.

67. CINM, National Shipwreck Inventory files and Wreck of the Ten Sail Project field notes and maps.

68. Norwegian Maritime Museum, "*August*," in the Malmstein Register.

69. Norwegian Maritime Museum, "*Glamis*," in the Malmstein Register; Margaret Leshikar-Denton and Bert Ho, *The Probable* Glamis *Site: Archaeological Mapping and Potential for a Shipwreck Preserve, Grand Cayman, Cayman Islands*, Cayman Islands National Museum Shipwreck Preserve Series, no. 1 (Cayman Islands: CINM, 2004); Bert Ho, "An Archaeological Study of *Glamis*: The Role of a 19th-Century Iron Barque" (master's thesis, Florida State University, 2004).

Appendix C

1. *Gentleman's Magazine*, "Admiral Sir John Lawford, K.C.B." (obituary), April 1843, 426; wills of Admiral Sir John Lawford, KCB (1757–1842), and Lady Anna Maria Lawford, née Holden (ca. 1758–1853), and Lawford's family tree, http://www.clivesfamily.co.uk.

2. D. Steel, *Original and Correct List of the Royal Navy* (London: 1793–1815); Pitcairn-Jones, "The Commissioned Sea Officers of the Royal Navy, 1660–1815," vol. 2, part 2 (manuscript, NMM/PRO); William L. Clowes, *The Royal Navy, A History from the Earliest Times to the Present*, vols. 4–5 (New York: AMS Press, 1966; reprint of earlier edition: London, Sampson Low, Marston and Company, 1900).

3. There are some discrepancies between the listings in Pitcairn-Jones and other naval biographical sources regarding the ships on which John Lawford served. For example, John Marshall's biography and an obituary notice (detailed later in appendix C) suggest that Lawford removed from the *Polyphemus* into the *Audacious*, and do not mention that he served on the *Invincible*.

4. Lawford was actually made post captain on 1 December 1793 into the *Convert*.

5. Pitcairn-Jones, "Commissioned Sea Officers," vol. 2, part 2.

6. HMS *Convert* was actually lost on 8 February 1794.

7. John Marshall, *Royal Naval Biography*, vol. 1, part 2 (London, 1823), 496–99.

8. *Gentleman's Magazine*, "Admiral Sir John Lawford, K.C.B.," 426.

9. Pitcairn-Jones, "Commissioned Sea Officers," vol. 2, part 2.

10. Thomas Southey, *Chronological History of the West Indies*, vol. 2 (London, Frank Cass, 1968; reprint of the original edition: London, 1827), 522–27.

11. P. L. Dickinson, College of Arms, letter to Margaret Leshikar-Denton, 14 July 1992. Dickinson also confirmed that John Lawford's wife's maiden name was Holden, rather than Holder, as printed in the obituary notice in the *Gentleman's Magazine*.

12. Wills of Admiral Lawford and wife (see appendix C, note 1).

Bibliography

MANUSCRIPT AND ARCHIVAL SOURCES

France

ARCHIVES NATIONALES, PARIS

C/7 276, *Dossier personnel de Alexandre Joseph Riouffe.*
Marine BB/4/28, fol. 86–95, *Dossier L'Inconstante.*

ARCHIVES DU PORT DE ROCHEFORT, ROCHEFORT

1 A 122, *Correspondance du Commandant de la Marine à Rochefort avec la Cour,* 1790–91.

1 E 256, *Correspondance de la Cour avec l'Intendant de la Marine à Rochefort, Direction général Port R pour l'Intendance, No. 18*, 14 March 1789; *No. 34*, 16 May 1789; *No. 43*, 13 June 1789; *No. 69*, 21 November 1789.

1 E 256, *Correspondance de la Cour avec l'Intendant de la Marine à Rochefort, Pour modèle, comparaison du résumé de l'etat de situation des vaisseaux du 1 Mai 1789 avec l'inventaire du magasin général.*

1 E 261, *Correspondance de la Cour avec l'Intendant de la Marine à Rochefort, Direction des constructions*, Rochefort, 26 June 1789.

1 E 261, *Correspondance de la Cour avec l'Intendant de la Marine à Rochefort, Intendance général, No. 75*, 25 September 1789.

1 E 262, *Correspondance de la Cour avec l'Intendant de la Marine à Rochefort, Direction du port, No. 1*, Rochefort, 10 January 1790; *No. 2*, Rochefort, 10 January 1791.

1 E 262, *Correspondance de la Cour avec l'Intendant de la Marine à Rochefort, Intendance général pour l'Intendance, No. 20*, 26 March 1790; *No. 27*, 23 April 1790; *No. 31*, 30 April 1790; *No. 165*, 28 December 1790.

1 E 268, *Correspondance de la Cour avec l'Intendant de la Marine à Rochefort, Officier militaire pour l'Intendance, No. 293*, 17 November 1791.

1 E 268, *Correspondance de la Cour avec l'Intendant de la Marine à Rochefort, Commis aux revues aux approvisionnement, No. 316*, 27 November 1791.

1 E 271, *Correspondance de la Cour avec l'Intendant de la Marine à Rochefort, Extrait de l'equipage de deux frégates armées en flûte, et celui d'une flûte*, 17 November 1791.

1 E 271, *Correspondance de la Cour avec l'Intendant de la Marine à Rochefort, Port R*

et arsenaux pour l'Intendance, No. 294, 17 November 1791; *No. 322*, 3 December 1791.
[1 E 271], *Correspondance de la Cour avec l'Intendant de la Marine à Rochefort, Artillerie et colonies, No. 330*, 8 December 1791; *No. 353*, 17 December 1791.
2 G2 25 & 34, *Devis d'armement et de campagne, la frégate la Gracieuse, devis de retour de campagne.*
3 E2 35, *Rôle d'équipage, la frégate l'Inconstante, commandée par M. Riouffe Major de Vaisseau, rôle de bord*, 21 November 1791 to 25 November 1793.

Ministère de la Défense, Service Historique de la Marine, Château de Vincennes

CC7 ALPHA 2151, *Dossier individuel de Alexandre Joseph Riouffe.*

Cayman Islands

Cayman Islands National Archive

"An Accurate Map of the West Indies, from the Latest Improvements." London, R. Wilkinson, 1 January 1794.
"A Map of the Island of Jamaica Divided into Counties and Parishes, for *The History of the British West Indies* by Bryan Edwards Esqr. 1794." In *The History, Civil and Commercial, of the British Colonies in the West Indies*, vol. 1, 3rd ed. London: Printed for John Stockdale, 1801.
Admiralty Chart of Grand Cayman. London, published under the Superintendence of Captain Sir Frederick J. Evans, 30 December 1882.
The Caymanian 1, no. 1, 2 March 1908.

Cayman Islands National Museum

Grand Cayman Cannon Survey files.
National Shipwreck Inventory files.
Terrestrial Site Inventory files.
Institute of Nautical Archaeology communications and reports.
Indiana University Scuba Research and Development Group communications and reports.

United States

Hornbake Library, University of Maryland

Microfilm AN41.16.M3—Reel 5, *Maryland Journal and Baltimore Advertiser*, 21 March 1794.

Jamaica

Jamaica Archives, Spanish Town

High Court of Vice Admiralty, Ships' Papers, "*L'Inconstant* to HMS *Penelope*, Taken 25th November 1793, Condemned."
1B/5/3/18, Council of Jamaica Minutes, 1771–84.
1B/5/3/20, Council of Jamaica Minutes, May 1792 to May 1799.

National Library of Jamaica, Institute of Jamaica, Kingston

[Microfilm] *The Royal Gazette* 15 (1793), 29 December 1792 to 5 January 1793, No. 1; 26 October to 28 December 1793, Nos. 44 to 52.

MS. 72, Nugent Papers, Report on the Cayman Islands by Edward Corbet, 21 June 1802.

United Kingdom

Ministry of Defense, Hydrography Department, Somerset

q43 Ag 1, Admiralty Chart of Grand Cayman with Notations by George Gauld, 1773.

Ag 1 196 fol. 2, Admiralty Chart of Grand Cayman with Notations by George Gauld, 1773.

U 10 AG1, Admiralty Chart of Grand Cayman with Notations by George Gauld, 1773.

National Maritime Museum, London

Ships' Draughts, *L'Unité*, Reg. No. 6247 (digital reproduction ID J6091), Stern and Profile, As Taken; Reg. No. 6248, Profile, As Fitted; Reg. No. 6249, Decks, As Fitted; Reg. No. 6250 (digital reproduction ID J6088), Decks, As Taken.

Public Record Office, Kew (now National Archives, Kew)

Admiralty Records

ADM 1/245, Admiralty and Secretariat Papers, "Jamaica 1793 & 94 Admiral John Ford Esqr.": dispatches and enclosures from John Ford, Commodore and Commander in Chief of His Majesty's Ships and Vessels at Jamaica, to Philip Stephens, Secretary of the Admiralty, 13 January 1793 to 3 April 1794.

ADM 1/2059, Captain's Letters, 1793–94, "L," John Lawford's dispatches and enclosures.

ADM 1/3992, Lloyds 1793–1804, Extract of a personal letter from Jérémie dated 27 November 1793 and received in London on 27 January 1794, forwarded by Thomas Taylor of Lloyd's Coffee House to Philip Stephens, 27 January 1794.

ADM 1/5331, Courts-Martial, February to December 1794, April 1—Captain John Lawford, the Officers and Company of the *Convert.*

ADM 7/112, Register of Passes 1792–95.

ADM 7/113, Register of Passes 1792–95, Index.

ADM 7/141, Register of Foreign Passes 1784–94.

ADM 7/142, Register of Foreign Passes 1784–94, Index.

ADM 7/782, Registers of Convoys 1793–97, the *Proserpine* Convoy; the *Hector* Convoy; the *Hannibal* Convoy.

ADM 36/11476, Ships' Muster Books, Muster-Table of HMS *Convert*, 1793–94.

ADM 51/1158, Captains' Logs, Francis Roberts' Log of HMS *Success*, 13 February to 31 August 1794.

ADM 52/3276, Masters' Logs, John Douglas's Log of HMS *Penelope*, 31 August 1793 to 10 June 1794.

ADM 52/3427, Masters' Logs, Richard Davy's Log of HMS *Success*, 19 February to 20 July 1794.

Board of Trade Records

BT 107/8, Transcripts and Transactions: Series I, Register of Shipping, London Foreign Trade 1787–89.

BT 107/9, Transcripts and Transactions: Series I, Register of Shipping, London Foreign Trade 1790–93.

BT 111/1, Indexes to Transcripts, Ships Registered in London 1786–1854, Index 1786–1802, A–Z, London.

Colonial Office Records

CO 137/92, Jamaica Original Correspondence, 18 November 1793 to 7 February 1794, dispatches and enclosures from Adam Williamson, Lieutenant Governor and Commander in Chief in Jamaica, to Henry Dundas, Secretary of State for War.

CO 141/1, Government Gazettes, *The Royal Gazette*, XVI (1794), 28 December 1793 to 28 June 1794, Nos. 1 to 26.

CO 142/21, Jamaica Miscellaneous, Shipping Returns, 1783–1804.

CO 142/22, Jamaica Miscellaneous, Shipping Returns, 1784–1807.

CO 142/23, Jamaica Miscellaneous, Shipping Returns, 1795–98.

CO 700/West Indies 23, Maps and Plans in PRO II: America and the West Indies, Catalog No. 2972, West Indies (1773–75) 1790.

PRINTED SOURCES

Abandoned Wreck Law (5 of 1966) (1997 Revision). Government of the Cayman Islands.

Augier, F. R., S. C. Gordon, D. G. Hall, and M. Reckord. *The Making of the West Indies*. Trinidad and Jamaica: Longman Caribbean, 1990.

Bamford, Paul W. *Forests and French Sea Power, 1660–1789*. Toronto: University of Toronto Press, 1956.

Barskett, James. *History of the Island of St. Domingo: From Its First Discovery by Columbus to the Present Period*. 1818. Reprint, London: Frank Cass, 1972.

Black, Clinton V. *The Story of Jamaica from Prehistory to Present*. London: Collins, 1965.

Blackmore, H. L. *The Armouries of the Tower of London*. Vol. 1, *Ordnance*. London: Her Majesty's Stationery Office, 1976.

Boudriot, Jean. "La frégate dan la marine royage, 1660–1750, la frégate légère." *Neptunia* 181 (1991): 27–31.

———. "Propos sur les bois de marine sous l'Ancien Régime." *Neptunia* 182 (1991): 12–18.

———. *The Seventy-Four Gun Ship*. 4 vols. Translated by David H. Roberts. Annapolis: Naval Institute Press, 1986–88.

Boudriot, Jean, and Hubert Berti. *Frégate* La Belle-Poule *1765 de l'ingénieur Guignace, historique des frégates de 12 et monographie*. Paris: A.N.C.R.E., 1985.

———. *The History of the French Frigate, 1650–1850*. Translated by David H. Roberts. East Sussex, England: Jean Boudriot Publications, 1993.

Bridges, George Wilson, *The Annals of Jamaica*. Vol. 2. 1828. Reprint, London: Frank Cass, 1968.

Burns, Alan. *History of the British West Indies*. London: George Allen and Unwin, 1954.

Charnock, John. *An History of Marine Architecture*. 3 vols. London: R. Faulder and 28 other publishers, 1800–1802.

Clowes, William L. *The Royal Navy: A History from the Earliest Times to the Present*. Vols. 4–5. 1900. Reprint, New York: AMS Press, 1966.

Colledge, J. J. *Ships of the Royal Navy*. Annapolis: Naval Institute Press, 1987.

Craton, Michael, and the New History Committee. *Founded upon the Seas: A History of the Cayman Islands and Their People*. Kingston, Jamaica: Ian Randle Publishers, 2003.

Cros, Bernard. "Les ingénieurs de la marine aux XVII et XVIII siècles." *Neptunia* 170 (1988): 7–18.

Doran, Edwin B. "A Physical and Cultural Geography of the Cayman Islands." PhD diss., University of California at Berkeley, 1953.

Doyle, William. *The Oxford History of the French Revolution*. Oxford: Oxford University Press, 1990.

Dunn, Richard S. *Sugar and Slaves: The Rise of the Planter Class in the English West Indies, 1624–1713*. London: W. W. Norton, 1973.

European Magazine: A Collection of Papers on Naval Architecture, Originally Communicated through the Channel of the European Magazine. London: European Magazine, 1791–93.

Falconer, William. *Falconer's Marine Dictionary*. New York: Augustus M. Kelley, 1970. Reprint of *An Universal Dictionary of the Marine*, 1780 edition.

———. *An Universal Dictionary of the Marine*. London: T. Cadell, 1769.

Feiling, Keith. *A History of England*. [London?]: Book Club Associates, 1974.

Forfait, Pierre Alexandre Laurent. *Traité élémentaire de la mâture des vaisseaux: À l'usage des élèves de la marine*. Paris: Clousier, 1788.

Gentleman's Magazine, "Admiral Sir John Lawford, K.C.B." (obituary), April 1843, 426.

Gordon, Arnold L. "Circulation of the Caribbean Sea." *Journal of Geophysical Research* 72, no. 24 (1967): 6207–23.

Hampson, Norman. *La marine de l'an II, mobilisation de la flotte de l'océan, 1793–1794*. Paris: Librairie Narcel Rivière, 1959.

Herbin de Halle, P. E. *Des bois propres au service des arsenaux de la marine et de la guerre, ou développement et rapprochement des lois, règlemens et instructions concernant la recherche, le martelage et l'exploitation des arbres propres aux constructions navales, de l'artillerie, etc*. Paris: S. C. L'Huillier, 1813.

Hirst, George S. S. *Notes on the History of the Cayman Islands*. Kingston, Jamaica: P. A. Benjamin, 1910.

Ho, Bert. "An Archaeological Study of *Glamis*: The Role of a 19th-Century Iron Barque." Master's thesis, Florida State University, 2004.

Hopkins, Fred W., and Donald G. Shomette. "The *Debraak* Legacy: An Analysis of Eighteenth Century Rigging." *American Neptune* 51, no. 3 (1991): 156–63.

James, C. L. R. *The Black Jacobins, Toussaint L'Ouverture, and the San Domingo Revolution*. London: W. H. Allen, 1989.

Jones, Brian. "A Field Guide to the Geology of the Cayman Islands." Manuscript, University of Alberta, 1988.

———. "Geology of the Cayman Islands." In *The Cayman Islands: Natural History and Biogeography*, edited by M. A. Brunt and J. E. Davies, 13–49. Boston: Kluwer Academic, 1994.

Jones, Brian, E. B. Lockhart, and C. Squair. "Phreatic and Vadose Cements in the

Tertiary Bluff Formation of Grand Cayman Island, British West Indies." *Bulletin of Canadian Petroleum Geology* 32 (1984): 382–97.

Jones, Olive R. *Cylindrical English Wine and Beer Bottles, 1735–1850*. Ottawa, Ontario: Parks Canada, 1986.

Jones, Olive R., and E. Ann Smith. *Glass of the British Military, 1755–1820*. Ottawa, Ontario: Parks Canada, 1985.

Keeler, Mary Frear, ed. *Sir Francis Drake's West Indian Voyage, 1585–1586*. London: Hakluyt Society, 1981.

Lavery, Brian. *Nelson's Navy: The Ships, Men, and Organization, 1793–1815*. London: Conway Maritime Press, 1989.

Lescallier, Daniel. *Traité pratique du gréement des vaisseaux et autres batimens de mer: Ouvrage publié par ordre du Roi, pour l'instruction des élèves de la marine, sous le Ministère de M. de Fleurieu*. Paris: Clousier, 1791.

———. *Vocabulaire des termes de marine, anglois et françois*. Paris: L'Imprimerie Royale, 1777.

Leshikar-Denton, Margaret. "Caribbean Maritime Archaeology." In *Encyclopedia of Global Archaeology*, edited by Claire Smith, 1160–68. New York: Springer, 2014.

———. "Caribbean Maritime Archaeology." In *The Oxford Handbook of Maritime Archaeology*, edited by A. Catsambis, B. Ford, and D. L. Hamilton, 629–59. New York: Oxford University Press, 2011.

———. "Foundations in Management of Maritime Cultural Heritage in the Cayman Islands." In *Underwater Cultural Heritage at Risk*, edited by R. Grenier, D. Nutley and I. Cochran, 23–25. Paris: International Council on Monuments and Sites. http://www.icomos.org/risk/2006/fulldocan.pdf (accessed 3 April 2019), 2006.

———. "Problems and Progress in the Caribbean." In *International Handbook of Underwater Archaeology*, edited by C. Ruppé and J. Barstad, 279–98. New York: Kluwer Academic / Plenum Press, 2002.

———. "The Situation in the Caribbean." In *Patrimonio cultural subacuático / Underwater Cultural Heritage*, edited by V. Marín, 80–85. Havana: UNESCO, 2004.

———. "Tracing the Wreck of the Ten Sail." In *Beneath the Seven Seas*, edited by G. F. Bass, 206–9. London: Thames and Hudson, 2005.

Leshikar-Denton, Margaret E., and Pilar Luna Erreguerena, eds. *Underwater and Maritime Archaeology in Latin America and the Caribbean*. Walnut Creek, CA: Left Coast Press, 2008.

Leshikar-Denton, Margaret, and Bert Ho. *The Probable* Glamis *Site: Archaeological Mapping and Potential for a Shipwreck Preserve, Grand Cayman, Cayman Islands*. Cayman Islands National Museum Shipwreck Preserve Series, no. 1. Cayman Islands: CINM, 2004.

Leshikar-Denton, Margaret E., and Philip Pedley, eds. *Our Islands' Past*. Vol. 2, *The Wreck of the Ten Sails*. George Town, Grand Cayman: Cayman Islands National Archive and Cayman Free Press, 1994.

Leshikar-Denton, Margaret E., Matthew A. Russell, and Amanda M. Evans, eds. "Special Issue: Navigating Contentious Waters: International Responses to the 2001 UNESCO Convention on the Protection of the Underwater Cultural Heritage." *Journal of Maritime Archaeology* 5, no. 2 (2010).

Leshikar-Denton, Margaret E., and Della A. Scott-Ireton. "The Cayman Islands Experience: Yesterday, Today, and Tomorrow." In *Underwater and Maritime Ar-*

chaeology in Latin America and the Caribbean, edited by Margaret E. Leshikar-Denton and Pilar Luna Erreguerena, 221–44. Walnut Creek, CA: Left Coast Press, 2008.

———. "Underwater Archaeology." In *Encyclopedia of Caribbean Archaeology*, edited by Basil A. Reid and Grant Gilmore III, 341–48. University Press of Florida, 2014.

———. "Creativity in Maritime Heritage Management in the Cayman Islands." In *Caribbean Heritage*, edited by Basil A. Reid, 345–55. Kingston, Jamaica: University of the West Indies Press, 2012.

———. "A Maritime Heritage Trail and Shipwreck Preserves for the Cayman Islands." In *Out of the Blue: Public Interpretation of Maritime Cultural Resources*, edited by J. H. Jameson and D. A. Scott-Ireton, 64–84. New York: Springer, 2007.

Lewis, Michael. *The History of the British Navy*. Baltimore: Penguin Books, 1962.

———. *A Social History of the Navy, 1793–1815*. London: George Allen and Unwin, 1960.

Lloyd's List, 1793–94. Farnborough, Hants: Gregg International Publishers, 1969. Reprint, Nos. 2581 to 2620, 28 January to 13 June 1794.

Lloyd's Register, 1794. London: Gregg Press. Reprint.

Long, E. *The History of Jamaica*. London: T. Lowndes, 1774.

MacGregor, David. *Fast Sailing Ships, Their Design and Construction, 1775–1875*. Annapolis: Naval Institute Press, 1988.

———. *Merchant Sailing Ships, 1775–1815*. London: Conway Maritime Press, 1985.

Marshall, John. *Royal Naval Biography*. Vol. 1, part 2. London: Longman, Hurst, Rees, Orme, Brown and Green, 1823.

Molinari, Robert L., Michael Spillane, Irving Brooks, Donald Atwood, and Carol Duckett. "Surface Currents in the Caribbean Sea as Deduced from Lagrangian Observations." *Journal of Geophysical Research* 86, no. C7 (1981): 6537–42.

Morison, Samuel Eliot. *Admiral of the Ocean Sea: A Life of Christopher Columbus*. London: Little, Brown, 1970.

Morrison, John M., and Worth D. Nowlin Jr. "General Distribution of Water Masses within the Eastern Caribbean Sea during the Winter of 1972 and Fall of 1973." *Journal of Geophysical Research* 87, no. C6 (1982): 4207–29.

Norwegian Maritime Museum. "*August*," "*Glamis*," in the Malmstein Register.

Pares, Richard. *War and Trade in the West Indies, 1739–1763*. London: Frank Cass, 1963.

Pinet, Paul. Acetates to Accompany *Oceanography: An Introduction to the Planet's Oceans*. New York: West Publishing, 1992.

Pitcairn-Jones. "The Commissioned Sea Officers of the Royal Navy, 1660–1815." Vol. 2, part 2. Manuscript, National Maritime Museum, London/Public Record Office, Kew, England.

Richards, Denis. *An Illustrated History of Modern Europe, 1789–1984*. Harlow: Longman Group UK, 1974.

Smith, Roger C. *The Maritime Heritage of the Cayman Islands*. Gainesville: University Press of Florida, 2000.

———. "The Maritime Heritage of the Cayman Islands: Contributions in Nautical Archaeology." Master's thesis, Texas A&M University, 1981.

———. "Treasure Ships of the Spanish Main: The Iberian-American Maritime Empires." In *Ships and Shipwrecks of the Americas*, edited by George F. Bass. London: Thames and Hudson, 1988.

Southey, Thomas. *A Chronological History of the West Indies*. Vols. 2–3. 1827. Reprint, London: Frank Cass, 1968.

Stalkartt, Marmaduke. *Naval Architecture.* 2 vols. London: J. Boydell, J. Dodsley, and J. Sewell, 1781–87.

Steel, D. *Original and Correct List of the Royal Navy*. London, 1793–1815.

Steel, David. *The Elements and Practice of Naval Architecture*. 2 vols. 1805. Reprint, London: Sim Comfort Associates, 1977.

———. *The Elements and Practice of Rigging and Seamanship*. 2 vols. 1794. London: Sim Comfort Associates, 1978.

Sutherland, William. *The Ship Builder's Assistant*. London: Mount and Davidson Tower Hill, 1794.

Vial de Clairbois, Honore Sebastien. *Traité élémentaire de la construction des vaisseaux, à l'usage des élèves de la marine*. Paris: Clousier, 1787.

Villiers, Patrick. *La marine de Louis XVI de Choiseul à Sartine*. Vol. 1. Grenoble: J. P. Debbane, 1985.

Williams, Eric. *From Columbus to Castro: The History of the Caribbean, 1492–1969*. London: Andre Deutsch, 1989.

Williams, Neville. *A History of the Cayman Islands*. Grand Cayman: Government of the Cayman Islands, 1970.

ORAL SOURCES

Cayman Islands National Archive

Memory Bank Tapes (now part of the Oral History Program)

Narrator Weddy Connolly, interviewed by Margaret E. Leshikar-Denton and Jeanne Masters, 10 December 1990.

Narrator Edison Jackson, interviewed by Margaret E. Leshikar-Denton, 4 January 1991.

Narrator Mary Antoinette Wood Levy, interviewed by Margaret E. Leshikar-Denton, 24 January 1991.

Narrator Phoebe Watler Spence, interviewed by Margaret E. Leshikar-Denton, 14 November 1990.

Narrator Marshall Watler, interviewed by Margaret E. Leshikar-Denton, 4 January 1991.

Subject: Wreck of the Ten Sail, Narrators Barrett Welcome, Ethellen Jackson, William Allen McLaughlin, William Warren Conolly, Phoebe Watler Spence, Nina Watler Conolly, [Katy Rochelle Wood? or Lydia Rachel Rankine?], Mary Antoinette Wood Levy, Doris Wood, interviewed by Anita Ebanks, 1982–83.

ONLINE SOURCES

Amlwch History, Amlwch Port Heritage Trail, www.amlwchhistory.co.uk (accessed 3 April 2019).

International Council on Monuments and Sites. 1996. *ICOMOS International Charter on the Protection and Management of Underwater Cultural Heritage*. Paris: ICOMOS. Available at https://www.icomos.org/charters/underwater_e.pdf (accessed 3 April 2019).

United Nations Educational, Scientific, and Cultural Organization. 2001. *UNESCO*

Convention on the Protection of the Underwater Cultural Heritage. Paris: UNESCO. Available at http://portal.unesco.org/en/ev.phpURL_ID=13520&URL_DO=DO_TOPIC&URL_SECTION=201.html (accessed 3 April 2019).

Wills of Admiral Sir John Lawford, KCB (1757–1842), and Lady Anna Maria Lawford, née Holden (ca. 1758–1853), and Lawford's family tree, www.clivesfamily.co.uk (accessed 12 May 2019).

Index

Page numbers in italics refer to illustrations.